Serverless Programmi Cookbook

Practical solutions to building serverless applications using Java and AWS

Heartin Kanikathottu

BIRMINGHAM - MUMBAI

Serverless Programming Cookbook

Copyright © 2019 Packt Publishing

All rights reserved. No part of this book may be reproduced, stored in a retrieval system, or transmitted in any form or by any means, without the prior written permission of the publisher, except in the case of brief quotations embedded in critical articles or reviews.

Every effort has been made in the preparation of this book to ensure the accuracy of the information presented. However, the information contained in this book is sold without warranty, either express or implied. Neither the author, nor Packt Publishing or its dealers and distributors, will be held liable for any damages caused or alleged to have been caused directly or indirectly by this book.

Packt Publishing has endeavored to provide trademark information about all of the companies and products mentioned in this book by the appropriate use of capitals. However, Packt Publishing cannot guarantee the accuracy of this information.

Commissioning Editor: Merint Mathews
Acquisition Editor: Karan Sadawana
Content Development Editor: Anugraha Arunagiri
Technical Editor: Divya Vadhyar
Copy Editor: Safis Editing
Project Coordinator: Ulhas Kambali
Proofreader: Safis Editing
Indexer: Rekha Nair
Graphics: Tom Scaria
Production Coordinator: Deepika Naik

First published: January 2019

Production reference: 1310119

Published by Packt Publishing Ltd.
Livery Place
35 Livery Street
Birmingham
B3 2PB, UK.

ISBN 978-1-78862-379-7

www.packtpub.com

To my wife, Sneha; baby girl, June Grace; mother, Dr. Gresamma Mathew; and above all, God almighty.

– Heartin Kanikathottu

mapt.io

Mapt is an online digital library that gives you full access to over 5,000 books and videos, as well as industry leading tools to help you plan your personal development and advance your career. For more information, please visit our website.

Why subscribe?

- Spend less time learning and more time coding with practical eBooks and Videos from over 4,000 industry professionals
- Improve your learning with Skill Plans built especially for you
- Get a free eBook or video every month
- Mapt is fully searchable
- Copy and paste, print, and bookmark content

Packt.com

Did you know that Packt offers eBook versions of every book published, with PDF and ePub files available? You can upgrade to the eBook version at www.packt.com and as a print book customer, you are entitled to a discount on the eBook copy. Get in touch with us at customercare@packtpub.com for more details.

At www.packt.com, you can also read a collection of free technical articles, sign up for a range of free newsletters, and receive exclusive discounts and offers on Packt books and eBooks.

Contributors

About the author

Heartin Kanikathottu is a senior software engineer and blogger with around 11 years of IT experience. He is currently working as a Senior Member of Technical Staff at VMware. He has previously worked with companies including Software AG, SAP Ariba and TCS. He has a masters degree in cloud computing and bachelors degree in computer science. He has completed 10 professional certifications on the areas of cloud computing, coding and design from companies including AWS, Pivotal, Oracle, Microsoft, IBM and Sun. He likes to share his technical knowledge through his blogs such as Heartin.tech, CloudMaterials.com and JavaJee.com. He also likes to mentor juniors and take technical sessions at work, meetups and conferences.

> *I want to thank God almighty for giving me this wonderful opportunity. My wife Sneha helped me to great lengths during every phase of writing this book both as a supportive wife as well as an excellent reviewer. My baby girl June sacrificed dada time a lot while I was writing. I also want to thank my current employer VMware, colleagues, family members especially my mother Dr. Gresamma Mathew and friends who supported me with advice and prayers.*

About the reviewer

Sneha Thomas is a full stack developer with 8 years of IT experience. She considers herself to be an excellent UI developer with good backend skills. She has worked on technologies such as Angular, Java, Spring, Hibernate, databases and various web technologies such as HTML, JavaScript and CSS. She also has good knowledge of the cloud platforms such as AWS and Google Cloud Platform. She has got a masters degree with specialization in cloud computing and a bachelors degree in electronics and communications. During her free times she like to experiment with new technologies and write blogs on JavaJee.com.

Packt is searching for authors like you

If you're interested in becoming an author for Packt, please visit `authors.packtpub.com` and apply today. We have worked with thousands of developers and tech professionals, just like you, to help them share their insight with the global tech community. You can make a general application, apply for a specific hot topic that we are recruiting an author for, or submit your own idea.

Table of Contents

Preface — 1

Chapter 1: Getting Started with Serverless Computing on AWS — 7
  Introduction — 7
  Getting started with the AWS platform — 8
    Getting ready — 8
    How to do it... — 9
    How it works... — 11
      AWS Identity and Access Management (IAM) — 11
      Amazon CloudWatch — 11
      Multi-Factor Authentication (MFA) — 11
    There's more... — 12
    See also — 12
  Your first AWS Lambda — 13
    Getting ready — 13
      Code repository usage guidelines — 14
    How to do it... — 15
    How it works... — 18
      About the parent POM — 18
      Lambda roles — 18
      Lambda runtimes — 18
      Extra dependencies — 19
    There's more... — 19
      Other ways to create Lambda functions from the management console — 20
      Other ways to deploy code in a Lambda function — 20
      Passing JSON to and from Lambda handler — 20
    See also — 20
  Your first Lambda with AWS CLI — 21
    Getting ready — 21
      Configuring AWS CLI — 22
      Creating S3 bucket — 24
      Note for Windows users — 24
    How to do it... — 25
    How it works... — 29
      Creating a role and attaching a policy — 30
      Lambda memory-size and timeout — 30
      S3 Bucket and Key — 30
      Cleaning up — 30
    There's more... — 31
    See also — 31
  Your first Lambda with Amazon CloudFormation — 31
    Getting ready — 32

Table of Contents

Set up the project and S3 bucket	32
Understanding YAML and JSON	32
How to do it...	32
Cleaning up roles, policy, and Lambda	36
How it works...	36
There's more...	37
CloudFormation Template Components	37
Resource component	38
Intrinsic functions	38
CloudFormation Designer	39
Additional benefits of CloudFormation	39
Cloud Formation alternatives	40
See also	40

Using AWS SDK, Amazon CloudFormation, and AWS CLI with Lambda — 40

Getting ready	40
How to do it...	41
Creating the POJOs for requests and response.	42
How it works...	47
There's more...	47
Pseudo-parameters	48
See also	48

Dev Practices – dependency injection and unit testing — 48

Getting ready	49
Code refactoring	49
How to do it...	50
How it works...	53
There's more...	53
See also	54

Your first Lambda with serverless framework — 54

Getting ready	54
How to do it...	54
How it works...	57
There's more...	58
See also	58

Chapter 2: Building Serverless REST APIs with API Gateway — 59

Introduction	59

Building your first API using the AWS CLI — 60

Getting ready	60
How to do it...	60
How it works...	64
HTTP essentials	65
REST essentials	66
Parts of a URL	66
There's more...	67
See also	67

Building your first API using Amazon CloudFormation — 67
- Getting ready — 67
- How to do it... — 68
- How it works... — 72
- There's more... — 72
- See also — 72

Building your first API with Lambda integration — 73
- Getting ready — 73
- How to do it... — 74
  - Creating the Lambda — 74
  - Creating a REST API with AWS CLI commands — 75
  - Creating a REST API with a CloudFormation template — 78
- How it works... — 79
  - CLI commands — 80
  - CloudFormation template components — 81
- There's more... — 81
- See also — 81

Building and testing your first POST API method — 82
- Getting ready — 82
- How to do it... — 82
  - Creating the API with CLI commands — 83
  - Creating the API with a CloudFormation template — 85
  - Testing with Postman — 86
- How it works... — 87
  - Passthrough behavior — 88
- There's more... — 88
- See also — 88

Mapping requests and responses with mapping templates — 89
- Getting ready — 89
- How to do it... — 89
  - Mapping requests — 90
  - Mapping responses — 90
  - Creating the API using CLI commands — 91
  - Creating the API with a CloudFormation template — 92
  - Testing the API — 93
- How it works... — 94
  - Mapping templates and variables — 94
  - Using #set — 95
- There's more... — 95
  - The Apache Velocity Language — 96
  - JSONPath expressions — 96
- See also — 96

Validating request payloads with models — 96
- Getting ready — 97
- How to do it... — 97
  - The request data format — 97
  - Creating the API with CLI commands — 98

Table of Contents

The CloudFormation template	100
Testing the API	101
How it works...	102
There's more...	102
See also	102

Lambda and API with proxy integration — 103

Getting ready	103
How to do it...	103
Creating a Lambda function for proxy integration	104
Deploying the Lambda	105
Creating the Proxy API with CLI commands	105
Creating the API using CloudFormation templates	108
How it works...	110
The greedy path, the ANY HTTP method, and proxy integration	110
RequestStreamHandler versus RequestHandler	110
The input and output format of a Lambda function for proxy integration	111
There's more...	111
See also	112

Chapter 3: Data Storage with Amazon DynamoDB — 113

Introduction — 113
Your first DynamoDB table — 114

Getting ready	114
How to do it...	114
Creating a table using CLI commands	115
Creating a table using a CloudFormation template	117
How it works...	119
DynamoDB data model	119
Data model limits	119
DynamoDB keys and partitions	120
Read and write capacity units	120
Waiting for asynchronous operations	120
Other ways to create tables	121
There's more...	121
DynamoDB features	121
DynamoDB general limitations	122
Local and global secondary indexes	122
See also	122

Throughput provisioning examples — 123

Getting ready	123
How to do it...	123
Scenario 1	123
Scenario 2	124
Scenario 3	124
How it works...	125
Strongly consistent reads versus eventually consistent reads	125
Limits on throughput updates within a day	125
There's more...	126

See also	126
Working with data from the CLI	**126**
Getting ready	126
How to do it...	127
Adding items	127
Reading items	127
Updating items	131
Deleting items	131
How it works...	132
Add, update, and delete operations	132
Reading data from DynamoDB	132
return-consumed-capacity	133
There's more...	133
See also	133
Using the DynamoDB SDK from Lambda	**134**
Getting ready	134
How to do it...	134
How it works...	139
AmazonDynamoDB client versus DynamoDB wrapper client	139
IAM policy and actions	139
Single Lambda versus multiple Lambdas	140
There's more...	141
See also	141
Creating tables from Lambda	**141**
Getting ready	141
How to do it...	142
How it works...	145
There's more...	145
See also	145
Adding data items from Lambda	**145**
Getting ready	145
How to do it...	146
How it works...	148
There's more...	148
See also	149
Reading data from Lambda	**149**
Getting ready	149
How to do it...	150
How it works...	154
There's more...	154
See also	155
Chapter 4: Application Security with Amazon Cognito	**157**
Introduction	157
Creating a Cognito user pool	158
Getting ready	158

How to do it...	158
Creating Cognito user pool with AWS CLI	158
Creating Cognito user pool with CloudFormation template	161
How it works...	165
Generating and using JSON templates with CLI commands	165
AliasAttributes versus UsernameAttributes	166
There's more...	166
See also	166
Server-side authentication flow	**167**
Getting ready	167
How to do it...	167
Creating Cognito user pool client	167
Creating a Cognito user pool client with AWS CLI	168
Creating a Cognito user pool client with CloudFormation template	168
Server-side authentication flow	169
How it works...	172
Server-side, client-side, and custom authentication flows	172
Secure Remote Password protocol	172
The access token, refresh token, and ID token	173
ADMIN_NO_SRP_AUTH versus USER_PASSWORD_AUTH	173
There's more...	174
See also	174
Client-side authentication flow	**174**
Getting ready	174
How to do it...	174
Creating a Cognito user pool client	175
Creating a Cognito user pool client with AWS CLI	175
Creating a Cognito user pool client with CloudFormation template	175
Client-side authentication flow	176
How it works...	177
There's more...	178
See also	178
User sign-up flow with Cognito	**178**
Getting ready	179
How to do it...	179
User sign-up with self-confirmation	179
User sign-up with admin confirmation	182
How it works...	183
There's more...	183
See also	183
Working with groups	**183**
Getting ready	184
How to do it...	184
How it works...	186
There's more...	186
See also	186
Integrating Cognito with the API gateway	**187**

Getting ready	187
How to do it...	187
The AWS CLI	187
The CloudFormation template	192
How it works...	194
Claim-based identity	194
There's more...	195
See also	195
User sign-up with SMS verification and MFA	**195**
Getting ready	195
How to do it...	196
Creating the user pool	196
Creating a Cognito user pool client with AWS CLI	196
Creating a Cognito user pool client with CloudFormation template	200
User sign-up with SMS and MFA verification	202
How it works...	205
There's more...	205
See also	205
Chapter 5: Web Hosting with S3, Route53, and CloudFront	**207**
Introduction	**207**
Setting up an S3 static website	**208**
Getting ready	208
How to do it...	208
AWS CLI commands	208
The CloudFormation template	211
How it works...	213
There's more...	214
See also	214
Setting up CloudFront for an S3 website	**214**
Getting ready	214
How to do it...	214
AWS CLI commands	215
Understanding the DistributionConfig defaults in the response	216
The CloudFormation template	218
How it works...	220
There's more...	220
See also	220
Registering a domain name with Route 53	**220**
Getting ready	221
How to do it...	221
Registering a domain with AWS CLI commands	221
How it works...	224
Hosted zones	225
There's more...	225
Registering a domain from AWS Management Console	225
See also	227

Table of Contents

Using domains registered with other registrars	227
Getting ready	227
How to do it...	227
AWS CLI commands	228
The CloudFormation template	229
How it works...	230
DNS propagation	230
There's more...	230
Steps for configuring DNS from the AWS Management Console	230
See also	232
Using custom domains with S3 static websites	232
Getting ready	232
How to do it...	232
AWS CLI commands	232
The CloudFormation template	235
How it works...	238
There's more...	238
See also	239
Using custom domain names with CloudFront	239
Getting ready	239
How to do it...	239
AWS CLI commands	239
The CloudFormation template	243
The CloudFront distribution stack	244
The RecordSet stack	246
How it works...	248
There's more...	248
Using HTTPS to secure your domain URL	248
Disabling and deleting a CloudFront distribution	249
See also	250
Using HTTPS with a CloudFront domain	250
Getting ready	251
How to do it...	251
Associating a certificate with a domain using AWS CLI commands	251
Associating a certificate with a domain using CloudFormation template	253
How it works...	255
Server Name Identification (SNI)	256
There's more...	256
See also	256
Chapter 6: Messaging and Notifications with SQS and SNS	257
Introduction	257
Your first SQS queue (AWS CLI + CloudFormation)	258
Getting ready	258
How to do it...	258
Creating an SQS queue	258
AWS CLI commands	258

The CloudFormation template	259
Sending and receiving data (AWS CLI)	260
How it works...	261
There's more...	261
See also	262

Creating an SQS queue and sending messages with SDK (Java) — 262
Getting ready	262
How to do it...	262
Lambda project code (Java)	263
Provisioning and testing the Lambda (AWS CLI)	265
How it works...	269
There's more...	269
See also	269

Receiving and sending SQS messages in batches with SDK (Java) — 269
Getting ready	270
How to do it...	270
Lambda project code (Java)	270
Setting up queues and data	273
Provisioning and testing the Lambda (AWS CLI)	273
How it works...	276
There's more...	277
See also	277

Invoking the Lambda with an SQS event (Java) — 277
Getting ready	277
How to do it...	278
Lambda project code (Java)	278
Setting up queues and data	280
Provisioning the Lambda (AWS CLI)	280
Testing the Lambda (AWS CLI)	283
How it works...	283
There's more...	283
See also	284

Your first SNS topic for email and SMS (AWS CLI + CloudFormation) — 284
Getting ready	285
How to do it...	285
Creating an SNS topic	285
AWS CLI	285
The CloudFormation template	285
Creating email and SMS subscriptions (AWS CLI)	286
SMS subscription	286
Email subscription	287
Publishing a message	288
How it works...	289
There's more...	289
See also	289

Publishing to an SNS topic with SDK (Java) — 289

[ix]

Getting ready	290
How to do it...	290
Lambda project code (Java)	290
Provisioning and testing the Lambda (AWS CLI)	292
How it works...	294
There's more...	294
See also	294
Invoking a Lambda with SNS events (Java)	294
Getting ready	294
How to do it...	295
Lambda project code (Java)	295
Provisioning the Lambda (AWS CLI)	297
Testing the Lambda (AWS CLI)	298
How it works...	299
There's more...	299
See also	299
Chapter 7: Redshift, Amazon ML, and Alexa Skills	**301**
Introduction	301
Your first Kinesis data stream (AWS CLI)	302
Getting ready	302
How to do it...	302
Step 1 - Creating a Kinesis data stream	302
Using AWS CLI	302
Using the CloudFormation template	304
Step 2 - Adding and retrieving data	305
How it works...	307
Kinesis shard iterator types	308
There's more...	310
See also	310
Writing data into Kinesis Stream with SDK (Java)	310
Getting ready	311
How to do it...	311
Step 1 - Creating the Lambda project (Java)	311
Step 2 - Provisioning and testing Lambda (AWS CLI)	315
How it works...	318
There's more...	319
See also	319
Invoking Lambda with Kinesis events (Java)	319
Getting ready	320
How to do it...	320
Step 1 - Creating a Lambda project (Java)	320
Step 2 - Provisioning and testing Lambda (AWS CLI)	322
How it works...	324
There's more...	325
See also	325
Using Amazon ML for binary classification (AWS CLI)	326

Getting ready	326
How to do it...	327
How it works...	335
Types of models	336
DataSource object	336
Receiver Operating Characteristic and Area Under the ROC	336
There's more...	337
See also	337
Building and testing an Alexa skill (Java for Lambda, CLI for Alexa skill)	**337**
Getting ready	338
Installing and configuring the ASK CLI	338
Configuring ask-cli for the first time	339
How to do it...	340
Step 1 - Creating the Lambda project (Java)	341
Step 2 - Provisioning Lambda (AWS CLI)	346
Step 3 - Building an Alexa skill with ASK CLI	347
How it works...	353
Alexa skill invocation basics	354
Explaining the Lambda project (Java)	355
Explaining the ASK CLI steps	356
There's more...	356
Voice app platforms	357
See also	357
Chapter 8: Monitoring and Alerting with Amazon CloudWatch	**359**
Introduction	**359**
Checking logs, insights, and metrics (Console)	**360**
Getting ready	360
How to do it...	361
Step 1: Logging in to the CloudWatch dashboard	361
Logs	362
Log insights	364
Metrics	365
How it works...	367
Log groups	367
Log streams	368
Log insights	368
Metrics	368
There's more...	368
See also	369
Your first custom metric (AWS CLI)	**369**
Getting ready	369
How to do it...	369
Step 1–Create a simple metric without dimensions	369
Step 2—Add dimensions to metric data	371
How it works...	373
There's more...	374

Table of Contents

See also	374
Setting up CloudWatch alarms (AWS CLI)	374
Getting ready	374
How to do it...	375
How it works...	380
There's more...	381
See also	381
CloudWatch alarms with dimensions (AWS CLI)	382
Getting ready	382
How to do it...	382
How it works...	384
There's more...	384
See also	384
Using CloudWatch metric log filters	384
Getting ready	384
How to do it...	385
Creating metric filters from AWS CLI	385
Creating metric filters from the console	387
How it works...	390
There's more...	390
See also	390
Chapter 9: Serverless Programming Practices and Patterns	391
Introduction	391
Enabling CORS for the API and testing with CodePen	392
Getting ready	392
Getting familiar with CodePen	393
How to do it...	394
How it works...	398
There's more...	400
See also	400
Implementing and testing Cognito operations with the JavaScript SDK	401
Getting ready	401
Download the amazon-cognito-identity.min.js file	401
Create an S3 bucket and upload the amazon-cognito-identity.min.js file	402
Creating a Cognito user pool and client	403
How to do it...	404
How it works...	409
There's more...	409
See also	409
Federated identity with Amazon Cognito	409
Getting ready	410
How to do it...	410
Step 1 - Configuring Google Plus	410
Step 2 - Creating and Configuring an Identity Pool	414

[xii]

Step 3 - Preparing and uploading code files	416
Preparing the index.html file	416
Deploying and testing the index.html file	418
How it works...	419
There's more...	419
See also	420
Creating SSL/TLS certificate with ACM	**420**
Getting ready	420
How to do it...	420
AWS CLI Commands	421
CloudFormation Template	425
How it works...	427
There's more...	428
See also	428
Fan-in and fan-out architectural patterns with AWS	**428**
Getting ready	429
How to do it...	429
Scenario 1 - Pub-Sub with multiple producers and consumers	429
Scenario 2 - Parallel processing without duplicates	430
Scenario 3 - Streaming real-time data for processing	430
Scenario 4 - Streaming real-time data for storing	430
How it works...	431
Real-world example scenarios	431
Scenario 1 - Pub-Sub scenario with multiple producers and consumers	431
Scenario 2 - Parallel processing	431
Scenario 3 - Streaming real-time data for processing	431
Scenario 4 - Streaming real-time data for storage	432
There's more...	432
Building a full stack web application on AWS	432
See also	433
Chapter 10: Other Cloud Providers	**435**
Introduction	**435**
Your first Serverless application in Azure	**436**
Getting ready	436
How to do it...	436
Deploying the function to Azure	438
Getting function info from UI and verifying the deployment	439
How It works...	440
There's more...	441
See also	443
Your first serverless application on Google Cloud Platform	**444**
Getting ready	444
How to do it...	444
How it works...	446
There's more...	447
See also	448
Your first Serverless application on IBM cloud	**449**

Getting ready	449
How to do it...	450
How It works...	454
There's more...	454
See also	456

Other Books You May Enjoy — 459

Index — 463

Preface

Managing physical servers will be a thing of the past once you're able to harness the power of Serverless computing. This recipe-based guide provides solutions to problems you might face while building Serverless applications.

You'll begin by setting up **Amazon Web Services** (**AWS**), the primary cloud provider used for most recipes. The next set of recipes will teach you about the components you need to build a Serverless web application, such as REST APIs, database, user management, authentication, domain registration, DNS management, website hosting, and CDN. The book also provides you with a fresh perspective by introducing you to the latest technology trends with recipes based on messaging, notifications, data analytics, machine learning, and NLP. Further, the book contains recipes on DevOps practices such as logging and monitoring. AWS discussion ends with some real-world practices and patterns. Finally, to broaden your understanding of Serverless computing, you'll also cover *getting started* guides for other cloud providers, such as Azure, Google Cloud Platform, and IBM cloud.

The Serverless architecture allows you to build and run applications and services without having to manage the necessary infrastructure, which reduces expenditure and improves scalability. In this book, you will learn how to harness Serverless technology to reduce production time, minimize cost, and gain the freedom to customize your code, all without hindering functionality.

By the end of this book, you'll have acquired the skills you need to build Serverless applications efficiently using various public cloud offerings.

Who this book is for

This book is aimed at developers looking for practical solutions to common problems encountered while building a Serverless application, providing helpful recipes to solve these problems. To get started with this intermediate-level book, knowledge of basic programming is a must.

What this book covers

Chapter 1, *Getting Started with Serverless Computing on AWS*, covers building Serverless applications with AWS Lambda. We will also get familiar with AWS IAM and AWS CloudFormation, two services that we will be using a lot in the coming chapters.

Chapter 2, *Building Serverless REST APIs with API Gateway*, will show you how to create reliable and scalable API Gateway REST APIs. Some of the API Gateway functionality, such as **Cross Origin Resource Sharing** (**CORS**), will be covered later.

Chapter 3, *Data Storage with Amazon DynamoDB*, contains recipes for Amazon DynamoDB, a fully managed NoSQL database, integrating DynamoDB with AWS Lambda, along with some example scenarios and solutions for throughput provisioning.

Chapter 4, *Application Security with Amazon Cognito*, covers how to use Amazon Cognito for user signup, user login, and user management. We will cover real-world applications of Cognito, such as federated logins, in a later chapter.

Chapter 5, *Web Hosting with S3, Route53, and CloudFront*, outlines recipes related to hosting a website, including registering domain names, hosting a static website with Amazon S3, attaching a custom domain for our S3 bucket, and using CloudFront CDN.

Chapter 6, *Messaging and Notifications with SQS and SNS*, discusses how Amazon SQS and Amazon SNS are generally used for interprocess communications within Serverless applications. We will also see how these services can be triggered in AWS Lambda.

Chapter 7, *Redshift, Amazon ML, and Alexa Skills*, explores how the following services can bring value to Serverless computing in the areas of analytics and natural language processing, covering Amazon Kinesis, Amazon Machine Learning, and Amazon Alexa Skill Sets.

Chapter 8, *Monitoring and Alerting with Amazon CloudWatch*, discusses monitoring and alerting, both of which are essential DevOps practices. We will also see CloudWatch alarms, CloudWatch metrics, and CloudWatch metric log filters.

Chapter 9, *Serverless Programming Practices and Patterns*, explores some patterns and practices for Serverless applications within the AWS platform. We will see how some of the services covered previously interact together, and how they are implemented in real-world projects.

Chapter 10, *Other Cloud Provider Services*, provides a basic understanding and some *getting started* guides for Serverless computing with a few other cloud providers. The main intention of this section is to explore the popular alternatives and learn to do quick setups for proof-of-concept demonstrations.

To get the most out of this book

Readers should be familiar with Java, Maven, Git, and Unix/Mac terminal or the Windows Command Prompt. To work with the JavaScript recipes you also need to be familiar with JavaScript. Additional links are provided within the *See more* section of the recipes to explain the prerequisite technologies. To make best use of the book you should first read the book from beginning until the end, at least once. After this, or along with reading the book, you may execute the code provided within the code files following the directions given within the book, and within the repository's `readme` files. Example codes should specify names or IDs. You will have to replace them with the name and ID that you create. Finally, you should build the projects on your own following the book's content.

Download the example code files

You can download the example code files for this book from your account at `www.packt.com`. If you purchased this book elsewhere, you can visit `www.packt.com/support` and register to have the files emailed directly to you.

You can download the code files by following these steps:

1. Log in or register at `www.packt.com`.
2. Select the **SUPPORT** tab.
3. Click on **Code Downloads & Errata**.
4. Enter the name of the book in the **Search** box and follow the onscreen instructions.

Once the file is downloaded, please make sure that you unzip or extract the folder using the latest version of:

- WinRAR/7-Zip for Windows
- Zipeg/iZip/UnRarX for Mac
- 7-Zip/PeaZip for Linux

Preface

The code bundle for the book is also hosted on GitHub at `https://github.com/PacktPublishing/Serverless-Programming-Cookbook`. In case there's an update to the code, it will be updated on the existing GitHub repository.

We also have other code bundles from our rich catalog of books and videos available at `https://github.com/PacktPublishing/`. Check them out!

Conventions used

There are a number of text conventions used throughout this book.

`CodeInText`: Indicates code words in text, database table names, folder names, filenames, file extensions, pathnames, dummy URLs, user input, and Twitter handles. Here is an example: "Mount the downloaded `WebStorm-10*.dmg` disk image file as another disk in your system."

A block of code is set as follows:

```
Resources:
 MyFirstRestAPI:
  Type: AWS::ApiGateway::RestApi
  Properties:
   Name: Greeting API
```

When we wish to draw your attention to a particular part of a code block, the relevant lines or items are set in bold:

```
GreetingResource:
   Type: AWS::ApiGateway::Resource
   Properties:
      RestApiId: !Ref MyFirstRestAPI
      ParentId: !GetAtt MyFirstRestAPI.RootResourceId
```

Any command-line input or output is written as follows:

```
aws apigateway create-resource \
    --rest-api-id c82tpsb7ka \
```

Preface

Bold: Indicates a new term, an important word, or words that you see onscreen. For example, words in menus or dialog boxes appear in the text like this. Here is an example: "Select **System info** from the **Administration** panel."

Warnings or important notes appear like this.

Tips and tricks appear like this.

Get in touch

Feedback from our readers is always welcome.

General feedback: If you have questions about any aspect of this book, mention the book title in the subject of your message and email us at `customercare@packtpub.com`.

Errata: Although we have taken every care to ensure the accuracy of our content, mistakes do happen. If you have found a mistake in this book, we would be grateful if you would report this to us. Please visit `www.packt.com/submit-errata`, selecting your book, clicking on the Errata Submission Form link, and entering the details.

Piracy: If you come across any illegal copies of our works in any form on the Internet, we would be grateful if you would provide us with the location address or website name. Please contact us at `copyright@packt.com` with a link to the material.

If you are interested in becoming an author: If there is a topic that you have expertise in and you are interested in either writing or contributing to a book, please visit `authors.packtpub.com`.

Reviews

Please leave a review. Once you have read and used this book, why not leave a review on the site that you purchased it from? Potential readers can then see and use your unbiased opinion to make purchase decisions, we at Packt can understand what you think about our products, and our authors can see your feedback on their book. Thank you!

For more information about Packt, please visit `packt.com`.

Getting Started with Serverless Computing on AWS

This chapter will cover the following topics:

- Getting started with the AWS platform
- Your first AWS Lambda
- Your first Lambda with AWS CLI
- Your first Lambda with Amazon CloudFormation
- Using AWS SDK, Amazon CloudFormation, and AWS CLI with Lambda
- Dev practices: dependency injection and unit testing
- Your first Lambda with Serverless framework

Introduction

Cloud computing introduced a pay-per-use model and abstracted physical servers with virtual machines and managed services. Cloud computing execution models include **Infrastructure as a Service (IaaS)**, **Platform as a service (PaaS)**, **Software as a Service (SaaS)**, and Serverless computing (or **Function as a Service (FaaS)**).

IaaS provides services that form the basic building blocks of cloud computing, such as virtual machines, storage, network, and so on. PaaS provides platforms on which we can develop applications such as execution runtime, databases, web servers, and so on. Saas provides completed software that we can use for various needs such as Gmail's email service.

Getting Started with Serverless Computing on AWS

Serverless computing allows us to run functions (code) without worrying about servers and pay only for the time we execute code. Despite the name, servers are still present, however, the provider does all the server management including starting and stopping them to serve requests, patching and more. Serverless computing comes roughly in between PaaS and SaaS.

This book focuses on AWS cloud (except in the last chapter), but most concepts apply to any cloud provider. Within AWS recipes, we will specify the AWS CLI commands for most of the use cases. In addition, we will use Java for all use cases where we generally use AWS Lambda such as working with DynamoDB database, Kinesis streams, SQS and SNS, and building backend for an Alexa skill. For services that are generally integrated into the UI such as Cognito we will discuss JavaScript SDK code. For one-time activities such as account creation and domain registration, and monitoring, we will also discuss AWS Management console steps.

Getting started with the AWS platform

Amazon provides you with Free Tier to get started with AWS on production quality servers. Free Tier provides you with free access to many services and features with decent limits.

Free Tier policies may change anytime. So, to avoid accidental costs, do check the Free Tier policies regularly at https://aws.amazon.com/free.

Getting ready

To work with AWS Free Tier, you need a decent computer, a reasonable internet connection, a working credit card, and basic knowledge of computers and the internet.

How to do it...

Let's get started on the AWS platform by creating a Free Tier account. We will then do some basic IAM settings as suggested by AWS. Finally, we will also create a billing alarm to keep track of any unexpected costs. If you already have a working account with basic setup done, you may skip this part of the recipe:

1. Go to `https://aws.amazon.com` and create a new Free Tier account (if you do not already have one) as follows:
    1. Provide login credentials.
    2. Provide personal information such as address, phone number, and other required details, if you have selected **Personal account**, or **Corporate information** if you have selected company account.
    3. Provide credit card details.
    4. Proceed with telephonic verification.
    5. Select **Basic plan** for Free Tier account with community support (or select a paid plan if you want to).

   After logging in for the first time, it is recommended that you complete the basic **Identity and Access Management (IAM)** security settings listed under the **Security Status** heading. If you have previously logged in, the options might not be displayed as shown next. If so, you need to manually go to IAM service from the **Services** dropdown.

2. Click on **Activate Multi-Factor Authentication (MFA) on your root account** and do as follows:
    1. Click **Manage**.
    2. Select **A Virtual MFA Device**.
    3. Click Continue on the message for installing an MFA-compatible application (assuming you have installed Google Authenticator along with barcode scanner, or any similar applications).
    4. Scan the barcode shown on screen using Google Authenticator, and enter two consecutive codes for confirmation.

3. Click on **Create individual IAM users** and do as follows:
    1. **Enter Username**.
    2. **Select Access Type** (`Programmatic access and AWS Management Console access`).
    3. Download the credentials `.csv` file to a secure area in your local machine. You will not be able to download it later, but you can regenerate it.

Getting Started with Serverless Computing on AWS

4. Click on **Use groups** to assign permissions and assign some random permissions.
5. Click on **Apply an IAM password policy** to set up a basic password policy.

 It is a good practice to assign permissions through groups even if there is only one user.

IAM dashboard should now show all security status items as green:

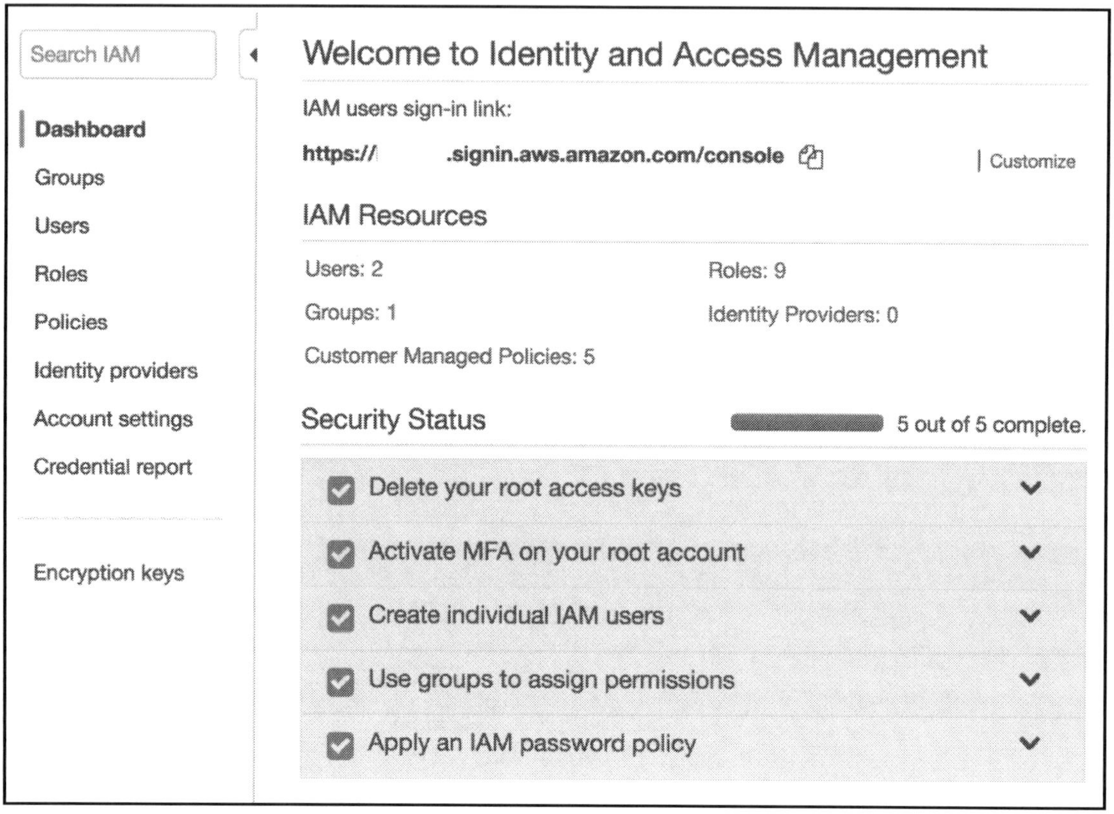

6. Create a billing alarm to have a check on accidental costs:
    1. Go to **My Billing Dashboard** (by clicking the drop-down arrow near to your name).
    2. Under **Alerts and Notifications**, click on **Enable Now to Monitor your estimated charges**.
    3. After going to **Preferences**, select **Receive Billing Alerts** and click on

[10]

Chapter 1

> **Manage Billing Alerts** link within the contents, which will take you to CloudWatch.
> 4. Click on **Billing** and create an alarm.

 You may also use the **budgets** feature to keep track of your costs. Read more at https://docs.aws.amazon.com/awsaccountbilling/latest/aboutv2/budgets-managing-costs.html.

If you followed all previous steps successfully, you are ready to get started with further recipes in this book.

How it works...

Most of the steps in this recipe are self-explanatory and similar to registering for any other paid online service. The following are the important AWS services and concepts that were introduced in this recipe.

AWS Identity and Access Management (IAM)

IAM enables secure access to AWS resources. IAM supports standard security concepts such as users, groups, roles, and permissions. The user is an individual who wants to use AWS services. Users can be added to groups. Users and groups are assigned with permissions. Roles are used by a service (for example, Amazon Ec2) for accessing other services.

Amazon CloudWatch

Amazon CloudWatch is a service that helps in monitoring your applications, responding to changes (such as performance changes and billing alarms), optimizing resource utilization, and providing you a unified view of the health of services in your account. We will see more use cases of Amazon CloudWatch in later recipes.

Multi-Factor Authentication (MFA)

Multi-Factor Authentication provides additional levels of authentication. In addition to passwords, it also requires you to authenticate using a token generated by a virtual or physical authenticator. It is a good practice to set up MFA even for personal accounts, as the password is the same as the e-commerce portal and Prime Video.

[11]

Getting Started with Serverless Computing on AWS

There's more...

The following are some of the common AWS services that are used in building Serverless applications on the AWS:

- **AWS Lambda** lets you write code without configuring any server.
- **Amazon API Gateway** lets you create REST APIs without coding.
- **Amazon Simple Storage Service (S3)** is an object store that helps you store and retrieve data. S3 can also be used for hosting **single-page applications** (**SPA**) such as an angular or react application.
- **Amazon DynamoDB** is a scalable NoSQL database.
- **Amazon CloudFront** is a **Content Delivery Network** (**CDN**) service.
- **Amazon CloudWatch** is a service to monitor your applications and respond to changes.
- **AWS CloudFormation** templates written in JSON or YAML can be used to provision and model our infrastructure.
- **AWS Identity and Access Management** (**IAM**) provides access control for AWS resources.
- **Amazon Cognito** helps you build access control for your application with features such as user sign-up, sign-in, and more.
- **Other services** can be used alongside these services for advanced use cases, such as natural language processing (for example, Alexa Skills kit, and Lex), Analytics (Amazon Kinesis Streams), Machine Learning (Amazon Machine Learning), and so on.

Apart from using the AWS management console from a browser, we can also interact with AWS services from AWS **CLI (command line)** and AWS SDK (programmatic access). Except for the first few recipes, we will mostly focus on using Amazon CloudWatch with AWS CLI for modeling and provisioning our infrastructure.

See also

- https://aws.amazon.com/getting-started

Chapter 1

Your first AWS Lambda

AWS Lambda is the core service in AWS for building serverless applications. You can run code without provisioning servers. You pay only for the time you run your code, unlike EC2 where you pay for the time the server is up. Lambda also takes care of high availability. You can invoke Lambdas from other AWS services, console, or AWS CLI.

In this recipe, we will create a Lambda in Java and deploy it using the AWS management console. In the next recipe, we will also explore AWS CLI to deploy Lambda. In later recipes and chapters, we will see how we can automate most of the deployment tasks using Amazon CloudWatch templates similar to how most enterprise projects do.

Getting ready

To follow the example in this recipe, you need a working AWS account. You should also set up **Java Development Kit (JDK)** and Maven in your local machine. I am currently using Java 8 and Maven 3.5.4.

Example projects in this book uses a maven parent project, `serverless-cookbook-parent-aws-java`. The versions of libraries used within each Lambda project (for example, `aws.sdk.version`) are defined in the parent project `POM` file.

> If you want to extend any recipe for your particular use case without needing to have the parent project, you can easily get rid of the parent project by moving the required properties and dependencies into the individual projects.

It is a good idea to create a folder within your operating system to manage the code files for this book. I will use a folder with the name `serverless`. You need to make sure that you can execute the following commands from this folder:

```
javac -version
mvn -version
```

You can set up the parent project inside our parent folder (`serverless` in my case) by executing the following commands from the command line:

1. Clone our book's Github repository:

    ```
    git clone
    https://github.com/PacktPublishing/Serverless-Programming-Cookbook.git
    ```

[13]

Getting Started with Serverless Computing on AWS

2. Go inside the repository folder, go inside our project-specific parent project, and run `mvn clean install`:

```
cd Serverless-Programming-Cookbook
cd serverless-cookbook-parent-aws-java
mvn clean install
```

The code repository of this book already has working code for all the recipes, where applicable. You may also create another folder within the parent folder (`serverless` is the parent folder in my case) to practice the examples within this book, and look into the code repository files only, when in doubt.

Code repository usage guidelines

Each chapter has a directory of its own (for example, `Chapter 01`). Inside the chapter's directory there will be sub-directories for each recipe. The recipe specific directory has names corresponding to the recipe's title. For example, the directory for this chapter, recipe titled *Your first Lambda* is `your-first-lambda`.

Inside the recipe's directory, there will be a directory for storing all resources including the AWS CLI commands called `resources`. Long AWS CLI commands are split into multiple lines for better readability using the \ symbol. If you are using a Windows machine you can use the ^ symbol instead of the \ symbol in the code files or make a single line command without the \ symbol.

The recipe's directory also contains a sub-directory for each Lambda project. You need to run `mvn clean package` for generating the Lambda JAR from within this directory. The Lambda JAR is generated within the target directory inside this directory. Every Lambda project inherits from the common Lambda parent project's directory `serverless-cookbook-parent-aws-java` and hence needs to be built before any Lambda project, following the steps outlined in the previous section.

Code examples within the book follows the AWS documentation style and is tested primarily on Mac operating system. It should also work on most Unix based operating systems such as Linux. For alternative solutions you may refer to the code files repository. Please refer to the heading *Alternative Solutions* in the repository's readme file for more details.

[14]

Chapter 1

Various user specific parameter values such as IDs, AWS account numbers, generated JAR file names etc. given within the examples has to be replaced with valid values based on previous steps executed and your account specific details. Copy pasting and executing the commands without verifying and replacing such parameter values can result in error.

How to do it...

We will create our first Lambda with Java as a Maven project. The javadoc comments and `package-info.java` files required for checkstyle checks from the parent are not shown here. We are also making use of the Maven shade plugin from the parent for generating the JAR files. You may refer to the code files for each recipe for the complete code:

1. Create the Java project based on Maven.

    Create a Java project based on Maven with our common parent, declared as shown next in the POM file:

You may use an IDE such as Intellij IDEA or Eclipse for working with the examples in this book.

```
<groupId>tech.heartin.books.serverless-cookbook</groupId>
<artifactId>helloworld-lambda</artifactId>
<version>0.0.1-SNAPSHOT</version>
<parent>
    <groupId>tech.heartin.books.serverlesscookbook</groupId>
    <artifactId>serverless-cookbook-parent-aws-java</artifactId>
    <version>0.0.1-SNAPSHOT</version>
</parent>
```

2. Also, declare the only dependency we need for our `hello world lambda` project in the POM file:

```
<dependencies>
  <dependency>
      <groupId>com.amazonaws</groupId>
      <artifactId>aws-lambda-java-core</artifactId>
      <version>${aws.lambda.java.core.version}</version>
  </dependency>
</dependencies>
```

[15]

Getting Started with Serverless Computing on AWS

The dependency versions (for example, `aws.lambda.java.core.version`) are defined in the POM file for the parent project `serverless-cookbook-parent-aws-java`.

3. Create the Lambda handler class and package it as a JAR.

   Create a class, `HelloWorldLambdaHandler`, that implements the interface, `RequestHandler`:

   ```
   package tech.heartin.books.serverlesscookbook;

   import com.amazonaws.services.lambda.runtime.Context;
   import com.amazonaws.services.lambda.runtime.RequestHandler;

   public final class HelloWorldLambdaHandler implements
   RequestHandler<String, String> {
       public String handleRequest(final String s, final Context
   context) {
           context.getLogger().log("input: " + s + "\n");
           String greeting = "Hello " + s;
           return greeting;
       }
   }
   ```

   To package the Lambda as a JAR file, from the project root folder, run the following:

   mvn clean package

   Two JARS will be created: one with only class files (starting with `original-`) and an Uber JAR with dependencies (starting with `serverless-`). You can easily differentiate between one and the other looking at their sizes. We will use the JAR file that starts with `original-` and that has only the class files for this recipe.

4. Deploy the Lambda handler to the AWS:
   1. Log in to the AWS console, and go to Lambda dashboard by clicking on **Services** and searching or selecting **Lambda**. Currently, it is under the compute category.
   2. Create a Lambda function as follows:
      1. Click on **Create Function.**
      2. Select `Author From Scratch`, which is the default.
      3. Give a name, such as `myHelloWorldLambda`.
      4. Select `Java 8` as the runtime.

[16]

Chapter 1

2. Under Role, select `Create new role from one or more templates`.
3. Give a role name, such as `myHelloWorldLambda`.
4. Leave the field for specifying **Policy templates** blank.
5. Click on **Create Function**. You should see a success message after a while.

5. Upload the Lambda JAR:

   Go to the **Function code** section and do the following:

   1. Select **Code entry type** as `Upload a .zip or .jar file`.
   2. Select `Java 8` as the runtime.
   3. Specify the fully qualified class name with handler method name as the following:
      `tech.heartin.books.serverlesscookbook.HelloWorldLambdaHandler::handleRequest`.
   4. Click on **Upload** under **Function package** and select the `JAR` file. You can select the JAR whose name starts with `original-`.
   5. Click on **Save** to save with defaults for other fields.

6. We can test the uploaded JAR:
   1. Select `Configure test events` from the **Select a test event** dropdown next to the **Test** button.
   2. Select **Create new test event.**
   3. Give a name for the event: `MyHelloWorldTest`.
   4. Within the JSON request content area, just specify your name, such as `Heartin`.
   5. Click on **Create**. If successful, it will take you to the `myHelloWorldLambda` function page.
   6. From the `myHelloWorldLambda` function page, select the test event, `MyHelloWorldTest`, next to the **Test** button, and click the **Test** button.
   7. You should see the message `Hello Heartin` after expanding the **details of execution result.**

[17]

7. We can also check the logs printed using `context.getLogger().log()`:
   1. Under the **Log output** section, you can see the log you printed.
   2. You can also see the log in the CloudWatch service. There should be a **Click here** link to view the CloudWatch log group. Click on the link, wait or refresh for a stream that matches your invocation time, and click on the stream link to see the log statement within CloudWatch.

How it works...

The following are the in detail information about the role and functionality of Lambda plays and concepts that were introduced in this recipe.

About the parent POM

Example projects in this book use the Maven parent project `serverless-cookbook-parent-aws-java` that defines the dependency versions for our examples. The actual dependencies are defined within each example project to help you understand the dependencies needed for each use case. All dependency definitions are shown within comments in the parent `POM` for quick reference.

Our parent project `serverless-cookbook-parent-aws-java` is also dependent on two open source projects: `simple-starter-parent-java` for the common Java dependencies, and `simple-starter-build-tools` for the common build file, such as the code style plugin definitions.

Lambda roles

In this recipe, we selected the **Create new role from template(s)** and did not select any policy. The basic permissions required (logging to CloudWatch) are added by default. We can also choose an existing role or create a custom role.

Lambda runtimes

AWS Lambda supports various runtimes, such as C# (.NET Core 1.0), C# (.NET Core 2.0), C# (.NET Core 2.1), Go 1.x, Java 8, Node.js 4.3, Node.js 6.10, Node.js 8.10, Python 2.7, and Python 3.6. Inline code editing is only allowed for Node.js and Python.

Extra dependencies

Our parent project, `serverless-cookbook-parent-aws-java`, defines a few more dependencies than I have. You can download them automatically through Maven (these projects are already available in Maven Central) or set these up manually in your local machine (to examine or modify) by executing the following commands from the command line.

1. Go inside the parent folder (`serverless` in my case) and clone the `simple-starter-build-tools` project:

    ```
    git clone https://github.com/heartin/simple-starter-build-tools.git
    ```

2. Go inside the project folder and run `mvn clean install`, as follows:

    ```
    cd simple-starter-build-tools
    mvn clean install
    ```

3. Go back to the parent folder (`serverless` in my case) and clone the `simple-starter-parent-java` project:

    ```
    git clone https://github.com/heartin/simple-starter-parent-java.git
    ```

4. Go inside the project folder and run `mvn clean install`:

    ```
    cd simple-starter-parent-java
    mvn clean install
    ```

> For more details on the preceding project dependencies, refer to the respective `Readme` files.

There's more...

The following are the in detail information about the other ways to create Lambda and to deploy its functions:

Other ways to create Lambda functions from the management console

Apart from the **Author from scratch** option, we can create Lambdas using **Blueprints** and **Serverless Application Repository**. **Blueprints** allow you to choose a preconfigured template as a starting point. Currently, blueprints are available only for Node.js and Python. **Serverless Application Repository** allows you to find and deploy Serverless apps developed by developers, companies and partners on AWS.

Other ways to deploy code in a Lambda function

In this recipe, we developed our code outside AWS and uploaded it to our AWS Lambda function as a `JAR` file. You can also upload the file to Amazon S3 by selecting **Code entry type** as `Upload a file from Amazon S3`, and providing the S3 link. For some languages such as Node.js and Python, you can also write the code inline within the Lambda function.

Passing JSON to and from Lambda handler

In this recipe, we passed simple Strings to and from our Lambda handler. We can instead pass a JSON and get back a JSON. To do this, we need to create two POJOs that represent our input and output, and specify them as generic types within our Handler declaration. We will see this approach in the next recipe.

See also

- Read about the *Programming Model for Authoring Lambda Functions in Java* at `https://docs.aws.amazon.com/lambda/latest/dg/java-programming-model.html`
- Read about the *Lambda permissions model* at `https://docs.aws.amazon.com/lambda/latest/dg/intro-permission-model.html`
- If you find any issues while setting up and using AWS, you can visit this page for troubleshooting help: `http://cloudmaterials.com/en/book/troubleshooting-aws-cloud-beginners`
- If you are new to Java, Maven or Git you may read my notes on those from these links:
    - `https://javajee.com/book/java-101-core-java-essentials`

- `https://javajee.com/book/maven-101-maven-build-automation-tool-essentials`
- `https://javajee.com/book/git-101-git-distributed-version-control-system-essentials`

Your first Lambda with AWS CLI

The AWS **Command Line Interface** (**CLI**) is a command line tool provided by AWS to manage AWS services. You can save your credentials and config into profiles, and then specify a profile while executing a command. The more you get familiar with the CLI commands, the faster you can work with AWS services, making you more productive.

In this recipe, we will deploy an AWS Lambda using AWS CLI. We will use an updated hello world. In the last recipe, we had sent and received back simple text. In this recipe, we will demonstrate the use of POJOs for sending to and retrieving JSON data from the Lambda handler.

In most of the later recipes within this book, I will be including AWS CLI commands along with either Management Console or CloudFormation steps to provide an overview of various API usages in a programming language-independent way. You can follow these API usages along with any particular programming language SDK documentation to implement it in that language. The CLI commands also help us better understand the CloudFormation templates.

Getting ready

Following are the prerequisites for this recipe:

1. Install and configure JDK, Maven and the parent project, `serverless-cookbook-parent-aws-java`, and read the section as outlined in
2. Follow the *Getting ready* section of the recipe *Your first AWS Lambda* to install and configure JDK, Maven and the parent project, `serverless-cookbook-parent-aws-java`, and follow the notes given in that section for code usage guidelines
3. Configure AWS CLI as given later in this section
4. Create an S3 bucket

Configuring AWS CLI

We can use `pip` or `pip3` to install AWS CLI.

> In a Windows machine, you can also install AWS CLI using the MSI installer following the steps at https://docs.aws.amazon.com/cli/latest/userguide/awscli-install-windows.html#install-msi-on-windows.

You use `pip` or `pip3` to install AWS CLI as:

```
pip install awscli --upgrade --user
```

Pip is a Python package management tool that can be installed along with Python. You may replace `pip` with `pip3` if you have installed `pip3`. The `--upgrade` option upgrades any installed requirements. The `--user` option installs the program to a sub-directory of your user directory to avoid modifying libraries used by operating system.

> The ids or keys shown within the examples in this book should be replaced with your own ids wherever applicable. Simply copy pasting the commands will not work in such cases.

We can configure our AWS credentials in our local machine by running `aws configure`. This will setup a default AWS profile. You can have more named profiles if you want.

> **TIP**: It is recommended that you create the default profile with credentials of a user with basic permissions. You can then create additional profiles for other use cases. We will be creating a user profile called `admin` later within this section for a user with admin permissions.

Run the below command to configure AWS CLI for the default profile. If `aws` command is not recognized, you will need to add it to the path.

```
aws configure
```

Provide your **AWS Access Key ID**, **AWS Secret Access Key**, **Default region name**, and **Default output format**:

```
AWS Access Key ID [None]: AKIAJMLZ7HO5RLH3NB7A
AWS Secret Access Key [None]: J4fk9Jlf+r3LBSX4HkR+QKRJgnPzvZbZ2/lmddtS
Default region name [None]: us-east-1
Default output format [None]: json
```

Chapter 1

AWS Access Key ID and **AWS Secret Access Key** is generated by AWS when you create a user with programmatic access. We had created an user and generated these credentials in the recipe *Getting started with the AWS platform*. You can also regenerate them later if you forget or miss them following the below steps:

1. Log in to AWS.
2. Go to IAM service.
3. Click on **Users** from the sidebar. This will show you the user summary page.
4. From within the user summary page, click on **Security Credentials** tab.
5. Click on **Create access key** to create a new key. You may make the old key inactive or delete it.

The **AWS Access Key ID** and **AWS Secret Access Key** entered is stored in a file, `~/.aws/credentials`, and the region name and output format is stored in a file, `~/.aws/config`.

> If you are using a Windows machine please refer to the sub heading *Note for Windows users* at the end of this section.

Verify the configuration as given as follows:

`cat ~/.aws/credentials`

```
[default]
aws_access_key_id = AKIAJMLZ7HO5RLH3NB7A
aws_secret_access_key = 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
```

And next, run `cat ~/.aws/config`:

```
[default]
region = us-east-1
output = json
```

Getting Started with Serverless Computing on AWS

AWS documentation recommends creating a named profile for your `admin` user (for instance, a user with administrator access policy) and then using it with AWS CLI. You can add an additional profile in `~/.aws/credentials`, as shown here:

```
[default]
aws_access_key_id = AKIAJMLZ7HO5RLH3NB7A
aws_secret_access_key = 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

[admin]
aws_access_key_id = BKIAJMLZ7HO5RLH3NB7B
aws_secret_access_key = K4fk9Jlf+r3LBSX4HkR+QKRJgnPzvZbZ2/1mddtT
```

You can add an additional profile by editing the file `~/.aws/config`, as shown here:

```
[default]
region = us-east-1
output = json

[profile admin]
region = us-east-1
output = json
```

Creating S3 bucket

We will be using Amazon **Simple Storage Service (S3)** to upload our JAR files. Therefore it would be good to do some reading on basic S3 concepts, such as S3 buckets and S3 keys.

You can create a bucket using the below command:

```
aws s3 mb s3://<bucket name> --profile admin
```

Replace the `<bucket name>` with your bucket's name. Remember that the S3 bucket name has to be unique across AWS.

Note for Windows users

If you are using a Windows machine the `.aws` folder should be present inside your user profile folder and may be found as `dir %UserProfile%\.aws`. You may also use the notepad command to edit files in a notepad instead of the `cat` command. Remember to save the notepad file if you are editing:

Chapter 1

```
C:\2018\AWS_Serverless>dir %UserProfile%\.aws
 Volume in drive C is Windows
 Volume Serial Number is 2275-89FB

 Directory of C:\Users_____\.aws

23/09/2018  21:58    <DIR>          .
23/09/2018  21:58    <DIR>          ..
26/09/2018  23:27                98 config
04/10/2018  23:47               362 credentials
               2 File(s)            460 bytes
               2 Dir(s)  181,064,708,096 bytes free

C:\2018\AWS_Serverless>notepad C:\Users_____\.aws\credentials
```

```
credentials - Notepad
File Edit Format View Help
[default]
aws_access_key_id = AKIAIAT2YWL5GAHGERGA
aws_secret_access_key = 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

[admin]
aws_access_key_id = AKIAIUW6CSOA4QDNP2YA
aws_secret_access_key = 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[serverless-admin
```

> CLI commands that feature in this book should work on the terminals of a UNIX-style operating system, such as Linux or Mac, without any or many changes. Minor modifications may be needed to execute them in other platforms. For example, specifying multi-line commands using \ has to be replaced with ^ for the Windows OS command prompt, and ` for PowerShell.

How to do it...

We will create our Lambda, similar to in the `Your First AWS Lambda` recipe, but using POJOs for input and output. We will not go deep into concepts discussed previously. If in doubt, please refer to the *Your First AWS Lambda* recipe.

1. Create the Maven project with only the core dependency, `aws-lambda-java-core`:

    ```xml
    <groupId>tech.heartin.books.serverless-cookbook</groupId>
    <artifactId>lambda-handler-with-pojos</artifactId>
    <version>0.0.1-SNAPSHOT</version>

    <parent>
     <groupId>tech.heartin.books.serverlesscookbook</groupId>
     <artifactId>serverless-cookbook-parent-aws-java</artifactId>
     <version>0.0.1-SNAPSHOT</version>
    </parent>

    <dependencies>
     <dependency>
      <groupId>com.amazonaws</groupId>
      <artifactId>aws-lambda-java-core</artifactId>
      <version>${aws.lambda.java.core.version}</version>
     </dependency>
    </dependencies>
    ```

[25]

2. Create POJO for input:

   ```
   import lombok.Data;

   @Data
   public class HandlerRequest {
       private String name;
   }
   ```

3. Create POJO for output:

   ```
   import lombok.AllArgsConstructor;
   import lombok.Data;

   @Data
   @AllArgsConstructor
   public class HandlerResponse {
       private String message;
   }
   ```

   > I have used project `lombok` within the POJOs to autogenerate setters, getters, and all-arguments constructor. The `lombok` dependencies are defined in the parent project, `simple-starter-parent-java`.

4. Create a Lambda handler with input and output POJOs:

   ```
   public final class MyLambdaHandler implements RequestHandler<HandlerRequest, HandlerResponse> {
       public HandlerResponse handleRequest(final HandlerRequest request,
                                            final Context context) {
           context.getLogger().log("Hello " + request.getName());
           return new HandlerResponse("Hello " + request.getName());
       }
   }
   ```

5. Package the JAR.

   We can generate JARs by running `mvn clean package`. Two JARs are created: one with only class files (starting with `original-`) and an Uber JAR with dependencies (starting with `serverless-`). In this recipe, we will use the original JAR.

Chapter 1

6. Upload the JAR file to your S3 bucket using AWS CLI:

   ```
   aws s3 cp target/original-serverless-cookbook-lambda-handler-with-pojos-0.0.1-SNAPSHOT.jar s3://serverless-cookbook/lambda-handler-with-pojos-0.0.1-SNAPSHOT.jar --profile admin
   ```

   > Replace the bucket name `serverless-cookbook` with your bucket's name. We saw the steps to create a bucket in the *Getting ready* section. Also, `--profile admin` is the profile we created in the *Getting ready* section.

7. Create a policy with the `aws iam create-policy` command:

   ```
   aws iam create-policy \
   --policy-name lambda_iam_policy_test \
   --policy-document file://basic-lambda-permissions.txt \
   --profile admin
   ```

   Replace `<account_id>` with your account id. You can get your account number by going to the **My Account** page after clicking on your name on the top right of your AWS management console. The policy file is also available in the resources folder of the recipe. If successful, you should get a response with the ARN of the policy created.

   > **TIP**
   > You may create a more restricting policy after checking the basic Lambda permissions template at `https://docs.aws.amazon.com/lambda/latest/dg/policy-templates.html`.

8. Create a role using the `aws iam create-role` command:

   ```
   aws iam create-role \
   --role-name lambda_iam_role_test \
   --assume-role-policy-document file://iam-role-trust-relationship.txt \
   --profile admin
   ```

   The policy file is available in the resources folder of the recipe. If successful, you should get a response with the `arn` of the role created.

   > Trust relationship policies allow the Lambda service to assume this role whereas the standard policy document is attached to a role to allow or deny access to resources.

9. Attach the policy to the role:

    ```
    aws iam attach-role-policy \
    --role-name lambda_iam_role_test \
    --policy-arn
    arn:aws:iam::<account_id>:policy/lambda_iam_policy_test \
    --profile admin
    ```

    Replace `<account_id>` with your account number.

10. Create a Lambda function providing the role and the S3 location:

    ```
    aws lambda create-function \
    --function-name demo-lambda-with-cli \
    --runtime java8 \
    --role arn:aws:iam::<account_id>:role/lambda_iam_role_test \
    --handler
    tech.heartin.books.serverlesscookbook.MyLambdaHandler::handleReques
    t \
    --code S3Bucket=serverless-cookbook,S3Key=lambda-handler-with-
    pojos-0.0.1-SNAPSHOT.jar \
    --timeout 15 \
    --memory-size 512 \
    --profile admin
    ```

    Replace `<account_id>` with your account number. The code option can accept the shorthand form as used here, or a JSON.

11. Invoke our Lambda from CLI:

    ```
    aws lambda invoke \
    --invocation-type RequestResponse \
    --function-name demo-lambda-with-cli \
    --log-type Tail \
    --payload '{"name":"Heartin"}' \
    --profile admin \
    outputfile.txt
    ```

    In certain platforms, you might have to add escaping for the payload specified in the command line. This is not required as the payload is specified as a file, as here:

    ```
    --payload file://input.txt \
    ```

Chapter 1

The output can be viewed in the `outputfile.txt` file:

```
$ cat outputfile.txt
{"message":"Hello Heartin"}$
```

12. Note the following regarding cleanup roles, policy, and Lambda.

    To delete Lambda, perform the following:

    ```
    aws lambda delete-function \
    --function-name demo-lambda-with-cli \
    --profile admin
    ```

    To detach policy from the role, perform the following:

    ```
    aws iam detach-role-policy \
    --role-name lambda_iam_role_test \
    --policy-arn
    arn:aws:iam::<account_id>:policy/lambda_iam_policy_test \
    --profile admin
    ```

    Replace `<account_id>` with your account number.

    To delete a role, note the following:

    ```
    aws iam delete-role \
    --role-name lambda_iam_role_test \
    --profile admin
    ```

    To delete policy, perform the following:

    ```
    aws iam delete-policy \
    --policy-arn
    arn:aws:iam::<account_id>:policy/lambda_iam_policy_test \

    --profile admin
    ```

    Replace `<account_id>` with your account number.

How it works...

The following are the important details and concepts that were introduced in this recipe:

Creating a role and attaching a policy

You need to create a role with a trust policy that allows our Lambda to assume the role. You also need to attach a policy that has CloudWatch permissions for logging.

Lambda memory-size and timeout

When creating a function from CLI, the default value of timeout is 3 seconds, and default value memory-size is 128 MB, which may not be sufficient for Lambdas with Uber JARs, and you may get a timeout exception or **Process exited before completing request**. Hence, I have set a higher timeout and memory-size. Other parameters are mostly self-explanatory.

S3 Bucket and Key

Amazon S3 is an object store. Objects (files) are stored as simple key-value pairs within containers called buckets. Bucket names have to be unique across AWS. There is no folder hierarchy within the buckets like traditional file systems. However, we can simulate folder structure with hierarchical key names. For example, consider the `folder1/folder2/file.txt` key, that simulates a folder-like structure. Read more about simulating folders in S3 at `https://docs.aws.amazon.com/AmazonS3/latest/user-guide/using-folders.html`.

Cleaning up

You need to do a cleanup in the following order:

1. Delete Lambda that uses the role
2. Detach policy from role
3. Delete role and policy

> We cannot delete a role without detaching all policies. We can however delete a role without deleting the Lambda. If you try to invoke the Lambda before attaching another role, it will give you an error such as—The role defined for the function cannot be assumed by Lambda.

There's more...

Once you get familiar with the AWS CLI commands, it is much faster and easier to work with AWS CLI, rather than navigate through the pages of AWS management console. This chapter covers only a very basic use case. Please follow the links in the *See also* section and try out more examples with AWS CLI and Lambda.

See also

- More details on installing AWS CLI using `pip` can be found at https://docs.aws.amazon.com/cli/latest/userguide/installing.html
- AWS documentation on CLI configuration can be found at https://docs.aws.amazon.com/cli/latest/userguide/cli-chap-getting-started.html
- AWS CLI command reference can be found at https://docs.aws.amazon.com/cli/latest/reference
- If you find any issues while setting up and using AWS, you can visit this page for troubleshooting help: http://cloudmaterials.com/en/book/troubleshooting-aws-cloud-beginners

Your first Lambda with Amazon CloudFormation

Amazon CloudFormation lets you provision and model your AWS service infrastructure declaratively. Instead of using interactive tools such as management console or CLI directly, you can declare the configuration with expected order, dependencies, input, and output in a template, and CloudFormation will provision it for you.

The concept of writing code to manage infrastructure is referred to as **Infrastructure as Code (IaC)** and is a practice that most enterprise companies follow. You can also maintain the provisioning code in a code repository and follow practices such as code reviews like any other code. Thus, it lets you reuse the provisioning code.

In this recipe, we will use CloudFormation to provision the infrastructure for the Lambda we created in the *Your Lambda with AWS CLI* recipe.

Getting ready

You need to read and follow to the *Getting ready* section of the recipes *Your first AWS Lambda* and *Your first Lambda with AWS CLI* before proceeding.

Set up the project and S3 bucket

In this recipe, we are reusing the Lambda we created in the *Your Lambda with AWS CLI* recipe. Generate a JAR by running `mvn clean package` inside that project, and upload the JAR to S3:

```
aws s3 cp target/original-serverless-cookbook-lambda-handler-with-
pojos-0.0.1-SNAPSHOT.jar s3://serverless-cookbook/lambda-handler-with-
pojos-0.0.1-SNAPSHOT.jar --profile admin
```

Replace the bucket name `serverless-cookbook` with your bucket's name. Refer to the *Getting ready* section of the recipe *Your First AWS CLI* to create the S3 bucket.

Understanding YAML and JSON

CloudFormation templates are written in JSON or YAML. Both support data in key-value pairs, objects, arrays, and so on .YAML also supports additional features such as multi-line strings, comments, and so on. I will also be using YAML for the examples. Since YAML support was introduced later for CloudFormation, you will also see a lot of JSON templates in the web. So, it is also good to have a decent understanding of YAML and JSON. If you are familiar with one, you may also use one of the *JSON to YAML* or *YAML to JSON* converters available online.

How to do it...

1. Create the CloudFormation template.

    Resources components specify the AWS resources used. We need two resources for our use case: a role and a Lambda function with that role. The following is the basic structure of our CloudFormation template:

    ```
    ---
    AWSTemplateFormatVersion: '2010-09-09'
    Description: Building Lambda with AWS CloudFormation
    Resources:
      IamRoleLambdaExecution:
    ```

```
    Type: AWS::IAM::Role
    Properties:
       # Properties for the role are shown later.
  LambdaFunctionWithCF:
    Type: AWS::Lambda::Function
    Properties:
       # Properties for the Lambda are shown later.
    DependsOn:
    - IamRoleLambdaExecution
```

I have also defined `AWSTemplateFormatVersion` and `Description` as a general practice, but they are optional. Note that properties for the `IamRoleLambdaExecution` and `LambdaFunctionWithCF` are not shown here. You may refer to further steps or use the template from the code files.

The role needs a trust relationship policy that allows the lambda to assume that role, and we need to attach a policy to the role that provides CloudWatch logging permissions. The `AssumeRolePolicyDocument` property specifies the trust relationship policy for the role:

```
AssumeRolePolicyDocument:
  Version: '2012-10-17'
  Statement:
  - Effect: Allow
    Principal:
      Service:
      - lambda.amazonaws.com
    Action:
    - sts:AssumeRole
```

The policy is specified inline within the **Policies** property of the role:

```
Policies:
- PolicyName: 'lambda-with-cf-policy'
  PolicyDocument:
    Version: '2012-10-17'
    Statement:
    - Effect: Allow
      Action:
      - logs:CreateLogGroup
      - logs:CreateLogStream
      - logs:PutLogEvents
      Resource: arn:aws:logs:*:*:*
```

We will also define two more properties for the role, namely path and name:

```
Path: "/"
RoleName: "lambda-with-cf-role"
```

Our Lambda function will have the following basic configuration:

```
LambdaFunctionWithCF:
  Type: AWS::Lambda::Function
  Properties:
    Code:
      S3Bucket: 'serverless-cookbook'
      S3Key: lambda-handler-with-pojos-0.0.1-SNAPSHOT.jar
    FunctionName: first-lambda-with-cloud-formation
    Handler:
tech.heartin.books.serverlesscookbook.MyLambdaHandler::handleReques
t
    MemorySize: 512
    Role:
      Fn::GetAtt:
      - IamRoleLambdaExecution
      - Arn
    Runtime: java8
    Timeout: 15
  DependsOn:
  - IamRoleLambdaExecution
```

We specify the role as a dependency for the Lambda function, and use `Fn::GetAtt` to retrieve the role dynamically instead of hardcoding the name. Most of the other properties are self-explanatory.

A CloudFormation stack is a collection of AWS resources that you need to manage as a single unit. All the resources in a stack are defined by a CloudFormation template. When you delete the stack, all of its related resources are also deleted.

We can create a CloudFormation stack in different ways, including the following:

1. Going through the **Create Stack** option within the CloudFormation service inside AWS Management Console
2. Uploading directly from the **Template Designer** within the CloudFormation service inside AWS Management Console
3. AWS CLI

Chapter 1

In this recipe, I will use Designer, but in all other recipes I will be using AWS CLI. AWS CLI is the best way to deploy CloudFormation templates. Designer is also a good tool to visualize and validate your scripts.

2. Create CloudFormation stack from Designer:
    1. Log in to AWS and go to CloudFormation service.
    2. Click on the **Design template** button to go to **Designer**. Within designer, you may do the following:
    3. Choose template language as YAML in the editor. (If you are using a JSON template, use JSON instead.)
    4. Select the **Template tab** in the editor.
    5. Copy and paste your template into the template editor window.
    6. Click on **refresh** on the Designer to see the template in the **Design view**.
    7. If any changes are required, you can either make changes within the **Template** tab or use the **Components** tab.
    8. If everything looks good, click on the upload button on the top left of the designer to launch the **Stack creation wizard** with the current template.
    9. Follow the wizard with defaults, and select the checkbox for **I acknowledge that AWS CloudFormation might create IAM resources with custom names**. Finally, click on **Create Stack**.
    10. Invoke our Lambda with AWS CLI as follows and verify:

```
aws lambda invoke \
--invocation-type RequestResponse \
--function-name first-lambda-with-cloud-formation \
--log-type Tail \
--payload '{"name":"Heartin"}' \
--profile admin \
outputfile.txt
```

Output can be viewed in the `outputfile.txt` file:

```
$ cat outputfile.txt
{"message":"Hello Heartin"}$
```

Cleaning up roles, policy, and Lambda

To clean up resources created by CloudFormation, you just need to delete the stack. This is the default setting. Since we have used AWS management console for stack creation, we will use it for deletion as well.

You can delete a CloudFormation stack from the management console as follows: go to CloudFormation service, select the stack, click on **Actions**, and click **Delete Stack**.

How it works...

In this recipe, we used the following CloudFormation template components: `Resource`, `AWSTemplateFormatVersion`, and `Description`. Resources are the AWS resources used in the template. `AWSTemplateFormatVersion` is the version of CloudFormation template the template conforms to.

> **TIP**
> The only mandatory section in a CloudFormation template is `Resource`. However, it is a good practice to always define a version and a description for a template.

We used two resources: a role (`IAMRoleLambdaExecution`) and a Lambda function (`LambdaFunctionWithCF`) that depends on that role. `Resource` names can be anything. `Type` specifies the type of the resource. We used two types, namely `AWS::IAM::Role` and `AWS::Lambda::Function`.

The properties of the `AWS::IAM::Role` resource type that we used are as follows:

- `AssumeRolePolicyDocument` specifies the trust relationship policy for the role
- Policies specify the policies inline

The properties of the `AWS::Lambda::Function` resource type that we used are as follows:

- `Code` property specifies the S3 bucket and the key. You can also specify a reference to an S3 Bucket resource type so that a new bucket is created dynamically and its name is used here.
- `FunctionName` specifies the name of the Lambda function.
- `Handler` specifies the fully qualified name of the handler class with the handler method.
- `MemorySize` specifies the memory in MB. The number of CPU cores is decided by AWS based on the memory.

- `Role` specifies the role.
- `Runtime` specifies the runtime (for instance, java8).
- `TimeOut` specifies the timeout.

To get the role **Arn**, we used the `GetAtt` function passing the logical name of the **Role** and the property name `Arn`:

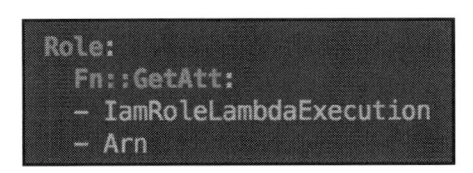

```
Role:
    Fn::GetAtt:
    - IamRoleLambdaExecution
    - Arn
```

`Fn::GetAtt` is an intrinsic function that returns the value of an attribute from a resource in the template.

We used CloudFormation designer in the recipe to see our template in design view, and then uploaded the template into a stack from the designer. You can also use the **Designer** to design CloudFormation templates from scratch.

There's more...

You can check the documentation and study related components within Lambda code if interested:

CloudFormation Template Components

CloudFormation templates are composed of the following primary components:

- `AWSTemplateFormatVersion` is the version of CloudFormation template the template conforms to
- `Description` is a text that describes the template
- `Resource` components are the AWS resources used in the template
- `Parameter` components are the input (dynamic) to your template
- `Mapping` components are variables (static) for your template
- `Output` components describe the values that are returned
- `Condition` components control resource provisioning
- `Metadata` provides additional information about the template

- `Transform` specifies the version of the **AWS Serverless Application Model** (**AWS SAM**) for Serverless applications

> `Resource` is the only mandatory section of a CloudFormation template.

We will talk about the components in the recipe in which they are introduced. Read more about template components at `https://docs.aws.amazon.com/AWSCloudFormation/latest/UserGuide/template-anatomy.html`.

Resource component

The following are some of the important features of `Resource` component:

- `Resource` component of the template specifies the AWS resources used in the template
- `Resource` can reference each other using the `ref` element
- Resource names can be anything
- `Type` specifies the type of the resource
- Each type has its own set of properties that you can refer to from the documentation, given under the properties element
- `DependsOn` specifies the other resources that the current resource is dependent on

Intrinsic functions

Intrinsic functions are built-in functions provided by AWS to use within a template for dynamically adding values. Common intrinsic functions used within CloudFormation templates are as follows: `Fn::Base64`, `Fn::Cidr`, `Fn::FindInMap`, `Fn::GetAtt`, `Fn::GetAZs`, `Fn::ImportValue`, `Fn::Join`, `Fn::Select`, `Fn::Split`, `Fn::Sub`, and `Ref`.

CloudFormation also supports the following conditional functions: `Fn::And`, `Fn::Equals`, `Fn::If`, `Fn::Not`, and `Fn::Or`.

We can specify the functions in the standard forms as mentioned here or in the short-hand form (for instance, `!Base64`, `!Cidr`, `!Ref`, and so on) if you are using YAML. We used the standard syntax for this recipe for reference, but will use the short-hand syntax in later recipes.

We will discuss the functions introduced in each chapter. You can read more about all intrinsic functions at `https://docs.aws.amazon.com/AWSCloudFormation/latest/UserGuide/intrinsic-function-reference.html`.

CloudFormation Designer

The following are some of the important features of the CloudFormation Designer:

- Create templates from scratch visually, validate, and upload
- Copy existing templates, see them visually, validate, and upload
- Drag and drop the resources you need
- Define relationships between resources
- Right-click on the service and click on the appropriate context menu option to go directly to the CloudFormation documentation for that service
- Edit logical name and other properties in the auto-generated template
- Copy and paste an existing template and see it in design view
- Directly upload the script to S3 and launch **Create stack wizard** in a single click

Additional benefits of CloudFormation

Apart from automated provisioning of resources through code and enabling reuse, CloudFormation also has other important usages, including the following:

- Lets you estimate costs based on the templates
- Enables tracking costs effectively
- Helps in saving costs by automated deletion of resources when not needed
- Diagrams generated based on templates can help in understanding the system better, and can be used in design discussions

Cloud Formation alternatives

Important alternatives to using CloudFormation include Ansible, Terraform, Chef, AWS OpsWorks, and AWS Elastic Beanstalk.

See also

- All resources supported by CloudFormation are available at `https://docs.aws.amazon.com/AWSCloudFormation/latest/UserGuide/aws-template-resource-type-ref.html`

Using AWS SDK, Amazon CloudFormation, and AWS CLI with Lambda

AWS SDK allows you to write code that interacts with AWS services. In this recipe, we will use AWS Java SDK for IAM to do some basic IAM operations to form a Lambda programmatically. We will use it along with Amazon CloudWatch and AWS CLI, which is a general practice followed in most real-world projects.

> The aim of this recipe is to understand the use of AWS Java SDK inside Lambda. Therefore, we will not go deep into the details of the IAM operations discussed in the recipe. The IAM operations details are available at `https://docs.aws.amazon.com/sdk-for-java/v1/developer-guide/examples-iam-users.html`.

Getting ready

You need an active AWS account, and read and follow the *Getting started* section of the recipes, *Your first AWS Lambda* and *Your first Lambda with AWS CLI* to set up Java, Maven, the parent project, `serverless-cookbook-parent-aws-java`, and AWS CLI, and other code usage guidelines.

How to do it...

We will create a Java Maven project and set the parent as `serverless-cookbook-parent-aws-java`.

1. Create a Java Maven project and set dependencies:

    ```
    <parent>
        <groupId>tech.heartin.books.serverlesscookbook</groupId>
        <artifactId>serverless-cookbook-parent-aws-java</artifactId>
        <version>0.0.1-SNAPSHOT</version>
    </parent>
    ```

2. Specify dependencies in the POM file:

    ```
    <dependencies>
        <dependency>
            <groupId>com.amazonaws</groupId>
            <artifactId>aws-lambda-java-core</artifactId>
            <version>${aws.lambda.java.core.version}</version>
        </dependency>

        <dependency>
            <groupId>com.amazonaws</groupId>
            <artifactId>aws-java-sdk-iam</artifactId>
            <version>${aws.sdk.version}</version>
        </dependency>

    </dependencies>
    ```

    > Do not directly define the whole AWS Java SDK (`aws-java-sdk`) dependency for a Lambda handler. Instead, only declare the dependencies you need (such as `aws-java-sdk-iam`). I tried adding `aws-java-sdk` to our Lambda and generated the Uber JAR. It was around 93 MB. AWS console did not allow me to upload the file manually into the Lambda function as the limit was 50MB. So, I uploaded it to S3. However, it failed again while extracting the JAR as the size of the extracted contents exceeded the allowed size of 262144000 bytes.

Creating the POJOs for requests and response.

1. Create a request POJO for accepting requests:

   ```
   import lombok.Data;

   @Data
   public class IAMOperationRequest {
     private String operation;
     private String userName;
   }
   ```

2. Create a POJO for sending back the response from the handler:

   ```
   import lombok.AllArgsConstructor;
   import lombok.Data;

   @AllArgsConstructor
   @Data
   public class IAMOperationResponse {
     private String message;
     private String errorMessage;
   }
   ```

> For our POJOs, we use project `lombok` (`@Data`) to auto-generate getters, setters, and so on. Project `lombok` dependency is added to the parent project `simple-starter-parent-java`. If you are using an IDE for development, you will have to install a plugin for your IDE to recognize project `lombok` annotations.

Creating a service class to implement the IAM Operations using AWS SDK:

1. Import the required classes:

   ```
   import com.amazonaws.services.identitymanagement.AmazonIdentityManagement;
   import com.amazonaws.services.identitymanagement.AmazonIdentityManagementClientBuilder;
   import com.amazonaws.services.identitymanagement.model.CreateUserRequest;
   import com.amazonaws.services.identitymanagement.model.CreateUserResult;
   import com.amazonaws.services.identitymanagement.model.DeleteConflictException;
   import
   ```

Chapter 1

```
com.amazonaws.services.identitymanagement.model.DeleteUserRequest;
import
com.amazonaws.services.identitymanagement.model.ListUsersRequest;
import
com.amazonaws.services.identitymanagement.model.ListUsersResult;
import com.amazonaws.services.identitymanagement.model.User;
```

2. Create and initialize a client object of `AmazonIdentityManagement` type:

    ```
    private final AmazonIdentityManagement iamClient;

    public IAMService() {
        iamClient =
    AmazonIdentityManagementClientBuilder.defaultClient();
    }
    ```

3. Write code for creating a user in a method:

    ```
    CreateUserRequest request = new
    CreateUserRequest().withUserName(userName);
        CreateUserResult response = iamClient.createUser(request);
    // get user details from response.
    ```

4. Write code for checking if a `user` is present in another method:

    ```
    boolean done = false;
    ListUsersRequest request = new ListUsersRequest();
    while (!done) {
        ListUsersResult response = iamClient.listUsers(request);

        for (User user : response.getUsers()) {
            if (user.getUserName().equals(userName)) {
                //return success message
            }
        }
        request.setMarker(response.getMarker());
        if (!response.getIsTruncated()) {
            done = true;
        }
    }
    // return error message
    ```

5. Write code for deleting a `user` in another method:

    ```
    DeleteUserRequest request = new DeleteUserRequest()
            .withUserName(userName);
        try {
            iamClient.deleteUser(request);
    ```

[43]

```
        } catch (DeleteConflictException e) {
            // Handle exception
        }
```

Let us now see how to create a handler.

1. Create a handler class with input and output POJOs:

    ```
    public final class HelloWorldLambdaHandler implements
    RequestHandler<IAMOperationRequest, IAMOperationResponse> {
    ```

2. Implement the `handleRequest` method with a switch statement to invoke an appropriate service method:

    ```
    public IAMOperationResponse handleRequest(final IAMOperationRequest
    request, final Context context) {
        context.getLogger().log("Requested operation = " +
    request.getOperation()
                + ". User name = " + request.getUserName());

        switch (request.getOperation()) {
            case "CREATE" :
                return this.service.createUser(request.getUserName());
            case "CHECK" :
                return  this.service.checkUser(request.getUserName());
            case "DELETE" :
                return this.service.deleteUser(request.getUserName());

            default:
                return new IAMOperationResponse(null,
                        "Invalid operation " +
    request.getOperation()
                                + ". Allowed: CREATE, CHECK,
    DELETE.");
        }
    }
    ```

3. Package the dependencies into an uber JAR using `mvn clean package`.

    Two JARs will be created: one with only class files (starting with `original-`) and an Uber JAR with all dependencies (starting with `serverless-`). We will use the Uber JAR in this recipe.

4. Upload the JAR to S3:

    ```
    aws s3 cp target/serverless-cookbook-iam-operations-0.0.1-
    SNAPSHOT.jar s3://serverless-cookbook/iam-operations-0.0.1-
    SNAPSHOT.jar --profile admin
    ```

5. Create a CloudFormation template for our lambda function.

   You need to create a role with a trust policy that allows our Lambda to assume the role. You also need to create a policy with CloudFormation and IAM permissions.

   We need to add permissions for IAM operations in our policies:

   ```
   - Effect: Allow
     Action:
     - iam:CreateUser
     - iam:DeleteUser
     - iam:ListUsers
     Resource:
     - Fn::Sub: arn:aws:iam::${AWS::AccountId}:user/*
   ```

   We have used a pseudo-parameter, `AWS::AccountId`, within a sub-intrinsic function to dynamically populate the account ID. I also improved the CloudWatch logging permission policy from the previous recipe using the pseudo-parameters:

   ```
   - Effect: Allow
     Action:
     - logs:CreateLogStream
     Resource:
     - Fn::Sub:
     arn:${AWS::Partition}:logs:${AWS::Region}:${AWS::AccountId}:log-group:/aws/lambda/aws-sdk-iam-with-cf-cli:*
   - Effect: Allow
     Action:
     - logs:PutLogEvents
     Resource:
     - Fn::Sub:
     arn:${AWS::Partition}:logs:${AWS::Region}:${AWS::AccountId}:log-group:/aws/lambda/aws-sdk-iam-with-cf-cli:*:*
   ```

   You should be able to complete this recipe by referring to the previous recipe, *Your First Lambda using CloudFormation*.

   > The completed template file is available in the resources folder as `cf-template-iam-operations.yml`.

Getting Started with Serverless Computing on AWS

6. Upload the CloudFormation template to S3:

   ```
   aws s3 cp ../resources/cf-template-iam-operations.yml
   s3://serverless-cookbook/cf-template-iam-operations.yml --profile
   admin
   ```

7. Create a CloudFormation stack using the CloudFormation template from AWS CLI:

   ```
   aws cloudformation create-stack --stack-name myteststack --
   template-url
   https://s3.amazonaws.com/serverless-cookbook/cf-template-iam-operat
   ions.yml --capabilities CAPABILITY_NAMED_IAM --profile admin
   ```

   This immediately responds with `StackId`. Note that you used a parameter, `--capabilities CAPABILITY_NAMED_IAM`. This is a security-related precaution. You are explicitly telling CloudFormation that you know what you are doing.

   You can check the status of stack creation using the `describe-stacks` command:

   ```
   aws cloudformation describe-stacks --stack-name <StackId> --profile
   admin
   ```

   StackStatus: `CREATE_COMPLETE` means stack creation was successful.

8. Verify the deployment with AWS CLI Lambda invoke:

   ```
   aws lambda invoke --invocation-type RequestResponse --function-name
   aws-sdk-iam-with-cf-cli --log-type Tail --payload
   '{"operation":"CREATE", "userName":"abcd"}' --profile admin
   outputfile.txt
   ```

   You can replace `CREATE` in the payload with `CHECK` for checking if the user was created, and `DELETE` for deleting the user.

9. Delete the CloudFormation stack:

   ```
   aws cloudformation delete-stack --stack-name <StackId> --profile
   admin
   ```

How it works...

AWS SDKs are used to interact with AWS services programmatically. There are SDKs available for programming languages such as Java, .Net, Node.js, PHP, Python, Ruby, Browser, Go, and C++.

We uploaded our CloudFormation template to S3 and provided the location using `--template-url`. You can also specify the template contents directly or from a file using `file://` with another option `--template-body`.

We created our roles for Lambda manually. If we are using Management console, we can create custom Lambda roles from within our Lambda create function page, or directly from IAM.

We used one new intrinsic function in our CloudFormation template, `Fn::Sub`. `Fn::Sub`, which substitutes variables in an input string with values that you specify. We used it to substitute the AWS Account ID and a few other values rather than hard-coding them.

We also used the following pseudo-`parameters`: `AWS::AccountId`, `AWS::Partition`, and `AWS::Region`, which represents the current account ID, partition, and region respectively. For most regions, the partition is `aws`. For resources in other partitions, the partition is named as `aws-partitionn` (for instance, `aws-cn` for China and `aws-us-gov` for the AWS GovCloud (US) region). Using pseudo-parameters lets us avoid worrying about the actual partition name.

There's more...

We used only basic IAM operations in this recipe. You can check the documentation and implement more complex operations from within Lambda code if interested.

> **TIP**: We will use CloudFormation and AWS CLI for most of our recipes. However, you may follow these steps to try to do the same in the management console. Doing things visually will help you remember the concepts for a longer time.

Pseudo-parameters

Pseudo-parameters are predefined parameters provided by AWS CLoudFormation. You can use them within a Ref or a Sub function to dynamically populate values. Pseudo-parameters available to use within a CloudFormation template include `AWS::AccountId`, `AWS::NotificationARNs`, `AWS::NoValue`, `AWS::Partition`, `AWS::Region`, `AWS::StackId`, `AWS::StackName`, and `AWS::URLSuffix`.

Read more about pseudo-parameters at `https://docs.aws.amazon.com/AWSCloudFormation/latest/UserGuide/pseudo-parameter-reference.html`.

See also

- `https://aws.amazon.com/sdk-for-java`
- `https://docs.aws.amazon.com/IAM/latest/UserGuide/access_policies_manage.html`
- `https://docs.aws.amazon.com/IAM/latest/UserGuide/access_policies_examples.html`
- `https://docs.aws.amazon.com/lambda/latest/dg/limits.html`
- `https://docs.aws.amazon.com/cli/latest/reference/cloudformation/index.html#cli-aws-cloudformation`

Dev Practices – dependency injection and unit testing

In this recipe, I will implement some of the common dev practices for creating Lambdas, such as using lightweight frameworks for dependency injection and writing unit tests for your code.

For dependency injection, we will use Guice, which is one of the dependency injection (IoC) frameworks suggested by AWS at `https://docs.aws.amazon.com/lambda/latest/dg/best-practices.html`. For unit testing, we will use JUnit and Mockito libraries.

Getting ready

You need an active AWS account, and read and follow the *Getting started* section of the recipes, *Your first AWS Lambda* and *Your first Lambda with AWS CLI* to set up Java, Maven, the parent project, `serverless-cookbook-parent-aws-java`, and AWS CLI, and other code usage guidelines.

This recipe also assumes you are familiar with general software development concepts and practices such as dependency injection, unit testing, and coding to interfaces. Familiarity with libraries such as JUnit and Mockito will be good to have.

Code refactoring

We will be improving the code we created in the *Using AWS SDK, Amazon CloudWatch and AWS CLI with Lambda* recipe. Before doing Dependency Injection, you need to refactor your code to follow the principle of programming to interfaces.

Refactor the service class into an interface and its implementation. I will also add `lombok`'s `@AllArgsConstructor` annotation to generate an all args constructor, which will be used during unit testing to inject the mock object.

1. We will first create an interface `IAMService`:

    ```
    /**
     * Interface for IAM operations.
     */
    public interface IAMService {
    ```

    We will define the corresponding implementation as `IAMServiceImpl`:

    ```
    /**
     * Implementation of {@link IAMService}.
     */
    @AllArgsConstructor
    public class IAMServiceImpl implements IAMService {
    ```

2. Extract the methods as well, and then replace the usage of the implementation with an interface:

    ```
    private IAMService service;

    public MyLambdaHandler() {
        service = new IAMServiceImpl();
    }
    ```

> Most IDEs will provide refactoring support to extract an interface from an implementation. IDEs will also help you in replacing the usages of your implementation with interface wherever possible.

How to do it...

Let us do dependency injection with `Guice`, which is a lightweight framework suggested by AWS.

1. Add Maven dependency for `Guice`:

   ```
   <dependency>
       <groupId>com.google.inject</groupId>
       <artifactId>guice</artifactId>
       <version>4.2.0</version>
   </dependency>
   ```

2. Create the `Guice` configuration class to bind interfaces to implementation:

   ```
   public class ApplicationModule extends AbstractModule {
       protected final void configure() {
           bind(IAMService.class).to(IAMServiceImpl.class);
       }
   }
   ```

3. Configure the handler class for using `Guice`:

   ```
   public final class MyLambdaHandler implements
   RequestHandler<IAMOperationRequest, IAMOperationResponse> {

       private static final Injector INJECTOR =
               Guice.createInjector(new ApplicationModule());

       private IAMService service;

       public MyLambdaHandler() {
           INJECTOR.injectMembers(this);
           Objects.requireNonNull(service);
       }

       @Inject
       public void setService(final IAMService service) {
           this.service = service;
       }
   ```

Chapter 1

I created a static Injector class and initialized it with our `Guice` configuration class. I added a default constructor to add this class to be injected by `Guice`. `Objects.requireNonNull` verifies if the implementation was injected successfully. I annotated it with Java's `@Inject` annotation for `Guice` to inject dependency.

Let us write unit tests for our code.

1. Add Maven dependency for `JUnit` and `Mockito`:

    ```
    <dependency>
        <groupId>junit</groupId>
        <artifactId>junit</artifactId>
        <version>4.12</version>
        <scope>test</scope>
    </dependency>

    <dependency>
        <groupId>org.mockito</groupId>
        <artifactId>mockito-core</artifactId>
        <version>2.21.0</version>
        <scope>test</scope>
    </dependency>
    ```

2. Create a simple test class for the handler that checks if the service implementation is injected:

    ```
    package tech.heartin.books.serverlesscookbook;

    import org.junit.Test;

    public class MyLambdaHandlerTest {
        @Test
        public void testDependencies() throws Exception {
            MyLambdaHandler testHandler = new MyLambdaHandler();
        }
    }
    ```

3. Create a test class for the service class that uses `Mockito` to mock AWS calls:

    ```
    @RunWith(MockitoJUnitRunner.class)
    public class IAMServiceImplTest {

        @Mock
        private AmazonIdentityManagement iamClient;

        private IAMService service;
    ```

[51]

Getting Started with Serverless Computing on AWS

```
    @Before
    public void setUp() {
        service = new IAMServiceImpl(iamClient);
        Objects.requireNonNull(service);
    }
    // Actual tests not shown here
}
```

4. Add the test method for create user:

```
@Test
public void testCreateUser() {
    IAMOperationResponse expectedResponse = new IAMOperationResponse(
            "Created user test_user", null);
    when(iamClient.createUser(any()))
            .thenReturn(new CreateUserResult()
                    .withUser(new User().withUserName("test_user")));
    IAMOperationResponse actualResponse
            = service.createUser("test_user");
    Assert.assertEquals(expectedResponse, actualResponse);
}
```

5. Add the test method to check user:

```
@Test
public void testCheckUser() {
    IAMOperationResponse expectedResponse = new IAMOperationResponse(
            "User test_user exist", null);
    when(iamClient.listUsers(any()))
            .thenReturn(getListUsersResult());
    IAMOperationResponse actualResponse
            = service.checkUser("test_user");
    Assert.assertEquals(expectedResponse, actualResponse);
}

private ListUsersResult getListUsersResult() {
    ListUsersResult result = new ListUsersResult();
    result.getUsers().add(new User().withUserName("test_user"));
```

6. Add the test method to delete user:

```
@Test
public void testDeleteUser() {
    IAMOperationResponse expectedResponse = new IAMOperationResponse(
```

```
        "Deleted user test_user", null);
when(iamClient.deleteUser(any()))
        .thenReturn(new DeleteUserResult());
IAMOperationResponse actualResponse
        = service.deleteUser("test_user");
Assert.assertEquals(expectedResponse, actualResponse);
}
```

7. To Package, deploy, and verify, follow the *Using AWS SDK, Amazon CloudFormation and AWS CLI with Lambda* recipe, and package, deploy, and verify by invoking the Lambda.

> **TIP**
> In real-world projects, you may follow the **Test Driven Development (TDD)** principle and write tests before actual code.

How it works...

We added a lightweight dependency injection framework, `Guice`, and modified code to incorporate it. We also used `JUnit` and `Mockito` to do unit testing of the code. Going deep into the working of `Guice`, `JUnit`, or `Mockito` is outside the scope of this book. But, you may ask any questions on the open source repository for the project (given in the introduction in `Chapter 1`, *Getting Started with Serverless Computing on AWS*).

There's more...

You may also use **Dagger** instead of `Guice` for dependency injection. Dagger is also a recommended framework from AWS for lightweight dependency injection. You can technically use Spring for dependency injection, but it is not recommended because of its bigger size.

You may use **TestNG** instead of JUnit for unit testing. TestNG provides additional features such as DataProviders. DataProviders allow you to supply an array with all possible inputs and their expected values for a single test method. With JUnit, you will have to write a test method per input combination. You may also use Hamcrest to create more flexible expressions in tests.

See also

- You may refer to other books at PacktPub to become familiar with the dependency injection and testing frameworks.

Your first Lambda with serverless framework

Serverless is an open source command line utility framework for building and deploying serverless applications. Serverless supports multiple cloud providers such as Amazon Web Services, Microsoft Azure, IBM OpenWhisk, Google Cloud Platform, Kubeless, Spotinst, Webtasks, and Fn.

In this recipe, we will use the Serverless framework to develop, deploy, invoke, check logs, and finally remove a simple hello world Lambda function on the AWS cloud platform.

Getting ready

Two dependencies are needed for the Serverless framework: node.js and AWS CLI. For installing AWS CLI, you may refer to the 'Deploying and Invoking Lambda with AWS CLI' recipe. You can install node using node packet as given at https://nodejs.org/en/download/package-manager.

You need to create a user for Serverless in AWS. It is a general practice to use the name `serverless-admin` and give administrator permission. It is not a very good practice to create users with administrator access, but currently that is the easiest way to work with Serverless. You should be careful about storing and using these credentials.

How to do it...

Let us create a simple Lambda using the Serverless framework:

1. Install Serverless in your machine using npm:

```
npm install -g serverless
```

2. Configure Serverless with user credentials:

```
serverless config credentials --provider aws --key <access key> --secret <secret access key> --profile serverless-admin
```

You should get a success message stating that keys were stored under the `serverless-admin` profile.

> The `sls` command is the shorthand of the Serverless command.

3. Create a Lambda function based on Java and Maven:

```
sls create --template aws-java-maven --path hello-world-java-maven
```

It creates a `hello-world-java-maven` folder, with `pom.xml` and `serverless.yml` files, and the `src` folder. You may open this Maven project in your IDE of choice. The auto-generated files looks as shown here in my IDE:

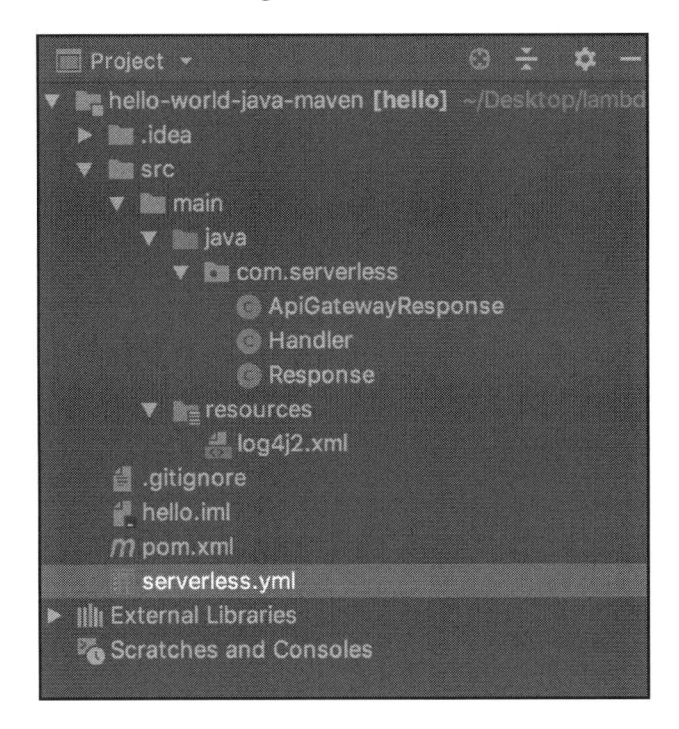

```
Project
▼ hello-world-java-maven [hello] ~/Desktop/lambd
  ► .idea
  ▼ src
    ▼ main
      ▼ java
        ▼ com.serverless
            ApiGatewayResponse
            Handler
            Response
      ▼ resources
          log4j2.xml
  .gitignore
  hello.iml
  pom.xml
  serverless.yml
► External Libraries
  Scratches and Consoles
```

[55]

Getting Started with Serverless Computing on AWS

As you can see, Serverless has created a bit more than a simple *hello world*. Serverless takes care of most of the things we did manually, including creating a role, setting memory, setting timeout, and so on.

Add a user profile and region to `serverless.yml`. The region is optional if you are using the default region:

```
provider:
  name: aws
  runtime: java8
  profile: serverless-admin
  region: us-east-1
```

Build the `jar` file with:

mvn clean package

4. Deploy the `jar` file to AWS:

    sls deploy -v

    You can log in to the AWS console and verify the new Lambda service. From the log statements, you can see that Serverless framework internally makes use of CloudFormation. You can verify the same from AWS Management console.

5. Invoke the function from `sls`:

    sls invoke -f hello -l

    Option `-f` specifies the function name, and `-l` specifies that logs need to be printed to terminal. The function name to invoke is `hello` and is available in the `serverless.yml` file. You can see the output and logs on the terminal.

6. Checking logs from the CLI:

    sls logs -f hello -t

    Option `-f` specifies the function name and `-t` denotes to tail the logs. You can now run the invoke command from the other terminal and see the logs being printed.

7. Now, clean up everything:

    sls remove

Chapter 1

8. Log in to AWS Management console and verify that everything is cleaned up.

How it works...

Serverless framework internally makes use of AWS CloudFormation for provisioning AWS resources. You can log in to **Management console**, go to **CloudFormation service**, select the stack named `hello-world-java-maven-dev`, and click on the **Template** tab for viewing the complete CloudFormation template.

You can further click on the **View/Edit template in Designer** option to see the template visually. The designer view of the CloudFormation template created for our example by the Serverless framework is shown here:

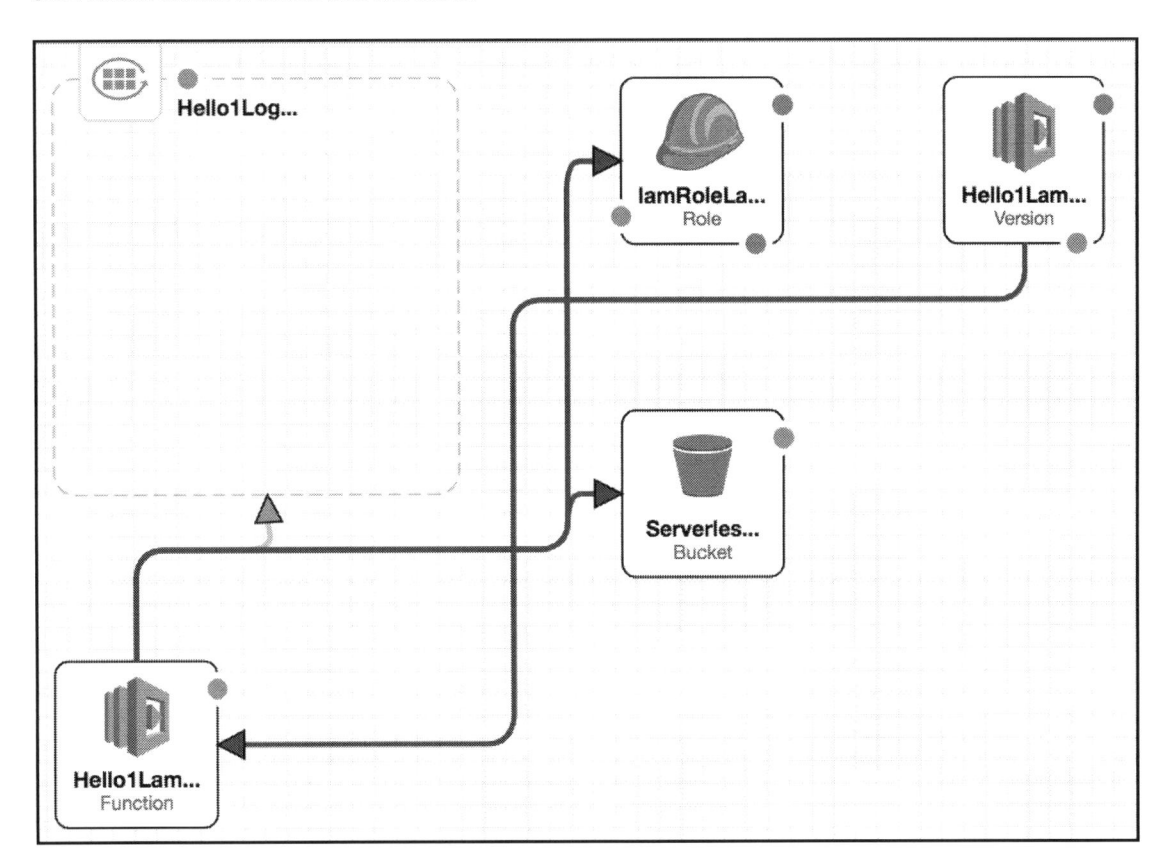

There's more...

Serverless framework is part of the `serverless.com` Serverless Platform. The other two components of the serverless platform are Serverless dashboard and event gateway. Serverless framework also integrates well with other processes and tools, such as CI and CD.

See also

- `https://serverless.com/framework/docs`.
- The last chapter, `Chapter 10`, *Serverless Computing with Other Cloud Providers, Tools and Frameworks* contains examples of other cloud providers.

Building Serverless REST APIs with API Gateway

This chapter will cover the following topics:

- Building your first API using the AWS CLI
- Building your first API using Amazon CloudFormation
- Building your first API with Lambda integration
- Building and testing your first POST API method
- Mapping requests and responses using mapping templates
- Validating request payloads with models
- Using Lambda and APIs with proxy integration

Introduction

An **application programming interface** (**API**) is a set of methods that allow us to programmatically access a component. APIs can be built for different layers, such as the web (`http/rest`), database, and operating system layers, and so on. A **representational state transfer** (**REST**) API is an API that uses REST principles and HTTP protocol to build web APIs that can be programmatically consumed by clients over a network, such as the internet.

Amazon API Gateway is the primary service within AWS for building serverless, scalable, and secure REST APIs. It acts as a gateway between your application and the outside world. You only pay for the API calls and data that are transferred out, and you do not have to maintain a server. It also provides support for testing, authorization, API version management, deployment, and maintaining and monitoring your REST APIs.

Building Serverless REST APIs with API Gateway

Amazon API Gateway is usually used with AWS Lambda, in order to build Serverless applications. In this chapter, we will discuss some core use cases of the API gateway, such as building, deploying, and testing APIs that interact with AWS Lambda. Additional use cases, such as security and integration with a user interface, will be discussed in later chapters. We will also discuss the REST principles and HTTP essentials.

Building your first API using the AWS CLI

In this recipe, we will create a simple REST API with mock integration, using CLI commands. We will specify a name as a path parameter, and the API will greet that person. In the next recipe, we will use CloudFormation templates to create the API. From that point, we will use both the CLI commands and the CloudFormation templates.

> In `Chapter 1`, *Getting Started with Serverless Computing on AWS*, we created Lambdas using the management console, the CLI, CloudFormation, and the serverless framework. From this chapter onward, we will mostly focus on using CloudFormation templates, but we will first discuss the corresponding CLI commands, as they can help us to better understand the templates.

Getting ready

A good understanding of REST, HTTP, and the HTTP mechanisms for the web (such as HTTP verbs, HTTP response codes, content negotiation, and so on) will help you to understand the various API gateway concepts that will be discussed in this chapter. You may refer to the *There's more...* section for notes on REST principles and HTTP essentials.

How to do it...

We will create our first REST API with API gateway by using CLI commands. Remember to replace the various IDs (`rest-api-id`, `parent-id`, and so on) in each command with your own, based on the previous step's result. As you will see in the next recipe, with CloudFormation templates, we do not have to manually specify IDs, unlike with the CLI commands:

1. Create a REST API in the `us-east-1` region, as follows:

    ```
    aws apigateway create-rest-api \
        --name 'API Gateway Hello World' \
    ```

Chapter 2

```
--region us-east-1 \
--profile admin
```

> The ID of the REST API from the response is used as the value for `rest-api-id` in later commands. Replace `c82tpsb7ka` in rest of the commands with the ID of the REST API you receive in this step.

2. Retrieve the ID of the root resource (/) of the REST API:

```
aws apigateway get-resources \
    --rest-api-id c82tpsb7ka \
    --region us-east-1 \
    --profile admin
```

> The ID of the root resource (/) from the response is used as the value for the `parent-id` of the sub-resource.

3. Create a child resource under the root resource (/):

```
aws apigateway create-resource \
    --rest-api-id c82tpsb7ka \
    --region us-east-1 \
    --parent-id rosgmsjlb5 \
    --path-part greeting \
    --profile admin
```

> The ID of the new resource (`greeting`) from the response is used as the `parent-id` for the path param resource that we will create next. replace `rosgmsjlb5` in next command with the ID of the resource you receive in this step.

4. Create a path param called '`{name}`' under the parent resource `greeting`, as follows:

```
aws apigateway create-resource \
    --rest-api-id c82tpsb7ka \
    --region us-east-1 \
    --parent-id oaslzo \
    --path-part '{name}' \
    --profile admin
```

Building Serverless REST APIs with API Gateway

> The ID of the new resource from the response is used as the `resource-id` for later commands. Replace `oas1zo` in next command with the ID of the resource you receive in this step.

5. Add an HTTP method, `GET`, on the resource '`{name}`':

```
aws apigateway put-method \
    --rest-api-id c82tpsb7ka \
    --resource-id lyb17y \
    --http-method GET \
    --authorization-type "NONE" \
    --region us-east-1 \
    --profile admin
```

> We set the `authorization-type` as `"NONE"`, so that everyone can access the API. We will look at authorization in a different chapter.

6. Set up a response status code of `200`, as follows:

```
aws apigateway put-method-response \
    --rest-api-id c82tpsb7ka \
    --resource-id lyb17y \
    --http-method GET \
    --status-code 200 \
    --region us-east-1 \
    --profile admin
```

7. Set up a `MOCK` integration, as follows:

```
aws apigateway put-integration \
    --rest-api-id c82tpsb7ka \
    --resource-id lyb17y \
    --http-method GET \
    --type MOCK \
    --integration-http-method GET \
    --request-templates '{ "application/json": "{\"statusCode\": 200}" }' \
    --region us-east-1 \
    --profile admin
```

Chapter 2

> The `request-templates` parameter hold a map where key is the content-type sent by the caller and value is a velocity template. When specifying a velocity template on the command line, it may have to be escaped as per operating system and the terminal used. This applies to other commands within this chapter that accept a velocity template such as the `response-templates` property.
>
> Code examples within the book follows the AWS documentation style and is tested primarily on Mac operating system. It should also work on most Unix based operating systems such as Linux. For alternative solutions you may refer to the code files repository. Please refer to the heading *Alternative Solutions* in the repository's `readme` file for more details.

8. Create a custom integration response by using the path param value, as follows:

```
aws apigateway put-integration-response \
    --rest-api-id c82tpsb7ka \
    --resource-id lyb17y \
    --http-method GET \
    --status-code 200 \
    --selection-pattern "" \
    --response-templates '{"application/json": "{\"message\": \"Hello $input.params('"'"'name'"'"')\"}"}' \
    --region us-east-1 \
    --profile admin
```

> If you are using a Windows Machine, please refer to the code files repository for alternative solutions where velocity template is escaped properly so that it can be executed on a Windows machine as well.

9. Deploy our API into a stage called `dev`, as follows:

```
aws apigateway create-deployment \
    --rest-api-id c82tpsb7ka \
    --region us-east-1 \
    --stage-name dev \
    --stage-description 'Dev stage' \
    --description 'First deployment' \
    --profile admin
```

10. Test the API by invoking the API URL (as follows) after replacing the `rest-api-id` (`c82tpsb7ka`) with your REST API ID:

    ```
    https://c82tpsb7ka.execute-api.us-east-1.amazonaws.com/dev/greeting/Heartin
    ```

    You should get a response that looks as follows:

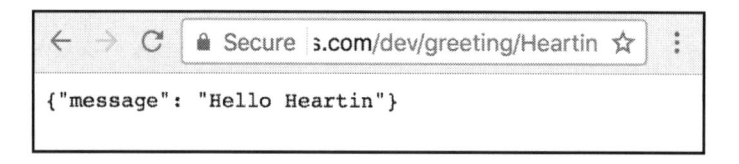

    ```
    {"message": "Hello Heartin"}
    ```

How it works...

First, we will explain the AWS CLI API gateway sub-commands used in this recipe, as follows:

- The `create-rest-api` command creates a REST API. We also need to specify a name and a region. An API setup with API gateway is region-specific.
- The `get-resources` command retrieves the root resource identifier of the REST API, which is the path `/`. You need the ID of this resource to create sub-resources.
- The `create-resource` command appends a child resource under a parent resource. We created a child, `greeting`, under the path `/`, and then created a child for the path param `'{name}'` under the path `greeting`, using the corresponding parent IDs. The `path-part` parameter specifies the path of the resource to add (for example, `greeting`, `{name}`).
- The `put-method` command specifies the HTTP verb. We added a `GET` verb on our resource `'greeting/{name}'`. The `authorization-type` specified was `'NONE'`, so everyone can access the resource. You could use IAM roles and policies, a custom Lambda authorizer, or an Amazon Cognito user pool instead. There is a chapter dedicated to security.
- The `put-method-response` command is used to set up the method response. We set up a response status code of `200` for successful `GET` requests. If you do not set up a method response and test, you will get an error, as the output mapping refers to an invalid method response.

- The `put-integration` command sets up an integration for the API. The following integration types are currently supported: `AWS`, `AWS_PROXY`, `HTTP`, `HTTP_PROXY`, and `MOCK`. We need to specify the `request-templates` property map, where the key is a `content-type` header (for example, `application/json`) and the value is a velocity template that will be applied to a request payload with that particular `content-type` header.
- The `put-integration-response` command represents a `put` integration. The `status-code` property is used to map the integration response to an existing method response (specified by the `put-method-response`). The `response-templates` specifies the `put` integration response's templates. We used `$input.params` to use the value of the path param.
- The `create-deployment` command deploys our API to a stage. Stages allow you to manage different versions of the API (for example, `dev`, `test`, `prod`, and so on). The endpoint URL of the generated API will be of the format `https://<rest-api-id>.execute-api.<region>.amazonaws.com/<stage>/<path>`.

Having a decent understanding of the HTTP and REST basics can help you to design good REST APIs. If you are familiar with the HTTP and REST basics, you can skip the remainder of this section.

HTTP essentials

HTTP stands for **Hypertext Transfer Protocol**, and it is used for exchanging documents (referred to as hypertext) over the internet. A hypertext is a text with links (hyperlinks) to other documents. HTTP provides a set of verbs for specifying the operations that we need to perform on a resource, and a set of response codes that the server can return to the client.

The following HTTP verbs (methods) are generally used with REST APIs: `GET`, for retrieving data; `HEAD`, for getting the header (similar to `GET`, but without the body); `POST`, for non-idempotent requests (for example, creating an ID); `PUT`, for idempotent requests (for example, override updates); `PATCH`, for partial updates; and `DELETE`, for deleting resources. `OPTIONS` is generally used for `CORS` pre-flight requests.

HTTP response codes are generally categorized as follows: 1xx for information, 2xx for success, 3xx for redirection, 4xx for client errors, and 5xx for server errors. The most commonly used codes are 200 (Success), 404 (Resource Not Found), 500 (Unhandled Internal Server Error), and so on. There is no hard rule on what a server can do when it receives an HTTP method or what response codes it can return, but the preceding are some general guidelines.

REST essentials

Representational State Transfer (**REST**) APIs exchange the representations of a resource in different formats (for example, `JSON`, `XML`, and others) between a server and client, using the existing mechanisms of the web, such as HTTP protocols, verbs, and response codes. The same APIs can be used as the backend for different apps (for example, web, mobile, and so on), based on different UI technologies (for example, Angular and React). Traditional MVC applications use a server-side view technology (such as JSP, ASP.net, PHP, and so on) that is tied to the backend code, and changing UI requires changing backend.

REST defines six architectural constraints, namely uniform interface, client-server, stateless, cacheable, layered system, and code on demand (optional). The uniform interface and client-server constraints are achieved by using the HTTP protocol, verbs, response codes, and so on. The client should take care of maintaining the state, and not the server (this is known as statelessness), which leads to cacheable URIs. APIs can be implemented in various layers, without letting the client know. Optionally, the server can respond with client-executable **code on demand** (**code**).

Richardson's Maturity Model can be used to check the level of RESTfulness. If we only use HTTP for transport, then the level is 0 (as in traditional SOAP services that use RPC over HTTP). Level 1 requires using URIs based on resources (for example, student/1). Level 2 requires using HTTP verbs to denote the operations (for example, `DELETE` to delete a resource). Level 3 requires using **hypermedia as the engine of application state** (**HATEOAS**), by providing links in responses (for example, URIs, for supported operations) to drive the application's state transitions.

Parts of a URL

Consider a URL: `http://www.heartin.tech/books/serverless-cookbook?format=pdf#index`. Here, `http` is the scheme, `www.heartin.tech` is the host, `books` and `serverless-cookbook` are resources, `format=pdf` is a query string, and `#index` is a fragment. You can specify a variable path param as `books/{book}`, and substitute a value for `{book}` when making requests. Path parameters should be preferred over query strings for specifying resources. Query strings are generally used for filtering results with `GET` requests (for example, pagination and sorting). The `#index` part is called a fragment, and it points to a location within an HTML file, but is less frequently used with REST.

> A more detailed discussion of REST and HTTP is beyond the scope of this book. Please read other books and articles to learn more.

There's more...

We have only discussed the limited AWS CLI commands and parameters that are required for our use case. For advanced use cases, refer to the AWS CLI documentation at `https://docs.aws.amazon.com/cli/latest/reference/apigateway/index.html`.

See also

- `https://www.ics.uci.edu/~fielding/pubs/dissertation/top.htm`
- `https://martinfowler.com/articles/richardsonMaturityModel.html`
- `https://docs.aws.amazon.com/apigateway/latest/developerguide/api-gateway-mapping-template-reference.html`
- `https://docs.aws.amazon.com/apigateway/latest/developerguide/api-gateway-known-issues.html`

Building your first API using Amazon CloudFormation

In the previous recipe, we built a simple REST API using the AWS CLI. In this recipe, we will use the CloudFormation template to create an API and understand the benefits of using CloudFormation over the AWS CLI. Most enterprise projects use CloudFormation templates for their infrastructure provisioning in AWS.

Getting ready

In this recipe, we will use the CloudFormation templates written in YAML. To deploy those templates, we will still use the AWS CLI. So, a basic understanding of CloudFormation, the AWS CLI, and YAML are good to have. If you are new to these, please refer to the respective *Your first AWS Lambda* recipe from `Chapter 1`, *Getting Started with Serverless Computing on AWS*.

How to do it...

Let's create the same API that we created in the previous recipe, but do it by using a CloudFormation template, and then deploy it using the AWS CLI. Finally, we will invoke the API from a browser. The CLI commands corresponding to the CloudFormation template components were already discussed in the previous recipe:

1. Start by defining the template with `AWSTemplateFormatVersion` and a description, as follows:

   ```
   ---
   AWSTemplateFormatVersion: '2010-09-09'
   Description: Building API with AWS CloudFormation
   ```

2. Define our REST API with the resource type `AWS::ApiGateway::RestApi`, as follows:

   ```
   Resources:
     MyFirstRestAPI:
       Type: AWS::ApiGateway::RestApi
       Properties:
         Name: Greeting API
         Description: API for greeting an user
         FailOnWarnings: true
   ```

   > The `FailOnWarnings` property tells CloudFormation to roll back the resource if a warning occurs during API creation.

3. Define the parent resource, `greeting`, under the root path, using the type `AWS::ApiGateway::Resource`:

   ```
   GreetingResource:
     Type: AWS::ApiGateway::Resource
     Properties:
       RestApiId: !Ref MyFirstRestAPI
       ParentId: !GetAtt MyFirstRestAPI.RootResourceId
       PathPart: 'greeting'
   ```

Chapter 2

> We do not have to copy and paste our REST API IDs. Instead, we refer to our REST API by using the `Ref` intrinsic function. Also, we are now using the shorthand form for the intrinsic functions.

4. Define a path parameter resource under `greeting` by using the type `AWS::ApiGateway::Resource`:

```yaml
NamePathParamResource:
  Type: AWS::ApiGateway::Resource
  Properties:
    RestApiId: !Ref MyFirstRestAPI
    ParentId: !Ref GreetingResource
    PathPart: '{name}'
```

> We are using the same properties from the AWS CLI commands, but in the CloudFormation way.

5. Create the method configuration with the resource type `AWS::ApiGateway::Method`, as follows:

```yaml
MyMockMethod:
  Type: AWS::ApiGateway::Method
  Properties:
    AuthorizationType: NONE
    HttpMethod: GET
    Integration:
      Type: MOCK
      IntegrationHttpMethod: GET
      IntegrationResponses:
      - StatusCode: 200
        ResponseTemplates:
          application/json: "{\"message\": \"Hello $input.params('name')\" }"
      RequestTemplates:
        application/json: "{\"statusCode\": 200}"
    ResourceId: !Ref NamePathParamResource
    RestApiId: !Ref MyFirstRestAPI
    MethodResponses:
    - StatusCode: 200
```

[69]

Building Serverless REST APIs with API Gateway

The CloudFormation template combines multiple CLI commands (`put-method`, `put-method-response`, `put-integration`, and `put-integration-response`) into a single and simple configuration.

6. Deploy our application using the resource type `AWS::ApiGateway::Deployment`, as follows:

```yaml
MyFirstDeployment:
  DependsOn: MyMockMethod
  Type: AWS::ApiGateway::Deployment
  Properties:
    Description: 'First Deployment'
    RestApiId: !Ref MyFirstRestAPI
    StageDescription:
      Description: 'Dev Stage'
    StageName: 'dev'
```

We have to specify that our `Deployment` resource depends on our `Method` resource, by using `DependsOn`. Otherwise, the `Deployment` resource may be executed before the `Method` resource.

7. Add an `Outputs` section to return the final URL for our REST API:

```yaml
Outputs:
  SampleEndpoint:
    Description: 'Sample Endpoint'
    Value: !Sub
      -
      https://${API_ID}.execute-api.${AWS::Region}.amazonaws.com/dev/greeting/Heartin
      - API_ID: !Ref MyFirstRestAPI
```

Here, we use the intrinsic function `Sub` to create the final endpoint, using the pseudo-variable `AWS::Region` and the intrinsic function `Ref`.

8. Create a `cloudformation` stack with our template, as follows:

```
aws cloudformation create-stack \
    --stack-name myteststack \
    --template-body file://your-first-rest-api-with-api-gateway-cf.yml \
    --region us-east-1 \
    --profile admin
```

Chapter 2

Here, I have used the `template-body` option to read the template file from the local machine. You can use the `template-url` option to read the template file from an S3 bucket.

The `create-stack` command will immediately return a `stack-id`, which we can use to check the stack creation status and delete the stack. We can also use the stack names for these operations:

```
{
    "StackId": "arn:aws:cloudformation:us-east-1:          :stack/myteststack/e8201060-ac40-11e8-8038-503acac5c0fd"
}
```

9. Check the status of the stack creation by using the `describe-stacks` sub-command, until it shows `CREATE_COMPLETE`:

    ```
    aws cloudformation describe-stacks \
        --stack-name myteststack \
        --region us-east-1 \
        --profile admin
    ```

    The `describe-stacks` command returns the current status of the stack (for example, `CREATE_IN_PROGRESS`, `CREATE_COMPLETE`, or `DELETE_COMPLETE`). If the stack creation completes successfully, it will return a status of <sphttps://packt-type-cloud.s3.amazonaws.com/uploads/sites/2819/2019/01/86d4cc9e-1a66-4aa3-ba42-f0d5dc363b52.pngan>`CREATE_COMPLETE`, along with the `Outputs` section with our sample URL:

```
"Stacks": [
    {
        "StackId": "arn:aws:cloudformation:us-east-1:          :stack/myteststack/e8201060-ac40-11e8-8038-503acac5c0fd",
        "StackName": "myteststack",
        "Description": "Building API with AWS CloudFormation",
        "CreationTime": "2018-08-30T10:41:34.755Z",
        "RollbackConfiguration": {},
        "StackStatus": "CREATE_COMPLETE",
        "DisableRollback": false,
        "NotificationARNs": [],
        "Outputs": [
            {
                "OutputKey": "SampleEndpoint",
                "OutputValue": "https://q3d7dw2dqq.execute-api.us-east-1.amazonaws.com/dev/greeting/Heartin",
                "Description": "Sample Endpoint"
            }
        ],
        "Tags": [],
        "EnableTerminationProtection": false
    }
```

You can verify the API by going to the URL in a browser. It should print the message `Hello Heartin`, as follows:

```
{"message": "Hello Heartin"}
```

10. You can delete the stack, and all of the resources that it created will automatically be cleaned up:

```
aws cloudformation delete-stack \
    --stack-name myteststack \
    --region us-east-1 \
    --profile admin
```

How it works...

In this recipe, we created our first REST API using Amazon CloudFormation. In the previous recipe, *Building your first API using the AWS CLI*, we created a similar API, but with the AWS CLI. Since the properties related to API Gateway API creation were already discussed in that recipe, I will not repeat them here.

We introduced a new CloudFormation template component: `Outputs`. We also used a sub-function in its value field, in order to derive a sample API endpoint. The maximum output that you can define in a template is 60. Its export parameter (not used here) can be used to specify an export name for the `Outputs` and reference it from another stack (a **cross-stack reference**).

There's more...

We deployed our CloudFormation template from the AWS CLI. You can also use the CloudFormation designer for template validation, or to see the template components visually, in a design view. We used the CloudFormation designer to validate and deploy our template in `Chapter 1`, *Getting Started with Serverless Computing on AWS*.

See also

- Refer to *Building your first API using the AWS CLI* recipe to learn about the API creation properties and REST and HTTP basics.
- To understand CloudFormation basics, you may refer to the *There's more* section of the recipe *Building your first Lambda with Amazon CloudFormation* from `Chapter 1`, *Getting Started with Serverless Computing on AWS*.
- For additional CloudFormation concepts, such as pseudo parameters, you can refer to the recipe *Using AWS SDK, Amazon CloudFormation and AWS CLI with Lambda* of `Chapter 1`, *Getting Started with Serverless Computing on AWS*.
- For additional theory on the *Outputs* section, you may refer to `https://docs.aws.amazon.com/AWSCloudFormation/latest/UserGuide/outputs-section-structure.html`.

Building your first API with Lambda integration

In the previous two recipes in this chapter, we created an API with mock integration. We also discussed REST principles, HTTP essentials, and the AWS CLI commands and CloudFormation template components used. In this recipe, we will integrate an API gateway API with Lambda. The API is similar to the previous one (with a path parameter), but we will use an AWS integration instead of mock integration.

Getting ready

You need an active AWS account. You need to follow the section *Getting started* in the recipes *Your first AWS Lambda* and *Your first Lambda with AWS CLI* from `Chapter 1`, *Getting Started with Serverless Computing on AWS*, to set up Java, Maven, the parent project, `serverless-cookbook-parent-aws-java`, and AWS CLI, and may also read other notes there including code usage guidelines, S3 bucket creation, and notes for Windows users.

We will discuss any newly introduced CLI command options or CloudFormation template components in detail. The complete commands and the CloudFormation template are available with the code files. You can also refer to the previous recipes for explanations of the concepts that were already discussed.

Since the focus of this chapter is API Gateway, we won't show you the complete Lambda code (Java and template) within the chapter content, unless we are introducing something new. The complete code (Java and template) is available in the project's code repository, for reference.

How to do it...

First, we will create a Lambda, and then we will invoke it from an API Gateway API by using AWS integration. We will look at how to use CLI commands, as well as a CloudFormation template, to create the API.

Creating the Lambda

We will create a Lambda similar to the simple greeting Lambda with **plain old Java objects** (**POJOs**) that we used in Chapter 1, *Getting Started with Serverless Computing on AWS*. We will first use the CLI, and then a CloudFormation template, but with a few changes, which as follows:

1. Add a field (time) to the HandlerRequest POJO, to represent the query parameter time (for example, Morning). The POJO already has a parameter, name, which represents the path parameter {name}.
2. Modify the handleRequest method to use both of the parameters passed within JSON to generate the greeting message. If a value is not provided for a param, we will add a default value.
3. We will also make a change to the previous CloudFormation template (lambda-with-pojos-cf-template.yml) by adding the Outputs component to the template, to export our Lambda's name, which will then be referred to from the API Gateway CloudFormation template through cross-stack reference:

    ```
    Outputs:
      LambdaOutput:
        Description: 'Lambda For API Gateway Reference'
        Value: !Ref MyLambdaFunction
        Export:
          Name: LambdaForApiGateway
    ```

4. Create the stack by using the create-stack sub-command, and verify the stack by using the describe-stacks sub-command. The complete template and commands are available in the code files.

Chapter 2

> We will use the exported stack name LambdaForApiGateway later in this recipe from another template. We won't be able to delete a CloudFormation stack until all of the referenced stacks are deleted.

Creating a REST API with AWS CLI commands

Let's first create the REST API by using AWS CLI commands. We will not show how to use the commands that we already discussed in previous recipes. However, the complete commands will be available with the code files:

1. Create a REST API with the name `API Gateway With Lambda`, using the `apigateway` sub-command `create-rest-api`.
2. Get the parent resource ID passing the REST API by using the `apigateway` sub-command `get-resources`.
3. Create a resource, `lambdagreeting`, under the root resource (/) by using the sub-command `create-resource`.
4. Create a path parameter, `{name}`, under the parent resource `lambdagreeting`, using the `apigateway` sub-command `create-resource`.
5. Create an `http-method GET` with the authorization type `'NONE'`, using the `apigateway` sub-command `put method`. Although it is not required for this recipe, we will add the property `request-parameters`, in order to specify that the path parameter is required:

   ```
   aws apigateway put-method \
       --rest-api-id 19sh9qhri2 \
       --resource-id n9iev1 \
       --http-method GET \
       --authorization-type "NONE" \
       --request-parameters method.request.path.name=true \
       --region us-east-1 \
       --profile admin
   ```

6. Set up a response status code of `200` for the `http-method GET`, using the `apigateway` sub-command `put-method-response`.

7. Set up an AWS integration, as follows:

   ```
   aws apigateway put-integration \
       --rest-api-id 19sh9qhri2 \
       --resource-id n9iev1 \
       --http-method GET \
   ```

[75]

Building Serverless REST APIs with API Gateway

```
    --type AWS \
    --integration-http-method POST \
    --uri 'arn:aws:apigateway:us-
east-1:lambda:path/2015-03-31/functions/arn:aws:lambda:us-
east-1:<account_id>:function:lambda-for-api-gateway/invocations' \
    --request-templates '{"application/json": "{\"name\":
\"$input.params('"'"'name'"'"')\" , \"time\":
\"$input.params('"'"'time'"'"')\"}"}' \
    --region us-east-1 \
    --profile admin
```

> The URI format for AWS Lambda integration
> is `arn:aws:apigateway:<region>:lambda:path/2015-03-31/funct
> ions/<lambda arn>/invocations`.

The `integration-http-method` (for the API request to Lambda) is `POST`, but `http-method` (for the client/browser request to the API) is `GET`. We have also defined the `request-templates` option, to specify a mapping template for the JSON sent to Lambda.

8. Define the integration response with a `selection-pattern`, `""`, but without the `response-templates` option:

```
aws apigateway put-integration-response \
    --rest-api-id 19sh9qhri2 \
    --resource-id n9iev1 \
    --http-method GET \
    --status-code 200 \
    --region us-east-1 \
    --selection-pattern "" \
    --profile admin
```

> We are no longer using the `response-templates` option to specify a dummy response, as the response is generated at the backend Lambda.

9. Deploy our Lambda to a stage, `dev1`, by using the `apigateway` sub-command `create-deployment`.

10. Give a `permission` for the API to invoke the `lambda`, as follows:

    ```
    aws lambda add-permission \
    --function-name lambda-for-api-gateway \
    --statement-id apigateway-st-1 \
    --action lambda:InvokeFunction \
    --principal apigateway.amazonaws.com \
    --source-arn "arn:aws:execute-api:us-east-1:<account_id>:tyu4dw36th/dev/GET/lambdagreeting/{name}" \
    --profile admin
    ```

11. Invoke the API from a browser with a path param value (`Heartin`):

    ```
    https://tyu4dw36th.execute-api.us-east-1.amazonaws.com/dev/lambdagreeting/Heartin
    ```

    > **TIP**: Remember to replace the REST API ID (`tyu4dw36th`) with your REST API ID.

    The preceding URL should show the following output:

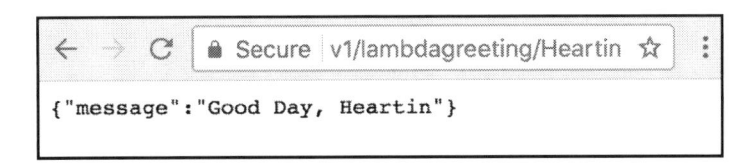

    ```
    {"message":"Good Day, Heartin"}
    ```

12. Invoke the API from a browser with path and query params, as follows:

    ```
    https://tyu4dw36th.execute-api.us-east-1.amazonaws.com/dev1/lambdagreeting/Heartin?time=Morning
    ```

    The preceding code will provide the following output:

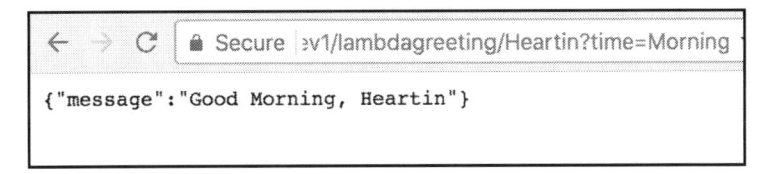

    ```
    {"message":"Good Morning, Heartin"}
    ```

Creating a REST API with a CloudFormation template

Now, let's create the API by using a CloudFormation template. We will not discuss the steps or components that were already discussed in previous recipes, nor will we discuss the theory behind commands that were already discussed within the section *Creating a REST API with AWS CLI commands*. The complete code is available in the code files:

1. Start to create the template by defining `AWSTemplateFormatVersion` and a suitable description (for example, `API with Lambda Integration`).
2. Define our REST API with a `FailOnWarnings` setting of `true`, using `AWS::ApiGateway::RestApi`.
3. Define a resource with the `PathPart` as `lambdagreeting`, using `AWS::ApiGateway::Resource`.
4. Define a path parameter (`PathPart`) of `'{name}'`, under the resource for the `PathPart` of `lambdagreeting`, by using `AWS::ApiGateway::Resource`.
5. Define an `http-method` `GET` with an `AWS` integration type and corresponding AWS (Lambda) integration URI, by using `AWS::ApiGateway::Method` (similar to what we did in the section *Creating a REST API with AWS CLI commands*):

```
MyMethod:
  Type: AWS::ApiGateway::Method
  Properties:
    AuthorizationType: NONE
    HttpMethod: GET
    Integration:
      Type: AWS
      IntegrationHttpMethod: POST
      IntegrationResponses:
      - StatusCode: 200
      RequestTemplates:
        application/json: "{\"name\": \"$input.params('name')\" , \"time\": \"$input.params('time')\"}"
      Uri:
        !Sub
          -
            'arn:aws:apigateway:${AWS::Region}:lambda:path/2015-03-31/functions/arn:aws:lambda:us-east-1:${AWS::AccountId}:function:${LAMBDA_NAME}/invocations'
          - LAMBDA_NAME: !ImportValue LambdaForApiGateway

    ResourceId: !Ref NamePathParamResource
    RestApiId: !Ref MyRestAPI
    MethodResponses:
    - StatusCode: 200
```

> We use the intrinsic function `ImportValue` to refer to an exported Lambda name. We had exported the name of our Lambda from a previous Lambda in the section *Creating the Lambda*.

6. Deploy our API to a stage, `dev`, by using `AWS::ApiGateway::Deployment`.
7. Add a permission for the API to invoke our Lambda, as follows:

```
LambdaInvokePermission:
  Type: AWS::Lambda::Permission
  Properties:
    FunctionName: !ImportValue LambdaForApiGateway
    Action: 'lambda:InvokeFunction'
    Principal: apigateway.amazonaws.com
    SourceArn: !Sub
      - arn:aws:execute-api:${AWS::Region}:${AWS::AccountId}:${API_ID}/*/GET/lambdagreeting/{name}
      - API_ID: !Ref MyRestAPI
```

8. Add an `Outputs` section that will return our final API endpoint of the form `https://<rest-api-id>.execute-api.<aws-region>.amazonaws.com/dev/lambdagreeting/Heartin`.
9. Create the stack by using the `create-stack` sub-command, and verify the stack by using the `describe-stacks` sub-command. The complete template and commands are available in the code files.
10. Test the API by running the URL from a browser, with and without the query parameters (see *Creating a REST API with AWS CLI commands* section for the expected output).

How it works...

In this recipe, we discussed how to integrate an API Gateway API with an AWS Lambda. Now, let's look at the important CLI commands and CloudFormation templates that were used.

CLI commands

The options for the following commands have not changed much, aside from their names and descriptions: `create-rest-api`, `get-resources`, `create-resource`, `put-method-response`, `put-integration-response`, and `create-deployment`. We also added `request-parameters` to `put-method`, to create the path param, as required.

We used the `AWS` integration type. We also specified the URI in the format required for AWS integrations: `arn:aws:apigateway:<region>:lambda:path/2015-03-31/functions/<lambda arn>/invocations`. The `2015-03-31` refers to the latest API version of the AWS Lambda service.

We defined the `request-templates` option of the `put-integration` sub-command to specify the mapping template for the JSON passed to Lambda from the API. Within the mapping template key is the content type, and the value is the mapping template for that content type. We also used the path and query parameter values within the mapping template. We will look at mapping templates in detail in a later recipe.

The `integration-http-method` of the `put-integration` command specifies the HTTP method used by API Gateway to connect with the Lambda. The `integration-http-method` should be `POST`, for Lambda integration. This is not the HTTP method that we use to access our API endpoint from a browser (which is `GET`, as specified by `http-method`).

We did not specify `iam` roles or policies for API Gateway to talk to Lambda; instead, we used Lambda's `add-permission` command to allow our API to invoke it. We specifically gave `lambda:InvokeFunction` permission, but you can also give all of the permissions by using `lambda:*`. For logging to CloudWatch, you will still need to add a role with the required permissions.

The `lambda add-permission` properties are as follows:

- `function-name` is the name of the Lambda function.
- `statement-id` is a unique number to identify this permission.
- `action` refers to the permitted actions.
- `principal` denotes the AWS service that is granted permission.
- `source-arn` is the `arn` of the resource invoking the function. You can specify `*` to denote that any of the part is matched (for example, `tyu4dw36th/*/*/lambdagreeting/{name}` matches any stage and any HTTP method).

CloudFormation template components

As always, we will start with the template version and description. The options for the following resource types have not changed much: `RestApi`, `Resource`, and `Deployment`. The `Outputs` section is also the same as before. Within the method declaration, we used the `AWS` integration type, along with a URI in the required format.

Within the management console, you have a separate `Lambda Integration` option and AWS integration option. However, with CLI commands and CloudFormation templates, the AWS integration option is used for both cases.

We have introduced a new intrinsic function: `Fn::ImportValue`. `Fn::ImportValue` gets the value of an output exported by another stack (in our case, the Lambda stack). Exports and imports are only allowed within regions, and export names must be unique within a region.

We also used a new type, `AWS::Lambda::Permission`, to add a permission to a Lambda. The options are similar to the CLI commands we used, but we have used CloudFormation intrinsic functions and variables to avoid any hardcoding. When working with API gateway, you only need to use `SourceArn` to specify the `SourceAccount`. However, if you are specifying a resource, such as an S3 bucket, you need to specify the `SourceAccount` option as well.

There's more...

We have now created our first API with a Lambda backend. We used API gateway's request and response modeling capabilities to structure the input and output from the Lambda. We can also configure API gateway to act as a proxy, in order to forward the request as it is to Lambda. We will see that in a later recipe.

See also

- For more information on the intrinsic function `Fn::ImportValue`, you can refer to https://docs.aws.amazon.com/AWSCloudFormation/latest/UserGuide/intrinsic-function-reference-importvalue.html
- For more information on `AWS::Lambda::Permission`, you can refer to https://docs.aws.amazon.com/AWSCloudFormation/latest/UserGuide/aws-resource-lambda-permission.html

Building and testing your first POST API method

In this recipe, we will create a simple POST API method that has an AWS integration with Lambda. A REST client will send a JSON request body to the API method in the format required by our Lambda, which will be passed through to the Lambda. We will use the same Lambda from the previous recipe.

GET is the default HTTP method for web browser requests; hence, we could invoke GET API methods from the browser in the previous recipes. To invoke other HTTP methods or override various HTTP options, we need to use a REST client. We will use the Postman REST client, which is available as a standalone app, as well as an extension to the Chrome browser.

Getting ready

You need an active AWS account. You need to follow the section *Getting started* in the recipes *Your first AWS Lambda* and *Your first Lambda with AWS CLI* from Chapter 1, *Getting Started with Serverless Computing on AWS*, to set up Java, Maven, the parent project, serverless-cookbook-parent-aws-java, and AWS CLI, and may also read other notes there including code usage guidelines, S3 bucket creation and notes for the Windows users.

As we are reusing the Lambda that was used in the recipe *Building your first API with Lambda integration*, you will need to build and deploy that Lambda using its CloudFormation template (if it was not already deployed). You can follow the steps in that recipe to build and upload JAR to S3, and use the provided CloudFormation template to deploy the Lambda.

How to do it...

As with the previous recipes, we will first look at how to create the API using CLI commands, and we will then look at how to use CloudFormation templates. We will also cover testing it with a REST client.

Creating the API with CLI commands

First, let's create the REST API by using AWS CLI commands. We will not show how to use the commands that we already discussed in previous recipes. However, the complete commands will be available with the code files:

1. Use the `aws apigateway` command to create a REST API in API Gateway, using the `apigateway` sub-command `create-rest-api`.
2. Get the root resource (/) of our API by using the `apigateway` sub-command `get-resources`.
3. Create our `path-part`, `lambdagreeting`, by using the `apigateway` sub-command `create-resource`.
4. Execute the `aws apigateway put-method` command with the `http-method` as POST, as follows:

   ```
   aws apigateway put-method \
       --rest-api-id 7uwav24q1f \
       --resource-id s6rij6 \
       --http-method POST \
       --authorization-type "NONE" \
       --region us-east-1 \
       --profile admin
   ```

5. Execute `aws apigateway put-method-response` with the `status-code` as 200 for the `http-method` POST, as follows:

   ```
   aws apigateway put-method-response \
       --rest-api-id 7uwav24q1f \
       --resource-id s6rij6 \
       --http-method POST \
       --status-code 200 \
       --region us-east-1 \
       --profile admin
   ```

6. Execute the `aws apigateway put-integration` command with the `http-method` as POST, the type as AWS, and a Lambda URI, as per the required format:

   ```
   aws apigateway put-integration \
       --rest-api-id 7uwav24q1f \
       --resource-id s6rij6 \
       --http-method POST \
       --type AWS \
       --integration-http-method POST \
       --uri 'arn:aws:apigateway:us-east-1:lambda:path/2015-03-31/functions/arn:aws:lambda:us-
   ```

Building Serverless REST APIs with API Gateway

```
    east-1:<account_id>:function:lambda-for-api-gateway/invocations' \
        --region us-east-1 \
        --profile admin
```

> We have omitted the `request-templates` property, and we are now passing parameters within the body of our `POST` request.

The default pass through behavior is to pass the request body to the Lambda as is (if no matching templates are defined), as you can see in the response of `put-integration`, as follows:

```
{
    "type": "AWS",
    "httpMethod": "POST",
    "uri": "arn:aws:apigateway:us-east-1:lambda:path/2015-03-31/functions/arn:aws:lambda:us-east-1:         :function:lambda-for-api-gateway/invocations",
    "passthroughBehavior": "WHEN_NO_MATCH",
    "timeoutInMillis": 29000,
    "cacheNamespace": "s6rij6",
    "cacheKeyParameters": []
}
```

7. Execute the `aws apigateway put-integration-response` command for the `http-method POST`, with a `selection-pattern` of `""`:

    ```
    aws apigateway put-integration-response \
        --rest-api-id 7uwav24q1f \
        --resource-id s6rij6 \
        --http-method POST \
        --status-code 200 \
        --region us-east-1 \
        --selection-pattern "" \
        --profile admin
    ```

8. Deploy our API to a stage, `dev`, using the `apigateway` sub-command `create-deployment`.

9. Give permission for the API to invoke the Lambda, as follows:

    ```
    aws lambda add-permission \
        --function-name lambda-for-api-gateway \
        --statement-id apigateway-st-2 \
        --action lambda:InvokeFunction \
        --principal apigateway.amazonaws.com \
        --source-arn "arn:aws:execute-api:us-east-1:<account_id>:7uwav24q1f/*/POST/lambdagreeting" \
        --profile admin
    ```

[84]

Chapter 2

Creating the API with a CloudFormation template

Now, let's create the API by using a CloudFormation template. We will not discuss the components that were already discussed in previous recipes, nor will we discuss the theory behind commands that were already discussed within the *CLI commands* section. The complete code is available in the code files:

1. Start to create the template by defining `AWSTemplateFormatVersion` and a suitable `Description`.
2. Create the REST API by using `AWS::ApiGateway::RestApi`.
3. Create the `path-part`, `lambdagreeting`, by using `AWS::ApiGateway::Resource`.
4. Define the method, with the `http-method` as `POST`, as follows:

   ```
   MyMethod:
     Type: AWS::ApiGateway::Method
     Properties:
       AuthorizationType: NONE
       HttpMethod: POST
       Integration:
         Type: AWS
         IntegrationHttpMethod: POST
         IntegrationResponses:
         - StatusCode: 200
         Uri:
           !Sub
             -
   'arn:aws:apigateway:${AWS::Region}:lambda:path/2015-03-31/functions/arn:aws:lambda:us-east-1:${AWS::AccountId}:function:${LAMBDA_NAME}/invocations'
             - LAMBDA_NAME: !ImportValue LambdaForApiGateway

       ResourceId: !Ref GreetingResource
       RestApiId: !Ref MyRestAPI
       MethodResponses:
       - StatusCode: 200
   ```

   > We have omitted the `request-templates` property, and we are now passing parameters within the body of our `POST` message.

5. Deploy our API to a stage, `dev`, by using `AWS::ApiGateway::Deployment`.

[85]

6. Add permission for the API to invoke the Lambda, as follows:

```
LambdaInvokePermission:
  Type: AWS::Lambda::Permission
  Properties:
    FunctionName: !ImportValue LambdaForApiGateway
    Action: 'lambda:InvokeFunction'
    Principal: apigateway.amazonaws.com
    SourceArn: !Sub
      - arn:aws:execute-api:${AWS::Region}:${AWS::AccountId}:${API_ID}/*/POST/lambdagreeting
      - API_ID: !Ref MyRestAPI
```

7. Add an `Outputs` section with the updated URI, as follows:

```
Outputs:
  SampleEndpoint:
    Description: 'POST Endpoint'
    Value: !Sub
      - https://${API_ID}.execute-api.${AWS::Region}.amazonaws.com/dev/lambdagreeting
      - API_ID: !Ref MyRestAPI
```

Testing with Postman

We will now look at how to test our API by using the Postman client. You can also use any other REST client that you are comfortable with:

1. Search for `Postman Chrome extension`, and follow the search results to install the Postman extension in Chrome.

   > Postman is also available as a native app, to download, install, and use. It will also be the preferred way to use the Postman client, from this point forward.

2. Once Postman has been added as an extension in Chrome, you can launch it from `chrome://apps/`. You can log in to your Google account, or skip logging in.

3. Select the **Request** option. You can specify a folder to save the request in, or close the **Save** dialog box.

4. Configure Postman to send requests to our API method, and click on **Send**:
   1. Select the **POST** method.
   2. Add our endpoint URL for the **POST** method.
   3. Go to the **Body** tab, click on **raw**, and select **JSON (application/json)** for the content type.
   4. Add our JSON payload, as follows:

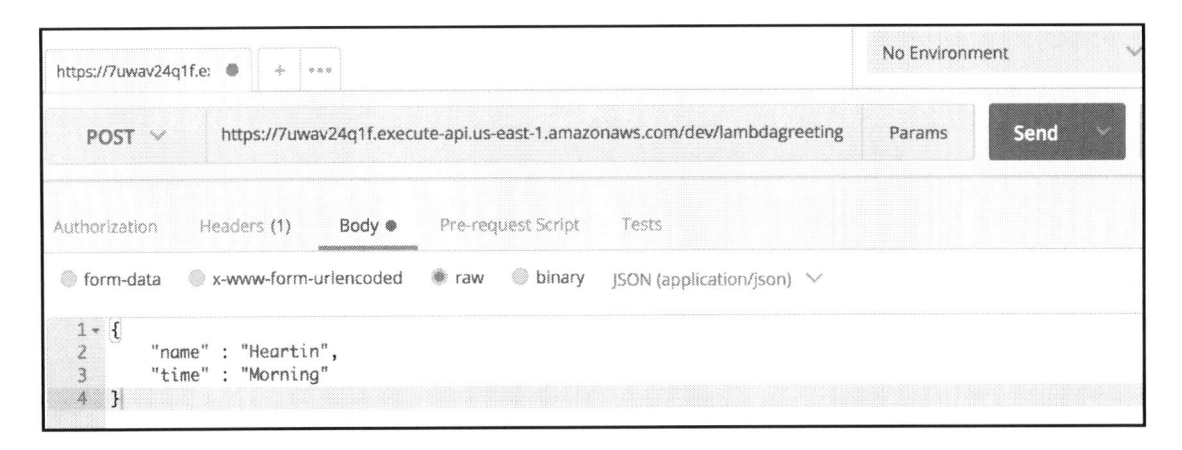

```
{
    "name" : "Heartin",
    "time" : "Morning"
}
```

5. Once you have configured the options and have clicked on send, you should get a successful response, as follows:

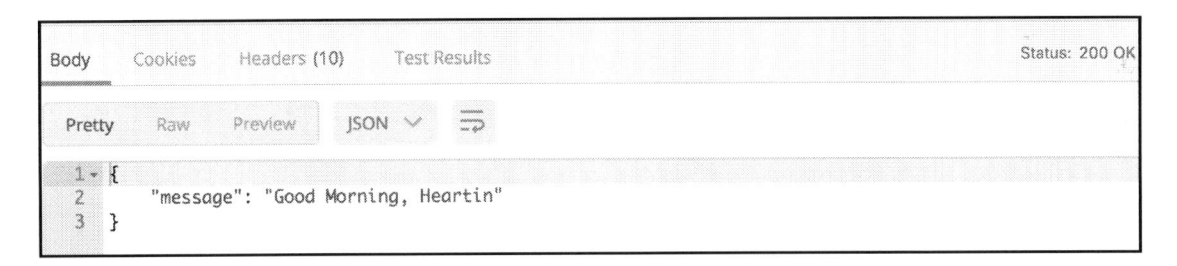

```
{
    "message": "Good Morning, Heartin"
}
```

How it works...

In this recipe, we created a POST API method whose request body is passed to the Lambda as is. To use the `POST` method, we used the `POST` HTTP method. To allow pass-through behavior, we did not use any `request-templates` property, and made use of the default passthrough behavior.

Passthrough behavior

In the `put-integration` response, you saw that the `passthroughBehavior` had the value `WHEN_NO_MATCH`, which means that, if we do not define a template for the request content type, API Gateway will `passthrough` the request body to the Lambda.

We can override the passthrough behavior with the `passthrough-behavior` parameter in the CLI, or with the `PassthroughBehavior` property within the CloudFormation template. The valid values for this parameter are as follows:

- `WHEN_NO_MATCH`: This option allows the pass through of the request body for unmapped content types to the backend.
- `WHEN_NO_TEMPLATES`: This option allows pass through only if the templates are not defined for any content type. If a template is defined for at least one content type, the others will be rejected with a `415` HTTP response status code. The HTTP `415` response status code stands for `Unsupported Media Type`. This is the recommended option.
- `NEVER`: This option rejects all unmapped content types with an HTTP `415` response code.

There's more...

Having a decent understanding of all of the common HTTP headers used with HTTP requests and HTTP responses can help you to design good REST APIs. To see the actual HTTP requests and responses for our `POST` method invocation, you can use a such as like Fiddler (www.telerik.com/fiddler) or Wireshark (www.wireshark.org).

See also

You can read more about using Fiddler and Wireshark for monitoring HTTP requests on their respective websites:

- https://www.telerik.com/fiddler
- https://www.wireshark.org

Mapping requests and responses with mapping templates

Amazon API Gateway allows us to map our incoming requests to a format that's required by our Lambda, and map the response from the Lambda into a format that's required by the client, all by using the mapping templates. The API Gateway body mapping templates are based on the Apache **Velocity Template Language** (**VTL**) and JSONPath expressions.

In this recipe, we will see how to map a JSON body coming from a request into another JSON structure, as required by the backend (Lambda). We will also map the JSON response from the backend (Lambda) into a different JSON response structure which is sent back as the response. We will use the same Lambda from the recipe *Building your first API with Lambda integration*, but the client will send the request in a different format.

Getting ready

You need an active AWS account. You need to follow the section *Getting started* in the recipes *Your first AWS Lambda* and *Your first Lambda with AWS CLI* from `Chapter 1`, *Getting Started with Serverless Computing on AWS* to set up Java, Maven, the parent project, `serverless-cookbook-parent-aws-java`, and AWS CLI, and may also read other notes there including code usage guidelines, S3 bucket creation, and notes for Windows users.

As we are reusing the Lambda that we used in the recipe *Building your first API with Lambda integration*, you will need to build and deploy that Lambda (if you have not done so already). You can follow the steps in that recipe to build the project and upload JAR to S3, and you can use the provided CloudFormation template to deploy the Lambda.

The body mapping templates are written based on VTL and JSONPath expressions. So, having a decent understanding of the Apache VTL language and JSONPath expressions will help you to better understand the sample templates and to develop templates that suit your project's needs.

How to do it...

We will map the client request with the expected request format for the Lambda, and we will also map the Lambda response to the expected response format for the client.

Mapping requests

The expected request structure for our Lambda, based on the request POJO, is as follows:

```
{
  "name" : "Heartin",
  "time" : "Morning"
}
```

The request payload sent from the client via the POST request is as follows:

```
{
  "user" : {
  "name" : "Heartin"
  },
  "greeting" : {
  "time" : "Morning"
  }
}
```

We can map the request payload to the expected JSON format by using the following mapping template:

```
{
  "name" : $input.json('$.user.name'),
  "time" : $input.json('$.greeting.time')
}
```

Mapping responses

The response from the Lambda is as follows:

```
{
  "message" : "Good Morning, Heartin"
}
```

The expected response from the client is as follows:

```
{
  "greeting" : "Good Morning, Heartin"
}
```

We can map the response returned from the Lambda into the expected response format by using the following mapping template:

```
{
 "greeting" : $input.json('$.message'),
}
```

Creating the API using CLI commands

First, let's create the REST API by using AWS CLI commands. We will not show how to use the commands that we already discussed in previous recipes. However, the complete commands will be available in the code files:

1. Create a REST API in API Gateway by using the `apigateway` sub-command `create-rest-api`.
2. Get the root resource (/) of our API by using the `apigateway` sub-command `get-resources`.
3. Create our `path-part`, `lambdagreeting`, by using the `apigateway` sub-command `create-resource`.
4. Create a `POST` method by using the `apigateway` sub-command `put-method`.
5. Set a response status code for our `POST` method by using the `apigateway` sub-command `put-method-response`.
6. Execute the `aws apigateway put-integration` command with the request mapping template, as follows:

```
aws apigateway put-integration \
    --rest-api-id y3yftanqp7 \
    --resource-id e4w7ka \
    --http-method POST \
    --type AWS \
    --integration-http-method POST \
    --uri 'arn:aws:apigateway:us-east-1:lambda:path/2015-03-31/functions/arn:aws:lambda:us-east-1:<account_id>:function:lambda-for-api-gateway/invocations' \
    --request-templates '{ "application/json" : "{ \"name\" : $input.json('"'"'$.user.name'"'"'), \"time\" : $input.json('"'"'$.greeting.time'"'"')}" }' \
    --passthrough-behavior WHEN_NO_TEMPLATES \
    --region us-east-1 \
    --profile admin
```

[91]

Building Serverless REST APIs with API Gateway

> Aside from the `request-template` property, we also set the value of `passthrough-behavior` with `WHEN_NO_TEMPLATES`.

7. Execute the `aws apigateway put-integration-response` command with the response mapping template, as follows:

```
aws apigateway put-integration-response \
    --rest-api-id y3yftanqp7 \
    --resource-id e4w7ka \
    --http-method POST \
    --status-code 200 \
    --region us-east-1 \
    --selection-pattern "" \
    --response-templates '{ "application/json" : "{ \"greeting\" : $input.json('"'"'$.message'"'"') }" }' \
    --profile admin
```

8. Deploy our API into a stage by using the `apigateway` sub-command `create-deployment`.
9. Give permission for the API method to invoke the Lambda function by using the command `aws lambda add-permission`.

Creating the API with a CloudFormation template

Now, let's create the API by using a CloudFormation template. We will not discuss the components that were already discussed in previous recipes, nor will we discuss the theory for commands that were already discussed within the *CLI commands* section. The complete code is available in the code files.

With the CloudFormation template, the major change is within the `Integration` property of the resource type `AWS::ApiGateway::Method`, as follows:

```
Integration:
  Type: AWS
  IntegrationHttpMethod: POST
  PassthroughBehavior: WHEN_NO_TEMPLATES
  RequestTemplates:
    application/json: "{ \"name\" : $input.json('$.user.name'), \"time\": $input.json('$.greeting.time') }"
  IntegrationResponses:
  - StatusCode: 200
    ResponseTemplates:
```

```
            application/json: "{ \"greeting\" : $input.json('$.message')}"
  Uri:
    !Sub
      -
'arn:aws:apigateway:${AWS::Region}:lambda:path/2015-03-31/functions/arn:aws
:lambda:us-east-1:${AWS::AccountId}:function:${LAMBDA_NAME}/invocations'
        - LAMBDA_NAME: !ImportValue LambdaForApiGateway
```

> All of the other components (for example, template version, description, API, resource, deployment, adding permission, and output) remain the same, except for the descriptions and names (in a few places), which are changed to match the current recipe.

Testing the API

You can test the API by using Postman (or any other REST/HTTP client), as follows:

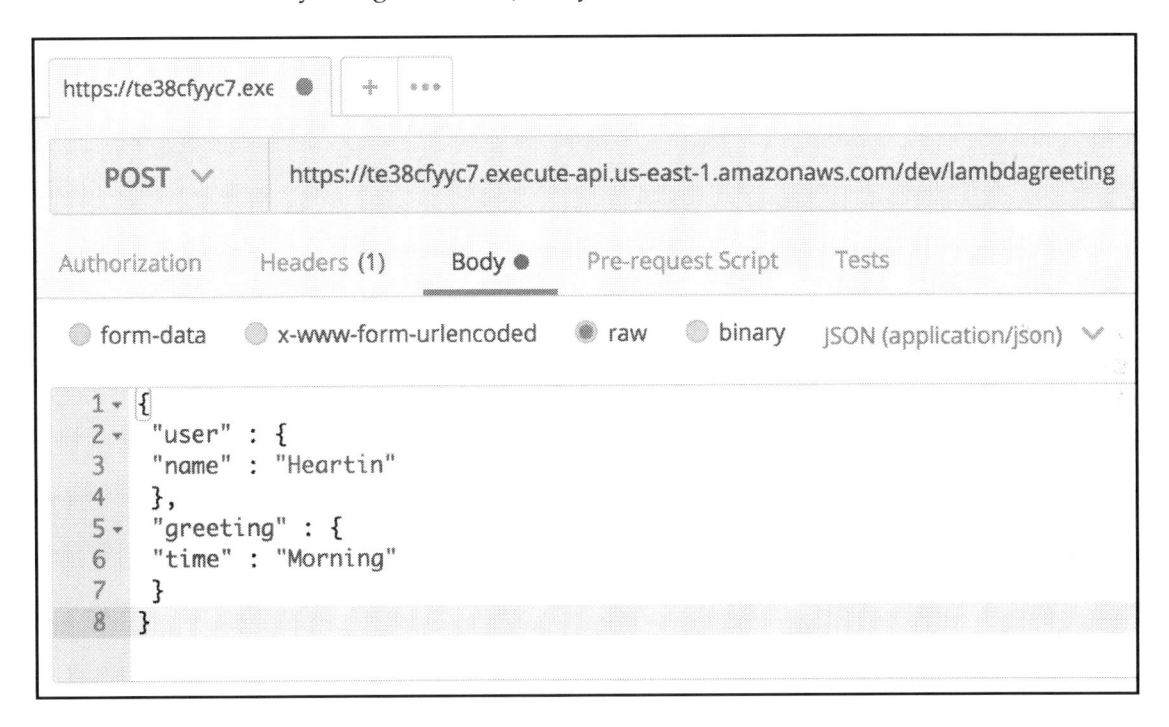

```
{
  "user" : {
    "name" : "Heartin"
  },
  "greeting" : {
    "time" : "Morning"
  }
}
```

Building Serverless REST APIs with API Gateway

The response should be the same as in the previous recipe, as shown in the following screenshot:

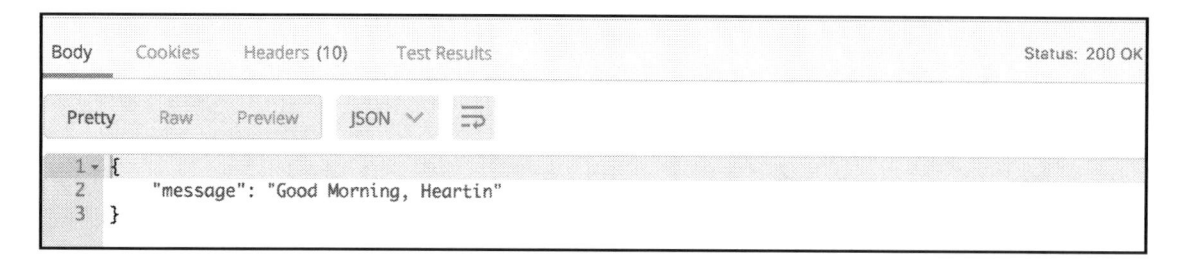

```
{
    "message": "Good Morning, Heartin"
}
```

How it works...

In this recipe, we used mapping templates with the variable `$input` that is provided by API gateway to transform the request JSON and response JSON. We also specified the recommended passthrough behavior of `WHEN_NO_TEMPLATES`, instead of the default `WHEN_NO_MATCH`. We discussed passthrough behavior in the previous recipe.

Mapping templates and variables

You can map the requests and responses in API Gateway by using API Gateway's body mapping templates, based on the Apache VTL and JSONPath expressions.

The `$input` variable provided by the API Gateway represents the input payload (a request payload or response payload, based on the case) and the parameters available to the template. The function `$input.json()` retrieves part of the JSON, as specified by a JSONPath expression. In JSONPath, `$` represents the outer-level JSON object. `$input.json('$.user.name')` returns the value of the field `name` within the `user` object, and `$input.json('$.greeting.time')` returns the value of the field `time` within the `greeting` object. Similarly, `$input.json('$.message')` returns the value of the `message` field.

Aside from `$input`, API Gateway also provides `$context`, `$stageVariables`, and `$util` variables. The `$context` variable holds the contextual information, such as the `apiId`, `authorizer properties`, `principalId`, `httpMethod`, `error details`, `accountId`, `apiKey`, `cognitoAuthenticationProvider details`, `sourceIp`, `path`, `protocol`, `status`, `stage`, and so on. The variable `$stageVariables` can be used to refer to stage variables. The `$util` variable has utility functions that can be used in mapping templates, such as `escapeJavaScript()`, `parseJson()`, `urlEncode()`, `urlDecode()`, `base64Encode()`, and `base64Decode()`.

Using #set

You can use `#set` to define a variable that can be used within the template.

Our (original) template is as follows:

```
{
  "name" : $input.json('$.user.name'),
  "time": $input.json('$.greeting.time')
}
```

The template, when rewritten by using `#set`, is as follows:

```
#set($inputRoot = $input.path('$'))
{
  "name" : "$inputRoot.user.name",
  "time": "$inputRoot.greeting.time"
}
```

> The `$inputRoot` is also the variable name that is autogenerated by API Gateway in the AWS Management Console. However, you are free to use any name.

There's more...

We have used Apache Velocity Language and JSONPath expressions within our recipe. You can read the following sections to learn more about them, for advanced use cases.

The Apache Velocity Language

Apache Velocity is a Java-based templating engine. It was developed for web designers, to get access to Java objects without knowing the Java programming language. Velocity is currently used as a templating engine for a variety of use cases, such as generating web pages, SQL, PostScript, and so on. API Gateway uses it for its mapping templates. You can learn more about the velocity language at `http://velocity.apache.org`.

JSONPath expressions

JSONPath expressions are used with a JSON object, similar to how XPath expressions are used with an XML document. `$` represents the root-level object, and `@` represents the current object. JSONPath expressions can use the dot notation or the square bracket notation. You can read more about JSONPath at `http://goessner.net/articles/JsonPath`.

See also

Read more about creating models and mapping templates at `https://docs.aws.amazon.com/apigateway/latest/developerguide/models-mappings.html`.

Variables available to use within API Gateway mapping template is available at `https://docs.aws.amazon.com/apigateway/latest/developerguide/api-gateway-mapping-template-reference.html`.

Validating request payloads with models

In this recipe, we will add validation to request payloads by using models. We will define a model by using the JSON schema draft language, and we will then use it to validate our payloads. We will use the same Lambda that we used in the recipe *Building your first API with Lambda integration*.

Getting ready

You need an active AWS account. You need to follow the section *Getting started* in the recipes *Your first AWS Lambda* and *Your first Lambda with AWS CLI* from Chapter 1, *Getting Started with Serverless Computing on AWS* to set up Java, Maven, the parent project, `serverless-cookbook-parent-aws-java`, and AWS CLI, and may also read other notes there including code usage guidelines, S3 bucket creation, and notes for the Windows users.

As we are reusing the Lambda from the recipe *Your first API with Lambda integration*, you will need to build and deploy that Lambda (if you have not done so already). You can follow the steps in that recipe to build the project and upload JAR to S3, and you can use the provided CloudFormation template to deploy the Lambda.

How to do it...

We will define a request in the JSON format, and then define a model schema for JSON, using both the CLI commands and the CloudFormation templates.

The request data format

We will use the same request format that we used in the previous recipe:

```
{
 "user" : {
 "name" : "Heartin"
 },
 "greeting" : {
 "time" : "Morning"
 }
}
```

Creating the API with CLI commands

First, let's create the REST API by using AWS CLI commands. We will not show how to use the commands that we already discussed in previous recipes. However, the complete commands will be available in the code files:

1. Create a REST API in API Gateway, using the `apigateway` sub-command `create-rest-api`.
2. Get the root resource (/) of our API, using the `apigateway` sub-command `get-resources`.
3. Create our `path-part`, `lambdagreeting`, using the `apigateway` sub-command `create-resource`.
4. Create a model schema for our JSON, using the `apigateway` sub-command `create-model`:

```
aws apigateway create-model \
    --rest-api-id dqnqdyb3z2 \
    --name 'greetingRequestModel' \
    --description 'Greeting Request Model' \
    --content-type 'application/json' \
    --schema '{
            "$schema": "http://json-schema.org/draft-04/schema#",
            "title": "greetingModel",
            "type": "object",
            "properties": {
                "user" : {"type": "object",
                    "properties": {
                        "name" : {"type" : "string"}
                    }
                },
                "greeting" : {"type": "object",
                    "properties" : {
                        "time" : {"type" : "string"}
                    }
                }
            },
            "required" : ["user", "greeting"]
        }' \
    --profile admin
```

[98]

5. Create a request validator for our JSON, using the `apigateway` sub-command `create-request-validator`:

   ```
   aws apigateway create-request-validator \
       --rest-api-id dqnqdyb3z2 \
       --name greetingRequestValidator \
       --validate-request-body \
       --profile admin
   ```

6. Execute the `aws apigateway put-method` command with our request model and request validator IDs, as follows:

   ```
   aws apigateway put-method \
       --rest-api-id dqnqdyb3z2 \
       --resource-id ffknxp \
       --http-method POST \
       --authorization-type "NONE" \
       --request-models application/json=greetingRequestModel \
       --request-validator-id 549e4h \
       --region us-east-1 \
       --profile admin
   ```

7. Set a response status code for our `POST` method by using the `apigateway` sub-command `put-method-response`.
8. Set up the integration type, `request-template`, and the passthrough behavior with the `apigateway` sub-command `put-integration`.
9. Set up the response mapping, using the `apigateway` sub-command `put-integration-response`.
10. Deploy our API into a stage, `dev`, using the `apigateway` sub-command `create-deployment`.
11. Give permission for the API method to invoke the Lambda function, using the command `aws lambda add-permission`.

The CloudFormation template

Now, let's create the API by using the CloudFormation template. We will not discuss the components that were already discussed in previous recipes, nor will we discuss the theory for commands that were already discussed within the *CLI commands* section. The complete code is available in the code files:

1. Start by defining the template version, `Description`, `RestApi`, and a `path-part lambdagreeting`.

2. Create a model for request validation, as follows:

```
MyRequestValidationModel:
  Type: AWS::ApiGateway::Model
  Properties:
    ContentType: application/json
    Description: Greeting Request Model
    Name: GreetingRequestModel
    RestApiId: !Ref MyRestAPI
    Schema: '{"$schema": "http://json-schema.org/draft-04/schema#",
             "title": "greetingModel",
             "type": "object",
             "properties": {
               "user" : {"type": "object",
                 "properties": {
                   "name" : {"type" : "string"}
                 }
               },
               "greeting" : {"type": "object",
                 "properties" : {
                   "time" : {"type" : "string"}
                 }
               }
             },
             "required" : ["user", "greeting"]
           }'
```

3. Create a request validator, as follows:

```
MyRequestValidator:
  Type: AWS::ApiGateway::RequestValidator
  Properties:
    Name: GreetingRequestValidator
    RestApiId: !Ref MyRestAPI
    ValidateRequestBody: true
    ValidateRequestParameters: false
```

4. Use the model and validator within the `AWS::ApiGateway::Method` resource, as follows:

```yaml
MyMethod:
  Type: AWS::ApiGateway::Method
  Properties:
    AuthorizationType: NONE
    HttpMethod: POST
    Integration:
      Type: AWS
      IntegrationHttpMethod: POST
      PassthroughBehavior: WHEN_NO_TEMPLATES
      RequestTemplates:
        application/json: "{ \"name\" : $input.json('$.user.name'), \"time\": $input.json('$.greeting.time') }"
      IntegrationResponses:
        - StatusCode: 200
          ResponseTemplates:
            application/json: "{ \"greeting\" : $input.json('$.message') }"
      Uri:
        !Sub
          -
            'arn:aws:apigateway:${AWS::Region}:lambda:path/2015-03-31/functions/arn:aws:lambda:us-east-1:${AWS::AccountId}:function:${LAMBDA_NAME}/invocations'
          - LAMBDA_NAME: !ImportValue LambdaForApiGateway
    RequestModels:
      application/json: !Ref MyRequestValidationModel
    RequestValidatorId: !Ref MyRequestValidator
    ResourceId: !Ref GreetingResource
    RestApiId: !Ref MyRestAPI
    MethodResponses:
      - StatusCode: 200
```

5. Add deployment, add Lambda permissions, and add an `Outputs` section, similar to the previous recipes.

Testing the API

You can test the API from Postman (or any other REST client of your choice) by passing the request in the expected format; you should get the expected response message. If you use the sample JSON method provided at the start of this section, you should get a response of `Good Morning, Heartin`.

If you send an invalid request (say, `{}`), you should get an error message with a response code of **400**, as shown in the following screenshot:

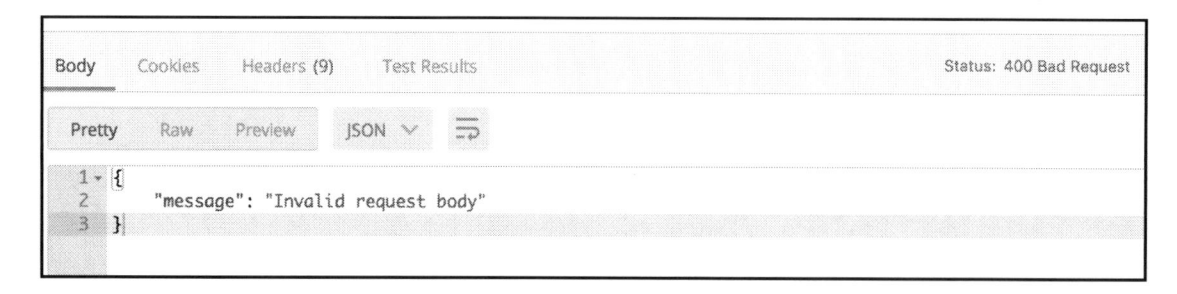

```
{
    "message": "Invalid request body"
}
```
Status: 400 Bad Request

How it works...

In this recipe, we added a model based on the JSON schema for our input message format. To use the model to reject payloads that do not conform to our format, we did the following:

1. We specified all of the fields that are required (this is optional)
2. We created a validator and assigned it to this method

There's more...

In our recipes, we created the template manually from AWS CLI. API Gateway Management Console also supports auto generating mappings, based on models. Once we define a model, we can create starter mappings from the integration request and integration response sections of the API gateway dashboard in the Management Console.

See also

- To learn more about JSON schema, you can refer to `https://json-schema.org/understanding-json-schema/index.html`.

Lambda and API with proxy integration

In this recipe, we will configure our API to act as a proxy for a Lambda. We will create a new Lambda function that extracts the required data from the incoming request. While using proxy integration, Lambda needs to implement the low-level `RequestStreamHandler` that gives us access to the `InputStream` and `OutputStream`.

Getting ready

You need an active AWS account. You need to follow the section *Getting started* in the recipes *Your first AWS Lambda* and *Your first Lambda with AWS CLI* from Chapter 1, *Getting Started with Serverless Computing on AWS* to set up Java, Maven, the parent project, `serverless-cookbook-parent-aws-java`, and AWS CLI, and may also read other notes there including code usage guidelines, S3 bucket creation, and notes for Windows users.

A basic understanding of HTTP, REST, Java, and Maven is required to understand and follow the steps within this recipe. Knowledge of a REST client, such as Postman, is also good to have. You can refer to the previous recipes if you do not have the required basic understanding of these technologies and/or tools.

How to do it...

We will use proxy integration for our API, in order to pass the request to the Lambda without any changes. We will use the greedy path param `{proxy+}` under the root resource \, in order to catch all of the requests to its sub-resources. We will also add the `ANY` HTTP method over the greedy path to match for any type.

> The requests to the root resource, \ are still not matched. If we need to match for \, as well, we should define and configure an `ANY` method over it.

Creating a Lambda function for proxy integration

We will use a simple Lambda function, following the Lambda proxy integration example provided by AWS. We will only discuss the important code snippets that are used inside of the Lambda function within this chapter. However, you can refer to the code files for the complete code.

The Lambda `Handler` class implements the `RequestStreamHandler` interface, as follows:

```
public class ProxyStreamHandlerLambda implements RequestStreamHandler {
```

Along with the `Context` object, the `handler` method accepts the `InputStream` and `OutputStream`:

```
public final void handleRequest(final InputStream inputStream,
                                final OutputStream outputStream,
                                final Context context) throws IOException {
```

We can parse the `InputStream` to extract the event details sent by API Gateway as a `JSONObject`:

```
JSONParser parser = new JSONParser();
BufferedReader reader = new BufferedReader(new
InputStreamReader(inputStream));
JSONObject event = (JSONObject) parser.parse(reader);
```

We are using the `JSONParser` from `json-simple` (`com.googlecode.json-simple`). The `path`, `query`, `headers`, and `body` can be extracted from the event, as follows:

```
JSONObject pathParams = (JSONObject) event.get("pathParameters");
String application = (String) pathParams.get("proxy");

JSONObject queryParams = (JSONObject) event.get("queryStringParameters");
String name = (String) queryParams.get("name");

JSONObject body = (JSONObject) parser.parse((String) event.get("body"));
String time = (String) body.get("time");

JSONObject headers = (JSONObject) event.get("headers");
String acceptHeader = (String) headers.get("Accept");
```

> The complete working code, with the necessary checks (such as the null pointer check), is available in the code files.

For the response, we defined the response body and headers, and we added them (along with other parameters) to a `JSONObject` (`responseJson`):

```
JSONObject responseBody = new JSONObject();
responseBody.put("message", greeting);

JSONObject headers = new JSONObject();
headers.put("Content-Type", "application/json");

JSONObject responseJson = new JSONObject();
responseJson.put("isBase64Encoded", false);
responseJson.put("statusCode", "200");
responseJson.put("headers", headers);
responseJson.put("body", responseBody.toString());
```

Finally, let's add the response object to the `OutputStream` by using an `OutputStreamWriter`:

```
OutputStreamWriter writer = new OutputStreamWriter(outputStream, "UTF-8");
writer.write(responseJson.toJSONString());
writer.close();
```

Deploying the Lambda

Upload the Lambda to our S3 bucket with the `aws s3 cp` command. Then, use the CloudFormation template that is provided to deploy the Lambda stack. There are not many changes in the template, except for the name and description. The export parameter name for the Lambda is defined as `LambdaForProxyIntegration`.

Creating the Proxy API with CLI commands

First, let's create the REST API by using AWS CLI commands. We will not show how to use the commands that we already discussed in previous recipes. However, the complete commands will be available in the code files:

1. Create a REST API in API Gateway, using the `apigateway` sub-command `create-rest-api`.
2. Get the root resource (/) of our API, using the `apigateway` sub-command `get-resources`.
3. Add a greedy path param, '{proxy+}', for the proxy resource:

   ```
   aws apigateway create-resource \
       --rest-api-id qacob6w4v7 \
   ```

```
    --region us-east-1 \
    --parent-id xitaiyjnuf \
    --path-part '{proxy+}' \
    --profile admin
```

> This resource will match any sub-resources for the parent /.

4. Use the ANY method over the proxy resource, in order to match any HTTP method, as follows:

```
aws apigateway put-method \
    --rest-api-id qacob6w4v7 \
    --resource-id k7zima \
    --http-method ANY \
    --authorization-type "NONE" \
    --region us-east-1 \
    --profile admin
```

5. Add a response code for the ANY method, as follows:

```
aws apigateway put-method-response \
    --rest-api-id qacob6w4v7 \
    --resource-id k7zima \
    --http-method ANY \
    --status-code 200 \
    --region us-east-1 \
    --profile admin
```

6. Execute put-integration with the AWS_PROXY integration type, as follows:

```
aws apigateway put-integration \
    --rest-api-id qacob6w4v7 \
    --resource-id k7zima \
    --http-method ANY \
    --type AWS_PROXY \
    --integration-http-method POST \
    --uri 'arn:aws:apigateway:us-east-1:lambda:path/2015-03-31/functions/arn:aws:lambda:us-east-1:<account_id>:function:lambda-for-proxy-integration/invocations' \
    --region us-east-1 \
    --profile admin
```

7. Execute `put-integration-response` for the `ANY` method, as follows:

   ```
   aws apigateway put-integration-response \
     --rest-api-id qacob6w4v7 \
     --resource-id k7zima \
     --http-method ANY \
     --status-code 200 \
       --region us-east-1 \
       --selection-pattern "" \
       --profile admin
   ```

8. Create a deployment with the `dev` stage, using the `apigateway` sub-command `create-deployment`.

9. Give permission for the API to invoke the Lambda, as follows:

   ```
   aws lambda add-permission \
       --function-name lambda-for-proxy-integration \
       --statement-id apigateway-st-3 \
       --action lambda:InvokeFunction \
       --principal apigateway.amazonaws.com \
       --source-arn "arn:aws:execute-api:us-east-1:<account_id>:qacob6w4v7/*/*/{proxy+}" \
       --profile admin
   ```

10. Execute the API from a REST client (for example, Postman), as shown in the following screenshot:

[107]

Building Serverless REST APIs with API Gateway

You should get a response similar to the following:

```
{
  "message": "Good Morning, Heartin. Welcome to MyApp. Client User-Agent is Mozilla/5.0 (Macintosh; Intel Mac
    OS X 10_13_6) AppleWebKit/537.36 (KHTML, like Gecko) Chrome/68.0.3440.106 Safari/537.36."
}
```

I sent a `POST` request from the Postman client, but a `GET` request from a browser will also work in this case, as the API's proxy resource has an `ANY` method, which can accept any HTTP method. Also, remember to replace the IDs with your own.

Creating the API using CloudFormation templates

Now, let's create the API using a CloudFormation template. We will not discuss the components that were already discussed in previous recipes, nor will we discuss the theory for commands that were already discussed within the *CLI commands* section. The complete code is available in the code files:

1. Start to create the template with the version, description, and RestApi resource.
2. Add the proxy resource, `'{proxy+}'`, as follows:

```
MyProxyResource:
  Type: AWS::ApiGateway::Resource
  Properties:
    RestApiId: !Ref MyRestAPI
    ParentId: !GetAtt MyRestAPI.RootResourceId
    PathPart: '{proxy+}'
```

3. Add the `Method` definition, with the `AWS_PROXY` integration type and `ANY` HTTP method, as follows:

```
MyMethod :
  Type : AWS::ApiGateway::Method
  Properties:
    AuthorizationType: NONE
    HttpMethod: ANY
    Integration:
      Type: AWS_PROXY
      IntegrationHttpMethod: POST
      IntegrationResponses:
      - StatusCode: 200
      Uri:
        !Sub
        -
```

```
'arn:aws:apigateway:${AWS::Region}:lambda:path/2015-03-31/functions
/arn:aws:lambda:us-
east-1:${AWS::AccountId}:function:${LAMBDA_NAME}/invocations'
        - LAMBDA_NAME: !ImportValue LambdaForProxyIntegration

    ResourceId: !Ref MyProxyResource
    RestApiId: !Ref MyRestAPI
    MethodResponses:
    - StatusCode: 200
```

> We are importing the Lambda `LambdaForProxyIntegration`. Therefore, the Lambda's CloudFormation template has to be executed first.

4. Add the deployment resource in a stage: `dev`.
5. Provide permission to the API to invoke the Lambda, as follows:

```
LambdaInvokePermission:
  Type: AWS::Lambda::Permission
  Properties:
    FunctionName: !ImportValue LambdaForProxyIntegration
    Action: 'lambda:InvokeFunction'
    Principal: apigateway.amazonaws.com
    SourceArn: !Sub
      - arn:aws:execute-
api:${AWS::Region}:${AWS::AccountId}:${API_ID}/*/*/{proxy+}
      - API_ID: !Ref MyRestAPI
```

6. Provide an `Outputs` section with a sample endpoint, as follows:

```
Outputs:
  SampleEndpoint:
    Description: 'Sample Endpoint'
    Value: !Sub
      -
https://${API_ID}.execute-api.${AWS::Region}.amazonaws.com/dev/MyApp
      - API_ID: !Ref MyRestAPI
```

7. Execute the `create-stack` command to deploy the API.

Since we are importing the Lambda `LambdaForProxyIntegration`, the Lambda's CloudFormation template has to be executed first.

8. Finally, test the API from a REST client, such as Postman (similar to what we did for the API that we created using the CLI commands). You can also use a browser for testing, which uses the GET method, as the API can accept any HTTP method.

How it works...

Let's try to understand the theory behind Lambda proxy integration. You will also see how to define Lambdas for proxy integration, and how they are different from the other Lambdas that you have seen.

The greedy path, the ANY HTTP method, and proxy integration

We can use the greedy path param, {proxy+}, under a resource, in order to catch all of the requests to the resource's sub-resources. For example, /hello/{proxy+} catches all of the resources under hello/. The ANY HTTP method matches for any HTTP method. Enabling proxy integration will make the API pass the raw request to the Lambda, as is.

We used all three of these together, but that is not a requirement. You can use any one of these, or a combination of them. For example, we can define a regular path parameter and a regular HTTP method, but enable proxy integration. This will forward raw requests to the Lambda only when the path and HTTP method matches.

RequestStreamHandler versus RequestHandler

Implementations of the interface RequestHandler<I, O> accept and return POJOs. JSON payloads are mapped to the request POJO, and the response POJO is mapped to a JSON response. It can also accept and return a string payload.

The interface RequestStreamHandler is used for low-level request handling. The handler method provides access to InputStream for input, and OutputStream for output. RequestStreamHandler is generally used along with proxy integration. However, a good practice is to use RequestHandler and do all of the mappings within the API, whenever possible.

The input and output format of a Lambda function for proxy integration

While using proxy integration with API Gateway, API Gateway passes the HTTP request to the Lambda in a particular format. Similarly, API Gateway expects the output in a particular format. Refer to the recipe to see how most of these are used in Java code.

The input format is as follows:

```
{
  "resource": "The resource path",
  "path": "The path parameter",
  "httpMethod": "Incoming request's method name"
  "headers": {request headers}
  "queryStringParameters": {query string parameters }
  "pathParameters": {path parameters}
  "stageVariables": {Available stage variables}
  "requestContext": {Request context with authorizer-returned key-value pairs}
  "body": "A JSON string of the request payload."
  "isBase64Encoded": "A boolean flag that indicate if the applicable request payload is Base64-encoded"
}
```

The output format is as follows:

```
{
  "isBase64Encoded": true|false,
  "statusCode": httpStatusCode,
  "headers": { headerName: headerValue key value pairs },
  "body": "body content"
}
```

There's more...

In this chapter, you learned about building API Gateway APIs with mock integration, Lambda integration (AWS integration), and Lambda proxy integration (`AWS_PROXY` integration). You can also do HTTP and HTTP proxy integrations, and you can integrate API Gateway with other AWS services. Try to experiment with other integrations.

There is more to learn about Lambda and API Gateway in the context of Serverless programming, in areas such as security, hosting, deployment, scalability, performance, and so on. We will focus on some of these in the upcoming chapters.

See also

You can learn more about API Gateway from the following links to the developer guide:

- https://docs.aws.amazon.com/apigateway/latest/developerguide/api-gateway-set-up-simple-proxy.html
- https://docs.aws.amazon.com/apigateway/latest/developerguide/set-up-lambda-proxy-integrations.html
- https://docs.aws.amazon.com/apigateway/latest/developerguide/api-gateway-create-api-as-simple-proxy-for-lambda.html

You may read more about REST principles and also understand the value provided by API Gateway by looking into how you would create them without API Gateway at https://javajee.com/book/introduction-to-restful-web-services-and-jax-rs.

3
Data Storage with Amazon DynamoDB

This chapter will cover the following topics:

- Your first DynamoDB table
- Throughput provisioning examples
- Working with data from the CLI
- Using the DynamoDB SDK from Lambda
- Creating tables from Lambda
- Adding data from Lambda
- Reading data from Lambda

Introduction

In this chapter, we will learn to build a data store for our serverless applications using Amazon DynamoDB. DynamoDB is a fully managed NoSQL database service and is the primary data store in AWS for building serverless applications. If you have strict relational use cases, you may also consider Amazon Aurora, which is a fully managed relational database service. If you need more analytical features, such as aggregations, along with NoSQL flexibility, you may explore the Amazon Elasticsearch service.

A relational data model table consists of rows (records) with a fixed number of columns, and is queried using **Structured Query Language** (**SQL**). Different NoSQL databases are classified into different families, such as key-value store, document store, columnar, graph, and so on, and have different query mechanisms. DynamoDB has characteristics of both key-value and document-databased NoSQL families. Relational databases follow the ACID model for consistency and NoSQL databases generally follow the BASE model.

In previous chapters, we saw different ways to work with Lambda and API gateway, such as the management console, the SDK, the CLI, and CloudFormation templates. From now on, our focus will be on using CloudFormation templates and the AWS SDK, along with essential CLI commands.

Your first DynamoDB table

In this recipe, we will create our first DynamoDB table. Amazon DynamoDB is the primary database in AWS for building serverless applications. DynamoDB is a fully managed NoSQL database and you do not have to manage any servers. Unlike most NoSQL databases, DynamoDB, also supports consistent reads, but with an additional cost.

Attributes in DynamoDB are synonymous with columns, and items are synonymous with rows in a relational database. However, there is no table-level schema in DynamoDB. You can have different set of attributes in different items (rows). You can also have an attribute with the same name but different types in different items.

Getting ready

You need a working AWS account and should have installed and configured the AWS CLI with a profile with the necessary permissions, as given in the *Your first Lambda with the AWS CLI* recipe of `Chapter 1`, *Building Serverless REST APIs with API gateway*. You are also expected to have a decent understanding of AWS CLI commands, Amazon CloudFormation, and basic database concepts.

How to do it...

We will create a simple table, check its properties, update it, and finally delete the table. We will first use CLI commands to create the table and then use a CloudFormation template to do the same. We will also use CLI commands to check the created table. We will use the AWS SDK to do this in a later recipe.

Creating a table using CLI commands

1. We can create a simple DynamoDB table using the `aws dynamodb create-table` CLI command as follows:

   ```
   aws dynamodb create-table \
   --table-name my_table \
   --attribute-definitions 'AttributeName=id, AttributeType=S'
   'AttributeName=datetime, AttributeType=N' \
   --key-schema 'AttributeName=id, KeyType=HASH'
   'AttributeName=datetime, KeyType=RANGE' \
   --provisioned-throughput 'ReadCapacityUnits=5,
   WriteCapacityUnits=5' \
   --region us-east-1 \
   --profile admin
   ```

   Here, we define a table named `my_table` and use the `attribute-definitions` property to add two fields: `id` of type string (denoted by `S`) and `datetime` of type number (denoted by `N`). We then define a partition key (or hash key) and a sort key (or range key) using the `key-schema` property. We also define the maximum expected read and write capacity units per second using the `provisioned-throughput` property. I have specified the region even though `us-east-1` is the default.

2. List tables using the `aws dynamodb list-tables` CLI command to verify our table was created:

   ```
   aws dynamodb list-tables \
   --region us-east-1 \
   --profile admin
   ```

3. Use the `aws dynamodb describe-table` CLI command to see the table properties:

   ```
   aws dynamodb describe-table \
   --table-name my_table \
   --profile admin
   ```

The initial part of the response contains the table name, attribute definitions, and key schema definition we specified while creating the table:

```
{
    "Table": {
        "AttributeDefinitions": [
            {
                "AttributeName": "datetime",
                "AttributeType": "N"
            },
            {
                "AttributeName": "id",
                "AttributeType": "S"
            }
        ],
        "TableName": "my_table",
        "KeySchema": [
            {
                "AttributeName": "id",
                "KeyType": "HASH"
            },
            {
                "AttributeName": "datetime",
                "KeyType": "RANGE"
            }
        ],
```

The later part of the response contains `TableStatus`, `CreationDateTime`, `ProvisionedThroughput`, `TableSizeBytes`, `ItemCount`, `TableArn` and `TableId`:

```
        "TableStatus": "ACTIVE",
        "CreationDateTime": 1536848737.732,
        "ProvisionedThroughput": {
            "NumberOfDecreasesToday": 0,
            "ReadCapacityUnits": 5,
            "WriteCapacityUnits": 5
        },
        "TableSizeBytes": 0,
        "ItemCount": 0,
        "TableArn": "arn:aws:dynamodb:us-east-1:          :table/my_table",
        "TableId": "ee1d4c5a-3ccb-4b43-bd05-2262903380a3"
    }
}
```

4. You may use the `aws dynamodb update-table` CLI command to update the table:

```
aws dynamodb update-table \
--table-name my_table \
--provisioned-throughput 'ReadCapacityUnits=10,
WriteCapacityUnits=10' \
--profile admin
```

5. Finally, you may delete the table using `aws dynamodb delete-table`:

```
aws dynamodb delete-table \
--table-name my_table \
--profile admin
```

> We will be reusing this table in a later recipe when we work with data. If you are continuing with other recipes in this chapter now, you may delete the table after completing those recipes.

Creating a table using a CloudFormation template

We will see the components of the CloudFormation template needed for this recipe. The completed template file is available with the code files.

1. Start creating the CloudFormation template by defining the template format, the version, and a description:

```
---
AWSTemplateFormatVersion: '2010-09-09'
Description: Your First DynamoDB Table
```

2. Define the `Resources` section with the `DynamoDB Table` type:

```
Resources:
  MyFirstTable:
    Type: AWS::DynamoDB::Table
```

3. Define the properties section with the essential properties: `TableName`, `ProvisionedThroughput`, `KeySchema`, and `AttributeDefinitions`:

```
Properties:
  TableName: my_table
  ProvisionedThroughput:
    ReadCapacityUnits: 1
    WriteCapacityUnits: 1
```

```
            KeySchema:
              -
                AttributeName: id
                KeyType: HASH
              -
                AttributeName: dateandtime
                KeyType: RANGE
            AttributeDefinitions:
              -
                AttributeName: id
                AttributeType: S
              -
                AttributeName: dateandtime
                AttributeType: N
```

> Properties and their values are the same as we saw with the AWS CLI commands earlier. You can use the AWS CLI dynamodb command actions `list-tables` and `describe-table` to check the created table.

4. Update the table properties with the CloudFormation template:

   Change `ReadCapacityUnits` and `WriteCapacityUnits` in the template to 5 for each. You can then update the stack using the `aws cloudformation update-stack` CLI command:

   ```
   aws cloudformation update-stack \
       --stack-name myteststack \
       --template-body file://resources/your-first-dynamodb-table-
   cf-template-updated.yml \
       --region us-east-1 \
       --profile admin
   ```

   > Whenever an update is made, CloudFormation compares the template with the existing stack and updates only those resources that are changed. This is the first time we are using the `update-stack` action in this book.

5. Verify the table update using the `aws dynamodb describe-table` CLI command.
6. Delete the stack using the `aws cloudformation delete-stack` CLI command. As mentioned earlier, the other recipes in the chapter use this table, so if you are planning to continue with other recipes now, you may delete the table after completing them.

How it works...

We used the following DynamoDB CLI command actions in this recipe: `create-table`, `list-tables`, `describe-table`, `update-table`, and `delete-table`. We use the corresponding components and properties within our CloudFormation template as well. Some of these options will become clear after you read the following notes.

DynamoDB data model

Data in DynamoDB is stored in tables. A table contains items (similar to rows), and each item contains attributes, (similar to columns). Each item can have a different set of attributes and the same attribute names may be used with different types in different items.

DynamoDB supports the datatypes string, number, binary, Boolean, string set, number set, binary set, and list.

DynamoDB does not have a JSON data type; however, you can pass JSON data to DynamoDB using the SDK and it will be mapped to native DynamoDB data types.

You can also define indexes (global secondary indexes and local secondary indexes) to improve read performance.

Data model limits

The following are some of the important limits in the DynamoDB data model:

- There is an initial limit of 256 tables per region for an AWS account, but this can be changed by contacting AWS support.
- Names for tables and secondary indexes must be at least three characters long, but no more than 255 characters. Allowed characters are A-Z, a-z, 0-9, _ (underscore), - (hyphen), and . (dot).
- An attribute name must be at least one character long, but no greater than 64 KB long. Attribute names must be encoded using UTF-8, and the total size of each encoded name cannot exceed 255 bytes.
- The size of an item, including all the attribute names and attribute values, cannot exceed 400 KB.
- You can only create a maximum of five local secondary indexes and five global secondary indexes per table.

For a complete list of DynamoDB limits, refer to `https://docs.aws.amazon.com/amazondynamodb/latest/developerguide/Limits.html`.

DynamoDB keys and partitions

Each item is identified with a primary key, which can be either only the partition key if it can uniquely identify the item, or a combination of partition key and sort key. The partition key is also called a **hash key** and the sort key is also called a **range key**. Primary key attributes (partition and sort keys) can only be string, binary, or number.

Initially, a single partition holds all table data. When a partition's limits are exceeded, new partitions are created and data is spread across them. Current limits are 10 GB storage, 3,000 RCU, and 1,000 WCU. Data belonging to one partition key is stored in the same partition; however, a single partition can have data for multiple partition keys. The partition key is used to locate the partition and the sort key is used to order items within that partition.

Read and write capacity units

We specified the maximum read and write capacity units for our application per second, referred to as **read capacity unit** (RCU) and **write capacity unit** (WCU). We also updated our RCU and WCU. Updating the table properties is an asynchronous operation and may take some time to take effect. We will see throughput provisioning in detail in another recipe.

Waiting for asynchronous operations

The CLI commands `create-table`, `update-table`, and `delete-table` are asynchronous operations. The control returns immediately to the command line, but the operation runs asynchronously.

To wait for table creation, you can use the `aws dynamodb wait table-exists --table <table-name` command, which polls the table until it is active. The `wait table-exists` command may be used in scripts to wait until the table is created before inserting data. Similarly, you can wait for table deletion using the `aws dynamodb wait table-not-exists --table <table-name>` command, which polls with `describe-table` until `ResourceNotFoundException` is thrown. Both the wait options poll every 20 seconds and exit with a 255 return code after 25 failed checks.

Other ways to create tables

In this recipe, we created our table by specifying the properties, such as `attribute-definitions`, `key-schema`, `provisioned-throughput`, and so on. Instead, you can specify a JSON snippet or JSON file using the `cli-input-json` option. The `generate-cli-skeleton` option returns a sample template as required by the `cli-input-json` option.

In this recipe, we created a table using the AWS CLI and CloudFormation. You can also create DynamoDB tables from Java code using the AWS SDK, as we will see in a later recipe. However, in most real-world cases, CloudFormation templates are used to create and provision tables, and the AWS SDK is used to work with data items.

There's more...

Let's first see some features and limitations of DynamoDB. We will also see some theory on the **LSI** and **GSI**.

DynamoDB features

The following are some of the important features of DynamoDB:

- DynamoDB is a fully managed NoSQL database service. There are no servers to manage.
- DynamoDB has the characteristics of both the key-value and the document-based NoSQL families.
- Virtually no limit on throughput or storage. It scales very well, but according to the provisioned throughout configuration.
- DynamoDB replicates data into three different facilities within the same region for availability and fault tolerance. You can also set up cross-region replication manually.
- It supports eventual consistency reads as well as strongly consistent reads.
- DynamoDB is schemaless at the table level. Each item (rows) can have a different set of elements. Even the same attribute name can be associated with different types in different items.
- DynamoDB automatically partitions and re-partitions data as the table grows in size.
- You can store JSON and then do nested queries on that data using the AWS SDK.

- Data is stored on SSD storage.
- DynamoDB supports atomic updates and atomic counters.
- DynamoDB supports conditional operations for put, update, and delete.

DynamoDB general limitations

Here are some of the general limitations of DynamoDB:

- DynamoDB does not support complex relational queries such as joins or complex transactions.
- DynamoDB is not suited for storing a large amount of data that is rarely accessed. S3 may be better suited for such use cases.
- You cannot select the Availability Zone for your DynamoDB table.
- Default replication of data for availability and fault tolerance is only within a region.

Local and global secondary indexes

You can define LSI and GSI for your tables to improve the read performance. An LSI can be considered as an alternate sort key for a given partition-key value. A GSI contains attributes from the base table and organizes them by a primary key that is different from that of the base table. Secondary indexes are useful when you want to query based on non-key parameters. You can create them with the CLI as well as CloudFormation templates. There is a limit of five LSIs and five GSIs per table.

You can read and learn more about LSIs and GSIs from the following links:

- https://docs.aws.amazon.com/amazondynamodb/latest/developerguide/LSI.html
- https://docs.aws.amazon.com/amazondynamodb/latest/developerguide/GSI.html

See also

- https://aws.amazon.com/rds/aurora

Throughput provisioning examples

Provisioned throughput is the maximum read and write capacity that an application can use within a table or index.

If we use more than the specified RCU or WCU, DynamoDB can throttle the requests, the requests will fail with a 400 (bad request) error, and DynamoDB throws `ProvisionedThroughputExceededException`. AWS SDKs can do automatic retries in the case of a throughput exception.

Apart from manual throughput provisioning, DynamoDB also supports features such as auto-scaling and reserved capacity. Having a decent understanding of throughput provisioning can help you configure these alternate options efficiently. We will discuss different throughput provisioning scenarios in this recipe.

Getting ready

In this recipe, we do not directly discuss writing any commands or code. We will instead discuss examples of how to derive on a RCU or WCU based on a requirement. However, you may try them out when following the commands and code discussed in other recipes.

How to do it...

Let's look at some scenarios to understand RCU and WCU better.

Scenario 1

Your application needs to perform 5 million writes and 5 million eventually consistent reads per day with item sizes of 1 KB:

```
Number of writes per day = 5,000,000
Number of writes per second = ceil (5,000,000 / (24 * 60 * 60))  = 58
1 WCU is required for each 1 KB of write. So writes required for each item
= ceil(1) = 1
Total WCU required  = 58 x 1 = 1.
Similarly 5,000,000 eventually consistent reads per day  = 58 eventually
consistent reads per second.
1 RCU is required for 2 eventually consistency reads. So RCU required for
58 eventually consistent reads  = 29
1 RCU is required for 4KB of read. So reads required for each data item =
```

Data Storage with Amazon DynamoDB

```
ceil(1/4) = 1
Total RCU required = 29 x 1 = 29.
```

This example is based on the pricing example given by Amazon. We will see some more scenarios to make the concept clearer.

Please note the following:

- The `ceil` function returns the smallest integer greater than the passed value, for example, ceil (1.5) is 2.
- The AWS Free Tier provides 25 RCU and 25 WCU per second for a whole month. Therefore, if you set and use 58 WCU and 29 RCU for a month, you will be billed for only 33 WCU and 4 RCU.
- The AWS Free Tier provides 25 RCU and 25 WCU per second for a whole month. If you are using DynamoDB only for half a month, you can use approximately 50 WCU and 50 RCU per second. Therefore, if you set and use 58 WCU and 29 RCU for only half of a month, you will be billed for only 8 WCU and 0 RCU.

Scenario 2

Your application needs to perform 5 million writes and 5 million strongly consistent reads per day with item sizes of 5.5 KB:

```
Number of writes per day = 5,000,000
Number of writes per second = ceil (5,000,000 / (24 * 60 * 60))  = 58
1 WCU is required for each 1 KB of write. So, writes required for each item
= ceil(5.5) = 6
Total WCU required   = 58 x 6 = 348
Similarly 5,000,000 strongly consistent reads per day  = 58 strongly
consistent reads per second.
1 RCU is required for 1 strongly consistency read. So RCU required for 58
strongly consistent reads  = 58
1 RCU is required for 4KB of read. So reads required for each data item =
ceil(5.5/4) = 2
Total RCU required = 58 x 2 = 116
```

Scenario 3

Your application needs to perform one write and one eventually consistent read per second with item sizes of 1 KB on a DynamoDB table:

```
Number of writes per second = 1
1 WCU is required for each 1 KB of write. So writes required for each item
```

```
= ceil(1) = 1
Total WCU required  = 1 x 1 = 1;
Similarly, the number of eventually consistent reads per second = 1
1 RCU is required for 1 strongly consistency read. So, the RCU required for
1 eventually consistent read  = .5
1 RCU is required for 4 KB of read. So reads required for each data item =
ceil(1/4) = 1
Total RCU required = .5 x 1 = .5.
```

Even though the required RCU is `.5`, we still have to set an RCU of `1`. This is because you can only set integers greater than `0` for WCU and RCU.

How it works...

Let us go through some of the throughput-provisioning related concepts in more detail.

Strongly consistent reads versus eventually consistent reads

DynamoDB replicates data in three different facilities within a region. When you read data from DynamoDB, by default they are eventually consistent reads and hence you may not always see the latest data. You can opt for strongly consistent reads at twice the cost of eventually consistent reads.

One RCU can be used for one strongly consistent read per second or two eventually consistent reads per second, for an item up to 4 KB in size. One WCU can be used for one write per second for an item up to 1 KB in size.

Limits on throughput updates within a day

There is a limit on the number of times you can decrease your throughput in a day. However, there is no limit on the number of throughput increases. Exact limits may be updated by Amazon. The latest limits are available at `https://docs.aws.amazon.com/amazondynamodb/latest/developerguide/Limits.html`.

Data Storage with Amazon DynamoDB

There's more...

Apart from manually provisioning throughput, DynamoDB supports the following ways to manage capacity: auto-scaling and reserved capacity. With auto-scaling, you define the upper and lower limits for RCU and WCU along with a target utilization percentage within those limits. DynamoDB auto-scaling will maintain your target utilization as your application workload increases or decreases. Reserve capacity allows you to reserve minimum capacity for longer periods with a one-time upfront payment. Reserving capacity can save cost considerably.

See also

- https://aws.amazon.com/dynamodb/pricing/
- https://docs.aws.amazon.com/amazondynamodb/latest/developerguide/HowItWorks.ProvisionedThroughput.html

Working with data from the CLI

In this recipe, we will create, read, update, and delete items. We will learn to query and scan data with eventual consistency, as well as strong consistency. We will discuss the AWS CLI commands to work with data in this recipe, followed by recipes that use Java code from Lambda function using AWS Java SDK for DynamoDB.

We discuss only the essential DynamoDB concepts and commands, to get you started working with DynamoDB to build serverless applications with DynamoDB as the data store. You may explore further in the AWS documentation, a dedicated book, or a course on DynamoDB to master DynamoDB concepts.

Getting ready

Table-creation commands are not repeated in this recipe. So, you may follow the previous recipe and create a table as required by this recipe. You also need to install the AWS CLI and configure a profile with the necessary permissions, as given in the *Your first Lambda with the AWS CLI* recipe from Chapter 1, *Getting Started with Serverless Computing on AWS*.

How to do it...

We will add, read, update, and delete data items in DynamoDB.

Adding items

1. Use the `aws dynamodb put-item` CLI command to add an item to the DynamoDB table:

    ```
    aws dynamodb put-item \
        --table-name my_table \
        --item '{"id":{"S":"001"}, "datetime":{"N":"1536898265"}, "field1":{"N":"20"}}' \
        --region us-east-1
        --profile admin
    ```

2. Add a data item with different sets of attributes:

    ```
    aws dynamodb put-item \
        --table-name my_table \
        --item '{"id":{"S":"001"},"datetime":{"N":"1536898285"}, "field1":{"N":"30"}, "field2":{"S":"ABC"}}' \
        --region us-east-1
        --profile admin
    ```

    We added an additional attribute, `field2`.

3. Add an item with an existing field, but different data type:

    ```
    aws dynamodb put-item \
        --table-name my_table \
        --item '{"id":{"S":"002"},"datetime":{"N":"1536898295"}, "field1":{"S":"DEF"}}' \
        --region us-east-1
        --profile admin
    ```

Reading items

We can read items using `get-item`, `query`, or `scan`:

1. Use the `aws dynamodb get-item` CLI command, passing all key fields:

    ```
    aws dynamodb get-item \
        --table-name my_table \
        --key '{"id":{"S":"002"},"datetime":{"N":"1536898295"}}' \
    ```

Data Storage with Amazon DynamoDB

```
    --return-consumed-capacity TOTAL \
    --region us-east-1
    --profile admin
```

This command will return a single item, along with metadata describing the result. The result part returned is shown in the following screenshot:

```
{
    "Item": {
        "id": {
            "S": "002"
        },
        "datetime": {
            "N": "1536898295"
        },
        "field1": {
            "S": "DEF"
        }
    },
```

The metadata part is shown in the following screenshot:

```
    "ConsumedCapacity": {
        "TableName": "my_table",
        "CapacityUnits": 0.5
    }
}
```

I had added the `return-consumed-capacity` option to return the aggregate `ConsumedCapacity`.

2. Use the `query` action, passing the partition key field and a filter expression:

```
aws dynamodb query \
    --table-name my_table \
    --key-condition-expression "id=:id" \
    --filter-expression "field1=:field1" \
    --expression-attribute-values '{":id":{"S":"001"},
":field1":{"N":"20"}}' \
    --return-consumed-capacity TOTAL \
    --region us-east-1
    --profile admin
```

[128]

The sort key is optional here. The previous command's execution will return a single matching item, along with the following metadata that describes the result:

```
"Count": 1,
"ScannedCount": 2,
"ConsumedCapacity": {
    "TableName": "my_table",
    "CapacityUnits": 0.5
```

It scans for the document within the whole current partition, as we specified only the partition key, and hence `ScannedCount` is 2.

3. Use this `query`, passing all key fields and a filter expression:

```
aws dynamodb query \
    --table-name my_table \
    --key-condition-expression "id=:id and dateandtime=:dateandtime" \
    --filter-expression "field1=:field1" \
    --expression-attribute-values '{":id":{"S":"001"}, ":field1":{"N":"20"}, ":dateandtime":{"N":"1536898265"}, ":field1":{"N":"20"}}' \
    --return-consumed-capacity TOTAL \
    --region us-east-1
    --profile admin
```

This command will return a single matching item along with the following metadata:

```
"Count": 1,
"ScannedCount": 1,
"ConsumedCapacity": {
    "TableName": "my_table",
    "CapacityUnits": 0.5
```

It scans for one document as we specified both partition key and sort key, and hence `ScannedCount` is 1. You may also `query` with only the partition key without the sort key or filter expression (usage available with code files), in which case the count will be the number of matching items (here 2) and the scanned count will be the partition size (here 2).

Data Storage with Amazon DynamoDB

4. Execute the same command as a strongly consistent read using the `consistent-read` option:

   ```
   aws dynamodb query \
     --table-name my_table \
     --key-condition-expression "id=:id and dateandtime=:dateandtime" \
     --filter-expression "field1=:field1" \
     --expression-attribute-values '{":id":{"S":"001"}, ":field1":{"N":"20"}, ":dateandtime":{"N":"1536898265"}, ":field1":{"N":"20"}}' \
     --consistent-read \
     --return-consumed-capacity TOTAL \
     --region us-east-1
     --profile admin
   ```

   This command will return a single matching item along with the following metadata:

   ```
   "Count": 1,
   "ScannedCount": 1,
   "ConsumedCapacity": {
       "TableName": "my_table",
       "CapacityUnits": 1.0
   ```

   Note that the command now utilizes one capacity unit for read with strong consistency, instead of 0.5 with eventual consistency.

5. Use `scan`, passing `key` fields and a filter expression:

   ```
   aws dynamodb scan \
       --table-name my_table \
       --filter-expression "id=:id and dateandtime=:dateandtime and field1=:field1" \
       --expression-attribute-values '{":id":{"S":"002"}, ":dateandtime":{"N":"1536898295"}, ":field1":{"S":"DEF"}}' \
       --return-consumed-capacity TOTAL \
       --region us-east-1
       --profile admin
   ```

   This command will return a single matching item along with the following metadata:

```
"Count": 1,
"ScannedCount": 3,
"ConsumedCapacity": {
    "TableName": "my_table",
    "CapacityUnits": 0.5
```

Here, the `ScannedCount` is 3, which is the table size. The scan command scans the entire table even if we specify both partition key and sort key. You may scan with the filter expression without the partition key or sort key (usage available with the code files), in which case the count will be the number of matching rows (here 1) and the scanned count will still be the table size, which is 3. You may scan without the filter expression (usage available with the code files), in which case the count and scanned count both will be the number of items in the table. You may also scan with strong consistency using the `consistent-read` option, similar to the `query` example we saw before.

Updating items

1. Update items using the `update-item` command:

    ```
    aws dynamodb update-item \
        --table-name my_table \
        --key '{"id":{"S":"001"},"dateandtime":{"N":"1536898265"}}' \
        --update-expression "SET field1=:field1" \
        --expression-attribute-values '{":field1":{"N":"30"}}' \
        --region us-east-1
        --profile admin
    ```

    For `update-item`, you need to specify all the keys available using the `key` option.

Deleting items

1. Delete items using the `delete-item` command and a `key`:

    ```
    aws dynamodb delete-item \
        --table-name my_table \
        --key '{"id":{"S":"002"},"dateandtime":{"N":"1536898295"}}' \
    ```

```
--region us-east-1
--profile admin
```

Similar to `update-item`, for `delete-item`, you also you need to specify all the keys available using the `key` option.

How it works...

We added, read, updated, and deleted data in this recipe.

Add, update, and delete operations

We add data using the `put-item` operation, update using `update-item`, and delete using `delete-item`. The `put-item`, `update-item`, and `delete-item` operations are idempotent operations. This means that you can execute the command any number of times without any side effects. However, capacity will be charged for all attempts.

Reading data from DynamoDB

DynamoDB supports three ways of querying data:

- Read the exact item using `get-item`, providing all the keys.
- Read the items using a `query`, providing at least the partition key. You may also provide a sort key and/or a filter expression.
- Read the items using a scan, providing a filter expression.

Each of these ways support strongly consistent reads, using an additional option of `consistent-read`. The default is eventual consistency. By default, all attributes are returned in a read operation. You can use a `ProjectionExpression` parameter to specify which attributes need to be returned.

The following are some of the important characteristics of `get-item`:

- We cannot use `get-item` against a local or global secondary index.
- All key attributes need to be provided, or a `ValidationException` is thrown.
- If no items match, it returns nothing (no exception is thrown).

The following are some of the important characteristics of a `query`:

- The partition key is mandatory.
- You can provide a sort key or a range for sort keys.
- You can filter non-key values, but discarded values are still charged for.
- If no items match, it returns an empty block.
- The `query` results are always sorted by the sort key. The default order is ascending, but we can reverse the order by setting the `ScanIndexForward` parameter to false.

The following are some of the important characteristics of a `scan`:

- Key fields are not mandatory, but may be provided along with filter expressions.
- It scans the entire table, unlike a `query`, which scans only the records matching the provided keys. Hence, we should try to use queries instead of scans when possible.
- DynamoDB supports parallel scans for improved performance.

return-consumed-capacity

The `return-consumed-capacity` option returns the capacity used by an operation. It can have three values: `TOTAL` returns the aggregate capacity units consumed, `ALL_OLD` returns the values of all items before updating (changed or not), and `ALL_NEW` returns the values of all items after updating (changed or not). These values apply to all operations, except `ALL_NEW`, which is not applicable for `delete-item`.

There's more...

DynamoDB also supports batch operations using `batch-get-item` and `batch-write-item`. Batch `get` and `write` operations are generally done from within applications, using a loop. We will not do batch operations in this chapter, but I will provide more theory and useful links for batch reads and writes in upcoming recipes.

See also

- https://docs.aws.amazon.com/cli/latest/reference/dynamodb/index.html

Data Storage with Amazon DynamoDB

Using the DynamoDB SDK from Lambda

In previous recipes, we saw how to work with tables and data in DynamoDB using CloudFormation and the AWS CLI. In this recipe, I will outline the general steps to use the AWS Java SDK for DynamoDB from Lambda, and there will be no code files. In later recipes, we will implement different DynamoDB operations in Lambda, following this outline.

We will create different Lambda for different DynamoDB operations such as create table, add item, and read item. When used with API gateway, each Lambda will be mapped to a particular HTTP method on a resource. You may also use the same Lambda for all operations using Lambda proxy integration.

Getting ready

You need an active AWS account. You need to follow the section *Getting started* in the recipes *Your first AWS Lambda* and *Your first Lambda with AWS CLI* from Chapter 1, *Getting Started with Serverless Computing on AWS*, to set up Java, Maven, the parent project, serverless-cookbook-parent-aws-java, and AWS CLI, and may also read other notes there including code usage guidelines, S3 bucket creation, and notes for Windows users.

If you are not familiar with developing and deploying Lambda with the Java runtime using a CloudFormation template and the AWS CLI, you may first refer to the respective recipes in Chapter 1, *Getting Started with Serverless Computing on AWS*. Complete CloudFormation templates and the required CLI commands are provided with the code files for reference.

How to do it...

I will list and explain the general steps for developing DynamoDB operations from Lambda using the SDK in this section:

1. Create a Maven project for the Lambda with the common parent and the DynamoDB Java SDK dependency

    We follow the same project structure for all our Lambda projects:

```
▼ ■ src
    ▼ ■ main
        ▼ ■ java
            ▼ ■ tech.heartin.books.serverlesscookbook
                ▼ ■ domain
                    ■ package-info.java
                    © Request
                    © Response
                ▼ ■ services
                    ① DynamoDBService
                    © DynamoDBServiceImpl1
                    © DynamoDBServiceImpl2
                    ■ package-info.java
                © MyLambdaHandler
                ■ package-info.java
```

In the `POM` file, define the parent project as `serverless-cookbook-parent-aws-java`. This parent project defines the common properties and inherits from another parent with basic Java project dependencies and configurations such as lombok, checkstyle configurations, and so on:

```
<parent>
    <groupId>tech.heartin.books.serverlesscookbook</groupId>
    <artifactId>serverless-cookbook-parent-aws-java</artifactId>
    <version>0.0.1-SNAPSHOT</version>
</parent>
```

We also need to add the dependency for the AWS Java SDK for DynamoDB in our `POM` file:

```
<dependency>
    <groupId>com.amazonaws</groupId>
    <artifactId>aws-java-sdk-dynamodb</artifactId>
    <version>${aws.sdk.version}</version>
</dependency>
```

The `aws.sdk.version` property is defined in the parent project.

2. Define the `Request` and `Response` domain objects

Data Storage with Amazon DynamoDB

The `Request POJO` and `Response POJO` are used for input and output mapping for our Lambda handler (`MyLambdaHandler`). While the Request object will be specific to each operation-specific Lambda, the Response object will be reused for all cases and is defined as follows:

```
@Data
@AllArgsConstructor
public class Response {
    private String message;
    private String errorMessage;
}
```

3. Create the service implementation

   Define a service class for implementing the logic behind DynamoDB operations such as create table, add data, and so on. You may split the service class into an interface and an implementation class, which is a general practice with Java projects. You may also directly put your application logic into the Lambda handler without a service class.

   I have defined an interface (`DynamoDBService`) and two implementations; one uses the DynamoDB wrapper client (`DynamoDBServiceImpl1`) and the other uses the AmazonDynamoDB client (`DynamoDBServiceImpl2`). I have used Lambda environment variable in the handler to decide the implementation to use.

   The AmazonDynamoDB client can be created as follows:

   ```
   AmazonDynamoDB dynamoDBClient =
   AmazonDynamoDBClientBuilder.defaultClient();
   ```

   The DynamoDB wrapper client can be created using the AmazonDynamoDB client as follows:

   ```
   DynamoDB dynamoDB = new DynamoDB(dynamoDBClient);
   ```

   The code for the operation in the service class is specific to each operation and is shown in the respective recipes.

4. Define the Lambda handler

   The Lambda handler implementation will also be similar for all operations, except for the service method name and log message:

   ```
   public final class MyLambdaHandler implements
   RequestHandler<Request, Response> {
   ```

```
        private DynamoDBService service;

    public Response handleRequest(final Request request, final
Context context) {
        context.getLogger().log("Creating table " +
request.getTableName());
        final String version = System.getenv("API_VERSION");
        if(version != null && version.equals("V2")) {
            service = new DynamoDBServiceImpl2();
        } else{
            service = new DynamoDBServiceImpl1();
        }
        return service.createTable(request);
    }
}
```

We will use the Lambda environment variable to determine the version of `DynamoDBServiceImpl` to use. The default is V1, which is the wrapper client-based code. The JavaDoc comments required to pass the checkstyle checks are not shown here. Refer to the code files repository for the complete code.

5. Package and deploy Lambda

    The steps to package and deploy Lambda are common for all projects. You can package a Maven project as follows:

    mvn clean package

    Once the `.jar` file is created, you can upload the JAR file to S3 as follows:

    ```
    aws s3 cp \
    target/lambda-dynamodb-create-table-0.0.1-SNAPSHOT.jar \
    s3://serverless-cookbook/lambda-dynamodb-create-table-0.0.1-
    SNAPSHOT.jar \
    --profile admin
    ```

6. Define the CloudFormation template

    The CloudFormation template to provision our Lambda is similar for all Lambdas in this chapter, except the names and IAM policy permissions required for the DynamoDB operations we do. The IAM policy permissions required by each Lambda are also discussed separately for each case.

Data Storage with Amazon DynamoDB

We start the template with the template version and description, define a log group for our Lambda, define a role that can be assumed by Lambda, and create a policy to write logs. The Lambda function's configuration is also similar to other recipes, except the names. You may also add all Lambdas into a single template file if you are planning to deploy them together.

7. Deploy the CloudFormation template

    The `deploy stack` command for the CloudFormation template is the same for all Lambdas, except the name changes:

    ```
    aws cloudformation create-stack \
      --stack-name myteststack \
      --template-body file://resources/lambda-dynamodb-create-table-cf-template.yml \
      --capabilities CAPABILITY_NAMED_IAM \
      --region us-east-1 \
      --profile admin
    ```

    How to use `describe-stack` and `delete-stack` is shown in the code files.

8. Invoke the Lambda

    The payload that is passed to the `aws lambda invoke` command is specific to each Lambda's `Request` object.

    Our Lambda selects whether to execute version 1 (one that uses a DynamoDB wrapper client) or version 2 (one that uses an AmazonDynamoDB client) based on the value of Lambda environment variable, `API_VERSION`. The version 2 service implementation can be executed after updating the `API_VERSION` Lambda environment variable to V2:

    ```
    aws lambda update-function-configuration \
        --function-name <lambda name> \
        --environment Variables={API_VERSION=V2} \
        --region us-east-1 \
        --profile admin
    ```

9. Cleanup
    The cleanup steps (if required) are provided with each operation-specific Lambda's recipe.

How it works...

AmazonDynamoDB client versus DynamoDB wrapper client

With the DynamoDB Java SDK, we can either use the AmazonDynamoDB client directly or the wrapper client for DynamoDB. The wrapper client abstracts away some of the complexity of using the AmazonDynamoDB client directly. I will show the use of the wrapper client in this book; however, I will add the corresponding use of the AmazonDynamoDB client in the code files for the book.

IAM policy and actions

If you are new to IAM policies, you may create them using the Policy Generator. Go to the IAM Dashboard, click **Policies** on the left, and click **Create Policy** at the top to go to the **Create Policy** page. You can search for the service you want (such as DynamoDB) and select the actions you need. You also need to select a resource, which is a table in our case.

Actions are classified into **List**, **Read**, and **Write** actions.

The list actions available to select in the policy generator are shown here:

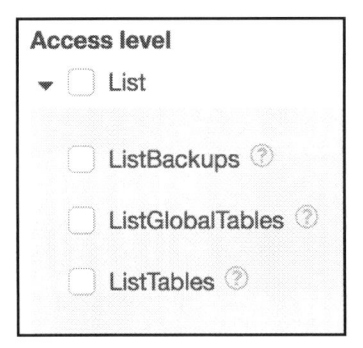

Data Storage with Amazon DynamoDB

The **Read** actions available to select in the policy generator are shown here:

- Read
  - BatchGetItem
  - DescribeBackup
  - DescribeContinuousBackups
  - DescribeGlobalTable
  - DescribeGlobalTableSettings
  - DescribeLimits
  - DescribeReservedCapacity
  - DescribeReservedCapacityOfferings
  - DescribeStream
  - DescribeTable
  - DescribeTimeToLive
  - GetItem
  - GetRecords
  - GetShardIterator
  - ListStreams
  - ListTagsOfResource
  - Query
  - Scan

The **Write** actions available to select in the policy generator are shown here:

- Write
  - BatchWriteItem
  - CreateBackup
  - CreateGlobalTable
  - CreateTable
  - DeleteBackup
  - DeleteItem
  - DeleteTable
  - PurchaseReservedCapacityOfferin...
  - PutItem
  - RestoreTableFromBackup
  - RestoreTableToPointInTime
  - TagResource
  - UntagResource
  - UpdateContinuousBackups
  - UpdateGlobalTable
  - UpdateGlobalTableSettings
  - UpdateItem
  - UpdateTable
  - UpdateTimeToLive

Single Lambda versus multiple Lambdas

We can use proxy integration to use the same Lambda for all HTTP methods and/or resources. However, it is a general practice to use smaller Lambdas for each HTTP method per resource and let API gateway invoke the right Lambda based on the HTTP method in the request.

There's more...

DynamoDB also provides a local downloadable version you can use for your local testing. You can find more details at https://docs.aws.amazon.com/amazondynamodb/latest/developerguide/DynamoDBLocal.html.

See also

- https://docs.aws.amazon.com/amazondynamodb/latest/APIReference/API_Operations.html
- https://docs.aws.amazon.com/lambda/latest/dg/tutorial-env_cli.html
- https://docs.aws.amazon.com/cli/latest/reference/lambda/update-function-configuration.html

Creating tables from Lambda

In this recipe, we will create tables from Lambda following the general steps outlined in the *Using the DynamoDB SDK from Lambda* recipe. We had already seen creating tables from the CLI and using a CloudFormation template in an earlier recipe. Tables are generally created in the real world using CloudFormation templates.

Getting ready

You need an active AWS account. You need to follow the section *Getting started* in the recipes *Your first AWS Lambda* and *Your first Lambda with AWS CLI* from Chapter 1, *Getting Started with Serverless Computing on AWS* to set up Java, Maven, the parent project, `serverless-cookbook-parent-aws-java`, and AWS CLI, and may also read other notes there including code usage guidelines, S3 bucket creation, and notes for Windows users.

It would be good to first go through the *Using the DynamoDB SDK with Lambda* recipe to understand the theory behind using the AWS SDK for DynamoDB from Lambda. Otherwise, refer back to that recipe whenever you have any doubts. It is also required to have decent knowledge of Java and Maven.

How to do it...

Let's discuss the steps to create a table from Lambda without repeating the common steps we already discussed:

1. Create a Maven project for the Lambda with the common parent and the DynamoDB Java SDK dependency
2. Define the `Request` and `Response` domain objects

   The `Request` object for the `lambda-dynamodb-create-table` Lambda is defined as follows:

   ```
   @Data
   public class Request {
       private String tableName;
       private String partitionKey;
       private String sortKey;
       private long readCapacityUnits;
       private long writeCapacityUnits;
       private boolean waitForActive;
   }
   ```

   The `Response` object is common to all Lambdas, as discussed in the *Using the DynamoDB SDK from Lambda* recipe.

3. Create the service implementation

   A table can be created using the DynamoDB wrapper client as follows:

   ```
   Table table = dynamoDB.createTable(request.getTableName(),
           Arrays.asList(
                   new KeySchemaElement(request.getPartitionKey(), KeyType.HASH),
                   new KeySchemaElement(request.getSortKey(), KeyType.RANGE)),
           Arrays.asList(
                   new AttributeDefinition(request.getPartitionKey(), ScalarAttributeType.S),
                   new AttributeDefinition(request.getSortKey(), ScalarAttributeType.N)),
               new ProvisionedThroughput(request.getReadCapacityUnits(), request.getWriteCapacityUnits()));
   ```

We can optionally wait until a table is created based on the value of `waitForActive` in the request object:

```
if (request.isWaitForActive()) {
    try {
        table.waitForActive();
    } catch (InterruptedException e) {
        e.printStackTrace();
    }
}
```

We can check the existence of a table and return an exception if the table already exists:

```
if (this.dynamoDB.getTable(tableName).getDescription() != null)
{
    return true;
}
```

The complete code is available with the code files.

4. Define Lambda handler to call the service method and return a response
5. Package and deploy Lambda
6. Define the CloudFormation template

    In the CloudFormation template, add permissions for Lambda to execute the `CreateTable` and `DescribeTable` actions:

    ```
    - Effect: Allow
      Action:
      - dynamodb:CreateTable
      - dynamodb:DescribeTable
      Resource:
      - Fn::Sub:
        arn:aws:dynamodb:${AWS::Region}:${AWS::AccountId}:table/*
    ```

    `CreateTable` permission is required to create the table and `DescribeTable` permission is required to wait for table creation.

7. Deploy the CloudFormation template
8. Invoke Lambda and test it

    Invoke our Lambda from the CLI as follows:

    ```
    aws lambda invoke \
        --invocation-type RequestResponse \
    ```

```
                --function-name lambda-dynamodb-create-table \
                --log-type Tail \
                --payload '{
                                "tableName":"my_table",
                                "partitionKey": "id",
                                "sortKey": "dateandtime",
                                "readCapacityUnits": 1,
                                "writeCapacityUnits": 1,
                                "waitForActive": false
                            }' \
                --region us-east-1 \
                --profile admin \
                outputfile.txt
```

The `waitForActive` input parameter is set as false here, and hence the request will return immediately. If you are waiting for table creation by setting `waitForActive` as true, you might want to raise the timeout for the lambda. Otherwise, your request might time-out with an error message as follows:

```
{"errorMessage":"2018-09-26T02:55:46.038Z 9fd63df2-
c137-11e8-9c78-e9dde91c7800 Task timed out after 15.01
seconds"}
```

We can now use the `aws dynamodb describe-table` CLI command to verify the new table's properties.

To execute the version 2 service implementation, update the `API_VERSION` Lambda environment variable to `V2`:

```
aws lambda update-function-configuration \
    --function-name lambda-dynamodb-create-table \
    --environment Variables={API_VERSION=V2} \
    --region us-east-1 \
    --profile admin
```

Now, execute the previous commands and verify the resultant output file.

9. Cleanup

To delete the table, you can use `aws dynamodb delete-table`.

How it works...

We discussed the steps to create tables from Lambda without repeating the theory behind using the AWS Java SDK for DynamoDB, which we already discussed in the *Using the DynamoDB SDK from Lambda* recipe. If you have any doubts about the common steps, refer to that recipe again.

There's more...

In real-world projects, tables are generally provisioned using CloudFormation templates, unless there is a use case to create tables dynamically. When a CloudFormation stack is deleted, all the provisioned resources, including tables, are also deleted. However, with the SDK or CLI, we need to take care of deleting the tables manually from within the code or through CLI commands.

See also

- https://docs.aws.amazon.com/amazondynamodb/latest/developerguide/AppendixSampleDataCodeJava.html

Adding data items from Lambda

In this recipe, we will add data items to our DynamoDB table from Lambda following the general steps outlined in the earlier recipe *Using the DynamoDB SDK from Lambda*. We have already seen how to work with data in DynamoDB from the AWS CLI in an earlier recipe.

Getting ready

You need an active AWS account. You need to follow the section *Getting started* in the recipes *Your first AWS Lambda* and *Your first Lambda with AWS CLI* from Chapter 1, *Getting Started with Serverless Computing on AWS* to set up Java, Maven, the parent project, serverless-cookbook-parent-aws-java, and AWS CLI, and may also read other notes there including code usage guidelines, S3 bucket creation, and notes for Windows users.

Data Storage with Amazon DynamoDB

It would be good to first go through the *Using the DynamoDB SDK from Lambda* recipe to understand the theory behind using the AWS SDK for DynamoDB from Lambda. Otherwise, refer back to that recipe whenever you have doubts. It is also assumed that you have decent knowledge of Java and Maven.

How to do it...

Let's discuss the steps to add data items from Lambda without repeating the common steps we already discussed:

1. Create a Maven project for the Lambda with the common parent and the DynamoDB Java SDK dependency.
2. Define the `Request` and `Response` domain objects.

   The Request object for the `lambda-dynamodb-put-item` lambda is defined as follows:

   ```
   @Data
   public class Request {
       private String tableName;
       private String partitionKey;
       private String sortKey;
       private String partitionKeyValue;
       private Integer sortKeyValue;
       private boolean waitForActive;
       private Map<String, String> stringData;
       private Map<String, Integer> integerData;
   }
   ```

   I have added two maps, one for string types and one for integer types. The Response object is common to all Lambdas, as discussed in the *Using the DynamoDB SDK from Lambda* recipe.

3. Create the service implementation.

   We can add an item into a DynamoDB table as follows:

   ```
   Table table = dynamoDB.getTable(request.getTableName());

   Item item = new Item()
           .withPrimaryKey(request.getPartitionKey(),
       request.getPartitionKeyValue(),
               request.getSortKey(),
       request.getSortKeyValue());
   ```

```
if (request.getStringData() != null) {
    request.getStringData().forEach((k, v) ->
item.withString(k, v));
}

if (request.getIntegerData() != null) {
    request.getIntegerData().forEach((k, v) -> item.withInt(k,
v));
}

table.putItem(item);
```

The complete code is available with the code files.

4. Define Lambda handler to call the service method and return a response.
5. Package and deploy Lambda.
6. Define the CloudFormation template.

    In the CloudFormation template, add permissions for Lambda to put items. If you are waiting for table creation, you also need the `DescribeTable` permission:

    ```
    - Effect: Allow
      Action:
      - dynamodb:PutItem
      - dynamodb:DescribeTable
      Resource:
      - Fn::Sub:
    arn:aws:dynamodb:${AWS::Region}:${AWS::AccountId}:table/*
    ```

7. Deploy the CloudFormation template.
8. Invoke Lambda and test it.

    We can invoke our Lambda from the CLI as follows:

    ```
    aws lambda invoke \
        --invocation-type RequestResponse \
        --function-name lambda-dynamodb-put-item \
        --log-type Tail \
        --payload '{
                    "tableName":"my_table",
                    "partitionKey": "id",
                    "sortKey": "dateandtime",
                    "partitionKeyValue": "p1",
                    "sortKeyValue": 1537963034,
                    "waitForActive": false,
                    "stringData" : {
    ```

```
                    "s1": "v1",
                    "s2": "v2"
                },
                "integerData" : {
                    "i1" : 1,
                    "i2" : 2
                }
            }
        }' \
    --region us-east-1 \
    --profile admin \
    outputfile.txt
```

To execute a version 2 service implementation, update the `API_VERSION` Lambda environment variable to V2:

```
aws lambda update-function-configuration \
    --function-name lambda-dynamodb-put-item \
    --environment Variables={API_VERSION=V2} \
    --region us-east-1 \
    --profile admin
```

9. Cleanup

    You can delete items using `aws dynamodb delete-item`.

How it works...

We discussed the steps to add items to a DynamoDB table from Lambda, without repeating the theory behind using the AWS Java SDK for DynamoDB, which we already discussed in the *Using the DynamoDB SDK from Lambda* recipe. If you have any doubts about the common steps, refer to that recipe again.

There's more...

DynamoDB also supports writing items in a batch using the `batch-write-item` command action.

`batch-write-item` has the following characteristics:

- Can write to one or more tables.
- Can write up to 25 items. If we try to write more than 25 items, the whole set will fail.

- Maximum request size is 16 MB.
- Any unprocessed items are returned.
- From a capacity unit calculation perspective, each item is treated separately. For example, if I have two items of 6 KB each, both items will take two units, making a total of four capacity units. See the *throughput provisioning* recipe for more clarity on throughput calculations.
- The `batch-write-item` can be used for `put` or `delete`. You cannot do `put` and `delete` for the same item.

See also

- https://docs.aws.amazon.com/amazondynamodb/latest/developerguide/batch-operation-document-api-java.html#JavaDocumentAPIBatchWrite

Reading data from Lambda

In this recipe, we will read data from Lambda, following the general steps outlined in the *Using the DynamoDB SDK from Lambda* recipe. We will read data using the `get-item`, `query`, and `scan` APIs. We have already seen reading data from the CLI in an earlier recipe, *Working with data from the CLI*.

Getting ready

You need an active AWS account. You need to follow the section *Getting started* in the recipes *Your first AWS Lambda* and *Your first Lambda with AWS CLI* from Chapter 1, *Getting Started with Serverless Computing on AWS* to set up Java, Maven, the parent project, `serverless-cookbook-parent-aws-java`, and AWS CLI, and may also read other notes there including code usage guidelines, S3 bucket creation, and notes for Windows users.

You need to follow the *Adding data items from Lambda* or *Working with data from the CLI* recipe and set up data before we can read them in this recipe. It would also be good to first go through the *Using the DynamoDB SDK from Lambda* recipe to understand the theory behind using the AWS SDK for DynamoDB from Lambda.

Data Storage with Amazon DynamoDB

How to do it...

Let's discuss the steps to read data from Lambda without repeating the common steps we already discussed:

1. Create a Maven project for the Lambda with the common parent and the DynamoDB Java SDK dependency.
2. Define the `Request` and `Response` domain objects.

   The `Request` object for the `lambda-dynamodb-read-item` lambda is defined as follows:

   ```
   @Data
   public class Request {
       private String tableName;
       private String partitionKey;
       private String sortKey;
       private String partitionKeyValue;
       private String sortKeyValue; // Will be stored integer.
       private boolean waitForActive;
       private Map<String, String> filterData;
   }
   ```

   The `filterData` map will contain the attributes to create filter expressions and their corresponding values. The Response object is common for all Lambdas, as discussed in the *Using the DynamoDB SDK from Lambda* recipe.

3. Create the service implementation.

   The service class will have implementations for `get-item`, `query`, and `scan` operations. Reading items using `get-item` can be done as follows:

   ```
   Table table = dynamoDB.getTable(request.getTableName());
   Item item = table.getItem(new PrimaryKey()
           .addComponent(request.getPartitionKey(),
   request.getPartitionKeyValue())
           .addComponent(request.getSortKey(),
   Integer.parseInt(request.getSortKeyValue())));
   ```

   Reading using a `query` can be done as follows:

   ```
   Table table = dynamoDB.getTable(request.getTableName());
   final String keyConditionExpression = request.getPartitionKey()
   + "=:" + request.getPartitionKey();
   QuerySpec querySpec = new QuerySpec()
           .withKeyConditionExpression(keyConditionExpression);
   ```

```
final Map<String, Object> valueMap = new HashMap<>();
StringBuilder filterExpressionBuilder;
if (request.getFilterData() != null) {
    filterExpressionBuilder = new StringBuilder();
    processFilterData(request, filterExpressionBuilder,
valueMap);
querySpec.withFilterExpression(filterExpressionBuilder.toString
());
}
valueMap.put(":" + request.getPartitionKey(),
request.getPartitionKeyValue());
querySpec.withValueMap(valueMap);
ItemCollection<QueryOutcome> items = table.query(querySpec);
```

You can also supply both the keys, instead of just the partition key. More examples are provided with the code files.

Reading using a `scan` can be done as follows:

```
final Table table =
dynamoDB.getTable(request.getTableName());
final String projectionExpression =
request.getPartitionKey() + " , " + request.getSortKey();
final ScanSpec scanSpec = new ScanSpec()
        .withProjectionExpression(projectionExpression);
StringBuilder filterExpressionBuilder;
Map<String, Object> valueMap;
if (request.getFilterData() != null) {
    filterExpressionBuilder = new StringBuilder();
    valueMap = new HashMap<>();
    processFilterData(request, filterExpressionBuilder,
valueMap);
scanSpec.withFilterExpression(filterExpressionBuilder.toStr
ing());
    scanSpec.withValueMap(valueMap);
}
ItemCollection<ScanOutcome> scanItems =
table.scan(scanSpec);
```

The `processFilter` data method creates the filter expression and value map iterating through the `filterData` map:

```
private void processFilterData(final Request request,
        final StringBuilder filterExpressionBuilder,
        final Map<String, Object> valueMap) {

    request.getFilterData().forEach((k, v) -> {
        final String var = ":" + k;
```

Data Storage with Amazon DynamoDB

```
            if (!filterExpressionBuilder.toString().isEmpty()) {
                filterExpressionBuilder.append(" and ");
            }
            filterExpressionBuilder.append(k + "=" + var);
            valueMap.put(var, v);
        });
    }
```

Instead of using the DynamoDB wrapper client, you can also use the AmazonDynamoDB client to do `get-item`, `query`, and `scan`. The complete code with both the options is available with the code files.

4. Define Lambda handler to call the service method and return a response.

   I have modified the Lambda handler implementation to call `get-item`, `query`, or `scan` as follows: if both key parameters have values, I call `get-item`; if only the partition key has a value, I call `query`; and if both keys' values are missing, I call `scan`. This is not a requirement, but only a convenient way to demonstrate.

5. Package and deploy Lambda.
6. Define the CloudFormation template.

   In the CloudFormation template, add permissions for Lambda to execute `get-item`, `query`, and `scan`:

   ```
   - Effect: Allow
     Action:
     - dynamodb:GetItem
     - dynamodb:Query
     - dynamodb:Scan
     Resource:
     - Fn::Sub:
     arn:aws:dynamodb:${AWS::Region}:${AWS::AccountId}:table/*
   ```

7. Deploy the CloudFormation template.
8. Invoke Lambda and test it.

   Invoke the Lambda, providing both keys to execute the `get-item` method:

   ```
   aws lambda invoke \
       --invocation-type RequestResponse \
       --function-name lambda-dynamodb-read-item \
       --log-type Tail \
       --payload '{
                   "tableName":"my_table",
   ```

[152]

```
                    "partitionKey": "id",
                    "sortKey": "dateandtime",
                    "partitionKeyValue": "p1",
                    "sortKeyValue": 1537963031,
                    "waitForActive": false
                }' \
    --region us-east-1 \
    --profile admin \
    outputfile.txt
```

Invoke Lambda, passing the partition key and a filter to execute the `query` method:

```
aws lambda invoke \
    --invocation-type RequestResponse \
    --function-name lambda-dynamodb-read-item \
    --log-type Tail \
    --payload '{
                    "tableName":"my_table",
                    "partitionKey": "id",
                    "sortKey": "dateandtime",
                    "partitionKeyValue": "p1",
                    "waitForActive": false,
                    "filterData" : {
                        "s1": "v1",
                        "s2": "v2"
                    }
                }' \
    --region us-east-1 \
    --profile admin \
    outputfile.txt
```

The filter expression is optional. Though not shown in this recipe, a `query` can accept both the keys, along with a filter.

Finally, we can invoke a `scan` as follows:

```
aws lambda invoke \
    --invocation-type RequestResponse \
    --function-name lambda-dynamodb-read-item \
    --log-type Tail \
    --payload '{
                    "tableName":"my_table",
                    "partitionKey": "id",
                    "sortKey": "dateandtime",
                    "waitForActive": false,
                    "filterData" : {
                        "s1": "v1",
```

Data Storage with Amazon DynamoDB

```
                "s2": "v2"
            }
    }' \
    --region us-east-1 \
    --profile admin \
    outputfile.txt
```

The filter expression is optional. DynamoDB will always do a full table scan. I have added more examples in the code files than shown in the book.

The version 2 service implementation can be executed after updating the `API_VERSION` Lambda environment variable to `V2`:

```
aws lambda update-function-configuration \
    --function-name lambda-dynamodb-read-item \
    --environment Variables={API_VERSION=V2} \
    --region us-east-1 \
    --profile admin
```

9. Clean up the resources.

   There is no cleanup required after reading data. However, you should have set up the data following the previous recipe or an earlier one. You may either delete that data or the whole table itself.

How it works...

We discussed the steps to read date from Lambda without repeating the theory behind using the AWS Java SDK for DynamoDB, which we have already discussed in the *Using the DynamoDB SDK from Lambda* recipe. If you have any doubts about the common steps, refer to that recipe again.

There's more...

DynamoDB also supports batch reads using `batch-get-item`.

`batch-get-item` has the following characteristics:

- Can provide one or more keys. Each key should contain all key fields (partition or partition and sort), similar to `get-item`.
- You may retrieve items from multiple tables.

- Maximum number of returned documents is 100. If more than 100 items are requested, a `ValidationException` occurs.
- Maximum size of returned record is 16 MB. The remaining items' keys are returned as unprocessed items, and we can retry them.
- `ProvisionedThroughputExceededException` occurs if all items fail. If only some fail, the failed items' keys are returned, along with the results, and we can retry them.
- Items can be retrieved in parallel, but the order may not be guaranteed.
- We can filter the attributes that are returned. It will not affect the cost, but it will allow more items to be returned within the 16 MB limit.

See also

We have learned enough about DynamoDB to create a backend for a serverless application. You can learn further from AWS documentation. You may also follow my notes on DynamoDB at `http://cloudmaterials.com/en/book/amazon-dynamo-db-essentials`.

Following are some useful links to AWS documentation:

- `https://docs.aws.amazon.com/amazondynamodb/latest/developerguide/JavaDocumentAPIItemCRUD.html`
- `https://docs.aws.amazon.com/sdk-for-java/v1/developer-guide/examples-dynamodb-items.html`
- `https://docs.aws.amazon.com/amazondynamodb/latest/developerguide/ScanJavaDocumentAPI.html`
- `https://docs.aws.amazon.com/amazondynamodb/latest/developerguide/QueryingJavaDocumentAPI.html`
- `https://docs.aws.amazon.com/amazondynamodb/latest/developerguide/Expressions.ExpressionAttributeNames.html`

4
Application Security with Amazon Cognito

This chapter will cover the following topics:

- Creating a Cognito user pool (AWS CLI, CloudFormation)
- Server-side authentication flow (AWS CLI, CloudFormation)
- Client-side authentication flow (AWS CLI, CloudFormation)
- User sign-up flow with Cognito (AWS CLI)
- Working with groups (AWS CLI)
- Integrating Cognito in an API gateway (AWS CLI, CloudFormation)
- User sign-up with SMS verification and MFA (AWS CLI, CloudFormation)

Introduction

In the previous chapters, we learned how to create serverless functions, REST APIs, and data stores. In this chapter, we will use Amazon Cognito to provide application-level security and user management, including user sign-in, sign-up, and access control. We will also discuss Cognito's integration with API gateway APIs.

Like we did in the other chapters, we will discuss provisioning resources using both AWS CLI commands and CloudFormation templates. For application flows, we will mostly use the AWS CLI, without Java Lambda code. In general, Cognito is used with the frontend, mostly using the JavaScript SDK, as we will see in `Chapter 9`, *Serverless Programming Practices and Patterns*.

The following are the prerequisites required for completing the recipes in this chapter:

1. A working AWS account
2. Configuring the AWS CLI, as discussed in the recipe *Your first Lambda with AWS CLI*, in Chapter 1, *Getting Started with Serverless Computing on AWS*
3. A basic understanding of security concepts

Creating a Cognito user pool

Amazon Cognito can be used as an identity provider, as well as an identity broker. In this chapter, we will create a simple Cognito user pool, and we'll explore the use of Cognito as an identity provider. In later recipes, we will look at some more customization for the Cognito user pool.

Getting ready

- There are no additional prerequisites for completing this recipe, other than the common requirements specified in the chapter's introduction.

How to do it...

The initial setup, such as the user pool creation, is generally done using CloudFormation templates; authentication and authorization are generally done with the SDK.

Creating Cognito user pool with AWS CLI

In this section, we will create a user pool by using CLI commands:

1. Generate the input JSON template, using the `generate-cli-skeleton` option:

   ```
   aws cognito-idp create-user-pool \
       --pool-name my-pool-from-cli \
       --generate-cli-skeleton
   ```

   This command will return a template with all of the supported properties for the `create-user-pool` sub-command, in the correct JSON format.

Chapter 4

2. Fill in the properties that are required within the JSON file, and remove the properties that are not required:
   1. Start the JSON file, specifying a name by using the `PoolName` property:

      ```
      {
        "PoolName": "MyFirstUserPool",
      ```

   2. Under the `Policies` section, we will define the password policy, using the `PasswordPolicy` sub-property:

      ```
      "Policies": {
        "PasswordPolicy": {
          "MinimumLength": 8,
          "RequireUppercase": true,
          "RequireLowercase": true,
          "RequireNumbers": true,
          "RequireSymbols": true
        }
      },
      ```

   3. Define `AutoVerifiedAttributes` and `AliasAttributes`, as follows:

      ```
      "AutoVerifiedAttributes": [
        "email"
      ],
      "AliasAttributes": [
        "email"
      ],
      ```

      Refer to the *How it works...* section for more details.

   4. Define an email verification message and an email verification subject:

      ```
      "EmailVerificationMessage": "Your verification code from MyApp is {####}.",
      "EmailVerificationSubject": "Your verification code from MyApp",
      ```

> In this recipe, we will only demonstrate email verification. In a later recipe, we will look at how to do SMS verification.

Application Security with Amazon Cognito

5. Define a tag by using the `UserPoolTags` property, as follows:

   ```
   "UserPoolTags": {
     "Team": "Dev"
   },
   ```

6. Define the `AdminCreateUserConfig` property, as follows:

   ```
   "AdminCreateUserConfig": {
     "AllowAdminCreateUserOnly": false,
     "UnusedAccountValidityDays": 7,
     "InviteMessageTemplate": {
       "EmailMessage": "Your username for MyApp is {username} and password is {####}.",
       "EmailSubject": "Your temporary password for MyApp"
     }
   }
   ```

   The `AllowAdminCreateOnly` property, if set to `true`, restricts creating accounts to administrators. We will set it to `false`, as we will be doing user sign-up with this user pool in a later recipe. The complete JSON file is available in the code files.

3. Execute the `aws congnito-idp create-user-pool` command, specifying this JSON file:

   ```
   aws cognito-idp create-user-pool \
       --cli-input-json file://resources/create-user-pool-cli-input.json \
       --profile admin
   ```

   Note the `user-pool-id`, for use in future commands.

   We can verify `user-pool-created` by using the `describe-user-pool` sub-command:

   ```
   aws cognito-idp describe-user-pool \
       --user-pool-id us-east-1_u0YJPtdpv \
       --profile admin
   ```

   Remember to replace the `user-pool-id` value with our `user-pool-id` from the previous command. The `describe-user-pool` sub-command returns the current properties of the `user-pool`.

Creating Cognito user pool with CloudFormation template

Various sections of the CloudFormation template correspond to the CLI commands that we saw in the previous section. The complete template YAML file is available in the code files:

1. Start the template with the template format version and a description (optional):

    ```
    ---
    AWSTemplateFormatVersion: '2010-09-09'
    Description: 'My First Cognito User Pool'
    ```

2. Start to define the user pool resource with the type, `AWS::Cognito::UserPool`:

    ```
    Resources:
      MyFirstUserPool:
        Type: AWS::Cognito::UserPool
    ```

3. Under `Properties`, first, define a `Policies` property with a `PasswordPolicy`, as follows:

    ```
    Properties:
      Policies:
        PasswordPolicy:
          MinimumLength: 8
          RequireLowercase: true
          RequireNumbers: true
          RequireSymbols: true
          RequireUppercase: true
    ```

4. Define `AutoVerifiedAttributes` and `AliasAttributes`, as follows:

    ```
    AutoVerifiedAttributes:
    - email
    AliasAttributes:
    - email
    ```

5. Define an email verification message and an email verification subject, as follows:

    ```
    EmailVerificationMessage: 'Your verification code from MyApp is {####}.'
    EmailVerificationSubject: 'Your verification code from MyApp'
    ```

6. Define the `AdminCreateUserConfig` property, as follows:

   ```
   AdminCreateUserConfig:
     AllowAdminCreateUserOnly: false
     InviteMessageTemplate:
       EmailMessage: 'Your username for MyApp is {username} and password is {####}.'
       EmailSubject: 'Your temporary password for MyApp'
     UnusedAccountValidityDays: 7
   ```

   `AllowAdminCreateOnly` restricts creating accounts to administrators.

7. Provide a name and add a tag for this user pool (this is optional):

   ```
   UserPoolName: 'MyApp User Pool'
   UserPoolTags:
     Team: Dev
   ```

8. In the `Outputs` section, return the `user-pool-id`. Also, export the user pool, so that we can reuse it in later recipes:

   ```
   Outputs:
     UserPoolId:
       Description: 'Cognito user pool'
       Value: !Ref MyFirstUserPool
       Export:
         Name: MyFirstUserPoolId
   ```

   Save the file as `cognito-user-pool-cf-template.yml`.

9. Execute the CloudFormation template by using `aws cloudformation create-stack`, in order to create a CloudFormation stack.

   We can run the `aws cloudformation describe-stacks` command to find the status and get the `user-pool-id`.

   We can also use the `describe-user-pool` sub-command, with the ID returned by the `describe-stacks` sub-command, to verify the new Cognito user pool:

   ```
   aws cognito-idp describe-user-pool \
       --user-pool-id us-east-1_fYsb1Gyec \
       --profile admin
   ```

If it is successful, this command will return the current state of the newly created user pool. The initial part of the response contains the `id`, `name`, `policies`, an empty `LambdaConfig`, the last modified date, and the creation date:

```
{
    "UserPool": {
        "Id": "us-east-1_LccU5yCbI",
        "Name": "MyApp User Pool",
        "Policies": {
            "PasswordPolicy": {
                "MinimumLength": 8,
                "RequireUppercase": true,
                "RequireLowercase": true,
                "RequireNumbers": true,
                "RequireSymbols": true
            }
        },
        "LambdaConfig": {},
        "LastModifiedDate": 1542740032.158,
        "CreationDate": 1542740032.158,
```

The `SchemaAttributes` section will contain the definitions for all of the attributes (including the default attributes), in the following format:

```
"SchemaAttributes": [
    {
        "Name": "sub",
        "AttributeDataType": "String",
        "DeveloperOnlyAttribute": false,
        "Mutable": false,
        "Required": true,
        "StringAttributeConstraints": {
            "MinLength": "1",
            "MaxLength": "2048"
        }
    },
```

Other attributes contained within the `SchemaAttributes` section include the `name`, `given_name`, `family_name`, `middle_name`, `nick_name`, `preferred_username`, `profile`, `picture`, `website`, `email`, `email_verified`, `gender`, `birthdate`, `zoneinfo`, `locale`, `phone_number`, `phone_number_verified`, `address`, and `updated_at`.

The remainder of the response is as follows:

```
"AutoVerifiedAttributes": [
    "email"
],
"AliasAttributes": [
    "email"
],
"EmailVerificationMessage": "Your verification code from MyApp is {####}.",
"EmailVerificationSubject": "Your verification code from MyApp",
"VerificationMessageTemplate": {
    "EmailMessage": "Your verification code from MyApp is {####}.",
    "EmailSubject": "Your verification code from MyApp",
    "DefaultEmailOption": "CONFIRM_WITH_CODE"
},
"MfaConfiguration": "OFF",
"EstimatedNumberOfUsers": 0,
"EmailConfiguration": {},
"UserPoolTags": {
    "Team": "Dev"
},
"AdminCreateUserConfig": {
    "AllowAdminCreateUserOnly": true,
    "UnusedAccountValidityDays": 7,
    "InviteMessageTemplate": {
        "EmailMessage": "Your username for MyApp is {username} and password is {####}.",
        "EmailSubject": "Your temporary password for MyApp"
    }
},
"Arn": "arn:aws:cognito-idp:us-east-1:          :userpool/us-east-1_LccU5yCbI"
}
```

10. To clean up, we can delete the user pool by deleting the stack, or keep the stack and reuse it in the next recipe.

How it works...

Cognito is the primary service in AWS that can be used as an identity provider, for securing applications with authentication, authorization, and access control. The important features of Cognito are as follows:

- User sign-up
- User sign-in
- User creation by an administrator
- A set of predefined attributes, as well as support for creating custom attributes
- **Multi-factor authentication (MFA)**
- User profile management
- Email and SMS verification
- Forgot password
- Forcing a change of password after first login (in the case of admin user creation)
- Support for guest users
- Prevention of man-in-the-middle attacks through **Secure Remote Password (SRP)** protocols
- Enabling or disabling of user accounts by an administrator
- Deleting user accounts
- Support for customization, using Lambdas invoked through predefined triggers
- Support for authentication from other identity providers, such as Google, Facebook, Twitter, and so on

Generating and using JSON templates with CLI commands

Most AWS CLI commands come with options either to specify the input parameters directly on the command line, or input them through a JSON file specified by the `cli-input-json` property. A template for this JSON file can be generated by using the `generate-cli-skeleton` property option.

For the `create-user-pool` sub-command, we used the `cli-input-json` property, specifying a JSON file created using the `generate-cli-skeleton` property option. The `create-user-pool` sub-command has many properties, and some of them have sub-properties. It would be easy (and less error-prone) to get the template generated in the right format.

AliasAttributes versus UsernameAttributes

The Cognito `create user pool` sub-command supports two properties that allow for additional properties, such as the username and email to be used for logging in. `AliasAttributes` defines the supported attributes to be used as an alias for this user pool. The possible values for `AliasAttributes` are the `phone_number`, `email`, or `Preferred_username`. `UsernameAttributes` defines the supported attributes that can be specified as usernames when a user signs up. The possible values for `UsernameAttributes` are the `phone_number` or `email`.

While the `AliasAttributes` property allows us to use additional attributes as aliases for our original username for `login`, the `UsernameAttributes` property allows us to use the specified attributes as usernames, instead of another username. We cannot specify both `AliasAttributes` and `UsernameAttributes` in a single configuration, or we will get an error (`InvalidParameterException`) stating that only one of the `aliasAttributes` or `usernameAttributes` can be set in a user pool.

The `AliasAttributes` or `UsernameAttributes` that we use has to be unique across our user pool.

There's more...

We created a Cognito user pool in this recipe. To start using the Cognito user pool, we also need to create an app client. An **app client** is an entity that has permission to call APIs as unauthenticated users; such API functions include `register`, `sign-in`, and `forgot password`. We will look at how to create a Cognito user pool, and then how to use it to perform unauthenticated calls, in the next recipe.

We explored the use of Cognito as an identity provider. Identity providers provide user pool management on their own. Cognito can also be used as an identity broker, where an external provider will maintain the user pool, and Cognito will just provide temporary credentials, after that provider verifies the user credentials. However, most of these external providers will need an actual domain name that we own, for security reasons.

See also

- https://aws.amazon.com/compliance/shared-responsibility-model/
- https://docs.aws.amazon.com/cognito/latest/developerguide/cognito-user-pools-cost-allocation-tagging.html

- `https://docs.aws.amazon.com/cognito/latest/developerguide/user-pool-settings-client-apps.html`
- `https://docs.aws.amazon.com/cli/latest/userguide/generate-cli-skeleton.html`

Server-side authentication flow

Cognito supports different authentication flow use cases, such as server-side authentication flow, client-side authentication flow, and custom authentication flow. We will look at server-side authentication flow in this recipe. Server-side authentication is mostly used with SDKs, for server-side languages like Java, Node.js, and so on.

To work with a Cognito user pool, we also need an app client for the user pool. In this recipe, we will first define an app client that supports username and password authentication for admins. After that, we will execute admin-specific API commands from the CLI, in order to demonstrate the server-side authentication flow.

Getting ready

The following are the prerequisites for completing this recipe:

- A Cognito user pool that was created via the recipe, *Creating a Cognito user pool*

How to do it...

We will first create the app client, and then, we'll execute the admin-specific API commands, to demonstrate the server-side authentication flow.

Creating Cognito user pool client

We will now look at how to create a Cognito user pool client, using both AWS CLI commands and CloudFormation templates.

Creating a Cognito user pool client with AWS CLI

Use the `cognito-idp create-user-pool-client` sub-command to create a user pool client, as follows:

```
aws cognito-idp create-user-pool-client \
    --user-pool-id us-east-1_fYsb1Gyec \
    --client-name my-user-pool-client \
    --explicit-auth-flows ADMIN_NO_SRP_AUTH \
    --profile admin
```

Here, I have specified `ADMIN_NO_SRP_AUTH` as an explicit auth flow. This will allow us to pass our username and password without SRP. Other options that are allowed include `CUSTOM_AUTH_FLOW_ONLY` and `USER_PASSWORD_AUTH`. A few other authentication flows, including `USER_SRP_AUTH` and `REFRESH_TOKEN_AUTH`, are supported by default. We will see `REFRESH_TOKEN_AUTH` within this recipe, and `USER_SRP_AUTH` within a different recipe.

Creating a Cognito user pool client with CloudFormation template

With AWS CLI commands we had to hardcode the user pool ID, however with CloudFormation template we will reference it from the user pool CloudFormation template from the previous recipe.

We may add a template format version and a description similar to what we did in previous recipes.

The `Resources` and `Outputs` sections should look as follows:

```
Resources:
  MyUserPoolClient:
    Type: AWS::Cognito::UserPoolClient
    Properties:
      ClientName: 'My Cognito User Pool Client'
      ExplicitAuthFlows:
      - ADMIN_NO_SRP_AUTH
      RefreshTokenValidity: 30
      UserPoolId: !ImportValue MyFirstUserPoolId
Outputs:
  ClientId:
    Description: 'Cognito user pool Client'
    Value: !Ref MyUserPoolClient
```

Create the CloudFormation stack by executing the `aws cloudformation create-stack` command.

Chapter 4

Server-side authentication flow

The server-side authentication flow is used with admin APIs, as follows:

1. Use admin APIs to create a user, as follows:

    ```
    aws cognito-idp admin-create-user \
        --user-pool-id us-east-1_fYsb1Gyec \
        --username testuser \
        --temporary-password Passw0rd$ \
        --profile admin
    ```

    Remember to replace the user-pool-id value with your user pool id. If it is successful, this command will provide the following output:

    ```
    {
        "User": {
            "Username": "testuser",
            "Attributes": [
                {
                    "Name": "sub",
                    "Value": "9613d37a-89b1-441f-b511-1f2e4e04fe74"
                }
            ],
            "UserCreateDate": 1542740830.808,
            "UserLastModifiedDate": 1542740830.808,
            "Enabled": true,
            "UserStatus": "FORCE_CHANGE_PASSWORD"
        }
    }
    ```

    Note that the default user status is `FORCE_CHANGE_PASSWORD`. The user will be provided with a `NEW_PASSWORD_REQUIRED` challenge after the first login.

2. Initiate the authentication flow as an admin, as follows:

    ```
    aws cognito-idp admin-initiate-auth \
        --user-pool-id us-east-1_fYsb1Gyec \
        --client-id 4o1kgtd4sj39nr36ouak5mhblt \
        --auth-flow ADMIN_NO_SRP_AUTH \
        --auth-parameters USERNAME=testuser,PASSWORD=Passw0rd$ \
        --profile admin
    ```

[169]

> Note that we have specified `ADMIN_NO_SRP_AUTH`. This call will fail if we do not configure this option within explicit `auth` flows during the client creation. Also, remember to replace the value for `client-id` with our client ID from the previous step.

The `initiate auth` command will return a `NEW_PASSWORD_REQUIRED` challenge and a session ID:

```
{
    "ChallengeName": "NEW_PASSWORD_REQUIRED",
    "Session": "7tcWlQog6Uc4x4Np2vyRwuy46Edj1YsYJezGZsDsChLONe4EJol5UwPyp4mecdnABU
B6TJlYpKmrFzY0MFtA3056tDTB3Xx9HQ148CA4rRl4cFrbfly7GMsXE1v0tp0ub0ScKkULWQPCPYKsq2mc
x_cYzzkWU7glP867iwYsUIGPYmjWQHB7-HTxgKB0xWMA5nJB0bdDKQRkjv-pn50KlmPgrc9xwMWUWA-LGy
cxiCbuAoibBzQcILPkpwxJHBqggMcQRroC98qDEw3LeA0T204m4TVaAfpe1G4FQ3fcqMHqnynS34K4vsxx
SJRyJGasg0ep5ekkMQ0KlpAEDqrGNb4Vjfrt0kv6DFpnyUMA0bTr-MkZJS45J12JWLyGuHRHOiZZMDyK",
    "ChallengeParameters": {
        "USER_ID_FOR_SRP": "testuser",
        "requiredAttributes": "[]",
        "userAttributes": "{}"
    }
}
```

3. We will then send a response to the `auth` challenge, as follows:

```
aws cognito-idp admin-respond-to-auth-challenge \
    --user-pool-id us-east-1_fYsb1Gyec \
    --client-id 5hh4v7nveu22vea74h8stt9238 \
    --challenge-name NEW_PASSWORD_REQUIRED \
    --challenge-responses
USERNAME=testuser,NEW_PASSWORD=NewPass0123$ \
    --session <session-id> \
    --profile admin
```

If it is successful, this command will return a response with three tokens (an access token, a refresh token, and an ID token):

```
{
    "ChallengeParameters": {},
    "AuthenticationResult": {
        "AccessToken": "eyJraWQiOiI0VTY1ZHNqWlgyRHZoUDNwVFhnaTVkNU4zNkhmUkdOOFFVZHFvd1pmTXVnPSIsImFsZy
IjA2MGMyMGRkLWVjZjktMTFlOC040Tg1LWNkMzIwOGIxODA5NSIsInRva2VuX3VzZSI6ImFjY2VzcyIsInNjb3BlIjoiYXdzLmNvZ2
aXRvLWlkcC51cy1lYXN0LTEuYW1hem9uYXdzLmNvbVwvdXMtZWFzdC0xX2ZZc2IxR3llYyIsImV4cCI6MTU0MjcwNTA5MiwiaWF0Ij
OiI1aGg0djdudmV1MjJ2ZWE3NGg4c3R0OTIzOCIsInVzZXJuYW1lIjoidGVzdHVzZXIifQ.Eg3Z1kAJyJ-NEXmWmbavMV325_Uh-UT
ecuFeXtYLKHjc_rD7gj8vp5ONfDQN5m_u8fP8Q8JRFTsLPaGR6C3qX6uOF_HR6BN_YWpHYtBudsShz2qGlryxcvqSzfpzbws8rMli5
xZNIxmwnaOcOCycbED8buKQ49Mj_g",
        "ExpiresIn": 3600,
        "TokenType": "Bearer",
        "RefreshToken": "eyJjdHki0iJKV1QiLCJlbmMi0iJBMjU2R0NNIiwiYWxnIjoiUlNBLU9BRVAifQ.BnFlQ7rap5v7g4
aapMvMJPUejJIwTkqnPpAYjRNJsECnIlKgVYa8gmfkVLmPaGT8p2NmuIicHDZoPhY60VwAHrtVBWzq9xXX4g-k4PKIerEaMK4vZGMc
LlMHcUNex7usnE0xvu0ryXrSniWAi3Sq940xjfEFgpfM2g.4WtMGmzXd8KEzU1P.g7zcSVH6RXguLWAeTaOALcJghunwYB7Z5gSAEf
bdCTXsWaAfddTlNyGweh0e6S34q4t4egQtgTZWjcUdBuCRkvcCUU_V3YC38SxENfNmxw9AzVfRg7PQKM4M5Pt2vU-CZx8Hklat31fo
jErd-3YBOLzgYIq8_0qMNhVWoeJCA3AjsB0vQ2R7z_qyaTXqbQBBpR0QfjaQDOpsT404xRJ_Blqxs_PEm2Ego7mXsjo6SoILgVRX5q
gZ0KjqXci91M-65MJB7HblOUXYouOYPLazE_J3P0npEEAUUc9hx2RCHbfh8EUyPFiHv890mNukhcuyfNlh5N8EPLyy5Gmxf8MGgfe0
jqPtnA4J5f380vD5mXF2Dx_iF1-1MNdcZnQzUG-1Z0yG9rTchnrPIk6JLMCXhUQFu9791plCSKRf1oLiZTSg0e0PB_h2lGTJaU2ULE
klYj6qpxKaryd-ysY7C1YDPf-ee_wO-MN5maUjwXuzpKrboiwEBsjfrGSnwd4M58GHHQtqUZMUbVQn6hoVElyYNvhgXdXByuVTxGKm
HdmBu28hbuhYt7Y1h409AqhBWAhqUFez2BqBeGYT_tsv3FELK1-s7qPrNvkwLQYPaXDooLgKNVMqjnVbpIsbLU4DW4nAHLWNx9dl65
saUwcaMUuw.Wa_lkFBRerl1zeoKjE32XA",
        "IdToken": "eyJraWQi0iJlVWh6bWYzR2BwNDcrVW01b3dybDdReHZuamdvYjFlbk9ZV3NnV1FvZEc0PSIsImFsZyI6Il
dmV1MjJ2ZWE3NGg4c3R0OTIzOCIsImV2ZW50X2lkIjoiMDYwYzIwZGQtZWNmOS0xMWU4LTg5ODUtY2Q2MjA4YjE4MDk1IiwidG9rZW
YXN0LTEuYW1hem9uYXdzLmNvbVwvdXMtZWFzdC0xX2ZZc2IxR3llYyIsImV2ZS5pdG86dXNlcm5hbWUi0iJ0ZXN0dXNlciIsImV4cC
IWJmPU2bVufgReMSnyPp84--c34rl9X1G83Akea-fajxbfneD4Pf7Ny1YhfWtMe2Vr54z0GzV2cMAF_88BKwP3PmwlVZQzPYQabX5Y
8NsD_ql1vLRKQ2l3-_4vIfEZn0WfeXqzgoRRnHL_zw-1kTTXsldRRjzUDP53_cfSy2KIRRtkKJ-NGy8SwWt_KTrNRvsH8vdD9E1oQ"
    }
}
```

We can try to run the `initiate auth` command with the new password; we will see that it does not ask for the password challenge. Instead, it returns the tokens.

4. From now on, we can use the refresh token to regenerate the access token and the ID token:

```
aws cognito-idp admin-initiate-auth \
    --user-pool-id us-east-1_fYsb1Gyec \
    --client-id 5hh4v7nveu22vea74h8stt9238 \
    --auth-flow REFRESH_TOKEN_AUTH \
    --auth-parameters REFRESH_TOKEN=<refresh-token> \
    --profile admin
```

5. To clean up, delete the user pool client, as follows:

```
aws cognito-idp delete-user-pool-client \
    --user-pool-id us-east-1_fYsb1Gyec \
    --client-id 5hh4v7nveu22vea74h8stt9238 \
    --profile admin
```

Delete the user that we created for this recipe, as follows:

```
aws cognito-idp admin-delete-user \
  --user-pool-id us-east-1_fYsb1Gyec \
  --username testuser \
  --profile admin
```

How it works...

To summarize, we did the following in this recipe:

1. Created a user
2. Initiated an authentication flow as an admin
3. Responded to password challenges from Cognito
4. Used the refresh token to regenerate the access token and the ID token

Server-side, client-side, and custom authentication flows

Server-side authentication is mostly used with SDKs, for server-side languages such as Java, Node.js, Ruby, and so on. Server-side authentication uses admin APIs, and can also be referred to as **admin authentication flow**.

Client-side SDKs, such as iOS, Android, and JavaScript, use client-side authentication flow.

Custom authentication flow uses custom Lambdas that get triggered during various life cycle stages of the authentication.

Secure Remote Password protocol

The **Secure Remote Password (SRP)** protocol tries to protect the password from being sent insecurely over the network, through alternate means like clients letting the server know that they have the correct password, without actually sending it over the network.

SRP is currently only supported in client-side SDKs for iOS, Android, and JavaScript. Backend SDKs, such as the ones for Java, Node.js, Ruby, and others, do not support SRP. Server-side authentication flows usually happen on secure backend servers; hence, SRP protocol calculations may not be required.

The access token, refresh token, and ID token

An **identity token (ID token)** is used to authenticate requests to the backend (for example, the API gateway). For example, to send a request to an API gateway API with Cognito Authorizer, we use the authorization type **Bearer Token** and pass the ID token. This will be demonstrated later, in the recipe on *Integrating Cognito with the API gateway*. The ID token will also contain additional information, such as the user ID and any other user attributes that we provide while generating it. We will demonstrate this in a later recipe.

The **access token** is used within Cognito APIs, in order to authorize updates to the users' parameters. The Cognito API commands that accept access tokens include `associate-software-token`, `change-password`, `confirm-device`, `delete-user`, `delete-user-attributes`, `forget-device`, `get-device`, `get-user`, `get-user-attribute-verification-code`, `global-sign-out`, `list-devices`, `set-user-mfa-preference`, `set-user-settings`, `update-device-status`, `update-user-attributes`, `verify-software-token`, and `verify-user-attribute`.

The **refresh token** is used to get new identity and access tokens. For example, the `initiate auth` sub-command can specify the auth flow as `REFRESH_TOKEN_AUTH`, and can pass a refresh token to get back the access token and the ID token. We can configure the refresh token expiration (in days) when creating the user pool.

ADMIN_NO_SRP_AUTH versus USER_PASSWORD_AUTH

Cognito authentication APIs support various authentication flow types, including `ADMIN_NO_SRP_AUTH` and `USER_PASSWORD_AUTH`. Both `ADMIN_NO_SRP_AUTH` and `USER_PASSWORD_AUTH` support sending the username and the password from the client to the IDP, without SRP protocol.

`USER_PASSWORD_AUTH` also supports user migration from a legacy application, without actually requiring them to reset their passwords. However, AWS documentation suggests that we should update our auth flow type to a more secure once (for example, using SRP) after the migration is complete.

`ADMIN_NO_SRP_AUTH` is only supported for server-side authentication using `admin-initiate-auth` and `admin-respond-to-auth-challenge`, and is not supported for client-side authentication using `initiate-auth` and `respond-to-auth-challenge`.

There's more...

In this recipe, we saw server-side authentication. There are other authentication flow use cases, including server-side authentication flow, client-side authentication flow, and custom authentication flow. We will look at some of these in later recipes.

In the real world, the admin APIs that we used for authentication in this recipe are mostly used along with SDKs, for server-side languages like Java, Node.js, and so on. We can refer to the respective SDK documentation and follow the API usages in this recipe to implement them using the SDK.

See also

- https://docs.aws.amazon.com/cognito/latest/developerguide/amazon-cognito-user-pools-authentication-flow.html

Client-side authentication flow

In the previous recipe, we demonstrated the use of server-side authentication flow, along with the authentication flow type `ADMIN_NO_SRP_AUTH`. In this recipe, we will demonstrate the use of client-side authentication flow, with the authentication flow type `USER_PASSWORD_AUTH`.

Getting ready

The following are the prerequisites for completing this recipe:

- Make sure that we have created a Cognito user pool, following the recipe *Creating a Cognito user pool*.

How to do it...

First, we will create the client, and then, we will execute various client-specific API commands, to demonstrate the client-side authentication flow.

Creating a Cognito user pool client

We will create a user pool client for client-side authentication flow both using AWS CLI. We will also see the template components to use within a CloudFormation template.

Creating a Cognito user pool client with AWS CLI

We use the `cognito-idp create-user-pool-client` sub-command to create a user pool client, as follows:

```
aws cognito-idp create-user-pool-client \
    --user-pool-id us-east-1_fYsb1Gyec \
    --client-name my-user-pool-client \
    --explicit-auth-flows USER_PASSWORD_AUTH \
    --profile admin
```

Here, I have specified `USER_PASSWORD_AUTH` as an explicit `auth` flow.

> `ADMIN_NO_SRP_AUTH` is only supported with the admin-initiated authentication used in the server-side authentication flow. Both `ADMIN_NO_SRP_AUTH` and `USER_PASSWORD_AUTH` allow us to pass our username and password without SRP, but `USER_PASSWORD_AUTH` also supports user migration from legacy applications.

Creating a Cognito user pool client with CloudFormation template

We will follow the AWS CLI command option to create the corresponding CloudFormation template, in order to create the app client.

The `Resources` and `Outputs` sections should look as follows:

```
Resources:
  MyUserPoolClient:
    Type: AWS::Cognito::UserPoolClient
    Properties:
      ClientName: 'My Cognito User Pool Client'
      ExplicitAuthFlows:
      -USER_PASSWORD_AUTH
      RefreshTokenValidity: 30
      UserPoolId: !ImportValue MyFirstUserPoolId
Outputs:
  ClientId:
    Description: 'Cognito user pool Client'
    Value: !Ref MyUserPoolClient
```

We can also add a template format version and a description.

We can now create the CloudFormation stack with the user pool client, by executing the `aws cloudformation create-stack` command.

Client-side authentication flow

As we discussed previously, the client-side authentication flow uses non-admin APIs.

> The output for most of the commands will be similar to the ones that we discussed in the recipe *Server-side authentication flow*, and need not be repeated here. Please refer to that recipe for the screenshots.

Follow the steps to demonstrate the client-side authentication flow. Remember to replace the `user-pool-id` value with your user pool id.

1. For creating the user, we will still use the admin APIs, as follows:

   ```
   aws cognito-idp admin-create-user \
       --user-pool-id us-east-1_fYsb1Gyec \
       --username testuser2 \
       --temporary-password Passw0rd$ \
       --profile admin
   ```

   The default user status will be FORCE_CHANGE_PASSWORD, as we saw in the previous recipe.

2. Initiate the authentication flow, as follows:

   ```
   aws cognito-idp initiate-auth \
       --client-id 3jiv1fi1rspotsst9m19hktu58 \
       --auth-flow USER_PASSWORD_AUTH \
       --auth-parameters USERNAME=testuser2,PASSWORD=Passw0rd$
   ```

   > As this is a non-admin API, we do not have to specify the admin profile from the command line. The `initiate auth` command will return a NEW_PASSWORD_REQUIRED challenge and a session ID.

3. Send a response to the `auth` challenge, as follows:

   ```
   aws cognito-idp respond-to-auth-challenge \
       --client-id 3jiv1fi1rspotsst9m19hktu58 \
       --challenge-name NEW_PASSWORD_REQUIRED \
       --challenge-responses
   USERNAME=testuser2,NEW_PASSWORD=NewPass0123$ \
       --session <session-id>
   ```

   If it is successful, this command will return a response with three tokens: an access token, a refresh token, and an ID token. We can try to run the `initiate auth` command with the new password, and check that it does not ask for the password challenge.

4. From now on, we can also use the refresh token to regenerate the access token and the ID token:

   ```
   aws cognito-idp initiate-auth \
       --client-id 3jiv1fi1rspotsst9m19hktu58 \
       --auth-flow REFRESH_TOKEN_AUTH \
       --auth-parameters REFRESH_TOKEN=<refresh token>
   ```

5. To clean up, delete the user pool client, as follows:

   ```
   aws cognito-idp delete-user-pool-client \
       --user-pool-id us-east-1_fYsb1Gyec \
       --client-id 3jiv1fi1rspotsst9m19hktu58 \
       --profile admin
   ```

   Delete the user that we created for this recipe, as follows:

   ```
   aws cognito-idp admin-delete-user \
       --user-pool-id us-east-1_fYsb1Gyec \
       --username testuser2 \
       --profile admin
   ```

How it works...

To summarize, we did the following in this recipe:

1. Created a user
2. Initiated authentication flow as a user
3. Responded to password challenges from Cognito
4. Used the refresh token to regenerate the access token and the ID token

The major differences, as compared to the server-side authentication flow API usage, are as follows:

1. Unlike with the server-side authentication APIs, we did not specify an admin profile while executing the CLI commands.
2. You do not have to specify the user pool ID with client-side authentication flow API calls; only the client ID needs to be specified.

> **TIP**
> In real-world applications, you generally choose client-side authentication if you are working with SDKs for client-side platforms (for example, iOS, Android, or JavaScript), and server-side authentication flows if you are working with SDKs for server-side language platforms (for example, Java and Node.js).

There's more...

In this recipe, we used a simple authentication flow type, based on a username and password. However, you can also utilize the additional security of Secure Remote Password protocol for additional security. Currently, SRP support is only available for the iOS, Android, and JavaScript SDKs.

We explored the use of server-side authentication flow and client-side authentication flow in the last two recipes. There are additional flows, such as the custom authentication flow and the user migration authentication flow. You can refer to the link to *Amazon Cognito User Pool Authentication Flow* provided in the *See also* section.

See also

- https://docs.aws.amazon.com/cognito/latest/developerguide/amazon-cognito-user-pools-authentication-flow.html

User sign-up flow with Cognito

In the previous recipes, we created our users as admins. However, many real-world applications, including most web applications, allow users to sign-up by themselves. During the sign-up, a user might have to verify their email or phone number. An admin might also confirm a user sign-up.

In this recipe, we will demonstrate the user sign-up flow with self-confirmation, as well as with admin confirmation, using CLI commands. You can follow the same steps while working with any SDK of your choice. You can refer to the documentation of the particular SDK for the exact usage.

Getting ready

The following are the prerequisites for completing this recipe:

- Ensure that you have created a Cognito user pool, following the recipe *Creating a Cognito user pool*.
- Ensure that you have created a Cognito app client with a `USER_PASSWORD_AUTH` explicit flow declaration, following the recipe *Client-side authentication*.

How to do it...

I will discuss two sign-up flows: one that requires the user to provide an email address and confirm sign-up based on a code received in their email, and one in which the admin will confirm the user. In real-world applications, these two are often combined.

User sign-up with self-confirmation

The following steps describe how to set up user sign-up with self-confirmation:

1. Use the `sign-up` sub-command to initiate the sign-up flow, providing your `username` and `password`:

   ```
   aws cognito-idp sign-up \
       --client-id 4s69op0v8es2cojl5ncjql2v4g \
       --username testuser4 \
       --password Passw0rd$ \
       --user-attributes Name=email,Value=testemail@heartin.tech
   ```

   Replace `testemail@heartin.tech` with your email address.

If this is successful, you should get the following response:

```
{
    "UserConfirmed": false,
    "CodeDeliveryDetails": {
        "Destination": "+*********4114",
        "DeliveryMedium": "SMS",
        "AttributeName": "phone_number"
    },
    "UserSub": "f8f7f918-23dc-43da-a88b-4a7364c78072"
}
```

You will also receive an email with the confirmation code, as shown in the following screenshot:

Your verification code from MyApp » Inbox ×

no-reply@verificationemail.com via amazonses.com
to me ▾

Your verification code from MyApp is 156202.

> The preceding message format was configured while creating the user pool. You can also use the email configuration section in the input CLI JSON, or within the CloudFormation template, to make additional customizations, such as a reply email address.

2. Confirm the user sign-up with the code received, as follows:

```
aws cognito-idp confirm-sign-up \
--client-id 4s69op0v8es2cojl5ncjql2v4g \
--username testuser4 \
--confirmation-code 156202
```

If it is successful, you should see no errors in the response.

3. Now, try to sign-in with your username and password, as follows:

```
aws cognito-idp initiate-auth \
    --client-id 4s69op0v8es2cojl5ncjql2v4g \
    --auth-flow USER_PASSWORD_AUTH \
    --auth-parameters USERNAME=testuser4,PASSWORD=Passw0rd$
```

If it is successful, you will get a response with the `AccessToken`, `RefreshToken`, and `IdToken`:

```
{
    "ChallengeParameters": {},
    "AuthenticationResult": {
        "AccessToken": "eyJraWQiOiI0VTY1ZHNqWlgyRHZoUDNwVFhnaTVkNU4zNkhmUkdOOFFVZHFvd1pm
ImFjYzIyNGYxLWVkYjgtMTFlOC04ZTFhLWQ3OWVjYzQ1ZDhmYSIsInRva2VuX3VzZSI6ImFjY2VzcyIsInNjb3Bl
aXRvLWlkcC51cy1lYXN0LTEuYW1hem9uYXdzLmNvbVwvdXMtZWFzdC0xX2ZZc2IxR3llYyIsImV4cCI6MTU0Mjgy
OiI0czY5b3AwdjhlczJjb2psNW5janFsMnY0ZyIsInVzZXJuYW1lIjoidGVzdHVzZXI0In0.PoCpT2vnP3cSz4rU
3erXF3JoDZo5Cvb4bwSp6HdfRVkyqIP074hzq_JCvaegobV7xry6tWT5NcoKwn9Q0Ed49aDfj87ZPoho__oMwcuP
RnvnlO8vqhC97n-kVznvlTgP5KaT1Q",
        "ExpiresIn": 3600,
        "TokenType": "Bearer",
        "RefreshToken": "eyJjdHkiOiJKV1QiLCJlbmMiOiJBMjU2R0NNIiwiYWxnIjoiUlNBLU9BRVAifQ.
MLP0029vmuAgik4QXXXJY31G2ogZcPwmOF1JMFM7-11S44UhsvYW6_qYlZDeqftrdFWcA7Vw3I80nVATYQtyGfKl
puufkmaYNxeufhotJLPI3z6HXEgpuGhpBX527VOCjSfPjg.W4a8UIfHjGE_u_4Z.HkeWrZmM8hT175dMgt4nFRT1
6oylZIQtgi6CpLkHb08d6NAGyIBZvUiLzr_uPdqWgIQ8D8mxMz6XmsLyc894TgrSBBA1qLuYH4LVPXgs0yE4Mi5i
tqpXiMmUZIxJ3sHwMFFtvm5NysYEbRwpvXeASG3eKqBkJmYFKsiybYka9xPgG7D14x5CRkVzC9jPAH-g62LKXiG1
ZgwCp7wzl-nNh_99epvsu2NGgGU_GWtS80itTwQvz-caevybZyMl20rfk_7rwP61H1caPa5aeNziA3cM-usC8iBt
pQ1IY9tU1DrNSV8lBHNDQf5e5Vj29cxk4FXWGSOI2cgI1KUFQVzvlvKR7c03P03dGKF-Neew8ShWyKbQ3Uq5Y3YZ
k-ri9ipSu9r6BpVLgJafWzeOIzugJOYkVSwlbICR38wWdKLj9dDpSx-mLv66oEDh6Gz81XBZJfwmBAsx4KHYoOF2
alRtmN-q-2nG95SiS5EQX5FXlAskxqW59dpbY0Dx_fWgoM4d9nwvVJZThne2J16rMoPFI4_tLUZj50TmLa008bzE
nXEJ9F77zBc.v9RkG7wF1rwUWIXD_sATYg",
        "IdToken": "eyJraWQiOiJlVWh6bWYzR28wNDcrVW01b3dybDdReHZuamdvYjFbk9ZV3NnV1FvZEc0
djhlczJjb2psNW5janFsMnY0ZyIsImVtYWlsX3ZlcmlmaWVkIjp0cnVlLCJldmVudF9pZCI6ImFjYzIyNGYxLWVk
czpcL1wvY29nbml0by1pZHAudXMtZWFzdC0xLmFtYXpvbmF3cy5jb21cL3VzLWVhc3QtMV9mWXNiMUd5ZWMiLCJj
bkBnbWFpbC5jb20ifQ.K92hVJMHEhDtVIn7u6VLhPOh_LHSMvwWQaIbDck3PgrKMJkRq2aJpqsQwQvx7PARqNeOS
yYusSQHk2Epo9IXSSw66kCtw6mXmcfPScG-yXFNmELrhWHMtrtV967mH4nDAUmA4oMAlwbmRY06x01naNQeI9wYt
    }
}
```

4. Use the access token to delete the user, as follows:

   ```
   aws cognito-idp delete-user \
       --access-token <access token>
   ```

   Replace the `AccessToken` with the access token received in the previous command response. If it is successful, you should see no response.

5. Verify that the user was actually deleted by trying to initiate the authentication flow again. This time, you should get an error that the user does not exist.

User sign-up with admin confirmation

User sign-up with admin confirmation is similar to self-confirmation, as indicated by the following steps:

1. Use the `sign-up` sub-command to initiate the `sign-up` flow, as follows:

   ```
   aws cognito-idp sign-up \
       --client-id 4s69op0v8es2cojl5ncjql2v4g \
       --username testuser4 \
       --password Passw0rd$
   ```

   The email is optional here, since the user will be confirmed by an admin. However, you may specify an email and it will send the verification code, as we had specified the email as an `AutoVerifiedAttributes` while creating the user pool.

   If this is successful, you should get the following response:

   ```
   {
       "UserConfirmed": false,
       "UserSub": "e9ff2a2a-f7d9-44d3-b5a3-24ef7ee5288a"
   }
   ```

2. Confirm the user as an admin, as follows:

   ```
   aws cognito-idp admin-confirm-sign-up \
       --user-pool-id us-east-1_fYsb1Gyec \
       --username testuser4 \
       --profile admin
   ```

   If this is successful, you should not see a response.

3. Now, try to sign-in with your username and password, as follows:

```
aws cognito-idp initiate-auth \
    --client-id 4s69op0v8es2cojl5ncjql2v4g \
    --auth-flow USER_PASSWORD_AUTH \
    --auth-parameters USERNAME=testuser4,PASSWORD=Passw0rd$
```

   If it is successful, you will get a response with the `AccessToken`, `RefreshToken`, and `IdToken`, similar to the one in the self-confirmation flow.

4. You can delete the user by using the `delete-user` sub-command (refer to the self-confirmation flow).

How it works...

We have discussed two flows for user sign-up. In the first flow, the user provided an email while signing up, and an email was sent with a passcode. The user then used this passcode to confirm the sign-up process. In the second flow, the user created an account without providing an email, and then an admin confirmed the user. In the second flow, the user can still provide email; in such cases, the user will get the passcode, and an admin can still confirm that user. Most real-world projects support both of these options in a single flow.

There's more...

We have discussed passing an email as a user attribute. You can also pass any of the other built-in user attributes, such as `name`, `given_name`, `family_name`, `middle_name`, `nick_name`, `preferred_username`, `profile`, `picture`, `website`, `email`, `email_verified`, `gender`, `birthdate`, `zoneinfo`, `locale`, `phone_number`, `phone_number_verified`, `address`, and `updated_at`. You can also define a custom attribute.

We only discussed email verification in this recipe. You can add phone verification by adding it to the `AutoVerifiedAttributes` list. We also did user sign-up with a text username. We could have also used an `email` or `phone_number` as usernames. In a later recipe, we will create a user pool to support SMS and MFA verification, and to support user sign-up with a `phone_number` as a username.

See also

- https://docs.aws.amazon.com/cognito/latest/developerguide/user-pool-settings-email-phone-verification.html

Working with groups

Cognito users can be added to different groups, and we can treat users differently based on those groups. For example, as admin user can be shown an admin menu, whereas a regular user can be shown a regular menu. In this recipe, we will look at how to create and use groups with Cognito user pools.

Getting ready

The following are the prerequisites for completing this recipe:

- Ensure that you have created a Cognito user pool, following the recipe *Creating a Cognito user pool*.

How to do it...

We will look at how to create a group, how to add users to it, and finally, how to check a user for their groups:

1. Create the following users: `admin_user` and `regular_user`.
2. Create a group called `administrators`, as follows:

   ```
   aws cognito-idp create-group \
       --group-name 'administrators' \
       --user-pool-id us-east-1_fYsb1Gyec \
       --description 'Administrator Group' \
       --profile admin
   ```

   If this is successful, it should return the following response:

   ```
   {
       "id": "dxr47i",
       "name": "First_Cognito_Custom_Authorizer",
       "type": "COGNITO_USER_POOLS",
       "providerARNs": [
           "arn:aws:cognito-idp:us-east-1:          :userpool/us-east-1_fYsb1Gyec"
       ],
       "authType": "cognito_user_pools",
       "identitySource": "method.request.header.Authorization"
   }
   ```

3. Create a group called `authenticated_users`, following the command in the previous step.

4. Add the user `regular_user` to the `authenticated_users`, as follows:

   ```
   aws cognito-idp admin-add-user-to-group \
       --user-pool-id us-east-1_fYsb1Gyec \
       --username regular_user \
       --group-name authenticated_users \
       --profile admin
   ```

5. Add the user `admin_user` to the groups `administrators` and `authenticated_users`, following the command in the previous step.

6. Check for the groups that `admin_user` belongs to, as follows:

   ```
   aws cognito-idp admin-list-groups-for-user \
       --username admin_user \
       --user-pool-id us-east-1_fYsb1Gyec \
       --profile admin
   ```

   If this is successful, it should return the details of the two groups to which the user `admin_user` belongs, as follows:

   ```
   {
       "Groups": [
           {
               "GroupName": "administrators",
               "UserPoolId": "us-east-1_fYsb1Gyec",
               "Description": "Administrator Group",
               "LastModifiedDate": 1544632026.41,
               "CreationDate": 1544632026.41
           },
           {
               "GroupName": "authenticated_users",
               "UserPoolId": "us-east-1_fYsb1Gyec",
               "Description": "Authenticated User Group",
               "LastModifiedDate": 1544632036.115,
               "CreationDate": 1544632036.115
           }
       ]
   }
   ```

7. Check for the groups that `regular_user` belongs to, following the command in the previous step.

    If this is successful, it should return the details of the one group to which the user `regular_user` belongs, as follows:

    ```
    {
        "Groups": [
            {
                "GroupName": "authenticated_users",
                "UserPoolId": "us-east-1_fYsb1Gyec",
                "Description": "Authenticated User Group",
                "LastModifiedDate": 1544632036.115,
                "CreationDate": 1544632036.115
            }
        ]
    }
    ```

How it works...

This was a small and simple recipe to add a user to a group, and to check the groups to which a user belongs. Once you know the group a user belongs to, you can treat that user in a certain way. I have not included the commands with syntax as they are the same as those of the previous ones; a complete set of commands is available in the code files.

There's more...

We can also associate an IAM role to a group, and allow the users to access different AWS services based on the role and its associated policies. To attach a role, you can use the `role-arn` property of the `aws cognito-idp admin-list-groups-for-user` command.

See also

- https://docs.aws.amazon.com/cognito/latest/developerguide/cognito-user-pools-user-groups.html
- https://aws.amazon.com/blogs/aws/new-amazon-cognito-groups-and-fine-grained-role-based-access-control-2/

Integrating Cognito with the API gateway

In this recipe, we will integrate Cognito Authorizer with the API gateway, and we will get one step closer to our goal of building an end-to-end Serverless web application. After integrating Cognito Authorizer with the API gateway, we will test it by using the Postman REST client.

Getting ready

The following are the prerequisites for completing this recipe:

- Ensure that you have created a Cognito user pool, following the recipe *Creating a Cognito user pool*.
- Ensure that you have created a Cognito app client with a `USER_PASSWORD_AUTH` explicit flow declaration, following the recipe *Client-side authentication*.

How to do it...

I will list the API gateway CLI commands and provide the CloudFormation templates. However, I will not discuss much theory around the API gateway, as we already discussed that in `Chapter 2`, *Building Serverless REST APIs with API Gateway*. If you are not familiar with API gateway, please refer to the recipes in `Chapter 2`, *Building Serverless REST APIs with API Gateway*.

The AWS CLI

We will cover the steps to create an API gateway API and integrate Cognito Authorizer with it, as follows:

1. Create an API gateway REST API, as follows:

    ```
    aws apigateway create-rest-api  \
        --name "API Gateway With Cognito" \
        --region us-east-1 \
        --profile admin
    ```

2. Call `get-resources` to get the root resource ID, as follows:

   ```
   aws apigateway get-resources \
       --rest-api-id 3t0t98ifdh \
       --region us-east-1 \
       --profile admin
   ```

3. Create a resource with the path `greeting` and the parent ID as the ID of the root resource:

   ```
   aws apigateway create-resource \
       --rest-api-id 3t0t98ifdh \
       --region us-east-1 \
       --parent-id ufgvoiu8yh \
       --path-part greeting \
       --profile admin
   ```

4. Create an `authorizer` for API gateway, of the type `COGNITO_USER_POOLS`, as follows:

   ```
   aws apigateway create-authorizer \
       --rest-api-id 3t0t98ifdh \
       --name First_Cognito_Custom_Authorizer \
       --type COGNITO_USER_POOLS \
       --provider-arns arn:aws:cognito-idp:us-east-1:<account id>:userpool/us-east-1_fYsb1Gyec \
       --identity-source method.request.header.Authorization \
       --profile admin
   ```

   Replace the user pool ID (`us-east-1_fYsb1Gyec`) with your user pool ID, and `account id` with your account ID.

   If this is successful, you should get the following response:

   ```
   {
       "id": "dxr47i",
       "name": "First_Cognito_Custom_Authorizer",
       "type": "COGNITO_USER_POOLS",
       "providerARNs": [
           "arn:aws:cognito-idp:us-east-1:            :userpool/us-east-1_fYsb1Gyec"
       ],
       "authType": "cognito_user_pools",
       "identitySource": "method.request.header.Authorization"
   }
   ```

5. Execute the `put-method` sub-command, with the `authorization-type` as `COGNITO_USER_POOLS` and the `authorizer-id` received as the response to the `create-authorizer` command, as follows:

```
aws apigateway put-method \
    --rest-api-id 3t0t98ifdh \
    --resource-id rebvv7 \
    --http-method GET \
    --authorization-type COGNITO_USER_POOLS \
    --authorizer-id dxr47i \
    --region us-east-1 \
    --profile admin
```

6. Execute the `put-method-response` sub-command:

```
aws apigateway put-method-response \
    --rest-api-id  3t0t98ifdh \
    --resource-id  rebvv7 \
    --http-method  GET \
    --status-code  200 \
    --region   us-east-1 \
    --profile  admin
```

7. Execute the `put-integration` sub-command:

```
aws apigateway put-integration \
    --rest-api-id 3t0t98ifdh \
    --resource-id rebvv7 \
    --http-method GET \
    --type MOCK \
    --integration-http-method GET \
    --request-templates '{"application/json": "{\"statusCode\":
200}" }' \
    --region us-east-1 \
    --profile admin
```

8. Execute the `put-integration-response` sub-command:

```
aws apigateway put-integration-response \
    --rest-api-id 3t0t98ifdh   \
    --resource-id b0549c \
    --http-method GET \
    --status-code 200 \
    --selection-pattern "" \
    --response-templates '{"application/json": "{\"message\":
\"Welcome $context.authorizer.claims.given_name\"}"}' \
    --region us-east-1 \
    --profile admin
```

We use `$context.authorizer.claims.given_name` to retrieve the user attribute `given_name` that was used when creating the user. The sub-commands `put-method`, `put-method-response`, `put-integration`, and `put-integration-response` are simplified into a single block within the CloudFormation template for creating the API. In any case, CloudFormation templates are the preferred way to provision resources in AWS programmatically. I have included the CLI commands for a better understanding of the CloudFormation templates.

9. Create the `deployment`, as follows:

    ```
    aws apigateway create-deployment \
        --rest-api-id 3t0t98ifdh \
        --region us-east-1 \
        --stage-name dev \
        --stage-description "Dev stage" \
        --description "First deployment" \
        --profile admin
    ```

    A sample URL for this deployment will look as follows: https://3t0t98ifdh.execute-api.us-east-1.amazonaws.com/dev/greeting

10. Create the user pool client, as follows:

    ```
    aws cognito-idp create-user-pool-client \
        --user-pool-id us-east-1_fYsb1Gyec \
        --client-name my-user-pool-client \
        --explicit-auth-flows USER_PASSWORD_AUTH \
        --profile admin
    ```

11. Create a user `sign-up`, as follows:

    ```
    aws cognito-idp sign-up \
        --client-id 4519ureterrdqt0drbphk4q3pd \
        --username testuser5 \
        --password Passw0rd$ \
        --user-attributes Name=given_name,Value=Heartin
    ```

12. Confirm the user as an administrator, as follows:

    ```
    aws cognito-idp admin-confirm-sign-up \
        --user-pool-id us-east-1_fYsb1Gyec \
        --username testuser5 \
        --profile admin
    ```

13. Do an `initiate-auth` API call with the `auth` flow as USER_PASSWORD_AUTH, to allow for simple authentication based on username and password:

```
aws cognito-idp initiate-auth \
    --client-id 45l9ureterrdqt0drbphk4q3pd \
    --auth-flow USER_PASSWORD_AUTH \
    --auth-parameters USERNAME=testuser5,PASSWORD=Passw0rd$
```

If it is successful, this command will return the access token, ID token, and refresh token.

14. Finally, you can execute the URL by using a REST client, such as Postman. You need to select the authorization type as `Bearer Token` and copy the ID token value that you received in the `initiate-auth` request into the token field, as follows:

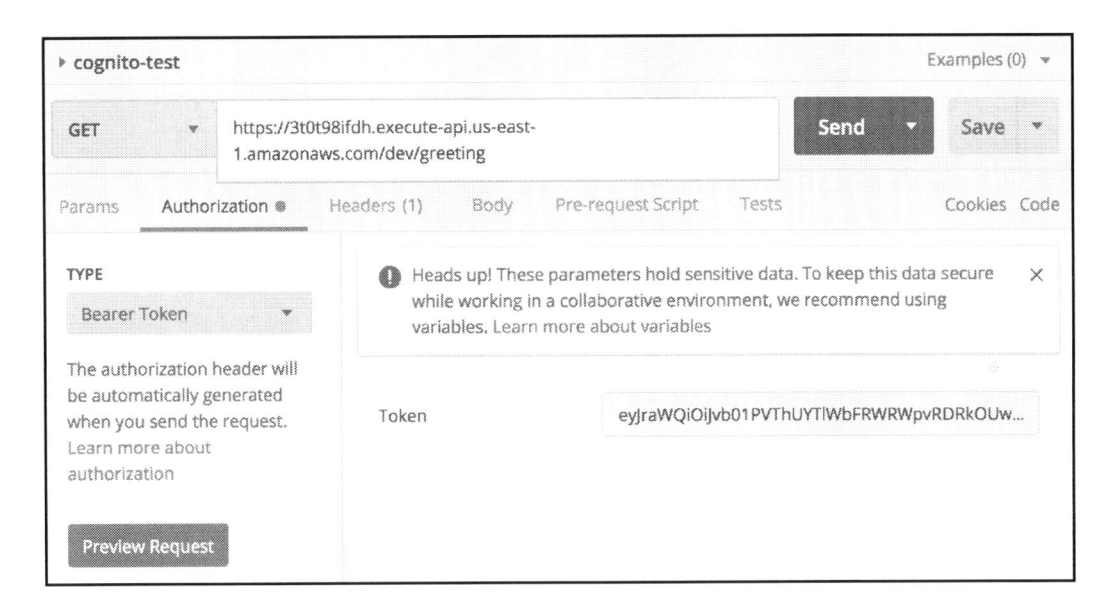

If it is successful, you should get the following results:

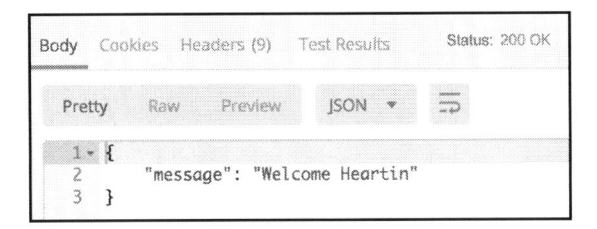

The CloudFormation template

The template starts as usual, with a template version and a description:

```
---
AWSTemplateFormatVersion: '2010-09-09'
Description: Building Cognito API with AWS CloudFormation
```

We will then create the `RestApi` resource, as follows:

```
Resources:
  MyFirstRestAPI:
    Type: AWS::ApiGateway::RestApi
    Properties:
      Name: Greeting API
      Description: API for greeting an user
      FailOnWarnings: true
```

Next, we will create an `authorizer` of the type `COGNITO_USER_POOLS`:

```
CustomCognitoAuthorizer:
  Type: AWS::ApiGateway::Authorizer
  Properties:
    Name: FirstCognitoAuthorizer
    RestApiId: !Ref MyFirstRestAPI
    Type: COGNITO_USER_POOLS
    ProviderARNs:
    - Fn::Sub:
      - arn:aws:cognito-idp:${AWS::Region}:${AWS::AccountId}:userpool/${UserPoolId}
      - UserPoolId: !ImportValue MyFirstUserPoolId
    IdentitySource: method.request.header.Authorization
```

The value for the `Name` property cannot contain spaces, unlike many other name properties. Also, note that we have imported the user pool stack from the first recipe of the chapter, to create the provider `ARN`.

The resource definition is similar to what you have seen before:

```
GreetingResource:
  Type: AWS::ApiGateway::Resource
  Properties:
    RestApiId: !Ref MyFirstRestAPI
    ParentId: !GetAtt MyFirstRestAPI.RootResourceId
    PathPart: 'greeting'
```

The method definition is also similar to what you have seen before, except that now, we specify the `AuthorizationType` as `COGNITO_USER_POOLS`, and reference the `AuthorizerId` from the `authorizer` resource that we defined previously:

```
MyMockMethod:
  Type: AWS::ApiGateway::Method
  Properties:
    AuthorizationType: COGNITO_USER_POOLS
    AuthorizerId: !Ref CustomCognitoAuthorizer
    HttpMethod: GET
    Integration:
      Type: MOCK
      IntegrationHttpMethod: GET
      IntegrationResponses:
      - StatusCode: 200
        ResponseTemplates:
          application/json: "{\"message\": \"Welcome $context.authorizer.claims.given_name\" }"
      RequestTemplates:
        application/json: "{\"statusCode\": 200}"
    ResourceId: !Ref GreetingResource
    RestApiId: !Ref MyFirstRestAPI
    MethodResponses:
    - StatusCode: 200
```

We use `context.authorizer.claims.given_name` to retrieve the user attribute `given_name` that we passed to the `initiate auth` API for retrieving the tokens. The ID token also contains this information, embedded inside of it.

The `Deployment` type definition and `Output` section are similar to what you have seen before:

```
    MyFirstDeployment:
      DependsOn: MyMockMethod
      Type: AWS::ApiGateway::Deployment
      Properties:
        Description: 'First Deployment'
        RestApiId: !Ref MyFirstRestAPI
        StageDescription:
          Description: 'Dev Stage'
        StageName: 'dev'

Output:
  SampleEndpoint:
    Description: 'Sample Endpoint'
    Value: !Sub
      -
```

[193]

```
https://${API_ID}.execute-api.${AWS::Region}.amazonaws.com/dev/greeting
      - API_ID: !Ref MyFirstRestAPI
```

Now, you need to run the following API CLI commands (from the previous section):

```
aws cognito-idp sign-up
aws cognito-idp admin-confirm-sign-up
aws cognito-idp initiate-auth
```

Finally, you can execute the URL by using a REST client, such as Postman. You need to select the authorization type as `Bearer Token`, and copy the ID token value that you received in the `initiate-auth` request into the **Token** field. Refer to the screenshots in the previous section for the CLI commands.

How it works...

In this recipe, we created an API gateway API and an authorizer of the type `COGNITO_USER_POOLS`, and integrated them together. The API gateway API CLI commands and the CloudFormation templates are similar to the ones that we discussed in `Chapter 2`, *Building Serverless REST APIs with API Gateway*; hence, we won't get into the related theory and concepts.

In addition to *Integrating Cognito with API Gateway*, we demonstrated the use of `context.authorizer.claims`, in order to retrieve additional user information from the ID token. The attributes that are used with `claims` need to be passed to the `initiate auth` API call that generates the ID token.

Claim-based identity

Claim-based identity is an approach to authentication in which the access tokens contain the access key information required for authentication, as well as additional information attributes (claims) about the users. Such tokens are referred to as **identity tokens**.

Claim-based authentication allows a user to use a single token to sign-in to multiple websites, which is referred to as **single sign-on**. Since some information attributes (claims) are already a part of the token, the user does not have to enter them again after signing in to the application.

There's more...

In this recipe, we returned the response by using mock integration. You can follow the recipes in `Chapter 2`, *Building Serverless REST APIs with API Gateway*, to do a Lambda integration instead of a mock integration. We will be building and hosting an application with end-to-end integration in the next chapter.

See also

- `https://docs.aws.amazon.com/apigateway/latest/developerguide/apigateway-enable-cognito-user-pool.html`
- `https://openid.net/specs/openid-connect-core-1_0.html#StandardClaims`

User sign-up with SMS verification and MFA

In the previous recipes, we did user sign-up with a text username and email verification. In this recipe, we will create a user pool to support SMS and MFA verification, and then do sign-up using a login with SMS and MFA verification.

We will also support user sign-up with a phone number as the username. However, you do not need to specify a phone number as the username to support SMS and MFA verification. Instead, you can specify `phone_number` as an auto-verified attribute, similar to how we specified `email` in the previous recipes.

Getting ready

The following are the prerequisites for completing this recipe:

- You will need a working phone number that can receive SMS to complete the steps within this recipe.

How to do it...

We will first create a user pool that supports SMS verification, and then, we will do user sign-up with SMS verification.

> I will not explain the theory behind the CLI commands or CloudFormation template parameters that we have already discussed in the previous recipes within this chapter. If you are not following the recipes in order, please refer to the previous recipes whenever you need extra details for those CLI commands or CloudFormation template parameters.

Creating the user pool

First, we will look at how to create a user pool that supports using a phone number as a username, with SMS and MFA verification.

Creating a Cognito user pool client with AWS CLI

We will now create a user pool using CLI commands. In the next section, we will create the user pool using a CloudFormation template:

1. Create a role that allows Cognito to send SMS messages:
    1. Create a policy JSON file with an action, `sns:publish`, as follows:

```
{
    "Version": "2012-10-17",
    "Statement": [
        {
            "Effect": "Allow",
            "Action": [
                "sns:publish"
            ],
            "Resource": [
                "*"
            ]
        }
    ]
}
```

Save this as `sns-publish-policy.txt`.

2. Create the policy, as follows:

   ```
   aws iam create-policy \
       --policy-name cognito_sns_iam_policy \
       --policy-document file://resources/sns-publish-policy.txt \
       --profile admin
   ```

3. Create a trust relationship document for the role, as follows:

   ```
   {
     "Version": "2012-10-17",
     "Statement": [
       {
         "Effect": "Allow",
         "Principal": {
           "Service": "cognito-idp.amazonaws.com"
         },
         "Action": "sts:AssumeRole"
       }
     ]
   }
   ```

   Save this as `assume-role-trust-relationship-policy-document.txt`.

4. Create the role, as follows:

   ```
   aws iam create-role \
       --role-name cognito_sns_iam_role \
       --assume-role-policy-document file://resources/assume-role-trust-relationship-policy-document.txt \
       --profile admin
   ```

   Note the role ARN.

5. Attach the policy to the role, as follows:

   ```
   aws iam attach-role-policy \
    --role-name cognito_sns_iam_role \
    --policy-arn arn:aws:iam::<account_id>:policy/cognito_sns_iam_policy \
    --profile admin
   ```

2. Generate the input JSON template by using the `generate-cli-skeleton` option, and fill in the properties that are required within the JSON file (remove the properties that are not required).

   1. We will start the JSON file by specifying a name, using the `PoolName` property:

      ```
      {
          "PoolName": "QnaTime.com User Pool",
      ```

      `QnaTime.com` is a domain that is bought in Chapter 5, *Web Hosting with S3, Route 53, and CloudFront*.

   2. Under the `Policies` section, we will define the password policy, using the `PasswordPolicy` sub-property:

      ```
      "Policies": {
        "PasswordPolicy": {
          "MinimumLength": 8,
          "RequireUppercase": true,
          "RequireLowercase": true,
          "RequireNumbers": true,
          "RequireSymbols": true
        }
      },
      ```

   3. Next, define `AutoVerifiedAttributes` and `UsernameAttributes`:

      ```
      "AutoVerifiedAttributes": [
        "phone_number"
      ],
      "UsernameAttributes": [
        "phone_number"
      ],
      ```

   4. Define an SMS verification message and email verification subject, as follows:

      ```
      "EmailVerificationMessage": "Your verification code from qnatime.com is {####}.",
      ```

5. Enable MFA, as follows:

   ```
   "MfaConfiguration": "ON",
   ```

You can set `MfaConfiguration` to `"OFF"` to disable MFA, or to `"OPTIONAL"` to make MFA optional for users.

6. Define the SMS configuration, as follows:

   ```
   "SmsConfiguration": {
     "SnsCallerArn": "arn:aws:iam::855923912133:role/cognito_sns_iam_role",
     "ExternalId": "some-unique-external-id-preferably-a-uuid"
   },
   ```

   Here, `SnsCallerArn` is the ARN of the role that you created in the previous step. The external ID is a unique external ID. If you are creating the user pool from the Management Console, AWS will generate a UUID value for this field.

7. Define any tags, if they are needed (optional).
8. Define the `AdminCreateUserConfig` property:

   ```
   "AdminCreateUserConfig": {
     "AllowAdminCreateUserOnly": false,
     "UnusedAccountValidityDays": 7,
     "InviteMessageTemplate": {
       "SMSMessage": "Your username for qnatime.com is {username} and password is {####}."
     }
   }
   ```

   We are not using `InviteMessageTemplate` in this recipe, as we are doing user sign-up, but it is shown for reference. Save this file as `create-user-pool-cli-input.json`. The complete JSON file is available in the code files.

Application Security with Amazon Cognito

3. Execute the `create-user-pool` sub-command, specifying this JSON file, as follows:

   ```
   aws cognito-idp create-user-pool \
    --cli-input-json file://resources/create-user-pool-cli-input.json \
    --profile admin
   ```

   Note the `user-pool-id`, for use in further commands.

4. You can verify `user-pool-created` by using the `describe-user-pool` sub-command.

Creating a Cognito user pool client with CloudFormation template

Creating Cognito user pools is more commonly done using CloudFormation templates. Various sections of the CloudFormation template correspond to the CLI commands that you saw in the previous section:

1. You can start the template with a description and a name. We will call our template file `cognito-user-pool-cf-template.yml`. You can find the file under the resources folder for this recipe:

   ```
   ---
   AWSTemplateFormatVersion: '2010-09-09'
   Description: Cognito User Pool with SMS and MFA Verification
   ```

2. Start to define the role for our resource with an inline policy definition, as follows:

   ```
   Resources:
     SNSRole:
       Type: "AWS::IAM::Role"
       Properties:
         AssumeRolePolicyDocument:
           Version: "2012-10-17"
           Statement:
           - Effect: "Allow"
             Principal:
               Service:
               - "cognito-idp.amazonaws.com"
             Action:
             - "sts:AssumeRole"
         Policies:
         - PolicyName: "CognitoSNSPolicy"
           PolicyDocument:
   ```

```
            Version: "2012-10-17"
            Statement:
            - Effect: "Allow"
              Action: "sns:publish"
              Resource: "*"
```

3. Define the user pool resource with the type `AWS::Cognito::UserPool`:

   ```
   UserPool:
     Type: "AWS::Cognito::UserPool"
   ```

4. Under `Properties`, define `AutoVerifiedAttributes` and `AliasAttributes`:

   ```
   Properties:
     AutoVerifiedAttributes:
     - phone_number
     UsernameAttributes:
     - phone_number
   ```

5. Define an SMS verification message and an email verification subject:

   ```
   SmsVerificationMessage: 'Your verification code from
   qnatime.com is {####}.'
   ```

6. Define MFA and SMS configuration, as follows:

   ```
   MfaConfiguration: "ON"
   SmsConfiguration:
     ExternalId: 'some-unique-external-id-preferably-a-uuid'
     SnsCallerArn: !GetAtt SNSRole.Arn
   ```

7. We will define the `AdminCreateUserConfig` property, as follows:

   ```
   AdminCreateUserConfig:
     AllowAdminCreateUserOnly: false
     InviteMessageTemplate:
       SMSMessage: 'Your username for qnatime.com is {username}
   and password is {####}.'
     UnusedAccountValidityDays: 7
   ```

   We are not using `InviteMessageTemplate` in this recipe, as we are performing user creation by admin, but it is given for reference.

Application Security with Amazon Cognito

8. Although it is not required, we will provide a name and add a tag for this user pool:

    ```
    UserPoolName: 'Qnatime.com User Pool'
    UserPoolTags:
       Team: Dev
    ```

9. In the `Outputs` section, we will return the user pool ID and the client ID, as follows:

    ```
    Outputs:
      UserPoolId:
        Value: !Ref UserPool
        Export:
          Name: "UserPool::Id"
      UserPoolClientId:
        Value: !Ref UserPoolClient
        Export:
          Name: "UserPoolClient::Id"
    ```

    The complete CloudFormation template is available in the code files.

10. Execute the CloudFormation template to create a CloudFormation stack.
11. You can run the `describe-stacks` sub-command to get the status and the `user-pool-id`. You can also use the `describe-user-pool` sub-command with the ID returned by the `describe-stacks` sub-command, in order to verify the new Cognito user pool.
12. To clean up, you can delete the user pool by deleting the stack, or you can keep the stack.

User sign-up with SMS and MFA verification

First, we will set up a user pool client for SMS verification; then, we will do user sign-up with SMS verification:

1. Create a user pool client, as follows:

    ```
    aws cognito-idp create-user-pool-client \
        --user-pool-id us-east-1_n5USdCHNf \
        --explicit-auth-flows USER_PASSWORD_AUTH \
        --client-name user-pool-client-signup \
        --profile admin
    ```

[202]

You can use `describe-user-pool-client` to get the details of the user pool client.

2. Do user sign-up with a phone number as the username, as follows:

```
aws cognito-idp sign-up \
    --client-id 6amm4ins1md8fo5tvhtmel183h \
    --username +917411174114 \
    --password Passw0rd$
```

You will need to start the phone number with a +, followed by the country code (for example, +44 for the United Kingdom and +91 for India).

If this is successful, you should get the following response:

```
{
    "UserConfirmed": false,
    "CodeDeliveryDetails": {
        "Destination": "+*******4114",
        "DeliveryMedium": "SMS",
        "AttributeName": "phone_number"
    },
    "UserSub": "f8f7f918-23dc-43da-a88b-4a7364c78072"
}
```

You will now get a confirmation code SMS at the phone number you specified.

If you do not receive a confirmation authentication code after waiting for some time, or if the one that you received expires, you can use the `resend-confirmation-code` command, as follows:

```
aws cognito-idp resend-confirmation-code \
    --client-id 6amm4ins1md8fo5tvhtmel183h \
    --username +917411174114
```

3. Confirm the user sign-up with the confirmation authentication code that was received in the previous step:

```
aws cognito-idp confirm-sign-up \
    --client-id 6amm4ins1md8fo5tvhtmel183h \
    --username +917411174114 \
    --confirmation-code 432348
```

Application Security with Amazon Cognito

4. Initiate the authentication flow, as follows:

   ```
   aws cognito-idp initiate-auth \
       --client-id 6amm4ins1md8fo5tvhtmel183h \
       --auth-flow USER_PASSWORD_AUTH \
       --auth-parameters USERNAME=+917411174114,PASSWORD=Passw0rd$
   ```

   As we have enabled MFA, you should get back an authentication challenge in the response, as shown in the following screenshot:

   ```
   {
       "ChallengeName": "SMS_MFA",
       "Session": "Ud3vrfFW0Xfx04tPDzE8rtGass4A1XnQIGrac-VcmSKVUDoC9FjiAbsAr3fyxwb577t4vCHBwMCad
   Sbcm6n_4-ypA0hxMfYTEfn4TjEdfs9jVkg4OegdvmXZ100lm9WFMVSb6f_CeYxxth1FsNiZiwxEOK2iLUIK74nzB0RAoh
   t4QKisydnFHwka82RvnewSwJF5vf6VnEuZOOb-qatdUN-B9kUWtYK8ImwDZuXZobxQwDcGtBGeyTzQynIGCxqB3xbRAv6
   Q1wp2RbRZNaiee2koHj9DybybVe0jL_kCmyjVNtPy06lHcSpV3AM4D007cOM-khuRLHFnKDIgkFTi90Dfu9KpQPlUKKXH
   lcfG5RKktU_6i6ulH9VDW2T3tROFXyxZRhGWzJ7Q5w69G45toUU0Fb_CYmGN9EKkD6HJ5SB8NneWj-sGN7dM7usALi080
   VAQCF0Lc8KOxYaWx9g2VNPHeosMFUW1-R0yE4HkJ0Q2YBsBg3BtVADadcVT8zsv1StPHhUKVyw4LGytq7oK32WQwh8GSu
   e32vWIXdTFzdN4MnqW8YeOidNW-4AxkBP6KC3ovlL9kGL60Q5ki7m-_5phFjexNzWVYUpqEEf1sIZP6h6Hbm2d3OmC29M
   wmqPSng0ot33UKyjE6_YE-FYYZpD4igZmt83cvjRlhCX_L_i7ZJltBe2xHlj7pq63Mn9IM0d0GAbkWw-ug-IKcku3hU",
       "ChallengeParameters": {
           "CODE_DELIVERY_DELIVERY_MEDIUM": "SMS",
           "CODE_DELIVERY_DESTINATION": "+*********4114",
           "USER_ID_FOR_SRP": "f8f7f918-23dc-43da-a88b-4a7364c78072"
       }
   }
   ```

   You will now receive an SMS with an authentication code.

5. Respond to the authentication challenge with the authentication code that you received in an SMS and the session value that you received in the previous step:

   ```
   aws cognito-idp respond-to-auth-challenge \
       --client-id 6amm4ins1md8fo5tvhtmel183h \
       --challenge-name SMS_MFA \
       --challenge-responses
   USERNAME=+917411174114,SMS_MFA_CODE=650598 \
       --session <session>
   ```

   If this is successful, you should get a response with the `AccessToken`, `RefreshToken`, and `IdToken`. You can use these for further operations, including deleting the user.

How it works...

To summarize, we did the following in this recipe:

1. Created a role with an inline policy that allowed Cognito to use SMS to send (publish) messages
2. Created a Cognito user pool to support using a `phone_number` as the username, SMS verification, and MFA
3. Performed user sign-up with a `phone_number` as the username
4. SMS verification
5. Multi-factor authentication (MFA)

Multi-factor authentication (MFA) is an authentication done in addition to the standard authentication. In our case MFA is done by sending a code through SMS and we send back that code in the response. In this recipe, I used both SMS verification and MFA; however, within the code files, I have also provided the CLI commands for scenarios where we perform sign-up and sign-in without MFA. You can disable MFA support while creating the user pool, by setting the `MfaConfiguration` parameter to `false`.

There's more...

Even though we only discussed using a phone number as a username with SMS verification for signing up, you could also use email, or a combination of email and SMS verification.

See also

You can read more about email and phone verification at: `https://docs.aws.amazon.com/cognito/latest/developerguide/user-pool-settings-email-phone-verification.html`.

5
Web Hosting with S3, Route53, and CloudFront

This chapter will cover the following topics:

- Setting up an S3 static website
- Setting up CloudFront for an S3 website
- Registering a domain with Route 53
- Using domains registered with other registrars
- Creating a custom domain with an S3 static website
- Creating a custom domain with CloudFront
- Using HTTPS with a CloudFront domain

Introduction

In the previous chapters, you saw how to create Serverless functions, add REST APIs, create data stores, and secure an application. In this chapter, we will look at recipes related to hosting a website, such as how to register domain names, host a static website, attach the custom domain for our S3 bucket, and use the CloudFront **Content Delivery Network** (**CDN**). You already saw S3 in previous recipes. **Amazon Route 53** is a new service that we will introduce in this chapter. The Route 53 service is Amazon's DNS management service for registering domains and implementing routing strategies.

Some Route 53 functionalities may be one-time activities (for example, domain registration), some may require user interaction at various stages (for example, domain ownership validation), and some may take a longer time to complete. For example, DNS propagation can take up to 24-48 hours. Therefore, these tasks are generally done from the AWS Management Console or by directly accessing the APIs, and less using CloudFormation. CloudFormation does not currently support domain registration, and it only has limited support for other DNS management activities.

Setting up an S3 static website

Simple Storage Service (S3) is an object store in AWS that allows us to store objects against keys. We already used S3 to deploy our Lambda code and within CloudFormation scripts, in earlier recipes. S3 can also be configured to host a static website. In this recipe, we will create an S3 bucket and configure it as a static website by using AWS CLI commands and CloudFormation scripts.

Getting ready

A basic understanding of Amazon S3 is required for this section. We used S3 to upload our Lambda code in Chapter 1, *Getting Started with Serverless Computing on AWS*, and we discussed a few of its properties. A decent understanding of web technologies, such as HTML, would be beneficial, but is not mandatory.

Up to this point, we have only been using the default region, `us-east-1`. An S3 bucket can be created in a region closer to you. To demonstrate this, I will be using a different region, Mumbai (`ap-south-1`), for this recipe. However, this is not a requirement for the recipe. We will use the CloudFront CDN later in this chapter, in order to cache the results across locations.

How to do it...

We will create one S3 static website bucket, and we will configure it as a website.

AWS CLI commands

I will use a bucket name (`qnatime`, or a variation thereof) for the AWS CLI commands within this chapter.

> S3 bucket names are unique across all regions. Please use a different domain name than the one I use in the recipes.

1. Create an S3 bucket, as follows:

   ```
   aws s3api create-bucket \
       --bucket qnatime \
       --create-bucket-configuration LocationConstraint=ap-south-1 \
       --region ap-south-1 \
       --profile admin
   ```

   We need to specify the `LocationConstraint` explicitly, in addition to the `--region` option for non-US regions. This command will provide you with the location of the S3 bucket:

   ```
   {
       "Location": "http://qnatime.s3.amazonaws.com/"
   }
   ```

   From this location and the knowledge of the region, you can derive the URL for our static website: `http://qnatime.s3-website.ap-south-1.amazonaws.com`. However, the website link will not work now, as we have not configured the bucket as a website.

   We are also using the `aws cli s3api` command, instead of the `aws cli s3` command that we were using hitherto. Some of the actions that we will perform will require more control, as provided by the `s3api` sub-command over the high-level `s3` sub-command.

2. Create an index document and an error document.

   An S3 static website requires you to provide two HTML files: an index document and an error document. The index document is the website landing page, and the error document is displayed in the case of an error.

   Create a simple `index.html` file, with only an `<h1>` tag inside the body:

   ```
   <body>
   <h1> Welcome to Q & A Time! </h1>
   </body>
   ```

Similarly, you can also create a simple `error.html` file, with a different text within the `<h1>` tag:

```
<body>
<h1> Error page for Q & A Time! </h1>
<body>
```

Refer to the code files for the complete `index.html` and `error.html` files.

3. Upload the index and error documents, as follows:

    ```
    aws s3 cp resources/index.html s3://qnatime/index.html \
    --profile admin
    aws s3 cp resources/error.html s3://qnatime/error.html \
    --profile admin
    ```

4. Create a website configuration JSON file specifying the index and error filenames, as follows:

    ```
    {
      "IndexDocument": {
        "Suffix": "index.html"
      },
      "ErrorDocument": {
        "Key": "error.html"
      }
    }
    ```

5. Create a static website specifying the website configuration JSON file, as follows:

    ```
    aws s3api put-bucket-website \
    --bucket qnatime.com \
    --website-configuration file://resources/s3-website-configuration.json \
    --profile admin
    ```

6. Create a bucket policy with read permission for everyone.

    By default, an S3 bucket and its objects do not provide read access to the public. However, for an S3 bucket to act as a website, all of the files need to be made accessible to the public. This can be done by using the following bucket policy:

    ```
    {
      "Version":"2012-10-17",
      "Statement":[
        {
          "Sid":"PublicReadGetObjectAccess",
          "Effect":"Allow",
    ```

```
            "Principal": "*",
            "Action":["s3:GetObject"],
            "Resource":["arn:aws:s3:::qnatime/*"]
        }
    ]
}
```

Execute the bucket policy, as follows:

```
aws s3api put-bucket-policy \
    --bucket qnatime \
    --policy file://resources/s3-website-policy.json \
    --profile admin
```

7. Execute the bucket website URL; the result will look like the following screenshot:

> ← → C ⓘ Not Secure | qnatime.s3-website.ap-south-1.amazonaws.com
>
> **Welcome to Q & A Time!**

The CloudFormation template

I will use a bucket named `quizzercloud` (or one of its variations) for all of the CloudFormation templates within this chapter:

1. Start the template with the template version and a description (optional).
2. Define a parameter for the bucket name:

```
Parameters:
  BucketName:
    Description: Bucket name for your website
    Type: String
```

3. Define a resource for the bucket:

```
Resources:
  MyBucket:
    Type: AWS::S3::Bucket
    Properties:
      BucketName: !Ref BucketName
      AccessControl: PublicRead
```

```
          WebsiteConfiguration:
            IndexDocument: index.html
            ErrorDocument: error.html
```

4. Define a bucket access policy that allows for everyone to access the bucket's contents:

```
      WebsitePublicAccessPolicy:
        Type: AWS::S3::BucketPolicy
        Properties:
          Bucket: !Ref MyBucket
          PolicyDocument:
            Statement:
              -
                Action:
                  - "s3:GetObject"
                Effect: "Allow"
                Resource:
                  Fn::Join:
                    - ""
                    -
                      - "arn:aws:s3:::"
                      - !Ref MyBucket
                      - "/*"
                Principal: "*"
```

5. Add an Outputs section to return the URL of the S3 website (optional):

```
      Outputs:
        S3WebsiteURL:
          Value: !Sub
            - http://${Bucket}.s3-website.${AWS::Region}.amazonaws.com
            - Bucket: !Ref MyBucket
          Description: URL for S3 static website
```

6. Execute the CloudFormation template by passing the values for the parameters:

```
aws cloudformation create-stack \
    --stack-name s3websitestack \
    --template-body file://resources/s3-static-website-cf-template.yml \
    --parameters ParameterKey=BucketName,ParameterValue=quizzercloud \
    --region ap-south-1 \
    --profile admin
```

7. Check the creation status by using the `aws cloudformation describe-stacks` command. If it is successful, you should get a response with an `Outputs` section, as follows:

```
"Outputs": [
    {
        "OutputKey": "S3WebsiteURL",
        "OutputValue": "http://quizzercloud.s3-website.ap-south-1.amazonaws.com",
        "Description": "URL for S3 static website"
    }
],
```

8. Once the stack creation has completed, you will need to upload the `index.html` and `error.html` files into the root bucket. Refer to the *AWS CLI commands* section or the code files for the command.
9. Finally, execute the S3 static website URL in a browser, as shown in the following screenshot:

> ← → C ⓘ Not Secure | quizzercloud.s3-website.ap-south-1.amazonaws.com
>
> **Welcome to Q & A Time!**

How it works...

To summarize, we did the following in this recipe:

1. We created an S3 bucket as a static website (for example, `qnatime`)
2. We added the `index.html` and `error.html` files
3. We added a bucket policy that allows for everyone to read the bucket
4. We verified the S3 static website from the browser

Web Hosting with S3, Route53, and CloudFront

There's more...

In the real world, an S3 website is usually pointed to by a custom domain (for example, `qnatime.com`). One restriction with this approach is that the bucket name and the custom domain have to be the same. We can work around this by using the CloudFront CDN. You will see that in a later recipe in this chapter.

S3 website endpoints do not currently support HTTPS. We can, however, work around this, by configuring the CloudFront CDN over our website configuration, and then adding SSL support, utilizing **Amazon Certificate Manager** (**ACM**). We will cover that in a later recipe within this book.

See also

- `https://docs.aws.amazon.com/cli/latest/reference/s3/index.html`
- `https://docs.aws.amazon.com/cli/latest/reference/s3api/index.html`

Setting up CloudFront for an S3 website

CloudFront is a CDN web service from Amazon that caches data across the globe, through data centers known as **edge locations**. These edge locations speed up the distribution of static and dynamic web content originating in one location in one region, such as an S3 bucket, to users in other regions.

Getting ready

You will need an S3 bucket configured as a website in order to follow this recipe. You can follow the recipe *Setting up an S3 static website* to set up an S3 bucket as a static website.

How to do it...

You can set up CloudFront through AWS CLI commands, CloudFormation, or the AWS Management Console. In this recipe, we will look at how to set up CloudFront for an S3 bucket configured as a static website, through CLI commands and CloudFormation template.

AWS CLI commands

You can create a CloudFront distribution with the AWS CLI by either passing a distribution config, or by specifying the original domain name (for example, an S3 bucket name). In this recipe, we will use the shorter option:

1. Create the CloudFront distribution by using the `create-distribution` command with `aws cloudfront`:

    ```
    aws cloudfront create-distribution \
      --origin-domain-name qnatime.s3.amazonaws.com \
      --default-root-object index.html \
      --profile admin
    ```

    This command will immediately return the ID of the distribution and the defaults that are considered:

    ```
    {
    "Location": "https://cloudfront.amazonaws.com/2018-06-18/distribution/E1ZX6JAV6EDQVO",
    "ETag": "E2D8OBE98ICCBH",
    "Distribution": {
        "Id": "E1ZX6JAV6EDQVO",
        "ARN": "arn:aws:cloudfront::218317422462:distribution/E1ZX6JAV6EDQVO",
        "Status": "InProgress",
        "LastModifiedTime": "2018-12-04T16:19:18.742Z",
        "InProgressInvalidationBatches": 0,
        "DomainName": "d39sfuvkc6hh8d.cloudfront.net",
        "ActiveTrustedSigners": {
            "Enabled": false,
            "Quantity": 0
        },
    },
    ```

    The `Etag` in the response from the CloudFront command is needed to make further commands, such as update or delete requests, from the CLI. The response also contains the `DistributionConfig` property, which contains all of the properties related to the distribution. This should take some time to complete.

2. Check the status by using the `aws cloudfront get-distribution` command:

    ```
    aws cloudfront get-distribution \
        --id E1ZX6JAV6EDQVO \
        --profile admin
    ```

Web Hosting with S3, Route53, and CloudFront

If it is successful, the status will change to `Deployed` in the response:

```
"Status": "Deployed",
```

The remainder of the response is similar to the previous one. The `DistributionConfig` property within the response will be discussed in detail later on.

3. Execute the CloudFront domain URL in a browser, as shown in the following screenshot:

```
← → C   ⓘ Not Secure | d39sfuvkc6hh8d.cloudfront.net
```

Welcome to Q & A Time!

Understanding the DistributionConfig defaults in the response

Let's go through the `DistributionConfig` property that we received as part of the response, and try to understand the structure and defaults for the important properties of `DistributionConfig`. I have only displayed screenshots from the response for the important sections, and will mention other properties by name.

`DistributionConfig` starts with the properties `CallerReference`, `Aliases`, and the `DefaultRootObject` (set as `index.html`). Next, it contains the `Origins` property, with our bucket details:

```
"Origins": {
    "Quantity": 1,
    "Items": [
        {
            "Id": "qnatime.s3.amazonaws.com-1543940355-477594",
            "DomainName": "qnatime.s3.amazonaws.com",
            "OriginPath": "",
            "CustomHeaders": {
                "Quantity": 0
            },
            "S3OriginConfig": {
                "OriginAccessIdentity": ""
            }
        }
    ]
},
```

Next, it contains the `DefaultCacheBehavior` section that starts with `TargetOriginId`, `ForwardedValues`, `TrustedSigners`, and `ViewerProtocolPolicy` (set as `allow-all`).

The `DefaultCacheBehavior` section continues with `MinTTL`, `AllowedMethods`, `SmoothStreaming`, `DefaultTTL`, `MaxTTL`, `Compress`, `LambdaFunctionAssociations`, and `FieldLevelEncryptionId`:

```
        "MinTTL": 0,
        "AllowedMethods": {
            "Quantity": 2,
            "Items": [
                "HEAD",
                "GET"
            ],
            "CachedMethods": {
                "Quantity": 2,
                "Items": [
                    "HEAD",
                    "GET"
                ]
            }
        },
        "SmoothStreaming": false,
        "DefaultTTL": 86400,
        "MaxTTL": 31536000,
        "Compress": false,
        "LambdaFunctionAssociations": {
            "Quantity": 0
        },
        "FieldLevelEncryptionId": ""
    },
```

Furthermore, we can see the `CacheBehaviors`, `CustomErrorResponses`, `Comment`, `Logging`, and `PriceClass` sections (set as `PriceClass_All`).

Web Hosting with S3, Route53, and CloudFront

Finally, there are the `Enabled`, `ViewerCertificate`, `Restrictions`, `WebACLId`, `HttpVersion`, and `IsIPV6Enabled` sections:

```
"Enabled": true,
"ViewerCertificate": {
    "CloudFrontDefaultCertificate": true,
    "MinimumProtocolVersion": "TLSv1",
    "CertificateSource": "cloudfront"
},
"Restrictions": {
    "GeoRestriction": {
        "RestrictionType": "none",
        "Quantity": 0
    }
},
"WebACLId": "",
"HttpVersion": "http2",
"IsIPV6Enabled": true
    }
  }
}
```

The CloudFormation template

Unlike with the CLI commands, there is no shorthand way to create a CloudFront distribution with a CloudFormation template without specifying the distribution config parameters. I will, however, only add the essential parameters in this recipe:

1. Start the template with the template version and a description (optional).
2. Create a resource of the type `AWS::CloudFront::Distribution`:

```
Resources:
  MyCloudFrontDistribution:
    Type: AWS::CloudFront::Distribution
    Properties:
      DistributionConfig:
        Origins:
        - DomainName: quizzer.cloud.s3.amazonaws.com
          Id: myS3Origin
          S3OriginConfig:
            OriginAccessIdentity: ''
        Enabled: 'true'
        Comment: 'CloudFront Distribution for S3 Bucket'
        DefaultRootObject: index.html
        DefaultCacheBehavior:
          TargetOriginId: myS3Origin
          ForwardedValues:
```

```
        QueryString: 'false'
        Cookies:
          Forward: none
    ViewerProtocolPolicy: allow-all
```

3. Add an `Outputs` section to return the CloudFront distribution ID and the CloudFront domain name:

    ```
    Outputs:
      CloudFrontDistributionId:
        Value: !Ref MyCloudFrontDistribution
        Description: 'CloudFront distribution id'
      CloudFrontDomain:
        Value: !GetAtt MyCloudFrontDistribution.DomainName
        Description: 'CloudFront distribution domain name'
    ```

4. Execute the stack, using the `create-stack` command.

    It will take some time for the distribution to be created. You can check the status by using the `describe-stacks` command. Once it has completed, you will get a response with the `Outputs` section, as follows:

    ```
    "Outputs": [
        {
            "OutputKey": "CloudFrontDistributionId",
            "OutputValue": "E3CNIY0N2WR354",
            "Description": "CloudFront distribution id"
        },
        {
            "OutputKey": "CloudFrontDomain",
            "OutputValue": "d130e9lj3phwkc.cloudfront.net",
            "Description": "CloudFront distribution domain name",
            "ExportName": "CloudFrontDomainName"
        }
    ],
    ```

5. Execute the CloudFront domain name in a browser, and verify whether the S3 static website has loaded:

    ← → C ① Not Secure | d1np6qfh9yzjps.cloudfront.net

    Welcome to Q & A Time!

How it works...

We created a CloudFront distribution for an existing bucket that was configured as a static website. We created the bucket in a previous recipe. With AWS CLI commands, you can either pass in just the original server and accept the defaults for the other options, or you can pass in a distribution config JSON file with all of the required configurations. These options are mutually exclusive. In this recipe, we only specified the original server S3 bucket for the AWS CLI command version. However, with the CloudFormation template, we still had to use the distributed config, with the essential parameters.

There's more...

We only specified the original server when creating the CloudFront distribution with AWS CLI commands. However, to update or delete a CloudFront distribution, you also need to specify the `Etag` received in the previous step, from the command line. For updates, including enabling or disabling the CloudFront distribution, we will need to provide the distribution configurations with the essential parameters. We will see them in the next recipe.

See also

- https://docs.aws.amazon.com/cli/latest/reference/cloudfront/index.html#cli-aws-cloudfront
- https://docs.aws.amazon.com/AmazonCloudFront/latest/DeveloperGuide/private-content-restricting-access-to-s3.html

Registering a domain name with Route 53

In this recipe, we will register a domain name for our Serverless application with the Amazon Route 53 service. Domain registration is usually a one-time activity, and hence, it is usually done from the AWS Management Console. You can also perform domain registration with AWS APIs. Currently, CloudFormation does not support domain registration; however, it does support a limited set of operations for domains that are already registered.

Now, we will look at how to register domains through the AWS Management Console and AWS CLI API commands.

Getting ready

You will need a working AWS account with a valid credit card in order to buy a domain name through Route 53. Buying a domain is outside of the free tier. You may want to do some research on selecting a good domain name should if you want to use it for a genuine use case later on.

How to do it...

We will register domain names using AWS CLI commands in this section. In the real world, people commonly register domains from the Management Console, as it is a one-time activity. Therefore, I have also included the steps to register from the Management Console, in the *There's more...* section.

Registering a domain with AWS CLI commands

If you need to register domains regularly, or if you are building a website (such as a domain registration website), you will need to use the APIs instead. You can register domain names with AWS CLI commands through the `register-domain` sub-command of the `route53domains` command:

1. We will first check the availability of the domain that we already registered:

    ```
    aws route53domains check-domain-availability \
        --domain-name qnatime.com \
        --profile admin
    ```

    This command will provide us with the following response:

    ```
    {
        "Availability": "UNAVAILABLE"
    }
    ```

    Now, check for another domain, which is not registered:

    ```
    aws route53domains check-domain-availability \
        --domain-name qnatime.net \
        --profile admin
    ```

This command will provide us with the following response:

```
{
  "Availability": "AVAILABLE"
}
```

In the real world, you may have to do some trials until you find a domain that is available. There are also websites that can help you find all available domains with a partial input, such as a prefix.

2. Create a contact information JSON file, as follows:

```
{
  "FirstName": "Heartin",
  "LastName": "Kanikathottu",
  "ContactType": "PERSON",
  "OrganizationName": "NA",
  "AddressLine1": "<Your AddressLine1>",
"AddressLine2": "<Your AddressLine1>",
  "City": "Bengaluru",
  "State": "KA",
  "CountryCode": "IN",
  "ZipCode": "<Your PIN>",
  "PhoneNumber": "+91.XXXXXXXXXX",
  "Email": "Your email"
}
```

> **TIP**: +91 is the country code for India. It has to be followed by a dot, and then the actual number. I will reuse the same contact JSON for all of the contacts. You can create different files, if necessary.

3. Finally, execute the `register-domain` sub-command:

```
aws route53domains register-domain \
    --domain-name 'qnatime.net' \
    --duration-in-years 1 \
    --no-auto-renew \
    --admin-contact file://resources/contact.json \
    --registrant-contact file://resources/contact.json \
    --tech-contact file://resources/contact.json \
    --privacy-protect-admin-contact \
    --privacy-protect-registrant-contact \
    --privacy-protect-tech-contact \
    --profile admin
```

This command will immediately return an operation ID:

```
{
    "OperationId": "ba6b494d-9e86-4acc-8904-3ba861228916"
}
```

You can check the status of your pending operation by using the `get-operation-detail` sub-command, as follows:

```
aws route53domains get-operation-detail \
    --operation-id ba6b494d-9e86-4acc-8904-3ba861228916 \
    --profile admin
```

This will return a response similar to the following:

```
{
    "OperationId": "ba6b494d-9e86-4acc-8904-3ba861228916",
    "Status": "IN_PROGRESS",
    "Message": "To finish registering your domain, you must verify your payment",
    "DomainName": "qnatime.net",
    "Type": "REGISTER_DOMAIN",
    "SubmittedDate": 1543554216.883
}
```

You can verify the payment from your AWS Management Console, as follows:

1. Log in to **AWS Management Console**, and go to **My Billing Dashboard**
2. Click on **Payment Methods**
3. Click on **Make Payment**
4. Click on the **Pay Now** action for the domain registration expense, and make the payment.

After the payment, you can wait, and then run the `get-operation-detail` sub-command again. This time, you should get a different message, as follows:

```
{
    "OperationId": "ba6b494d-9e86-4acc-8904-3ba861228916",
    "Status": "IN_PROGRESS",
    "DomainName": "qnatime.net",
    "Type": "REGISTER_DOMAIN",
    "SubmittedDate": 1543554216.883
}
```

You will get an email for verification. Verify your email address by clicking on the link.

As we mentioned at the beginning, the processes related to Route 53 may take some time to complete. So, you can wait for a while, and then try to run the `get-operation-detail` sub-command again. If everything goes fine, you will see something like the following:

```
{
    "OperationId": "ba6b494d-9e86-4acc-8904-3ba861228916",
    "Status": "SUCCESSFUL",
    "DomainName": "qnatime.net",
    "Type": "REGISTER_DOMAIN",
    "SubmittedDate": 1543554216.883
}
```

How it works...

In this recipe, we registered a domain from both the AWS Management Console and the AWS CLI.

Route 53 can be used for registering domain names, configuring DNS routing strategies, and even checking the health of resources. Route 53 is a global service, and it is Amazon's DNS management service. **DNS** stands for **Domain Name System**. DNS takes care of converting the domain name that you use over the internet to the corresponding host system IP address. Route 53 was named on the basis of DNS port 53.

You also saw that AWS supports privacy protection for supported domain names. `WHOIS` queries can be used by anyone to obtain basic information regarding a domain and its registrant. Privacy protection hides some of your information during `WHOIS` queries, such as your name, phone number, and email. Without privacy protection, this information could be used by spammers. However, privacy protection is restricted for some extensions, such as `.in`.

Hosted zones

A **hosted zone** is a collection of record sets for a particular domain. These record sets include **nameserver** (**NS**) records, **Start Of Authority** (**SOA**) records, MX records for configuring mail servers. Hosted zones can be public (for routing over the internet), or private (for routing within Amazon VPCs).

As you saw in the *How to do it...* section, AWS will automatically create a hosted zone for domains registered with the AWS Route 53 domain registrar, along with NS and SOA records.

There's more...

There are registrars other than Amazon Route 53 that can be used to register domain names. You can transfer domain names registered with other providers into AWS by using Route 53. You can also contact AWS to transfer domain names between AWS accounts.

Registering a domain from AWS Management Console

We can register a domain from AWS Management console by observing the following steps. In most cases, domains are registered from AWS Management Console:

1. First, you need to log in to your AWS Management Console and go to the Route 53 service.
2. From within the Route 53 dashboard, go to the **Domain Registration** page.
3. Click on **Register Domain** to go to the **Choose a domain name** page.
4. Enter the domain name, select the extension that you would like to buy, and click on **Check**. Route 53 will let you know if the domain name is available. It will also provide a number of suggestions.
5. Add the preferred domain name (or names) to the cart by clicking on **Add to cart**, and click on **Continue**.

6. You will need to enter the registrant contact details and select the tenure to register the domain. You can also scroll down and opt in to enable privacy protection. With privacy protection, some of your contact information will not be displayed publicly in a `Whois` search.
7. AWS will send an email confirmation link to the email that you specified. Click on it to verify your email. You will need to verify it within 15 days, or your domain will not be available publicly.
8. Read the terms, select the **terms and conditions** checkbox, and click on **Complete Purchase**.
9. You will then be redirected to the success page. AWS will now generate a bill for the domain registration, and will usually send you the update in an email. You can then make a payment with your credit card, just like paying a bill.

AWS automatically creates a hosted zone for domains registered with AWS. You can verify this by going to the **Hosted Zones** page in the left-hand sidebar, in the Route 53 dashboard:

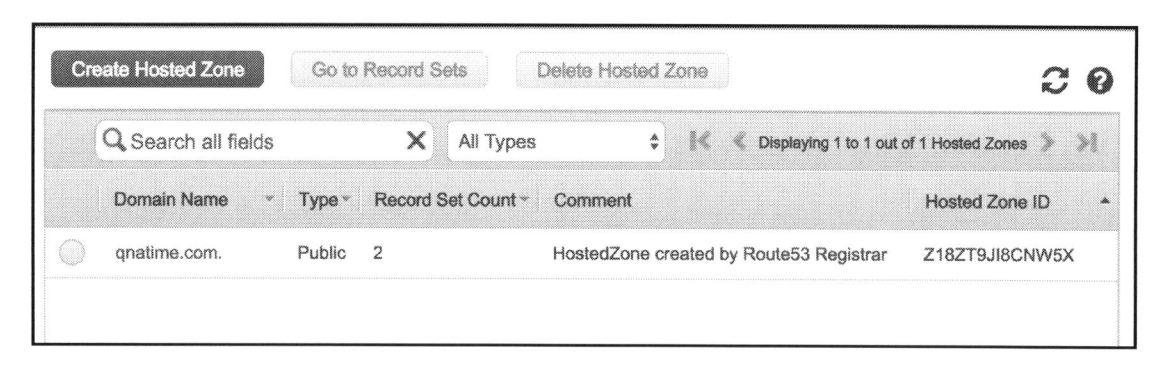

You can click on your domain name. AWS has also created two records for your domain, by default: a **Nameserver** (**NS**) record, and a **Start Of Authority** (**SOA**) record. This is shown in the following screenshot:

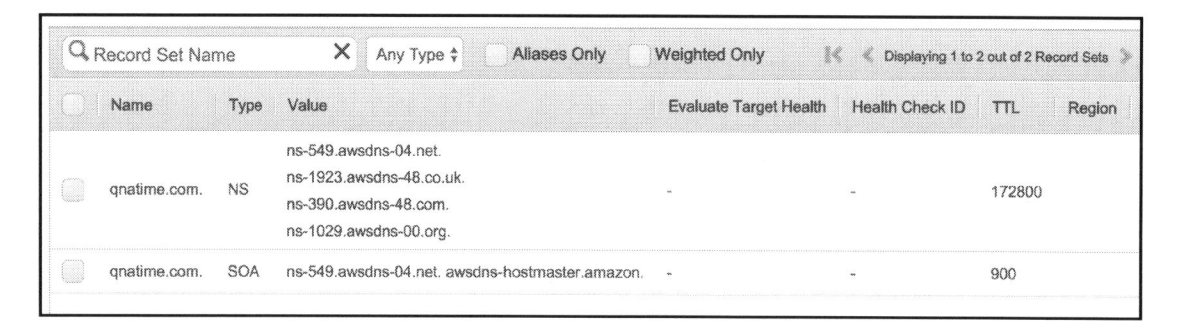

See also

- You may read more about working with DNS records at `https://docs.aws.amazon.com/Route53/latest/DeveloperGuide/rrsets-working-with.html`
- You may read more about Route 53 routing policies from my notes at `http://cloudmaterials.com/en/book/web-hosting-aws-route-53-s3-and-cloudfront`

Using domains registered with other registrars

We registered a domain name through Route 53 in the previous recipe. In this recipe, we will look at how Route 53 can be used with domains registered with other registrars, by creating hosted zones manually. It may be that you already have a domain registered with other registrars, or you may want to register one based on the cost of the extension that you want to register.

Getting ready

You will need a domain registered with any other registrar to follow the steps within this recipe. A decent knowledge of networking basics and DNS management concepts would also be a bonus.

How to do it...

We will create and configure hosted zone AWS CLI commands and CloudFormation templates. I have also included the steps for the AWS Management Console in the *There's more...* section.

AWS CLI commands

You can create a hosted zone from the AWS CLI by using the `create-hosted-zone` sub-command of the `route53` AWS CLI command. I will use a different domain this time:

```
aws route53 create-hosted-zone \
    --name quizzercloud.com \
    --caller-reference 2018-28-11-11:55 \
    --hosted-zone-config Comment="HostedZone for quizzercloud.com" \
    --profile admin
```

This command should immediately return a response, as follows; it might take some time for the changes to take effect:

```
{
    "Location": "https://route53.amazonaws.com/2013-04-01/hostedzone/Z1MSS6K1EB49B4",
    "HostedZone": {
        "Id": "/hostedzone/Z1MSS6K1EB49B4",
        "Name": "quizzercloud.com.",
        "CallerReference": "2018-28-11-11:55",
        "Config": {
            "Comment": "HostedZone for quizzercloud.com",
            "PrivateZone": false
        },
        "ResourceRecordSetCount": 2
    },
    "ChangeInfo": {
        "Id": "/change/CUOKDB5WJX02T",
        "Status": "PENDING",
        "SubmittedAt": "2018-11-30T06:26:03.989Z"
    },
    "DelegationSet": {
        "NameServers": [
            "ns-747.awsdns-29.net",
            "ns-1405.awsdns-47.org",
            "ns-268.awsdns-33.com",
            "ns-1867.awsdns-41.co.uk"
        ]
    }
}
```

This should be completed in a few minutes. You can get the hosted zone status or details by using the `route53 get-hosted-zone` command. You can also update the name servers in your domain registrar's control panel. It might take 24-72 hours for the DNS changes to be propagated.

The CloudFormation template

You can create hosted zones with CloudFormation templates by using the resource type `AWS::Route53::HostedZone`:

```
Resources:
  CloudMaterialsHostedZone:
    Type: "AWS::Route53::HostedZone"
    Properties:
      HostedZoneConfig:
        Comment: HostedZone for CloudMaterials.com
      Name: cloudmaterials.com
```

We will also add an `Outputs` section, for returning the `HostedZoneID` and nameservers:

```
Outputs:
  HostedZoneId:
    Value: !Ref CloudMaterialsHostedZone
    Description: HostedZone for cloudmaterials.com
  HostedZoneNameservers:
    Value: !Join
      - ','
      - !GetAtt CloudMaterialsHostedZone.NameServers
    Description: HostedZone Nameservers for cloudmaterials.com
```

The value of an `Outputs` field can only be of the string type. The property `Nameservers`, however, returns a list of nameservers. Therefore, we need to use a join function to add them to a string, separated by , .

Deploy the stack by using `deploy-stack`, and verify it by using `describe-stacks`. You can also verify this from the Route 53 dashboard in the AWS Management Console. The `Outputs` section of the response should appear as follows:

```
"Outputs": [
    {
        "OutputKey": "HostedZoneId",
        "OutputValue": "Z2CNT8T7RPHYHT",
        "Description": "HostedZone for cloudmaterials.com"
    },
    {
        "OutputKey": "HostedZoneNameservers",
        "OutputValue": "ns-820.awsdns-38.net,ns-355.awsdns-44.com,ns-1431.awsdns-50.org,ns-1543.awsdns-00.co.uk",
        "Description": "HostedZone Nameservers for cloudmaterials.com"
    }
],
```

You can now configure these nameservers with your domain registrar.

Web Hosting with S3, Route53, and CloudFront

How it works...

In this recipe, we created a `HostedZone` for a domain registered with another registrar. We can now use this domain like the other domain that was registered with Route 53.

When using domains registered with other domain registrars in Route 53, you need to manually create hosted zones. As you saw in the recipe, AWS will automatically create the NS and SOA records for your domain name. These NS records will then need to be updated with the other domain registrar, usually through a configuration page.

As you can see from the recipe, most of the tasks do not happen in real time, and some of them even need user input or user actions. Therefore, in many real-world project use cases, these are done manually, either from the console or through an application, using APIs.

DNS propagation

DNS is a hierarchical system involving many servers, starting with a root server. There are also caches at different locations. When you update nameservers on your domain control panel, it can take 24-72 hours, in general, for the changes to take effect. This time period is called the **DNS propagation time**.

There's more...

AWS Route 53 also supports various routing strategies, such as a simple routing policy, a failover routing policy, a geolocation routing policy, a geoproximity routing policy, a latency routing policy, a multivalue answer routing policy, and a weighted routing policy. With S3, we use the simple routing strategy, and the others are mostly useful when we are working with EC2 instances.

Steps for configuring DNS from the AWS Management Console

We can configure DNS from AWS Management Console as follows:

1. Log in to **AWS Management Console**, go to the **Route 53 dashboard**, and then go to the **Hosted Zones** page.
2. Click on the **Create Hosted Zone** button.

3. Fill in the domain name, a comment, and the type, and then click on **Create**:

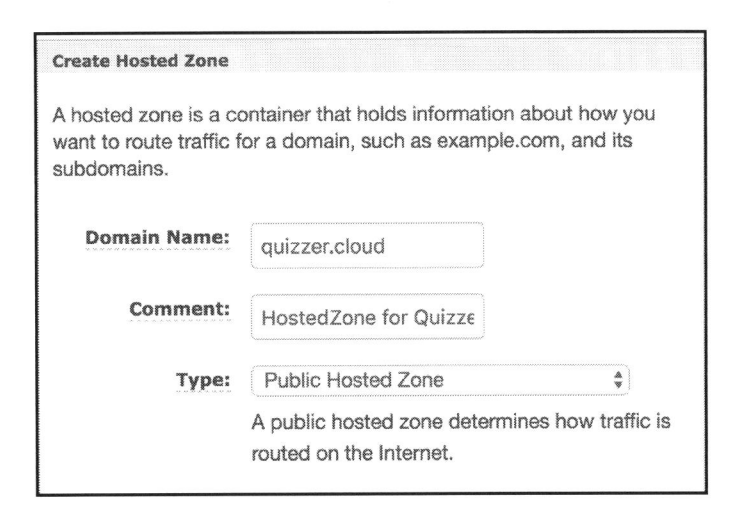

Create Hosted Zone

A hosted zone is a container that holds information about how you want to route traffic for a domain, such as example.com, and its subdomains.

Domain Name: quizzer.cloud

Comment: HostedZone for Quizze

Type: Public Hosted Zone

A public hosted zone determines how traffic is routed on the Internet.

The type denotes whether the hosted zone is public or private. This cannot be changed later.

AWS will autogenerate the NS and SOA records, along with the hosted zone:

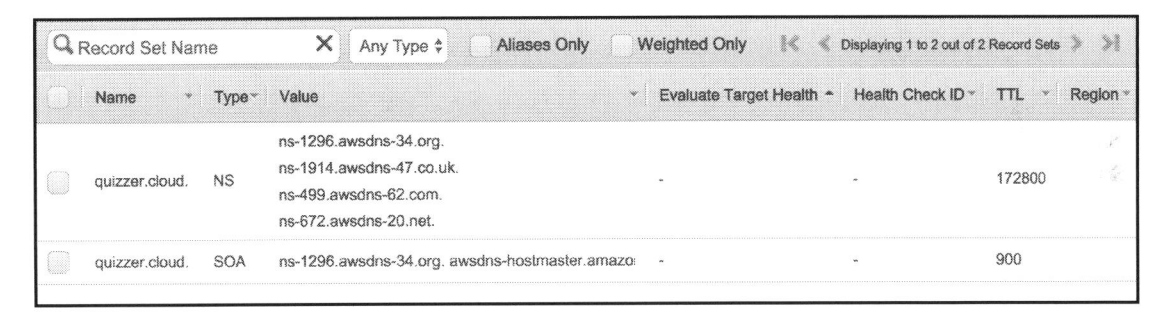

Name	Type	Value	Evaluate Target Health	Health Check ID	TTL	Region
quizzer.cloud.	NS	ns-1296.awsdns-34.org. ns-1914.awsdns-47.co.uk. ns-499.awsdns-62.com. ns-672.awsdns-20.net.	-	-	172800	
quizzer.cloud.	SOA	ns-1296.awsdns-34.org. awsdns-hostmaster.amazo	-	-	900	

4. Go to your other domain registrar (where you registered this domain) and update the preceding nameservers. Note that it can take some time for the DNS changes to propagate.

Using custom domains with S3 static websites

In this recipe, we will look at how to use custom domain names with S3. Using custom domains with S3 requires that the domain name (including the WWW sub-domain) is the same as that of the bucket name. We can have a bucket for a naked domain (for example, `qnatime.com`), and another bucket for its WWW sub-domain (for example, `www.qnatime.com`); the WWW sub-domain forwards the request to the naked domain.

Getting ready

You should have a public domain with a `HostedZone` configured in Route 53. Please refer to the recipes *Registering a domain name with Route 53* and *Using domains registered with other registrars*.

Also, we will not discuss the details related to the creation of an S3 static website, which was already discussed in the recipe *Setting up an S3 static website*. You can refer to that recipe, or refer to the code files for this recipe.

How to do it...

We will create one S3 static website bucket for the primary domain (`qnatime.com`) and another S3 static website bucket for the WWW sub-domain (`www.qnatime.com`). The WWW sub-domain bucket will simply redirect to the primary domain.

AWS CLI commands

I will be creating the bucket in the `ap-south-1 region`; you may choose any region of your choice:

See also

- You may read more about the `create-hosted-zone` CLI command at https://docs.aws.amazon.com/cli/latest/reference/route53/create-hosted-zone.html

1. Create a bucket, `qnatime.com`, for the primary domain.
2. Create an index document, `index.html`, and an error document, `error.html`, for the S3 website.
3. Upload the index and error documents.
4. Create a website configuration JSON file, specifying the index and error filenames.
5. Create a static website, specifying the website configuration JSON file.
6. Create a bucket policy, with read permission for everyone, for the bucket `qnatime.com`.
7. Create an S3 bucket with the name `www.qnatime.com`.
8. Configure the bucket as a website by using the `aws s3aoi put-bucket-website` command, with a configuration JSON file for redirection, as follows:

    ```
    {
      "RedirectAllRequestsTo": {
        "HostName": "qnatime.com",
        "Protocol": "http"
      }
    }
    ```

9. Create the `change-resource-record-sets` JSON file for creating alias records for the naked domain (`qnatime.com`) and the WWW sub-domain (`www.qnatime.com`).

    The changes for the naked domain are as follows:

    ```
    {
      "Comment": "change batch request for qnatime",
      "Changes": [
        {
          "Action": "CREATE",
          "ResourceRecordSet": {
            "Name": "qnatime.com",
            "Type": "A",
            "AliasTarget": {
              "HostedZoneId": "Z11RGJOFQNVJUP",
              "DNSName": "s3-website.ap-south-1.amazonaws.com",
              "EvaluateTargetHealth": false
            }
          }
        },
        ...
    ```

The DNS name and the hosted zone ID are available at `https://docs.aws.amazon.com/general/latest/gr/rande.html`.

The second part (to be added instead of the ... in the preceding snippet) is similar to the first, but with the name as `www.qnatime.com`.

This should return the following response:

```
{
    "ChangeInfo": {
        "Id": "/change/C1KSXLKZ4DWPPW",
        "Status": "PENDING",
        "SubmittedAt": "2018-11-29T22:18:29.160Z",
        "Comment": "change batch request for qnatime"
    }
}
```

10. You can check the status by using the `aws route53 get-change` command:

    ```
    aws route53 get-change \
        --id /change/C1KSXLKZ4DWPPW \
        --profile admin
    ```

    If it is successful, this should provide the following response:

    ```
    {
        "ChangeInfo": {
            "Id": "/change/C1KSXLKZ4DWPPW",
            "Status": "INSYNC",
            "SubmittedAt": "2018-11-29T22:18:29.160Z",
            "Comment": "change batch request for qnatime"
        }
    }
    ```

    You can also use the AWS Management Console to verify that two new alias records were created in the `HostedZone` for this domain.

11. Go to the domain names from the browser.

You should get a response from our bucket, as follows:

Welcome to Q & A Time!

Executing the sub-domain `www.qnatime.com` should redirect you to the naked domain (`qnatime.com`), and the final response should look the same as in the previous step.

The CloudFormation template

I will use a domain name, `quizzer.cloud`, to demonstrate how to use custom domains for S3 static websites with CloudFormation template:

1. Start the template with the template version and a description (optional).
2. Define two parameters for accepting the root domain name and the sub-domain name, as follows:

   ```
   Parameters:
     RootDomainName:
       Description: Domain name for your website (quizzer.cloud)
       Type: String
     SubDomainName:
       Description: Sub Domain name for your website
   (www.quizzer.cloud)
       Type: String
   ```

3. Define the root bucket resource, as follows:

   ```
   Resources:
     RootBucket:
       Type: AWS::S3::Bucket
       Properties:
         BucketName: !Ref RootDomainName
         AccessControl: PublicRead
         WebsiteConfiguration:
           IndexDocument: index.html
           ErrorDocument: error.html
   ```

4. Define a bucket access policy that allows everyone to access the bucket's contents, as follows:

```
WebsitePublicAccessPolicy:
  Type: AWS::S3::BucketPolicy
  Properties:
    Bucket: !Ref RootBucket
    PolicyDocument:
      Statement:
        -
          Action:
            - "s3:GetObject"
          Effect: "Allow"
          Resource:
            Fn::Join:
              - ""
              -
                - "arn:aws:s3:::"
                - !Ref RootBucket
                - "/*"
          Principal: "*"
```

5. Create the redirect bucket, as follows:

```
WWWBucket:
  Type: AWS::S3::Bucket
  Properties:
    BucketName: !Ref SubDomainName
    AccessControl: BucketOwnerFullControl
    WebsiteConfiguration:
      RedirectAllRequestsTo:
        HostName: !Ref RootDomainName
```

6. Create two A records within the HostedZone, for the root domain and the sub-domain, as follows:

```
myDNS:
  Type: AWS::Route53::RecordSetGroup
  Properties:
    HostedZoneName: !Sub
      - ${DomainName}.
      - DomainName: !Ref RootDomainName
    Comment: Zone apex alias.
    RecordSets:
      -
        Name: !Ref RootDomainName
        Type: A
        AliasTarget:
```

```
              HostedZoneId: 'Z11RGJOFQNVJUP'
              DNSName: 's3-website.ap-south-1.amazonaws.com'

          Name: !Ref SubDomainName
          Type: A
          AliasTarget:
              HostedZoneId: 'Z11RGJOFQNVJUP'
              DNSName: 's3-website.ap-south-1.amazonaws.com'
```

You can also use a `CNAME` record for sub-domains.

7. Add an `Outputs` section to return the URLs of the root domain and the sub-domain (this is optional):

```
Outputs:
  RootDomainURL:
    Value: !Sub
      - http://${DomainName}
      - DomainName: !Ref RootDomainName
    Description: URL for root domain
  SubDomainURL:
    Value: !Sub
      - http://${DomainName}
      - DomainName: !Ref SubDomainName
    Description: URL for redirect (sub) domain
```

8. Execute the preceding template by passing the parameters, as follows:

```
aws cloudformation create-stack \
    --stack-name mys3websitestack \
    --template-body file://resources/s3-static-website-cf-template.yml \
    --parameters ParameterKey=RootDomainName,ParameterValue=quizzer.cloud ParameterKey=SubDomainName,ParameterValue=www.quizzer.cloud \
    --region ap-south-1 \
    --profile admin
```

You can check the status of the CloudFormation stack creation by using the `describe-stacks` command.

9. Once the stack creation has completed, you will need to upload the `index.html` and `error.html` files into the root bucket.

Finally, execute the root domain and the WWW sub-domain in a browser.

You should see the same response from the root bucket in both cases, as follows:

> **Welcome to Q & A Time!**

How it works...

To summarize, we did the following in this recipe:

1. We created an S3 bucket as a static website (for example, `qnatime.com`)
2. We created another S3 bucket, with a WWW prefix, as a static website (for example, `www.qnatime.com`)
3. We added the files `index.html` and `error.html`
4. We added a bucket policy that allows for everyone to read the bucket
5. We created alias records for the primary domain and the WWW sub-domain, pointing to the S3 buckets (with and without a WWW prefix, respectively)

The S3 bucket names for static websites have to match the domain names exactly. For example, `qnatime.com` should point to a bucket named `qnatime.com`, and `www.qnatime.com` should point to a bucket named `www.qnatime.com`. Therefore, if someone has taken that bucket name, then you will not be able to use a custom domain to point to an S3 bucket. You can, however, overcome this limitation with the help of CloudFront, as you will see in a later recipe.

There's more...

S3 website endpoints do not currently support HTTPS. We can, however, work around this by using the CloudFront **Content Delivery Network** (**CDN**) over our website configuration, and then adding SSL support by utilizing **Amazon Certificate Manager** (**ACM**). We will look at this in a later recipe.

See also

You may read about `change-resource-record-sets` CLI command and its supported actions at https://docs.aws.amazon.com/cli/latest/reference/route53/change-resource-record-sets.html.

Using custom domain names with CloudFront

In this recipe, we will add a custom domain name to a CloudFront distribution. Without CloudFront, S3 bucket names have to be the same as the domain names. To demonstrate this, we will use a domain name, `qname.net`, to point to the CloudFront domain that is represented by the bucket `qname.com`.

Getting ready

You will need an S3 bucket configured as a website. You can follow the recipe *Setting up an S3 static website* to set up an S3 bucket as a static website.

How to do it...

I will create a CloudFront distribution for the S3 bucket `qnatime.com`, specifying the domain names that will be pointed against it as `Aliases`. After that, I will add the `A` records for these domain names to the domain's `HostedZone`.

AWS CLI commands

1. Create a CloudFront distribution `config` JSON file. Specify a caller reference to uniquely reference our request, as follows:

    ```
    {
      "CallerReference": "qnatime-distribution-2019-01-12-07-45",
    ```

Web Hosting with S3, Route53, and CloudFront

Specify the domains that will point to this CloudFront domain, as follows:

```
"Aliases": {
  "Quantity": 2,
  "Items": ["qnatime.net", "www.qnatime.net"]
},
```

You can only add a CNAME or alias to your domain record for CloudFront domain if it is added as Aliases for that CloudFront domain.

Specify the default root object and the origin details, as follows:

```
"DefaultRootObject": "index.html",
"Origins": {
  "Quantity": 1,
  "Items": [
    {
      "Id": "my-origin",
      "DomainName": "qnatime.com.s3.amazonaws.com",
      "S3OriginConfig": {
        "OriginAccessIdentity": ""
      }
    }
  ]
},
```

You can have multiple CloudFront distributions pointing to the same bucket.

Specify the other mandatory parameters, DefaultCacheBehaviour, Comment, and Enabled, as follows:

```
"DefaultCacheBehavior": {
    "TargetOriginId": "my-origin",
    "ForwardedValues": {
      "QueryString": true,
      "Cookies": {
        "Forward": "none"
      }
    },
    "TrustedSigners": {
      "Enabled": false,
      "Quantity": 0
    },
    "ViewerProtocolPolicy": "allow-all",
    "MinTTL": 3600
  },
  "Comment": "",
  "Enabled": true
```

    }

2. Create the distribution with the preceding `config` JSON file, as follows:

   ```
   aws cloudfront create-distribution \
       --distribution-config file://resources/distribution-config.json \
       --profile admin
   ```

   This will return immediately with a response, including the `Etag`, `Id`, and other defaults, as follows:

   ```
   {
   "Location": "https://cloudfront.amazonaws.com/2018-06-18/distribution/E18OUP1REXZHGA",
   "ETag": "EV3RMCDP8DYAA",
   "Distribution": {
       "Id": "E18OUP1REXZHGA",
       "ARN": "arn:aws:cloudfront::          :distribution/E18OUP1REXZHGA",
       "Status": "InProgress",
       "LastModifiedTime": "2018-12-01T02:39:52.072Z",
       "InProgressInvalidationBatches": 0,
       "DomainName": "d1obzjrl8ac1no.cloudfront.net",
       "ActiveTrustedSigners": {
           "Enabled": false,
           "Quantity": 0
       },
   ```

   The complete response has not been shown.

   It might take some time for the status to get changed to `Deployed`. You can check the status by using the `aws cloud-formation get-distribution` command. Once the status turns to `Deployed`, you can run the CloudFront domain from a browser, and check whether you can see the results from the `qnatime.com` bucket.

3. To create DNS A records for a domain, record we need to first create a change resource record sets JSON file as below and then execute it. First, create a change record set for the naked domain (`qnatime.net`):

   ```
   {
     "Comment": "change batch request for qnatime.net",
     "Changes": [
       {
         "Action": "CREATE",
         "ResourceRecordSet": {
   ```

```
            "Name": "qnatime.net",
            "Type": "A",
            "AliasTarget": {
              "HostedZoneId": "Z2FDTNDATAQYW2",
              "DNSName": "d1obzjrl8ac1no.cloudfront.net",
              "EvaluateTargetHealth": false
            }
          }
        },
```

`DNSName` is the domain name of your CloudFront distribution. You have to specify the hosted zone name for the domain. This is the domain name, followed by a dot. For CloudFront distribution domains, we use a constant hosted zone ID: `Z2FDTNDATAQYW2`.

Similarly, add a change record for the WWW sub-domain. You can also create a `CNAME` record for the sub-domain.

4. Execute the `change-resource-record-sets` sub-command with the preceding JSON file, in order to create the DNS A records:

   ```
   aws route53 change-resource-record-sets \
       --hosted-zone-id Z3G50MON7IDA18 \
       --change-batch file://resources/change-resource-record-sets.json \
       --profile admin
   ```

   Here, `hosted-zone-id` is the ID of the `HostedZone` for `qnatime.net`. This command will immediately return a response, with the status as `PENDING`:

   ```
   {
       "ChangeInfo": {
           "Id": "/change/C1P0E2LUACKQ6W",
           "Status": "PENDING",
           "SubmittedAt": "2018-12-01T03:07:56.716Z",
           "Comment": "change batch request for qnatime"
       }
   }
   ```

   You can check the status by using the `aws route53 get-change` command, until it changes to `INSYNC`:

Chapter 5

```
{
    "ChangeInfo": {
        "Id": "/change/C1P0E2LUACKQ6W",
        "Status": "INSYNC",
        "SubmittedAt": "2018-12-01T03:07:56.716Z",
        "Comment": "change batch request for qnatime"
    }
}
```

5. Execute `qnatime.net` to obtain the following:

> ← → C ⓘ Not Secure | qnatime.net
>
> # Welcome to Q & A Time!

Executing `www.qnatime.net` will produce the following result:

> ← → C ⓘ Not Secure | www.qnatime.net
>
> # Welcome to Q & A Time!

As we can see, we no longer have the restriction of using the same S3 bucket name and domain name. Note that we are not using the WWW redirect bucket (`www.qnatime.com`). Here, `www.qname.net` is also pointing to the same CloudFront domain, and there is no redirection from the bucket to the naked domain bucket behind the scenes.

> ⓘ If there is a **Not Secure** message in the browser, this is because we are using an HTTP request, and there are no valid certificates for our domain.

The CloudFormation template

We will create two CloudFormation stacks in this recipe. The first stack that we will create is the CloudFront distribution, with the aliases defined. The second stack will add the A records to our DNS configuration.

Web Hosting with S3, Route53, and CloudFront

The CloudFront distribution stack

Prepare a CloudFormation template using the following components:

1. Start the template with the template version and a description (optional).
2. We will define a `Parameters` section, to accept a comma-separated list of domain name aliases:

   ```
   Parameters:
     DomainNameAliases:
       Description: Domain name aliases for your website (quizzercloud.com,www.quizzercloud.com)
       Type: CommaDelimitedList
   ```

3. In the `Resources` section, we will define our CloudFront distribution:

   ```
   Resources:
     MyCloudFrontDistribution:
       Type: AWS::CloudFront::Distribution
       Properties:
         DistributionConfig:
           Origins:
           - DomainName: quizzer.cloud.s3.amazonaws.com
             Id: myS3Origin
             S3OriginConfig:
               OriginAccessIdentity: ''
           Enabled: 'true'
           Comment: 'CloudFront Distribution with Domain'
           DefaultRootObject: index.html
           Aliases: !Ref DomainNameAliases
           DefaultCacheBehavior:
             TargetOriginId: myS3Origin
             ForwardedValues:
               QueryString: 'false'
               Cookies:
                 Forward: none
             ViewerProtocolPolicy: allow-all
   ```

   Note that we can reference the parameter `DomainNameAliases` as a list.

4. We will also create an `Outputs` section, to return the CloudFront distribution ID and the domain name. We will also export the domain name and then import it later, into our `RecordSet` stack:

   ```
   Outputs:
     CloudFrontDistributionId:
       Value: !Ref MyCloudFrontDistribution
   ```

[244]

```
              Description: 'CloudFront distribution id'
            CloudFrontDomain:
              Value: !GetAtt MyCloudFrontDistribution.DomainName
              Description: 'CloudFront distribution domain name'
              Export:
                Name: CloudFrontDomainName
```

5. Create the stack. We will first create a JSON file to pass the parameter string, since passing a list through the CLI may require additional workarounds in a number of command prompts:

```
[
  {
    "ParameterKey": "DomainNameAliases",
    "ParameterValue": "quizzercloud.com,www.quizzercloud.com"
  }
]
```

Execute the stack, specifying the preceding parameters in JSON:

```
aws cloudformation create-stack \
    --stack-name mycloudfrontstackwithdomain \
    --template-body file://resources/create-cloud-front-distribution-with-domain.yml \
    --parameters file://resources/create-cloud-front-parameters.json \
    --region ap-south-1 \
    --profile admin
```

After executing the `create-stack` command, check the status by using the `describe-stacks` sub-command. Once it has completed successfully, it should return a response with the following `Outputs` section:

```
"Outputs": [
    {
        "OutputKey": "CloudFrontDistributionId",
        "OutputValue": "E36QJKF4NA03WG",
        "Description": "CloudFront distribution id"
    },
    {
        "OutputKey": "CloudFrontDomain",
        "OutputValue": "d14b6h6ajgyzgz.cloudfront.net",
        "Description": "CloudFront distribution domain name",
        "ExportName": "CloudFrontDomainName"
    }
],
```

Note that the complete `describe-stacks` output is not shown here, but only the `Outputs` section.

The RecordSet stack

We can create a template for `RecordSet`, given as follows:

1. Start the template with the template version and a description (optional).
2. Define the parameters (of the string type) for the root domain name, the sub-domain name, and the S3 hosted zone ID.

   Note that the S3 hosted zone is static, based on the region (for example, `Z2FDTNDATAQYW2` for `ap-south-1`).

3. Define a resource of the type `RecordSetGroup` type to add A records for the domains:

   ```
   Resources:
     QuizzerCloudDNS:
       Type: AWS::Route53::RecordSetGroup
       Properties:
         HostedZoneName: !Sub
           - ${DomainName}.
           - DomainName: !Ref RootDomainName
         Comment: Zone apex alias.
         RecordSets:
         -
           Name: !Ref RootDomainName
           Type: A
           AliasTarget:
             HostedZoneId: !Ref RecordHostedZoneId
             DNSName: !ImportValue CloudFrontDomainName
         -
           Name: !Ref SubDomainName
           Type: A
           AliasTarget:
             HostedZoneId: !Ref RecordHostedZoneId
             DNSName: !ImportValue CloudFrontDomainName
   ```

   The `HostedZoneName` is the domain name, followed by a dot (.), and the `RecordHostedZone` ID is a constant value for all of the CloudFront distributions

4. Define an `Outputs` section to return the URLs (optional).
5. Execute the `aws cloudformation create-stack` by passing the parameters, and then verify the following:

   After executing the `create-stack` sub-command, check the status by using the `describe-stacks` sub-command. Once it is successful, it should return a response with the following `Outputs` section:

   ```
   "Outputs": [
       {
           "OutputKey": "SubDomainURL",
           "OutputValue": "http://www.quizzercloud.com",
           "Description": "URL for redirect (sub) domain"
       },
       {
           "OutputKey": "RootDomainURL",
           "OutputValue": "http://quizzercloud.com",
           "Description": "URL for root domain"
       }
   ],
   ```

   We can verify that everything worked by going to `quizzercloud.com` and `www.quizzercloud.com` in a browser, as shown in the following screenshot:

   ← → C ⓘ Not Secure | quizzercloud.com

   Welcome to Q & A Time!

   Note that the URL is not secure. Even if we use HTTPS, we will still get a **Not Secure** message, as we do not have a valid certificate for this domain. We will look at how to fix this in the next recipe.

Web Hosting with S3, Route53, and CloudFront

How it works...

To summarize, we did the following in this recipe:

1. We created a CloudFront distribution, specifying the root domain and the WWW sub-domain
2. We created A records for the root domain and the WWW sub-domain
3. We then hit the root domain and the WWW sub-domain from a browser, and received a response from the file uploaded into the S3 bucket

To customize the input for creating a CloudFront distribution with the CLI, we have to first create a CloudFront distribution config JSON file, and then execute it. If there is no customization, we do not have to specify this JSON file, but we can only provide the original domain, as we saw in the previous recipe. With a CloudFormation template, we always have to specify the essential distribution config parameters in the template.

There's more...

We have only seen a limited customization of the properties for the distributed `config`. Explore more on your own to familiarize yourselves with all the options.

Using HTTPS to secure your domain URL

When building real-world web applications, we should always try to use HTTPS, instead of HTTP. If we try to execute `https://qnatime.net`, we will get the following response:

Whereas, executing `https://www.qnatime.net` will give us the following:

This is because we do not have a valid certificate, which can be verified by clicking on the **Not Secure** message:

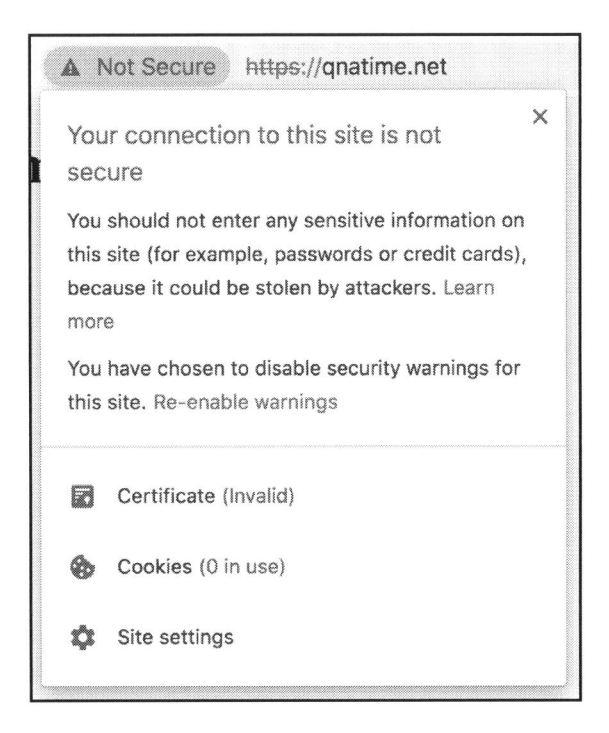

We will look at how to create and import a valid certificate to fix this error in the next recipe.

Disabling and deleting a CloudFront distribution

To delete a CloudFront distribution, we need to disable it first. To disable it, we need to use `update-distribution`, specifying a `distribution-config` JSON file with all of the existing properties, with the following change:

```
"Enabled": false,
```

For the initial JSON file for the update, we can copy and paste the value of `DistributionConfig` from the `get-distribution` sub-command response. Note that some properties, such as calling the reference or origin, cannot be updated.

Execute the `update-distribution` sub-command to disable the distribution.

```
aws cloudfront update-distribution \
    --id E18OUP1REXZHGA \
    --if-match EV3RMCDP8DYAA \
    --distribution-config file://resources/distr-config-disable.json \
    --profile admin
```

Here, the value for `id` is the ID of the distribution, and the value for `if-match` is the value of the `Etag` from the previous request. It will take some time to process the update request. We can check the status by using the `get-description` sub-command, until it changes from `InProgress` to `Deployed`. After that, we can delete the distribution:

```
aws cloudfront delete-distribution \
    --id E18OUP1REXZHGA \
    --if-match E2CDLHTOPGMT5J \
    --profile admin
```

Here, the value for `if-match` is the value of the `Etag` from the previous update request. For updates and deletes, we will also need to pass the `Etag` that we received in the previous step.

See also

- You may read more about Amazon Route 53 AliasTarget CloudFormation property at https://docs.aws.amazon.com/AWSCloudFormation/latest/UserGuide/aws-properties-route53-aliastarget.html

Using HTTPS with a CloudFront domain

In the *Using custom domain names with CloudFront* recipe, when we ran the URL in a browser using HTTPS, it showed a **Not Secure** message. In this recipe, we will associate an SSL certificate with our CloudFormation distribution so that we can access the URL through HTTPS. We will also configure automatically the redirection of any calls with an `http` prefix to a corresponding URL with an `https` prefix.

Getting ready

We can refer to *Creating SSL certificates with ACM* recipe in `Chapter 9`, *Serverless Architecture Patterns and Practices,* to obtain an ACM SSL certificate. We can also refer to the previous recipes in this chapter for details on the steps related to S3, CloudFront, and Route 53 that were already discussed.

How to do it...

We will create a CloudFront distribution with the ARN to the SSL certificate issued by AWS.

Associating a certificate with a domain using AWS CLI commands

We will use an ACM SSL certificate to enable HTTPS. For creating a certificate, you can refer *Creating SSL/TLS certificate with ACM* recipe in `Chapter 9`, *Serverless Programming Practices and Patterns.*

1. Obtain the ACM SSL certificate ARN to use with the domain (`www.qnatime.net`).
2. Create or update the CloudFront distribution with a `config` JSON file, similar to the one that was created in the *Using custom domain names with CloudFront,* recipe with the `ViewerCertificate` property, defined as follows:

   ```
   "ViewerCertificate": {
     "ACMCertificateArn": "arn:aws:acm:us-east-1:<account_id>:certificate/42b3ba99-66e9-4e71-8c1c-4239c1e81c84",
     "SSLSupportMethod": "sni-only",
     "MinimumProtocolVersion": "TLSv1.1_2016",
     "Certificate": "arn:aws:acm:us-east-1:<account_id>:certificate/42b3ba99-66e9-4e71-8c1c-4239c1e81c84",
     "CertificateSource": "acm"
   },
   ```

   The complete JSON file is also present in the book's code repository folder for this recipe.

Web Hosting with S3, Route53, and CloudFront

The SSL support method of `sni-only` indicates that CloudFront only serves our content over HTTPS to clients that support **Server Name Identification (SNI)**.

3. If you are creating a new distribution, `create-change-resource-record-sets` and add alias records in the domain's `HostedZone` (`qnatime.net.`), pointing to the new CloudFront distribution domain.
4. Once the certificate is successfully applied to the CloudFront distribution, try to visit the domain name for our website with `https`, as follows:

> ← → C 🔒 https://www.qnatime.net
>
> # Welcome to Q & A Time!

We can no longer see the **Not Secure** error message. If we click on the `lock` button and then click on **certificate** in the popup, we will see the certificate details:

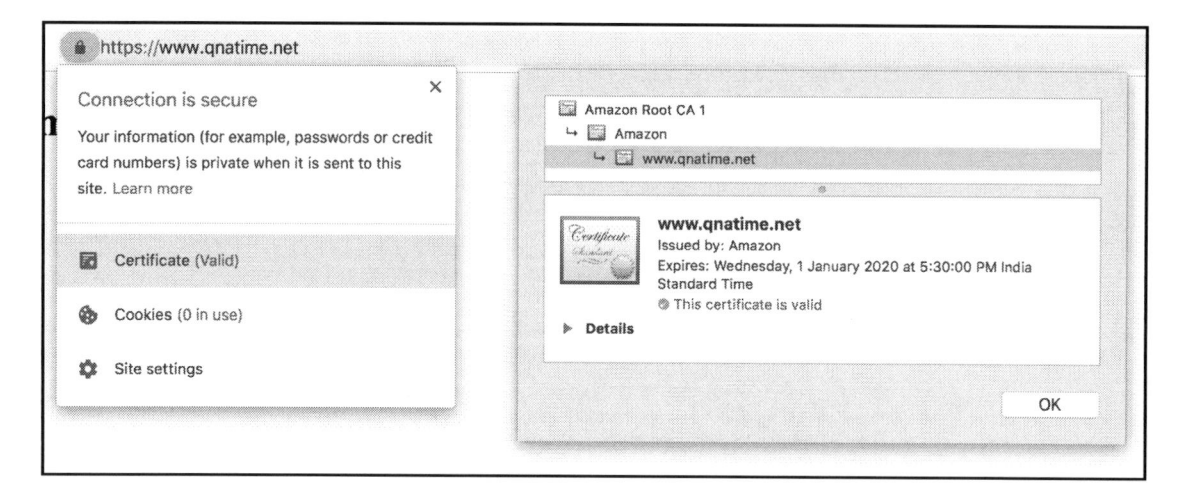

```
🔒 https://www.qnatime.net

Connection is secure                    ×
Your information (for example, passwords or credit
card numbers) is private when it is sent to this
site. Learn more

📄 Certificate (Valid)

🍪 Cookies (0 in use)

⚙ Site settings
```

```
Amazon Root CA 1
  └ Amazon
      └ www.qnatime.net

         www.qnatime.net
         Issued by: Amazon
         Expires: Wednesday, 1 January 2020 at 5:30:00 PM India
         Standard Time
         ⊘ This certificate is valid
  ▶ Details
                                                    OK
```

Note that we used a certificate generated with the WWW sub-domain; hence, even the naked domain request gets redirected to the one with a prefix.

Associating a certificate with a domain using CloudFormation template

We can either update our existing stack from the recipe *Using custom domain names with CloudFront*, if it is still available, or create a new stack. I will not be going over the template components that were already discussed in previous recipes, but the completed template will be available with the code files, for reference.

1. We can start the template with the template version and a description (optional).
2. Define a `Parameters` section to accept a comma-separated list of domain name aliases and the certificate ARN.
3. Under the `resources` property, define the `DistributionConfig` property with the requisite information.

   Define sub-properties under the `DistributionConfig` property for `Origins`, `Enabled`, `Comment`, `DefaultRootObject`, `Aliases`, `DefaultCacheBehaviour`, and `ViewerCertificate`:

   ```
   DistributionConfig:
     Origins:
     - DomainName: quizzer.cloud.s3.amazonaws.com
       Id: myS3Origin
       S3OriginConfig:
         OriginAccessIdentity: ''
     Enabled: 'true'
     Comment: 'CloudFront Distribution with Domain'
     DefaultRootObject: index.html
     Aliases: !Ref DomainNameAliases
     DefaultCacheBehavior:
       TargetOriginId: myS3Origin
       ForwardedValues:
         QueryString: 'false'
         Cookies:
           Forward: none
       ViewerProtocolPolicy: redirect-to-https
     ViewerCertificate:
       AcmCertificateArn: !Ref DomainNameCert
       SslSupportMethod: sni-only
   ```

   The `ViewerCertificate` property should have the sub-properties `AcmCertificateArn` and `SslSupportMethod`. I have also changed the `ViewerProtocolPolicy` to `redirect-to-https`. CloudFormation will now redirect any requests made with an HTTP URL to an HTTPS URL, with an HTTP status code of 301 (Moved Permanently).

Web Hosting with S3, Route53, and CloudFront

> We may also import an `AcmCertificateArn` from a CloudFormation template using its Outputs section, as shown in the *Creating SSL/TLS certificate with ACM* recipe in Chapter 9, *Serverless Programming Practices and Patterns*. However, note that we can only import output parameters from a template in the same region, and the certificates for the CloudFront distribution should be available in `us-east-1`.

4. Add an `Outputs` section that will return the distribution ID and the CloudFront distribution domain name. Export the CloudFront distribution domain name.
5. Create the CloudFront distribution by executing the `create-stack` CLI command, specifying the domains to be aliased as parameters.

   It might take some time for the changes to take effect. If the steps are followed as they were listed, the responded status would be `CREATE_COMPLETE`, and we would have an `Outputs` section similar to the following:

   ```
   "Outputs": [
       {
           "OutputKey": "CloudFrontDistributionId",
           "OutputValue": "E3CNIY0N2WR354",
           "Description": "CloudFront distribution id"
       },
       {
           "OutputKey": "CloudFrontDomain",
           "OutputValue": "d130e9lj3phwkc.cloudfront.net",
           "Description": "CloudFront distribution domain name",
           "ExportName": "CloudFrontDomainName"
       }
   ],
   ```

   Note that the complete response is not shown, just the relevant parts.

6. Create another CloudFormation stack for adding alias records to the `HostedZone` (`quizzercloud.com`).

   Refer to the *Using custom domains with CloudFront* recipe, but the `Outputs` section can now specify HTTPS URLs. The complete template is also available in the code files.

   If it is successful, the `aws cloudformation describe-stacks` command should return a response with a status of `CREATE_COMPLETE`, and an `Outputs` section with `https` URLs.

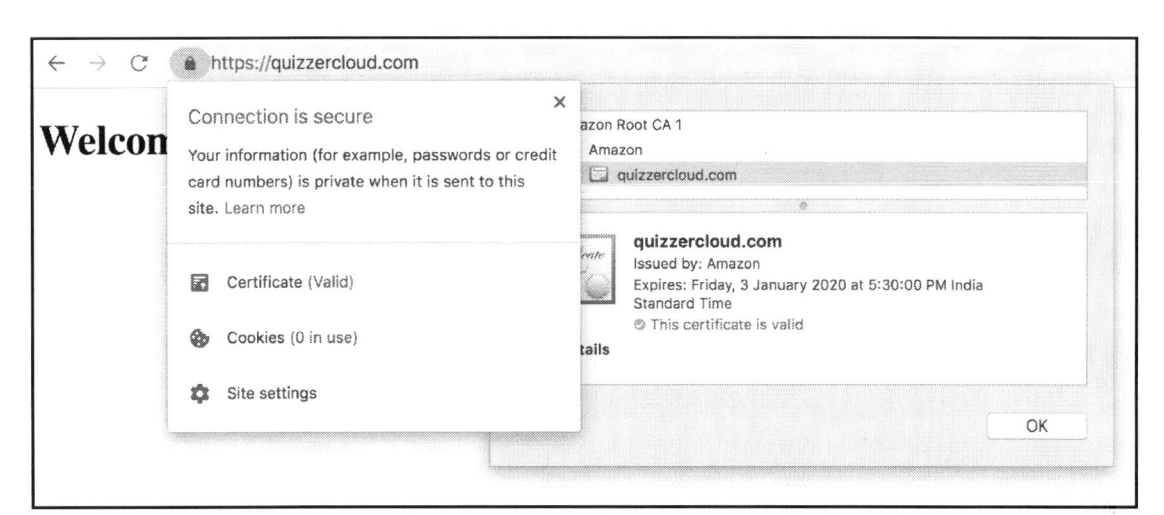

7. Finally, go to the domain name URL with the HTTPS prefix:

We generated the certificate without specifying the WWW prefix (the naked domain name); hence, even when we run the URL with a prefix, we will be redirected to the naked domain.

How it works...

To summarize, we did the following in this recipe:

1. We created a CloudFront distribution, specifying the root domain, the WWW sub-domain, and the ACM certificate ARN
2. We created `A` records for the root domain and the WWW sub-domain
3. We hit the root domain and the WWW sub-domain with an HTTPS prefix from a web browser, and received a response from the S3 bucket with a secure message in the browser

A CloudFront distribution supports SSL or TLS certificates in three ways: a default CloudFront certificate, an ACM certificate, and an IAM certificate. Previously, we used the default CloudFront certificate. In this recipe, we used an ACM SSL certificate, and that is the preferred way. An IAM certificate can only be used if a region does not support ACM. The steps to generate an IAM certificate are available in the *Creating SSL certificates with ACM* recipe, in `Chapter 9`, *Serverless Architecture Patterns and Practices*.

Server Name Identification (SNI)

SNI allows we to run multiple certificates on a single IP. An alternative approach is to use a dedicated IP address; CloudFront allocates dedicated IP addresses at each edge location in order to serve content over HTTPS. Any client can access our content with a dedicated IP; however, this option is costlier.

There's more...

So far, in all of the chapters of this book, we have discussed the essential services that are required for building a Serverless web application. A Serverless architecture can be used for non-web applications as well. A web application can also export data to another platform for analytics, perform activities such as machine learning on the data, and even add a **Natural Language Processing** (NLP) layer to it. In the next chapter, we will look at some additional services that extend the standard Serverless web application ecosystem.

For provisioning resources, we used CLI commands and CloudFormation templates. CloudFormation templates are always preferred, but CLI commands can help us to better understand the templates, and are helpful in quick prototyping. We looked at how to use Java Lambdas for writing Serverless functions in the backend. With service interactions, we used CLI commands that we could follow and implement in any supported language.

In `Chapter 9`, *Serverless Architecture Patterns and Practices*, we will use most of the services that we have discussed to build a standard web application with a JavaScript frontend.

See also

- To learn more about working with server certificates, you may refer to https://docs.aws.amazon.com/IAM/latest/UserGuide/id_credentials_server-certs.html

6
Messaging and Notifications with SQS and SNS

This chapter will cover the following topics:

- Your first SQS queue (AWS CLI + CloudFormation)
- Creating an SQS queue and sending messages with SDK (Java)
- Receiving and sending SQS messages in batches with SDK (Java)
- Invoking Lambda with SQS events (Java)
- Your first SNS topic for email and SMS (AWS CLI + CloudFormation)
- Publishing to SNS topic with SDK (Java)
- Invoking Lambda with SNS events (Java)

Introduction

In the previous chapters, we learned about various essential components for building a standard serverless web application such as functions, Rest API, datastore, user management, hosting, and domain registration. As discussed at the end of the previous chapter, a real-world application may not always be a web application, or may be extended with additional capabilities.

Until now, we were invoking Lambda from the API gateway. However, Lambdas may also be invoked reactively as a result of some triggers based on states of other services. In this chapter, we will first discuss adding messaging and notification support to serverless applications. Later, we will see how to trigger Lambdas based on state changes in various other services.

Messaging and Notifications with SQS and SNS

The following are the prerequisites for this chapter:

- A working AWS account
- Configuring AWS CLI as discussed in the *Your first Lambda with AWS CLI* recipe of Chapter 1, *Getting Started with Serverless Computing on AWS*

Your first SQS queue (AWS CLI + CloudFormation)

Amazon **Simple Queue Service (SQS)** is a fully managed messaging queue service in AWS that can be used with serverless as well as non-serverless microservices and distributed systems. In this recipe, we will create an SQS queue and use the queue to transfer data.

Getting ready

There are no additional prerequisites for completing this recipe, other than the common requirements specified in the chapter introduction.

How to do it...

We will first create the SQS queue and later test it using AWS CLI commands.

Creating an SQS queue

We will create an SQS queue first using CLI commands, and then using a CloudFormation template.

AWS CLI commands

You can create a simple SQS queue with defaults from AWS CLI as follows:

```
aws sqs create-queue \
  --queue-name 'my-first-queue' \
  --profile admin
```

If successful, this will give the output shown here:

```
{
    "QueueUrl": "https://queue.amazonaws.com/▇▇▇▇▇▇▇/my-first-queue"
}
```

The CloudFormation template

You can create a CloudFormation template file with the following `Resources` and `Output` sections to create a simple SQS queue with defaults:

```
Resources:
  SQSQueue:
    Type: AWS::SQS::Queue
    Properties:
      QueueName: my-first-sqs-queue-cf

Output:
  SQSQueueURL:
    Value: !Ref SQSQueue
    Export:
      Name: "SQSQueueURL"
  SQSQueueArn:
    Value: !GetAtt SQSQueue.Arn
    Export:
      Name: "SQSQueueArn"
```

You may also add a template version and description.

If stack creation (run using `aws cloudformation create-stack`) is successful, the `describe` command (run using `aws cloudformation describe-stacks`) will return a response with the `Output` section, as follows:

```
"Outputs": [
    {
        "OutputKey": "SQSQueueArn",
        "OutputValue": "arn:aws:sqs:us-east-1:▇▇▇▇▇▇▇:my-first-sqs-queue-cf",
        "ExportName": "SQSQueueArn"
    },
    {
        "OutputKey": "SQSQueueURL",
        "OutputValue": "https://sqs.us-east-1.amazonaws.com/▇▇▇▇▇▇▇/my-first-sqs-queue-cf",
        "ExportName": "SQSQueueURL"
    }
],
```

Sending and receiving data (AWS CLI)

1. We can send data to an AWS queue from the command line, as follows:

   ```
   aws sqs send-message \
       --queue-url https://queue.amazonaws.com/<account id>/my-first-queue \
       --message-body 'This is a test message' \
       --profile admin
   ```

   This command will return a response, as follows:

   ```
   {
       "MD5OfMessageBody": "fafb00f5732ab283681e124bf8747ed1",
       "MessageId": "dfc614e8-d5fb-4c00-98af-7c151483952d"
   }
   ```

2. We can get data from an AWS queue from the command line, as follows:

   ```
   aws sqs receive-message \
       --queue-url https://queue.amazonaws.com/<account id>/my-first-queue \
       --profile admin
   ```

   This command will return a response, as follows:

   ```
   {
       "Messages": [
           {
               "MessageId": "dfc614e8-d5fb-4c00-98af-7c151483952d",
               "ReceiptHandle": "AQEBqyEURarwr6VEp8POBaOfQZszTeR55Sf/c4C5NXuxF8i5HhebajL7HfIIL/O9QLD8jeqgwkjO/Uyy9PRoPtJJcA6i53fpxDkBnnzwVmuc+WV/Ytm9ilvCSEMzTcIgJ9gk24wPLFePdGHQ4IqkLoH+fQ==",
               "MD5OfBody": "fafb00f5732ab283681e124bf8747ed1",
               "Body": "This is a test message"
           }
       ]
   }
   ```

How it works...

In summary, we did the following in this recipe:

1. We created a queue using an AWS CLI command
2. We created a queue using a CloudFormation template
3. We sent a message to the queue from the AWS CLI
4. We retrieved a message from the queue from the AWS CLI

Both `send` and `receive` message commands returned the following properties:

- `Message id`: Message ID of the message
- `MD5ofBody`: This is the MD5 digest that can be used to verify when SQS received the message correctly

The `receive` message command also returned the following properties:

- `Body`: Body of the message.
- `MD5ofBody`: MD5 digest of the body.
- `ReceiptHandle`: There is a `ReceiptHandle` value associated with each instance of receiving a message. Every time you receive a message, the `ReceiptHandle` value will be different. To delete a message from the queue, you need to provide the latest `ReceiptHandle` value received.

There's more...

In this recipe, we created a simple queue with defaults. It has the following properties:

- `ContentBasedDeduplication`: Boolean
- `DelaySeconds`: Integer
- `FifoQueue`: Boolean
- `KmsMasterKeyId`: String
- `KmsDataKeyReusePeriodSeconds`: Integer
- `MaximumMessageSize`: Integer
- `MessageRetentionPeriod`: Integer
- `QueueName`: String
- `ReceiveMessageWaitTimeSeconds`: Integer

- `RedrivePolicy`: `RedrivePolicy` **object**
- `Tags`: **Resource tag**
- `VisibilityTimeout`: **Integer**

See also

- `https://docs.aws.amazon.com/cli/latest/reference/sqs/index.html#cli-aws-sqs`
- `https://docs.aws.amazon.com/AWSCloudFormation/latest/UserGuide/aws-properties-sqs-queues.html`
- `http://www.faqs.org/rfcs/rfc1321.html`

Creating an SQS queue and sending messages with SDK (Java)

In this recipe, we will create Lambda function in Java to create an SQS queue, get the URL of the queue using the queue name, and then send a message to that queue. We will not repeat the commands or steps required to create and invoke the Lambda that was already discussed earlier. Please refer to code files or earlier Lambda recipes for the complete code.

Getting ready

You need to follow the section *Getting started* in the recipes *Your first AWS Lambda* and *Your first Lambda with AWS CLI* from Chapter 1, *Getting Started with Serverless Computing on AWS* to set up Java, Maven, the parent project, `serverless-cookbook-parent-aws-java` and AWS CLI, and may also read other notes there including code usage guidelines, S3 bucket creation and notes for the Windows users.

How to do it...

We will first create our Java Lambda and then deploy and test it from the CLI.

Lambda project code (Java)

We will create a Lambda that gets triggered when messages are put into an SQS queue, and it will then send the message to another as a batch.

> Since we have already discussed Lambdas in detail earlier, I will show only important parts of the code and step details here. I will also not show error handling and other supportive code. Please refer to the code files for the complete code.

The Maven `pom.xml` file of the project should define the following dependency:

```
<dependency>
    <groupId>com.amazonaws</groupId>
    <artifactId>aws-java-sdk-sqs</artifactId>
    <version>${aws.sdk.version}</version>
</dependency>
```

The POM file also has dependencies for `aws-lambda-java-core`, and inherits from the parent project, `serverless-cookbook-parent-aws-java`.

We can create the Java Lambda project with the following structure:

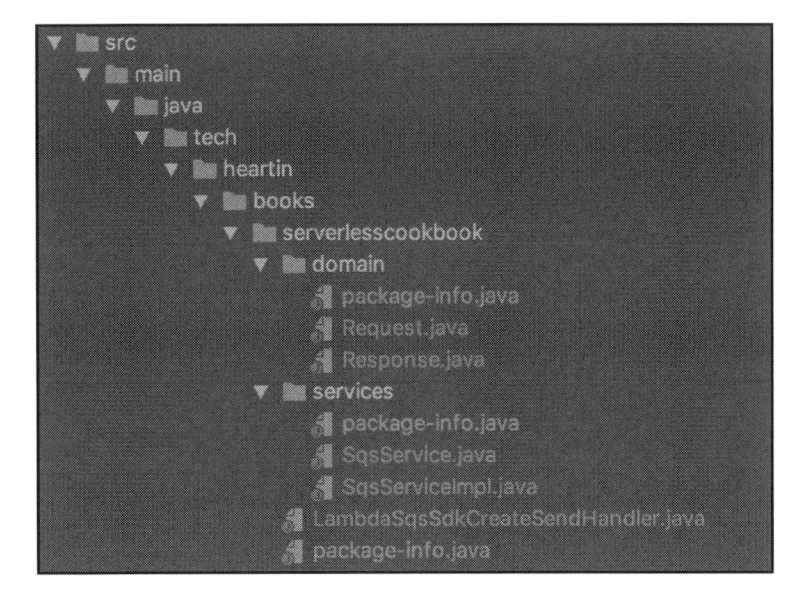

```
▼ src
  ▼ main
    ▼ java
      ▼ tech
        ▼ heartin
          ▼ books
            ▼ serverlesscookbook
              ▼ domain
                  package-info.java
                  Request.java
                  Response.java
              ▼ services
                  package-info.java
                  SqsService.java
                  SqsServiceImpl.java
                  LambdaSqsSdkCreateSendHandler.java
                  package-info.java
```

[263]

The `Request.java` class will correspond to our input JSON:

```
@Data
public class Request {
    private String queueName;
    private String message;
}
```

`Response.java` will contain a field to send the response back to the invoker:

```
@Data
@AllArgsConstructor
public class Response {
    private String message;
}
```

`SqsService.java` is the interface for our `service` class. This is not a requirement. You can directly use the implementation class or even embed all logic within the Lambda handler class itself:

```
public interface SqsService {
    Response createQueueAndSendMessage(Request request, LambdaLogger logger);
}
```

`SqsServiceImpl.java` is the actual `service` implementation.

We can create an SQS queue and retrieve its URL, as follows:

```
CreateQueueResult createResult =
this.sqsClient.createQueue(request.getQueueName());
logger.log("Created queue: " + createResult.getQueueUrl());
```

We can also get the URL, as follows:

```
String queueUrl =
this.sqsClient.getQueueUrl(request.getQueueName()).getQueueUrl();
```

We can create a `SendMessageRequest` and send a message, as follows:

```
SendMessageRequest sendMessageRequest = new SendMessageRequest()
        .withQueueUrl(queueUrl)
        .withMessageBody(request.getMessage())
        .withDelaySeconds(5);
this.sqsClient.sendMessage(sendMessageRequest);
```

`LambdaSqsSdkCreateSendHandler.java` is our Lambda handler class where we initialize the SQS client and pass it to the `service` class.

We can initialize the SQS client as follows:

```
private final AmazonSQS sqsClient;
public LambdaSqsSdkCreateSendHandler() {
    this.sqsClient = AmazonSQSClientBuilder.standard()
            .withRegion(System.getenv("AWS_REGION"))
            .build();
}
```

We then invoke the `service` method, passing the client along with the `Request` object:

```
public Response handleRequest(final Request request, final Context context)
{
    final SqsService sqsService =  new SqsServiceImpl(this.sqsClient);
    return sqsService.createQueueAndSendMessage(request, context.getLogger());
}
```

Provisioning and testing the Lambda (AWS CLI)

Follow these steps to deploy and invoke the Lambda. You may follow Chapter 1, *Getting Started with Serverless Computing on AWS* and use CloudFormation for Lambda provisioning:

1. Run `mvn clean package` from inside the Lambda project root folder to create the Uber JAR.
2. Upload the Uber JAR to S3:

   ```
   aws s3 cp \
       target/lambda-sqs-sdk-create-send-0.0.1-SNAPSHOT.jar \
       s3://serverless-cookbook/lambda-sqs-sdk-create-send-0.0.1-SNAPSHOT.jar \
       --profile admin
   ```

3. Create a role for the Lambda with an appropriate trust relationship definition:

   ```
   aws iam create-role \
       --role-name lambda-sqs-create-send-role \
       --assume-role-policy-document file://iam-role-trust-relationship.txt \
       --profile admin
   ```

The trust document, `iam-role-trust-relationship.txt`, is defined as follows:

```
{
  "Version": "2012-10-17",
  "Statement": [
    {
      "Effect": "Allow",
      "Principal": {
        "Service": "lambda.amazonaws.com"
      },
      "Action": "sts:AssumeRole"
    }
  ]
}
```

4. Create a policy for basic logging permissions and attach it to the role.

Create the policy document as follows:

```
{
    "Version":"2012-10-17",
    "Statement":[
        {
            "Effect":"Allow",
            "Action":[
                "logs:CreateLogGroup",
                "logs:CreateLogStream",
                "logs:PutLogEvents"
            ],
            "Resource":[
                "arn:aws:logs:*:*:*"
            ]
        }
    ]
}
```

Save this file as `basic-lambda-permissions.txt`.

Create the policy as follows:

```
aws iam create-policy \
    --policy-name lambda-basic-iam-policy \
    --policy-document file://basic-lambda-permissions.txt \
    --profile admin
```

Attach the policy to the role as follows:

```
aws iam attach-role-policy \
  --role-name lambda-sqs-create-send-role \
  --policy-arn arn:aws:iam::855923912133:policy/lambda-basic-iam-policy \
  --profile admin
```

5. Create a policy for required SQS permissions, and attach it to the role.

Create the policy document with the required SQS permissions as follows:

```
{
    "Version":"2012-10-17",
    "Statement":[
        {
            "Effect":"Allow",
            "Action":[
                sqs:CreateQueue,
                sqs:GetQueueUrl,
                "sqs:SendMessage"
            ],
            "Resource":[
                "arn:aws:sqs:*:*:*"
            ]
        }
    ]
}
```

Save the file as `lambda-sqs-create-send-permissions.txt`.

Create the policy and attach it to the role, as we did in the previous step.

6. Create the Lambda function as follows:

```
aws lambda create-function \
    --function-name lambda-sqs-create-send \
    --runtime java8 \
    --role arn:aws:iam::<account id>:role/lambda-sqs-create-send-role \
    --handler tech.heartin.books.serverlesscookbook.LambdaSqsSdkCreateSendHandler::handleRequest \
    --code S3Bucket=serverless-cookbook,S3Key=lambda-sqs-sdk-create-send-0.0.1-SNAPSHOT.jar \
    --timeout 15 \
```

Messaging and Notifications with SQS and SNS

```
    --memory-size 512 \
    --region us-east-1 \
    --profile admin
```

7. Invoke the Lambda function as follows:

```
aws lambda invoke \
    --invocation-type RequestResponse \
    --function-name lambda-sqs-create-send \
    --log-type Tail \
    --payload file://payload.json \
    --region us-east-1 \
    --profile admin \
outputfile.txt
```

The payload file should correspond to our input domain object (`Request.java`) as follows:

```
{
    "queueName" : "create-send-demo-queue",
    "message": "test payload 1"
}
```

If the `aws lambda invoke` command is successful, you should see a success message in the output file, `outputfile.txt` (assuming you return a success message from the Lambda similar to the code files).

8. Verify the invocation by retrieving the message from the queue:

```
aws sqs receive-message \
    --queue-url
https://queue.amazonaws.com/855923912133/create-send-demo-queue
\
    --profile admin
```

If successful, you should get the following message back:

```
{
    "Messages": [
        {
            "MessageId": "a1c1bac6-7bfc-4088-8202-f1ee3693882e",
            "ReceiptHandle": "AQEBeLA5/hVvWrOGb9+uEZ1aRBpxhv/0oY
Su/CbAlqEKKowCcXjcIWcuDncvYoyArEorOHfS5tlotN6DfgF6lXLAupHC63VLoN
KcDmA73ltN0all/6H18CcyRULUchdnwlWmpr3rIb1rqwSCh8zWwf7Uzg==",
            "MD5OfBody": "0709068de6e40356e7ed36037817bacd",
            "Body": "test payload 1"
        }
    ]
}
```

How it works...

In summary, we did the following in this recipe:

1. Created a Lambda function to perform the following:
    - Create an SQS queue
    - Get the queue URL from the queue
    - Send the message to the queue
2. Created the required policies and attached them to the role
3. Invoked Lambda with a payload as required by the input handler object (`Request.java`)
4. Verified data was posted to the queue using the `aws sqs receive-message` command

There's more...

We created a simple SQS queue and sent the message from within a Lambda. You can work on adding more features to the create queue code. Properties available for an SQS queue were listed in the previous recipe. We sent only a single message in this recipe, but you can also send multiple SQS messages together, as we will see in the next recipe.

See also

- `https://docs.aws.amazon.com/AWSSimpleQueueService/latest/SQSDeveloperGuide/sqs-api-permissions-reference.html`

Receiving and sending SQS messages in batches with SDK (Java)

In this recipe, we will create a Lambda function in Java to receive messages from an existing input SQS queue and send all the messages as a batch to another SQS output queue. We will also delete the messages from the input SQS queue.

Getting ready

You need to follow the section *Getting started* in the recipes *Your first AWS Lambda* and *Your first Lambda with AWS CLI* from Chapter 1, *Getting Started with Serverless Computing on AWS* to set up Java, Maven, the parent project, `serverless-cookbook-parent-aws-java` and AWS CLI, and may also read other notes there including code usage guidelines, S3 bucket creation and notes for the Windows users.

How to do it...

We will first create our Java Lambda. Next, we will create two queues as required for this recipe and place some data into one of them. After that, we will deploy the Lambda and test it from CLI.

Lambda project code (Java)

> Since we have already discussed Lambdas in detail earlier, I will show only important parts of the code and step details here. I will also not show error handling and other supportive code. Please refer to the code files for the complete code.

We will create a Lambda that will receive messages from one queue, send it to another as a batch, and then delete the retrieved messages.

The Maven `pom.xml` file of the project should also define the following dependency:

```xml
<dependency>
    <groupId>com.amazonaws</groupId>
    <artifactId>aws-java-sdk-sqs</artifactId>
    <version>${aws.sdk.version}</version>
</dependency>
```

We can create the Java Lambda project with the following structure:

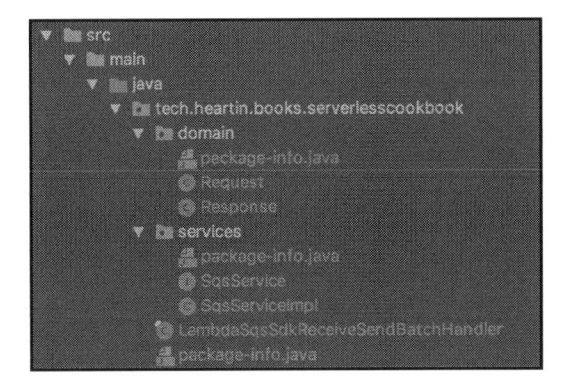

The `Request.java` class will correspond to our input JSON:

```
@Data
public class Request {
    private String inputQueueURL;
    private String outputQueueURL;
    private int maxMessagesToReceive;
    private int delay;
}
```

Here, `inputQueueURL` is the URL for the input queue from which the Lambda will receive messages, `outputQueueURL` is the URL for the output queue to which the Lambda will send messages, `maxMessagesToReceive` is the maximum number of messages retrieved from the queue in every receive call, and `delay` is the time for which delivery of messages to the queue is postponed.

`Response.java` will contain a field to send the response back to the invoker:

```
@Data
@AllArgsConstructor
public class Response {
    private String message;
}
```

`SqsService.java` is the interface for our service class. This is not a requirement; you can directly use the implementation class or even embed all logic within the Lambda handler class itself:

```
public interface SqsService {
    Response sendMessage(Request request, LambdaLogger logger);
}
```

`SqsServiceImpl.java` is the actual service implementation.

We can retrieve messages from the input queue as follows:

```
final ReceiveMessageRequest receiveMessageRequest = new ReceiveMessageRequest()
        .withQueueUrl(request.getInputQueueURL())
        .withMaxNumberOfMessages(request.getMaxMessagesToReceive());

final List<Message> messages =
this.sqsClient.receiveMessage(receiveMessageRequest).getMessages();
```

We can create and send a batch request to the output queue, as follows:

```
Collection<SendMessageBatchRequestEntry> entries = new ArrayList<>();

int idVal = 1;
for (Message m : messages) {
    logger.log("Adding message: " + m.getBody());
    entries.add(new SendMessageBatchRequestEntry("id_" + idVal,
            m.getBody()).withDelaySeconds(request.getDelay()));
    idVal++;
}

final SendMessageBatchRequest sendBatchRequest = new SendMessageBatchRequest()
        .withQueueUrl(request.getOutputQueueURL())
        .withEntries(entries);
this.sqsClient.sendMessageBatch(sendBatchRequest);
```

Finally, we delete all messages received, as follows:

```
for (Message m : messages) {
    this.sqsClient.deleteMessage(request.getInputQueueURL(),
m.getReceiptHandle());
}
```

`LambdaSqsSdkReceiveSendBatchHandler.java` is our Lambda handler class, where we initialize the SQS client and pass it to the service class.

We can initialize the SQS client as follows:

```
private final AmazonSQS sqsClient;
public LambdaSqsSdkReceiveSendBatchHandler() {
    this.sqsClient = AmazonSQSClientBuilder.standard()
            .withRegion(System.getenv("AWS_REGION"))
            .build();
}
```

We then invoke the `service` method, passing the client along with the `Request` object:

```
public Response handleRequest(final Request request, final Context context)
{
    final SqsService sqsService =  new SqsServiceImpl(this.sqsClient);
    return sqsService.sendMessage(request, context.getLogger());

}
```

Setting up queues and data

Before we can invoke our Lambda, we need to create an input and an output queue. We will also send messages to the input queue. When we invoke the Lambda, it will retrieve these messages.

Perform the following steps:

1. Create two SQS queues: an input queue, `my-input-queue`, and an output queue, `my-output-queue`, following the *Your first Simple Queue Service* (SQS) recipe.
2. Send six to seven messages to the queue from CLI.

Provisioning and testing the Lambda (AWS CLI)

Follow this steps to deploy and invoke the Lambda. You may follow Chapter 1, *Getting Started with Serverless Computing on AWS* and use CloudFormation for Lambda provisioning:

1. Run `mvn clean package` from inside the Lambda project root folder to create the Uber JAR.
2. Upload the Uber JAR to S3:

   ```
   aws s3 cp \
       target/lambda-sqs-sdk-receive-send-batch-0.0.1-SNAPSHOT.jar \
   ```

Messaging and Notifications with SQS and SNS

```
    s3://serverless-cookbook/lambda-sqs-sdk-receive-send-
batch-0.0.1-SNAPSHOT.jar \
    --profile admin
```

3. Create a role for the Lambda with an appropriate trust relationship definition:

```
aws iam create-role \
--role-name lambda-sqs-sdk-receive-send-batch-role \
--assume-role-policy-document file://iam-role-trust-
relationship.txt \
    --profile admin
```

The trust document, `iam-role-trust-relationship.txt`, is defined as follows:

```
{
  "Version": "2012-10-17",
  "Statement": [
    {
      "Effect": "Allow",
      "Principal": {
        "Service": "lambda.amazonaws.com"
      },
      "Action": "sts:AssumeRole"
    }
  ]
}
```

4. Create a policy for basic logging permissions and attach it to the role.
5. Create a policy for required SQS permissions and attach it to the role.

The policy document with required SQS permissions is shown as follows:

```
{
    "Version":"2012-10-17",
    "Statement":[
        {
            "Effect":"Allow",
            "Action":[
                "sqs:ReceiveMessage",
                "sqs:SendMessage",
                "sqs:SendMessageBatch",
                "sqs:DeleteQueue"
            ],
            "Resource":[
                "arn:aws:sqs:*:*:*"
            ]
```

                }
            ]
        }

6. Create the Lambda function, as follows:

   ```
   aws lambda create-function \
    --function-name lambda-sqs-sdk-receive-send-batch \
    --runtime java8 \
    --role arn:aws:iam::<account id>:role/lambda-sqs-sdk-receive-send-batch-role \
    --handler tech.heartin.books.serverlesscookbook.LambdaSqsSdkReceiveSendBatchHandler::handleRequest \
    --code S3Bucket=serverless-cookbook,S3Key=lambda-sqs-sdk-receive-send-batch-0.0.1-SNAPSHOT.jar \
    --timeout 15 \
    --memory-size 512 \
    --region us-east-1 \
    --profile admin
   ```

7. Invoke the Lambda function, as follows:

   ```
   aws lambda invoke \
       --invocation-type RequestResponse \
       --function-name lambda-sqs-sdk-receive-send-batch \
       --log-type Tail \
       --payload file://payload.json \
       --region us-east-1 \
       --profile admin \
       outputfile.txt
   ```

   The payload file should correspond to our input domain object (`Request.java`) as follows:

   ```
   {
       "inputQueueURL" : "https://queue.amazonaws.com/855923912133/my-input-queue",
       "outputQueueURL" : "https://queue.amazonaws.com/855923912133/my-output-queue",
       "maxMessagesToReceive" : 5,
       "delay": 10
   }
   ```

Messaging and Notifications with SQS and SNS

If the `aws lambda invoke` command is successful, you should see a success message in the output file, `outputfile.txt` (assuming you return a success message from the Lambda similar to the code files).

8. Verify the invocation by retrieving the message from the queue:

   ```
   aws sqs receive-message \
       --queue-url
   https://queue.amazonaws.com/855923912133/my-output-queue \
       --max-number-of-messages 7 \
       --profile admin
   ```

If successful, you should get between zero and seven (maximum) messages in a single `receive-message` call. Even if you have more messages than this value in the queue, the exact number of messages returned is not guaranteed, but the maximum returned will be as per the value of the `max-number-of-messages` property.

How it works...

In summary, we did the following in this recipe:

1. Created a Lambda function to perform the following:
   1. Retrieve multiple messages from an input queue
   2. Batch the messages and send it to an output queue
2. Created the input and output queues
3. Added data into the input queue
4. Created required policies and attached them to the role
5. Created the Lambda function specifying the role
6. Invoked the Lambda with a payload as required by the input handler object (`Request.java`)
7. Verified data was posted to the queue using the `aws sqs receive-message` command on the output queue

There's more...

We created a simple SQS queue, and messages were retrieved randomly. You can however configure the queue to act as a strict **first in, first out** (FIFO) queue using the Fifo queue property while creating the queue.

See also

- `https://docs.aws.amazon.com/AWSSimpleQueueService/latest/SQSDeveloperGuide/sqs-api-permissions-reference.html`
- `https://docs.aws.amazon.com/AWSJavaSDK/latest/javadoc/com/amazonaws/services/sqs/model/ReceiveMessageRequest.html#getMaxNumberOfMessages--`

Invoking the Lambda with an SQS event (Java)

Until now (in this recipe and recipes from previous chapters), we were invoking a Lambda either directly from the command line or from the API gateway. A Lambda can also be invoked (or triggered) as a response to an event (or trigger) from one of the supported event sources, such as SQS, Kinesis, DynamoDB, and so on.

In this recipe, we will invoke a Lambda with a trigger from an SQS event source. Similar to the previous recipe, we will then send all the messages as a batch to another SQS output queue. This way, we can easily verify the Lambda was triggered successfully from the other queue. You can also simply check the CloudWatch logs to verify this instead.

Getting ready

You need to follow the section *Getting started* in the recipes *Your first AWS Lambda* and *Your first Lambda with AWS CLI* from Chapter 1, *Getting Started with Serverless Computing on AWS* to set up Java, Maven, the parent project, `serverless-cookbook-parent-aws-java` and AWS CLI, and may also read other notes there including code usage guidelines, S3 bucket creation and notes for the Windows users.

How to do it...

We will first create our Java Lambda. Next, we will create two queues as required for this recipe and set up some data to one of them. After that, we will deploy the Lambda and test it from CLI.

Lambda project code (Java)

> Since we have already discussed Lambdas in detail earlier, I will show only important parts of the code and step details here. I will also not show error handling and other supportive code. Please refer to the code files for the complete code.

We will create a Lambda that gets triggered when messages are put into an SQS queue, and it will then send the message to another as a batch.

The Maven `pom.xml` file of the project should also define the following dependency:

```xml
<dependency>
    <groupId>com.amazonaws</groupId>
    <artifactId>aws-java-sdk-sqs</artifactId>
    <version>${aws.sdk.version}</version>
</dependency>
```

We can create a Java Lambda project with the following structure:

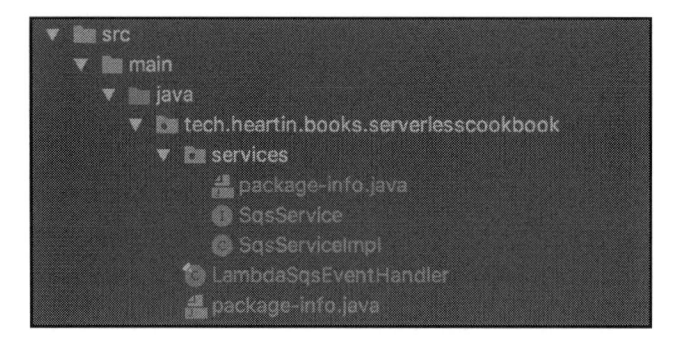

```
▼ src
    ▼ main
        ▼ java
            ▼ tech.heartin.books.serverlesscookbook
                ▼ services
                    package-info.java
                    SqsService
                    SqsServiceImpl
                LambdaSqsEventHandler
                package-info.java
```

Note that unlike previous recipes, we do not have request and response domain objects. While we were invoking the Lambda manually in previous recipes, in this recipe AWS will be invoking the Lambda and passing a predefined event object based on a trigger we configure.

`SqsService.java` is the interface for our service class. This is not a requirement; you can directly use the implementation class or even embed all logic within the Lambda handler class itself:

```
public interface SqsService {
    Boolean processEvent(SQSEvent event, String outputQueueURL,
LambdaLogger logger);
}
```

`SqsServiceImpl.java` is the actual service implementation.

We can retrieve messages from the input `SQSEvent` and create a collection of `SendMessageBatchRequestEntry` objects:

```
Collection<SendMessageBatchRequestEntry> entries = new ArrayList<>();

int idVal = 1;
for (SQSMessage m : event.getRecords()) {
    logger.log("Adding message: " + m.getBody());
    entries.add(new SendMessageBatchRequestEntry("id_" + idVal,
m.getBody()));
    idVal++;
}
```

We can create and send a batch request to the output queue, as follows:

```
final SendMessageBatchRequest sendBatchRequest = new
SendMessageBatchRequest()
        .withQueueUrl(request.getOutputQueueURL())
        .withEntries(entries);
this.sqsClient.sendMessageBatch(sendBatchRequest);
```

`LambdaSqsEventHandler.java` is our Lambda handler class, where we initialize the SQS client and pass it to the service class along with the `SQSEvent` we received.

We can initialize the SQS client as follows:

```
private final AmazonSQS sqsClient;
public LambdaSqsSdkReceiveSendBatchHandler() {
    this.sqsClient = AmazonSQSClientBuilder.standard()
            .withRegion(System.getenv("AWS_REGION"))
            .build();
}
```

We then invoke the `service` method, passing the client along with the `SQSEvent` object:

```
public Boolean handleRequest(final SQSEvent sqsEvent, final Context
context) {
```

```
            context.getLogger().log("Received SQS event: " + sqsEvent);

        final SqsService sqsService =  new SqsServiceImpl(this.sqsClient);
        return sqsService.processEvent(sqsEvent,
  System.getenv("SPC_OUTPUT_QUEUE_URL"), context.getLogger());

    }
```

We will use an environment variable to specify the name of the output queue. In the previous recipes, we were sending it through the request object. Also, it is a good practice to prefix environment variables with a project-specific constant. For example, SPC is a prefix that denote *Serverless Programming Cookbook*.

Setting up queues and data

Before we can invoke our Lambda, we need to create an input and an output queue. We will also send messages into the input queue. When we invoke the Lambda, it will retrieve these messages.

Perform the following:

1. Create two SQS queues: an input queue, `my-input-queue`, and an output queue, `my-output-queue`, following the *Your first SQS queue* recipe
2. Send six to seven messages into the queue from CLI

Provisioning the Lambda (AWS CLI)

Follow these steps to deploy and invoke the Lambda. You may follow Chapter 1, *Getting Started with Serverless Computing on AWS* and use CloudFormation for Lambda provisioning:

1. Run `mvn clean package` from inside the Lambda project root folder to create the Uber JAR
2. Upload the Uber JAR to S3:

    ```
    aws s3 cp \
        target/lambda-invoke-sqs-event-0.0.1-SNAPSHOT.jar \
        s3://serverless-cookbook/lambda-invoke-sqs-event-0.0.1-SNAPSHOT.jar \
        --profile admin
    ```

3. Create a role for the Lambda with an appropriate trust relationship definition:

```
aws iam create-role \
    --role-name lambda-invoke-sqs-event-role \
    --assume-role-policy-document file://iam-role-trust-relationship.txt \
    --profile admin
```

The trust document, `iam-role-trust-relationship.txt`, is defined as follows:

```
{
  "Version": "2012-10-17",
  "Statement": [
    {
      "Effect": "Allow",
      "Principal": {
        "Service": "lambda.amazonaws.com"
      },
      "Action": "sts:AssumeRole"
    }
  ]
}
```

4. Create a policy for basic logging permissions and attach it to the role
5. Create a policy for required SQS permissions and attach it to the role

The policy document with required SQS permissions is shown here:

```
{
    "Version":"2012-10-17",
    "Statement":[
        {
            "Effect":"Allow",
            "Action":[
                "sqs:GetQueueAttributes",
                "sqs:ReceiveMessage",
                "sqs:DeleteMessage",
                "sqs:SendMessage",
                "sqs:SendMessageBatch"
            ],
            "Resource":[
                "arn:aws:sqs:*:*:*"
            ]
        }
    ]
}
```

A Lambda configured to be invoked by an SQS even source should have the following permissions:

- `sqs:GetQueueAttributes`
- `sqs:ReceiveMessage`
- `sqs:DeleteMessage`

I have also added the send message permissions, as we will be forwarding the messages to another queue

6. Create the Lambda function, as shown here:

```
aws lambda create-function \
    --function-name lambda-invoke-sqs-event \
    --runtime java8 \
    --role arn:aws:iam::855923912133:role/lambda-invoke-sqs-event-role \
    --handler tech.heartin.books.serverlesscookbook.LambdaSqsEventHandler::handleRequest \
    --code S3Bucket=serverless-cookbook,S3Key=lambda-invoke-sqs-event-0.0.1-SNAPSHOT.jar \
    --environment Variables={SPC_OUTPUT_QUEUE_URL='https://queue.amazonaws.com/855923912133/my-output-queue'} \
    --timeout 15 \
    --memory-size 512 \
    --region us-east-1 \
    --profile admin
```

7. Configure an SQS event source for the Lambda:

```
aws lambda create-event-source-mapping \
    --event-source-arn arn:aws:sqs:us-east-1:855923912133:my-input-queue \
    --function-name lambda-invoke-sqs-event \
    --batch-size 4 \
    --profile admin
```

The `batch-size` parameter specifies the maximum number of messages to be retrieved from the queue together

Testing the Lambda (AWS CLI)

1. Send five messages to the input queue.
2. Verify the invocation by retrieving the message from the queue:

   ```
   aws sqs receive-message \
       --queue-url
   https://queue.amazonaws.com/855923912133/my-output-queue \
       --max-number-of-messages 5 \
       --profile admin
   ```

   If successful, you should get zero to five (maximum) messages in a single `receive-message` call. You may also check CloudWatch logs and verify the logs we printed.

How it works...

In summary, we did the following in this recipe:

1. Created a Lambda function to perform the following:
    1. Retrieve multiple messages from an input SQS event
    2. Batch the messages and send them to an output queue
2. Created the input and output queues
3. Created the required policies and attached them to the role
4. Created the Lambda function specifying the role
5. Added data into the input queue
6. Verified data was posted to the queue using the `aws sqs receive-message` command on the output queue

There's more...

We created an SQS queue event in this recipe using the `aws lambda create-event-source-mapping` command. We can also use this command to define the following event sources: Kinesis Data Streams and DynamoDB streams.

AWS supports the following triggers for Lambda:

- S3
- DynamoDB
- Kinesis Data Streams
- SNS
- SES
- SQS
- Cognito
- CloudFormation
- CloudWatch Logs
- CloudWatch Events
- CodeCommit
- Scheduled Events powered by CloudWatch Events
- AWS Config
- Alexa
- Lex
- API gateway
- AWS IoT Button
- CloudFront
- Kinesis Data Firehose

See also

- `https://docs.aws.amazon.com/lambda/latest/dg/invoking-lambda-function.html`

Your first SNS topic for email and SMS (AWS CLI + CloudFormation)

In this recipe, we will create a **Simple Notification Service** (**SNS**) topic for both email and SMS subscriptions. In the real world, you may use this for features such as **one time passwords** (**OTP**). We had already indirectly used SNS when we used SMS verification in `Chapter 4`, *Application Security with Amazon Cognito*.

Getting ready

The following are the prerequisites for this recipe:

- A working phone number and email address.

How to do it...

We will first create an SNS topic and then test email and SMS subscriptions.

Creating an SNS topic

We will create an SNS topic using both CLI commands and a CloudFormation template.

AWS CLI

You can create an SNS topic using the `aws sns create-topic` command:

```
aws sns create-topic \
    --name my-first-sns-topic \
    --profile admin
```

If successful, this will return the SNS topic ARN:

```
{
    "TopicArn": "arn:aws:sns:us-east-1:############:my-first-sns-topic"
}
```

The CloudFormation template

The `Resources` and `Output` sections of the template can include following:

```
Resources:
  SNSTopic:
    Type: AWS::SNS::Topic
    Properties:
      DisplayName: 'My first SNS topic'
      TopicName: my-first-sns-topic-cf

Output:
  SNSTopicARN:
```

```
      Value: !Ref SNSTopic
      Export:
        Name: "SNSTopicARN"
  SNSTopicName:
      Value: !GetAtt SNSTopic.TopicName
      Export:
        Name: "SNSTopicName"
```

You can also specify a list of subscriptions. However, in general practice subscriptions are added dynamically and hence we will demonstrate them using AWS CLI commands. You may also include a template format version and a description in the template file.

If the create stack command completes successfully, the stack description command's output will contain an `Output` section, as follows:

```
"Outputs": [
    {
        "OutputKey": "SNSTopicARN",
        "OutputValue": "arn:aws:sns:us-east-1:        :my-first-sns-topic-cf",
        "ExportName": "SNSTopicARN"
    },
    {
        "OutputKey": "SNSTopicName",
        "OutputValue": "my-first-sns-topic-cf",
        "ExportName": "SNSTopicName"
    }
],
```

Creating email and SMS subscriptions (AWS CLI)

We will create both SMS and email subscriptions.

SMS subscription

We can create an SMS subscription, as follows:

```
aws sns subscribe \
    --topic-arn arn:aws:sns:us-east-1:<account id>:my-first-sns-topic \
    --protocol sms \
    --notification-endpoint +917411174114 \
    --profile admin
```

If successful, this will return the Subscription ARN:

```
{
    "SubscriptionArn": "arn:aws:sns:us-east-1:<account id>:my-first-sns-topic:2f2934a3-c1f9-4192-9883-5057ed006d52"
}
```

Email subscription

You can create an email subscription as follows:

```
aws sns subscribe \
    --topic-arn arn:aws:sns:us-east-1:<account id>:my-first-sns-topic \
    --protocol email \
    --notification-endpoint serverlesscookbook@gmail.com \
    --profile admin
```

With email, the subscription ARN will not be confirmed until the user validates the subscription:

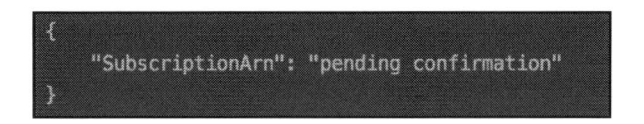

```
{
    "SubscriptionArn": "pending confirmation"
}
```

You will now get an email for confirmation of the specified email address:

AWS Notification - Subscription Confirmation Inbox

AWS Notifications <no-reply@sns.amazonaws.com>   4:04 PM
to me

You have chosen to subscribe to the topic:
arn:aws:sns:us-east-1:▮▮▮▮▮▮▮▮:my-first-sns-topic

To confirm this subscription, click or visit the link below (If this was in error no action is necessary):
Confirm subscription

Please do not reply directly to this email. If you wish to remove yourself from receiving all future SNS subscription confirmation requests please send an email to sns-opt-out

Once you click on **Confirm subscription**, you will be taken to a confirmation page:

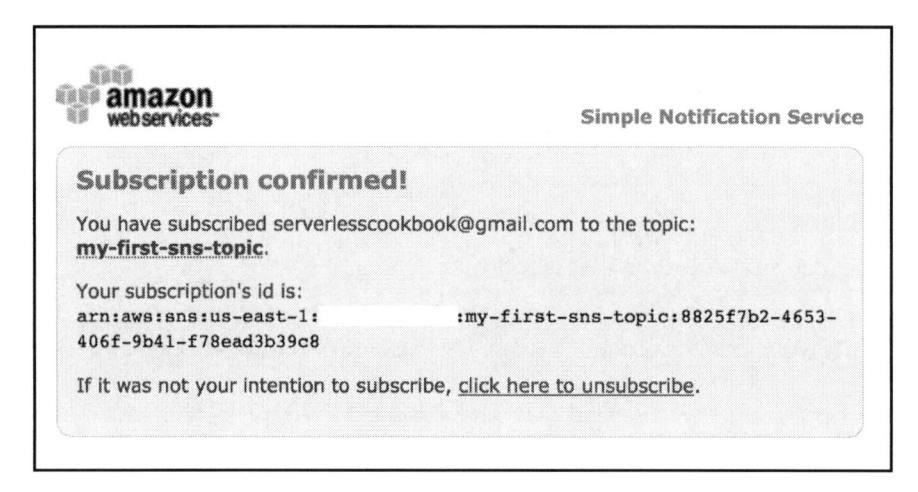

Publishing a message

You can publish a message to the topic as follows:

```
aws sns publish \
  --topic-arn arn:aws:sns:us-east-1:<account id>:my-first-sns-topic \
  --message "sending message to both mobile and email" \
  --profile admin
```

This will return the message ID in the console immediately. Actual delivery of the message to subscribers may take some time.

The email message received will look as shown here. Similarly, you will also get an SMS:

How it works...

In summary, we did the following in this recipe:

1. Created an SNS topic using AWS CLI command
2. Created an SNS topic with a CloudFormation template
3. Created an SMS subscription
4. Created an email subscription
5. Published a message to the topic

There's more...

We saw how to send an SMS and email to subscribers using SNS. SNS may be also used to fanout messages to a large number of subscribers by using SQS queues, AWS Lambda functions, and HTTP/S webhooks. We will see the fanout pattern with SNS and SQS in `Chapter 9`, *Serverless Architecture Patterns and Practices*.

See also

- https://docs.aws.amazon.com/cli/latest/reference/sns/index.html
- https://docs.aws.amazon.com/AWSCloudFormation/latest/UserGuide/aws-properties-sns-topic.html

Publishing to an SNS topic with SDK (Java)

In the previous recipe, we saw how to create an SNS topic, subscribe to that topic, and publish messages from AWS CLI. In this recipe, we will see how to publish a message to an SNS topic from Java Lambda code using the AWS Java SDK.

Getting ready

The following are the prerequisites for this recipe:

- You need to follow the section *Getting started* in the recipes *Your first AWS Lambda* and *Your first Lambda with AWS CLI* from Chapter 1, *Getting Started with Serverless Computing on AWS* to set up Java, Maven, the parent project, `serverless-cookbook-parent-aws-java` and AWS CLI, and may also read other notes there including code usage guidelines, S3 bucket creation and notes for the Windows users.
- You should have already created the SNS topic and subscriptions as discussed in the *Your first SNS topic for email and SMS* recipe.

How to do it...

We will first create our Java Lambda. We will then provision it and test it from AWS CLI.

Lambda project code (Java)

> In this recipe, we will write our logic within the Lambda handler itself without any service classes. I generally tend to create service classes as I primarily come from an enterprise Java development background. This is, however, not a requirement for Lambdas, and in many cases it might be better to simply code the logic within the Lambda handler itself. You can follow whatever approach you feel comfortable with. There might be also a preferred approach for most teams.

The Maven `pom.xml` file of the project should also define the following dependency:

```
<dependency>
    <groupId>com.amazonaws</groupId>
    <artifactId>aws-java-sdk-sns</artifactId>
    <version>${aws.sdk.version}</version>
</dependency>
```

We can create the Java Lambda project with the following structure:

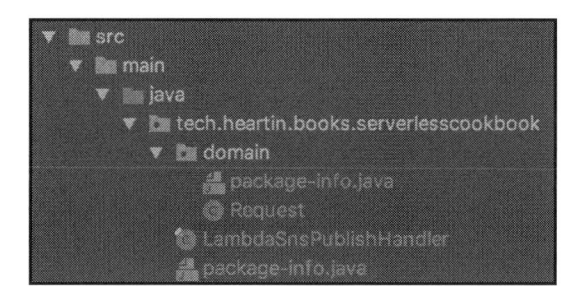

```
▼ src
  ▼ main
    ▼ java
      ▼ tech.heartin.books.serverlesscookbook
        ▼ domain
          package-info.java
          Request
        LambdaSnsPublishHandler
        package-info.java
```

The `Request.java` class will correspond to our input JSON:

```java
@Data
public class Request {
    private String topicArn;
    private String message;
}
```

There is no Response object as we are simply returning a String value as response.

`LambdaSnsPublishHandler.java` is our Lambda handler class, where we initialize the SNS client and publish the message.

We can initialize the SNS client as follows:

```java
private final AmazonSNS snsClient;
public LambdaSnsPublishHandler() {
    this.snsClient = AmazonSNSClientBuilder.standard()
            .withRegion(System.getenv("AWS_REGION"))
            .build();
}
```

We can then publish the message directly from the handler:

```java
public String handleRequest(final Request request, final Context context) {
    final PublishResult result;
    try {
        PublishRequest publishRequest = new PublishRequest(request.getTopicArn(), request.getMessage());
        result = snsClient.publish(publishRequest);
    } catch (Exception e) {
        return "Exception occurred: " + e.getMessage();
    }
```

```
        return "Message Id: " + result.getMessageId();
    }
```

Provisioning and testing the Lambda (AWS CLI)

Follow these steps to deploy and invoke the Lambda. You may follow Chapter 1, *Getting Started with Serverless Computing on AWS* and use CloudFormation for Lambda provisioning:

1. Run `mvn clean package` from inside the Lambda project root folder to create the Uber JAR.
2. Upload the Uber JAR to S3:

   ```
   aws s3 cp \
       target/lambda-sns-publish-with-sdk-0.0.1-SNAPSHOT.jar \
       s3://serverless-cookbook/lambda-sns-publish-with-sdk-0.0.1-SNAPSHOT.jar \
       --profile admin
   ```

3. Create a role for the Lambda with an appropriate trust relationship definition:

   ```
   aws iam create-role \
       --role-name lambda-sns-publish-with-sdk-role \
       --assume-role-policy-document file://iam-role-trust-relationship.txt \
       --profile admin
   ```

   Refer to the previous recipes or the code files for the trust relationship document file, `iam-role-trust-relationship.txt`.

4. Create a policy for basic logging permissions and attach it to the role.
5. Create a policy for required SNS permissions and attach it to the role.

   The policy document with required SNS permissions is shown as follows:

   ```
   {
       "Version":"2012-10-17",
       "Statement":[
           {
               "Effect":"Allow",
               "Action":[
                   "sns:Publish"
               ],
               "Resource":[
                   "arn:aws:sns:*:*:*"
   ```

```
            ]
        }
    ]
}
```

6. Create the Lambda function, as shown here:

```
aws lambda create-function \
    --function-name lambda-sns-publish-with-sdk \
    --runtime java8 \
    --role arn:aws:iam::855923912133:role/lambda-sns-publish-with-sdk-role \
    --handler tech.heartin.books.serverlesscookbook.LambdaSnsPublishHandler::handleRequest \
    --code S3Bucket=serverless-cookbook,S3Key=lambda-sns-publish-with-sdk-0.0.1-SNAPSHOT.jar \
    --timeout 15 \
    --memory-size 512 \
    --region us-east-1 \
    --profile admin
```

7. You can invoke the Lambda as follows:

```
aws lambda invoke \
    --invocation-type RequestResponse \
    --function-name lambda-sns-publish-with-sdk \
    --log-type Tail \
    --payload file://payload.json \
    --region us-east-1 \
    --profile admin \
    outputfile.txt
```

The `payload.json` file has the following contents:

```
{
    "topicArn" : "arn:aws:sns:us-east-1:<account id>:my-first-sns-topic",
    "message": "test payload 1"
}
```

If successful, you will get notifications to the configured email and SMS.

[293]

How it works...
In summary, we did the following in this recipe:
1. Created a Java Lambda to publish messages to a topic
2. Provisioned it and tested it from AWS CLI

There's more...
This was a small recipe to demonstrate the use of SNS Java SDK within a Lambda. You can extend it with additional functionality as per your requirements.

See also
- https://docs.aws.amazon.com/sns/latest/dg/using-awssdkjava.html

Invoking a Lambda with SNS events (Java)
In a previous recipe, we invoked a Lambda with a trigger from an SQS event source, and we configured SQS as an event source for the Lambda. With SNS, instead of defining an event source, Lambda has to subscribe to an SNS topic. Lambda will write the message received from the SNS topic into another queue, and we will verify the output queue after publishing messages to the topic.

Getting ready
You need to follow the section *Getting started* in the recipes *Your first AWS Lambda* and *Your first Lambda with AWS CLI* from Chapter 1, *Getting Started with Serverless Computing on AWS* to set up Java, Maven, the parent project, `serverless-cookbook-parent-aws-java` and AWS CLI, and may also read other notes there including code usage guidelines, S3 bucket creation and notes for the Windows users.

How to do it...

We will first create our Java Lambda. We will deploy the Lambda, subscribe the Lambda to the SNS topic, and test it from CLI.

Lambda project code (Java)

The Maven `pom.xml` file of the project should also define the following dependency:

```
<dependency>
    <groupId>com.amazonaws</groupId>
    <artifactId>aws-java-sdk-sqs</artifactId>
    <version>${aws.sdk.version}</version>
</dependency>
```

We can create a Java Lambda project with the following structure:

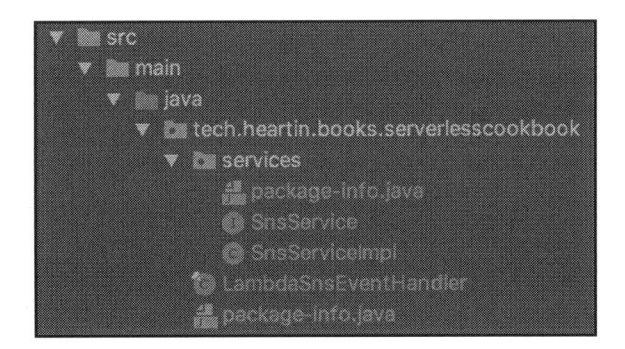

```
▼ src
  ▼ main
    ▼ java
      ▼ tech.heartin.books.serverlesscookbook
        ▼ services
            package-info.java
            SnsService
            SnsServiceImpl
          LambdaSnsEventHandler
          package-info.java
```

Note that we do not have request and response domain objects, as AWS will be invoking the Lambda and passing a predefined event object based on a trigger we configure.

`SnsService.java` is the interface for our service class. This is not a requirement—you can directly use the implementation class or even embed all logic within Lambda handler class itself:

```
public interface SnsService {
    Boolean processEvent(SNSEvent event, String outputQueueURL,
LambdaLogger logger);
}
```

`SqsServiceImpl.java` is the actual service implementation.

We can retrieve messages from the input `SNSEvent` and create a collection of `SendMessageBatchRequestEntry` objects:

```
Collection<SendMessageBatchRequestEntry> entries = new ArrayList<>();

int idVal = 1;
for (SNSRecord r : event.getRecords()) {
    logger.log("Adding message: " + r.getSNS().getMessage());
    entries.add(new SendMessageBatchRequestEntry("id_" + idVal, r.getSNS().getMessage()));
    idVal++;
}
```

We can create and send a batch request to the output queue, as follows:

```
final SendMessageBatchRequest sendBatchRequest = new SendMessageBatchRequest()
        .withQueueUrl(outputQueueURL)
        .withEntries(entries);
this.sqsClient.sendMessageBatch(sendBatchRequest);
```

`LambdaSnsEventHandler.java` is our Lambda handler class where we initialize the SQS client and pass it to the service class along with the `SNSEvent` we received.

We can initialize the SQS Client as follows:

```
private final AmazonSQS sqsClient;

public LambdaSnsEventHandler() {
    this.sqsClient = AmazonSQSClientBuilder.standard()
            .withRegion(System.getenv("AWS_REGION"))
            .build();
}
```

We then invoke the `service` method, passing the client along with the `SNSEvent` object:

```
public Boolean handleRequest(final SNSEvent snsEvent, final Context context) {
    context.getLogger().log("Received SQS event: " + snsEvent);

    final SnsService snsService =  new SnsServiceImpl(this.sqsClient);
    return snsService.processEvent(snsEvent, System.getenv("SPC_OUTPUT_QUEUE_URL"), context.getLogger());

}
```

We will use an environment variable to specify the name of the output queue.

Provisioning the Lambda (AWS CLI)

Follow these steps to deploy and invoke the Lambda:

1. Run `mvn clean package` from inside the Lambda project root folder to create the Uber JAR.
2. Upload the Uber JAR to `S3`:

   ```
   aws s3 cp \
       target/lambda-invoke-sns-event-0.0.1-SNAPSHOT.jar \
       s3://serverless-cookbook/lambda-invoke-sns-event-0.0.1-SNAPSHOT.jar \
       --profile admin
   ```

3. Create a role for the Lambda with an appropriate trust relationship definition:

   ```
   aws iam create-role \
       --role-name lambda-invoke-sns-event-role \
       --assume-role-policy-document file://iam-role-trust-relationship.txt \
       --profile admin
   ```

   The trust document, `iam-role-trust-relationship.txt`, is defined in previous recipes. You can also refer to the code files.

4. Create a policy for basic logging permissions and attach it to the role.
5. Create a policy for required SQS permissions and attach it to the role.

   The policy document with required SQS permissions is shown here:

   ```
   {
       "Version":"2012-10-17",
       "Statement":[
           {
               "Effect":"Allow",
               "Action":[
                   "sqs:SendMessage",
                   "sqs:SendMessageBatch"
               ],
               "Resource":[
                   "arn:aws:sqs:*:*:*"
               ]
           }
       ]
   }
   ```

These permissions are required since we are writing the messages received to the queue again, however if you are not using a queue, you will not need it.

6. Create the Lambda function as shown here:

```
aws lambda create-function \
    --function-name lambda-invoke-sns-event \
    --runtime java8 \
    --role arn:aws:iam::<account id>:role/lambda-invoke-sns-event-role \
    --handler tech.heartin.books.serverlesscookbook.LambdaSnsEventHandler::handleRequest \
    --code S3Bucket=serverless-cookbook,S3Key=lambda-invoke-sns-event-0.0.1-SNAPSHOT.jar \
    --environment Variables={SPC_OUTPUT_QUEUE_URL='https://queue.amazonaws.com/855923912133/my-output-queue'} \
    --timeout 15 \
    --memory-size 512 \
    --region us-east-1 \
    --profile admin
```

7. Subscribe the Lambda to the queue:

```
aws sns subscribe --topic-arn arn:aws:sns:us-east-1:<account id>:lambda-invoke-sns-topic \
    --protocol lambda \
    --notification-endpoint arn:aws:lambda:us-east-1:<account id>:function:lambda-invoke-sns-event \
    --profile admin
```

Testing the Lambda (AWS CLI)

We will now test the Lambda created in the previous section:

1. Send a messages to the topic.
2. Verify the invocation by retrieving the message from the output queue:

```
aws sqs receive-message \
    --queue-url https://queue.amazonaws.com/<account id>/my-output-queue \
    --max-number-of-messages 5 \
    --profile admin
```

If successful, you should get the message that you posted to the topic. You can also verify the invocation details from CloudWatch logs.

How it works...

In summary, we did the following in this recipe:

1. Created a Lambda function to perform the following:
    1. Retrieve messages from an input SNS event
    2. Batch the messages and send them to an output queue
2. Created the required policies and attached them to the role
3. Created the Lambda function, specifying the role
4. Added data into the topic
5. Verified that data was posted to the queue using the `aws sqs receive-message` command on the output queue

There's more...

We read a message from the topic and wrote it to an SQS queue. We can also configure an SQS queue with an SNS topic. One pattern that uses this combination is usually referred to as the fanout pattern. SNS can fanout messages to various SQS queues for various reasons, including parallel processing.

See also

- https://aws.amazon.com/blogs/compute/messaging-fanout-pattern-for-serverless-architectures-using-amazon-sns/

7
Redshift, Amazon ML, and Alexa Skills

This chapter will cover the following topics:

- Your first **Kinesis data stream** (**KDS**): AWS **Command Line Interface** (**CLI**)
- Writing data into KDS with SDK (Java)
- Invoking Lambda with a Kinesis event (Java)
- Using Amazon ML for binary classification (AWS CLI)
- Building and testing an Alexa skill (Java for Lambda, CLI for Alexa skills)

Introduction

In this chapter, I will introduce you to some services that can help you to perform analytics and **Natural Language Processing** (**NLP**) on the AWS cloud, such as Amazon KDS, the Amazon **Machine Learning** (**ML**) service, and the Alexa Skills Kit. KDS is primarily used for building data pipelines for big data applications. We will also look at a basic recipe each for the ML service and the Alexa Skills Kit. To learn more about these services, you can refer to any Packt book on data analytics, ML, and NLP.

You will require the following skill sets to complete the recipes in this chapter:

- Knowledge of how to work on AWS account
- Knowledge of how to configure AWS CLI, as discussed in the *Your first Lambda with AWS CLI* recipe in `Chapter 1`, *Getting Started with Serverless Computing on AWS*
- A basic understanding of data analytics, ML, and NLP concepts

> Keep in mind that not all services and features discussed in this chapter may be eligible for free use. Please refer to AWS Free Tier documentation for details.

Your first Kinesis data stream (AWS CLI)

In the previous chapter, we learned how we can use SQS for messaging. SQS is good for standard data transfer (messaging) within serverless microservice applications; however, applications that work on big data and data analytics demand more. KDS is a highly scalable data streaming service that is used for such use cases.

KDS consists of an ordered sequence of data records. A stream is composed of multiple shards with different unique sequences of data records. A partition key is used to group data into shards. In the following recipe, we will create a simple KDS, put data into the stream, and retrieve data from the stream, all using AWS CLI.

Getting ready

There are no additional prerequisites for completing this recipe other than the common requirements specified in this chapter's introduction.

How to do it...

We will first create the KDS and later test it using AWS CLI commands.

Step 1 - Creating a Kinesis data stream

We will create the KDS using both AWS CLI commands and the CloudFormation template.

Using AWS CLI

We can create a KDS from the AWS CLI as follows:

```
aws kinesis create-stream \
    --stream-name my-first-kinesis-stream \
    --shard-count 1 \
    --profile admin
```

This command will not return anything. You may use the `aws kinesis describe-stream` command to get the details of the stream:

```
aws kinesis describe-stream \
    --stream-name my-first-kinesis-stream \
    --profile admin
```

If stream creation happened successfully, you should see the `StreamStatus` as `ACTIVE`, as shown in the following screenshot:

```
{
    "StreamDescription": {
        "Shards": [
            {
                "ShardId": "shardId-000000000000",
                "HashKeyRange": {
                    "StartingHashKey": "0",
                    "EndingHashKey": "340282366920938463463374607431768211455"
                },
                "SequenceNumberRange": {
                    "StartingSequenceNumber": "49591020492899070200777637844347017508350464223327813634"
                }
            }
        ],
        "StreamARN": "arn:aws:kinesis:us-east-1:          :stream/my-first-kinesis-stream",
        "StreamName": "my-first-kinesis-stream",
        "StreamStatus": "ACTIVE",
        "RetentionPeriodHours": 24,
        "EnhancedMonitoring": [
            {
                "ShardLevelMetrics": []
            }
        ],
        "EncryptionType": "NONE",
        "KeyId": null,
        "StreamCreationTimestamp": 1544688253.0
    }
}
```

You can also list the streams available using `aws kinesis list-streams`, as shown in the following code:

```
aws kinesis list-streams \
    --profile admin
```

This should return the following response in our case (assuming you have only one stream):

```
{
    "StreamNames": [
        "my-first-kinesis-stream"
    ]
}
```

Using the CloudFormation template

You can create a CloudFormation template file with the following `Resource` and `Outputs` sections to create a simple KDS:

```
Resources:
  KinesisStream:
    Type: AWS::Kinesis::Stream
    Properties:
      Name: my-first-kinesis-stream
      RetentionPeriodHours: 24
      ShardCount: 1

Outputs:
  KinesisStreamId:
    Value: !Ref KinesisStream
    Export:
      Name: "KinesisStreamId"
  KinesisStreamArn:
    Value: !GetAtt KinesisStream.Arn
    Export:
      Name: "KinesisStreamArn"
```

You may also add a template version and description to the top of the template file and then execute the stack using the `aws cloudformation create-stack` command. The complete commands and the template are available with the code files.

If successful, the `describe-stacks` subcommand should return with an `Outputs` section, as shown in the following screenshot:

```
"Outputs": [
    {
        "OutputKey": "KinesisStreamId",
        "OutputValue": "my-first-kinesis-stream",
        "ExportName": "KinesisStreamId"
    },
    {
        "OutputKey": "KinesisStreamArn",
        "OutputValue": "arn:aws:kinesis:us-east-1:          :stream/my-first-kinesis-stream",
        "ExportName": "KinesisStreamArn"
    }
],
```

Step 2 - Adding and retrieving data

You can add data to a KDS from the CLI using the `aws kinesis put-record` command, as follows:

```
aws kinesis put-record \
    --stream-name my-first-kinesis-stream \
    --partition-key 12345 \
    --data sampledata01 \
    --profile admin
```

This will return the shard ID and the sequence number of the record, as shown in the following screenshot:

```
{
    "ShardId": "shardId-000000000000",
    "SequenceNumber": "49591020492899070200777638182537970916445021654921248770"
}
```

Similarly, you can add one more data item with a payload of `sampledata02`.

Retrieving data from a KDS is a two-step process:

1. Get the shard iterator:

   ```
   aws kinesis get-shard-iterator \
       --shard-id shardId-000000000000 \
       --shard-iterator-type TRIM_HORIZON \
       --stream-name my-first-kinesis-stream \
       --profile admin
   ```

This will return the following response:

```
{
    "ShardIterator": "AAAAAAAAAAEKqdNGz2fHKqvpf+q3Pjq/SAwh8sjh4o+ix88hW33Rdqv2SBbN3QTWzSZwjZN0nJkH1WAhb7Bbl
Kfqc7icOZaxfklnPdhanUDV/BpCoHqRktV3uso67gTB+A8k2ocYVBIwm65hgnu99nR5XyjPYSUKQ=="
}
```

2. Invoke the `aws kinesis get-records` command to pass the shard iterator, as shown in the following code:

   ```
   aws kinesis get-records \
       --shard-iterator <shard-iterator-value> \
       --profile admin
   ```

   Use the shard iterator value from the previous step. This should give the following response:

```
{
    "Records": [
        {
            "SequenceNumber": "49591022060730660638274567187983948851027405480717713410",
            "ApproximateArrivalTimestamp": 1544692680.484,
            "Data": "c2FtcGxlZGF0YTAx",
            "PartitionKey": "12345"
        },
        {
            "SequenceNumber": "49591022060730660638274567188104841432988868741785714690",
            "ApproximateArrivalTimestamp": 1544692685.119,
            "Data": "c2FtcGxlZGF0YTAy",
            "PartitionKey": "12345"
        }
    ],
    "NextShardIterator": "AAAAAAAAAAGILUFMLyqkIgvtDwjxqIjrvPRtHamPrkVePUh8QYx+wfeynNjk0R3VxnW6/TlcLgQjEHa0,
I4ZXe3NlhHaiwj0oCUv7l2wpNdfqh9zBX8/FVT5oXBRF8QIDC0cbIrIsJ6yCFTELhywPGSiVPvzAV2bQ==",
    "MillisBehindLatest": 1032000
}
```

The `TRIM_HORIZON` option return records from the oldest record. If you try to use the `get-records` command with the next shard iterator returned by this command, you will not get any records as it has retrieved all of the records already.

The data in the response is Base64 encoded, and so needs to be decoded. You can do a quick Google search to find an online decoder, or if you are using a Mac or a similar OS, you can also use the following command to decode the Base64-encoded string:

```
$ echo c2FtcGxlZGF0YTAx | base64 --decode
sampledata01$
$ echo c2FtcGxlZGF0YTAy | base64 --decode
sampledata02$
```

How it works...

In summary, we did the following in this recipe:

1. Created a KDS using AWS CLI commands and the CloudFormation template
2. Added two data records into the stream
3. Retrieved the stream iterator with the shard iterator type as `TRIM_HORIZON`
4. Retrieved the data records, passing the shard iterator value

You can add data to a KDS from the CLI using the `aws kinesis put-record` command, specifying the stream name and a partition key. The partition key determines which shard a given data record belongs to. A stream is composed of many shards and each shard has a fixed capacity. Based on the data rate capacity requirements, you can increase or decrease the number of shards.

The following are some of the limitations of a Kinesis shard:

- Five transactions per second for reads
- Total data read rate of 2 MBps
- 1,000 records per second for writes
- Data write rate of 1 MBps

Unlike adding records, retrieving records from a Kinesis stream is a two-step process:

1. You first need to retrieve the shard iterator, passing the stream name, the shard ID, and the shard iterator type.
2. Then you need to retrieve data records using the shard iterator. The shard iterator type determines how the shard iterator is used to start reading data records from the shard.

Let's look at the different shard types in detail.

Kinesis shard iterator types

You can specify one of the following shard iterator type values while retrieving the shard iterator value:

- AT_SEQUENCE_NUMBER: Use this to read from the position specified by the sequence number, as follows:

    ```
    aws kinesis get-shard-iterator \
        --shard-id shardId-000000000000 \
        --shard-iterator-type AT_SEQUENCE_NUMBER \
        --starting-sequence-number
    49591022060730660638274567187983948851027405480717713410 \
        --stream-name my-first-kinesis-stream \
        --profile admin
    ```

    I have specified the sequence number of record 1. Here, the `get-records` command will return both records 1 and 2.

- AFTER_SEQUENCE_NUMBER: Use this to read after the position specified by the sequence number, as follows:

    ```
    aws kinesis get-shard-iterator \
        --shard-id shardId-000000000000 \
        --shard-iterator-type AFTER_SEQUENCE_NUMBER \
        --starting-sequence-number
    49591022060730660638274567187983948851027405480717713410 \
        --stream-name my-first-kinesis-stream \
        --profile admin
    ```

    I have again specified the sequence number of record 1, however, here the `get-records` command will return only record 2.

- AT_TIMESTAMP: Use this to read from the specified timestamp, as follows:

    ```
    aws kinesis get-shard-iterator \
        --shard-id shardId-000000000000 \
        --shard-iterator-type AT_TIMESTAMP \
        --timestamp 1544692680.484 \
        --stream-name my-first-kinesis-stream \
        --profile admin
    ```

Provided the timestamp matches the first record, the `get-records` command will return both the records.

- `TRIM_HORIZON`: Use this to return records from the oldest record after the last commit. We already looked at how to use this in this recipe.
- `LATEST`: Use this to return the latest records that were added after the shard iterator was generated.

Let's look at how to use these types:

1. We will first get the shard iterator that specifies the shard iterator type as `LATEST`:

   ```
   aws kinesis get-shard-iterator \
       --shard-id shardId-000000000000 \
       --shard-iterator-type LATEST \
       --stream-name my-first-kinesis-stream \
       --profile admin
   ```

2. Note down the iterator value and add a new record, as shown in the following code:

   ```
   aws kinesis put-record \
       --stream-name my-first-kinesis-stream \
       --partition-key 12345 \
       --data sampledata03 \
       --profile admin
   ```

3. Invoke the `aws kinesis get-records` command, passing the shard iterator received in step 1:

   ```
   aws kinesis get-records \
       --shard-iterator <shard-iterator-value> \
       --profile admin
   ```

   This will return only the latest record that was added after the shard iterator was created, which is `sampledata03` (but encoded as before).

For more details, refer to the *get-shard-iterator* documentation reference link provided in the *See also* section.

There's more...

You can also add encryption to the stream by using the AWS **Key Management Service** (**KMS**).

If you exceed the limits when calling the `GetShardIterator` requests, it will throw a `ProvisionedThroughputExceededException`. For KDS limits, refer to the *service-sizes-and-limits* documentation reference link limits in the *See also* section.

See also

- https://docs.aws.amazon.com/streams/latest/dev/key-concepts.html
- https://docs.aws.amazon.com/cli/latest/reference/kinesis/get-shard-iterator.html
- https://docs.aws.amazon.com/streams/latest/dev/service-sizes-and-limits.html
- https://docs.aws.amazon.com/AWSCloudFormation/latest/UserGuide/aws-properties-kinesis-stream-streamencryption.html

Writing data into Kinesis Stream with SDK (Java)

In this recipe, we will develop an AWS Lambda function that write to KDS using AWS Java SDK for Kinesis. Kinesis producers may also be developed using the **Kinesis Producer Library** (**KPL**); this is the more common option for non-serverless applications. However, with AWS Lambda, SDK-based code is generally preferred as we will be using less libraries.

Getting ready

You will need to have the following prerequisites for this recipe:

- You need an active AWS account. You need to follow the *Getting started* section in the recipes *Your first AWS Lambda* and *Your first Lambda with AWS CLI* from Chapter 1, *Getting Started with Serverless Computing on AWS* to set up Java, Maven, the parent project, `serverless-cookbook-parent-aws-java`, and AWS CLI, and may also read other notes there, including code usage guidelines, S3 bucket creation, and notes for Windows users.
- Follow the recipe *Your first Kinesis data stream* and create a Kinesis stream named `my-first-kinesis-stream`.

How to do it...

We will learn how we can implement a Java Lambda function to write data into a Kinesis stream using AWS Java SDK for Kinesis. I will not show all the details of provisioning the Lambda; for these, you can refer to earlier recipes (as given in the *Getting ready* section).

Step 1 - Creating the Lambda project (Java)

We will create a Lambda that gets triggered from AWS CLI using `aws lambda invoke` command and send messages to an SQS queue as a batch.

> In this section, I will be discussing only the core application logic, and will not be discussing supporting code, such as imports, error handling, and Javadoc comments; however, the complete working code is provided in this book along with the code files.

Let's start by defining the dependency for AWS Kinesis SDK for Java in the POM file, as shown in the following code:

```
<dependency>
    <groupId>com.amazonaws</groupId>
    <artifactId>aws-java-sdk-kinesis</artifactId>
    <version>${aws.sdk.version}</version>
</dependency>
```

The POM file also has dependencies for `aws-lambda-java-core`. The `aws.sdk.version` property is defined, along with other properties in the parent project, POM `serverless-cookbook-parent-aws-java`.

We can create the `Java Lambda` project with the following package structure:

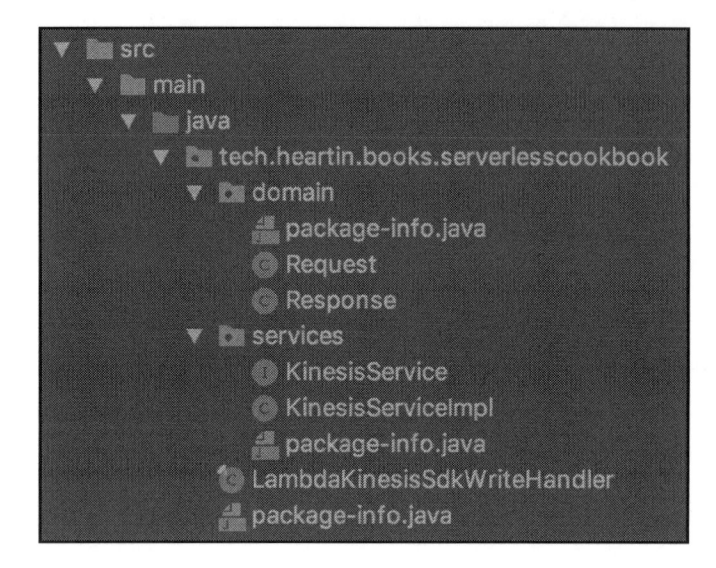

```
▼ src
  ▼ main
    ▼ java
      ▼ tech.heartin.books.serverlesscookbook
        ▼ domain
          ▪ package-info.java
          ◉ Request
          ◉ Response
        ▼ services
          ◉ KinesisService
          ◉ KinesisServiceImpl
          ▪ package-info.java
        ◉ LambdaKinesisSdkWriteHandler
        ▪ package-info.java
```

The `Request.java` class will correspond to our input JSON, as shown in the following code:

```
@Data
public class Request {
    private String streamName;
    private String partitionKey;
    private String payload;
    private int  count;
    private int batchSize;
}
```

`Response.java` class correspond to the output JSON from Lambda and will contain a field to send the response back to the invoker, as shown in the following code:

```
@Data
@AllArgsConstructor
public class Response {
    private String message;
    private int count;
}
```

The `KinesisService.java` is the interface for our `Service` class. This is not a requirement; you can directly use the implementation class or even embed all logic within the Lambda handler class itself, as shown in the following code:

```
public interface KinesisService {
    Response addRecords(Request request, LambdaLogger logger);
}
```

The `KinesisServiceImpl.java` class is the actual service implementation.

The following steps show how we can use it:

1. We first define and initialize the Kinesis client and a list of `PutRecordsRequestEntry`, as shown in the following code:

    ```
    private final AmazonKinesis kinesisClient;
    private final List<PutRecordsRequestEntry> kinesisBatch;

    public KinesisServiceImpl(final AmazonKinesis kinesisClient) {
        this.kinesisClient = kinesisClient;
        this.kinesisBatch = new ArrayList<>();
    }
    ```

2. Check the stream status at the start (optional) using the following code:

    ```
    public final Response addRecords(final Request request, final
    LambdaLogger logger) {

        this.documentAddedCount = request.getCount();

        DescribeStreamResult result =
    this.kinesisClient.describeStream(request.getStreamName());
        logger.log("Stream Status: " +
    result.getStreamDescription().getStreamStatus() + ". ");
    ```

3. Put the records into the stream in batches using the following code:

    ```
    for (int i = 1; i <= request.getCount(); i++) {

        payload = request.getPayload() + i;

        this.kinesisBatch.add(new PutRecordsRequestEntry()
                .withPartitionKey(request.getPartitionKey())
                .withData(ByteBuffer.wrap(payload.getBytes())));

        if (this.kinesisBatch.size() >= request.getBatchSize()) {

            try {
    ```

```
                logger.log("Flushing records to Stream...");
                flushBatch(request.getStreamName(), logger);
            } catch (Exception e) {
                logger.log("Exception occurred: " + e);
                this.isError = false;
            } finally {
                this.kinesisBatch.clear();
            }
        }
    }
}
```

4. The `flushBatch()` method actually writes to the stream, as shown in the following code:

```
private void flushBatch(final String streamName, final LambdaLogger logger) {
    final PutRecordsResult result =
this.kinesisClient.putRecords(new PutRecordsRequest()
            .withStreamName(streamName)
            .withRecords(this.kinesisBatch));
    result.getRecords().forEach(r -> {
        if (!(StringUtils.hasValue(r.getErrorCode()))) {
            String successMessage = "Successfully processed record with sequence number: " + r.getSequenceNumber()
                    + ", shard id: " + r.getShardId();
            logger.log(successMessage);
        } else {
            this.documentAddedCount--;
            String errorMessage = "Did not process record with sequence number: " + r.getSequenceNumber()
                    + ", error code: " + r.getErrorCode()
                    + ", error message: " + r.getErrorMessage();
            logger.log(errorMessage);
            this.isError = true;
        }
    });
}
```

You can also implement retry logic for failed records. Check the code files for additional suggestions.

5. Finally, return the `Response` object from the `addRecords` method using the following code:

```
if (this.isError) {
    return new Response(ERROR_MESSAGE, documentAddedCount);
} else {
```

The `LambdaKinesisSdkWriteHandler.java` is our Lambda handler class and has the following code:

```
public final class LambdaKinesisSdkWriteHandler implements
RequestHandler<Request, Response> {
    private final AmazonKinesis kinesisClient;

    public LambdaKinesisSdkWriteHandler() {
        this.kinesisClient = AmazonKinesisClientBuilder.standard()
                .withRegion(System.getenv("AWS_REGION"))
                .build();
    }

    public Response handleRequest(final Request request, final Context context) {
        context.getLogger().log("Received Request: " + request);

        final KinesisService kinesisService =  new
KinesisServiceImpl(this.kinesisClient);
        return kinesisService.addRecords(request, context.getLogger());
    }
}
```

Step 2 - Provisioning and testing Lambda (AWS CLI)

You can also go through the *Your first AWS Lambda* recipe in Chapter 1, *Getting Started with Serverless Computing on AWS*, and use CloudFormation for Lambda provisioning. Go through the following steps to deploy and invoke the Lambda function:

1. Run `mvn clean package` from inside the Lambda project root folder to create the Uber JAR.
2. Upload the Uber JAR to S3.
3. Create a role for the Lambda with an appropriate trust relationship definition.
4. Create a policy for basic logging permissions and attach it to the role.
5. Create a policy for the required Kinesis permissions and attach it to the role by going through the following steps:
   1. Create the policy document with the required Kinesis permissions using the following code:

      ```
      {
        "Version":"2012-10-17",
      ```

```
"Statement":[
{
"Effect":"Allow",
"Action":[
"kinesis:DescribeStream",
"kinesis:PutRecord",
"kinesis:PutRecords"
],
"Resource":[
"arn:aws:kinesis:*:*:*"
]
}
]
}
```

2. Save the file as `lambda-kinesis-producer-permissions.txt`.
3. Create the policy and attach it to the role.

6. Create the Lambda function as follows:

```
aws lambda create-function \
    --function-name lambda-kinesis-sdk-write \
    --runtime java8 \
    --role arn:aws:iam::<account id>:role/lambda_kinesis_write_role \
    --handler tech.heartin.books.serverlesscookbook.LambdaKinesisSdkWriteHandler::handleRequest \
    --code S3Bucket=serverless-cookbook,S3Key=lambda-kinesis-sdk-write-0.0.1-SNAPSHOT.jar \
    --timeout 15 \
    --memory-size 512 \
    --region us-east-1 \
    --profile admin
```

7. Invoke the Lambda function as follows:

```
aws lambda invoke \
    --invocation-type RequestResponse \
    --function-name lambda-kinesis-sdk-write \
    --log-type Tail \
    --payload file://resources/payload.json \
    --region us-east-1 \
    --profile admin \
    outputfile.txt
```

The payload file should correspond to our input domain object (`Request.java`), as shown in the following code:

```
{
    "streamName" : "my-first-kinesis-stream",
    "partitionKey": "12345",
    "payload": "testpayloadfromcli",
    "count": 10,
    "batchSize" : 5
}
```

If the `aws lambda invoke` command is successful, you should see a success message in the output file, `outputfile.txt` (assuming you return a success message from the Lambda similar to the code files).

Verify the invocation by retrieving the messages from the stream using the following steps:

1. First, retrieve the iterator, as shown in the following code:

   ```
   aws kinesis get-shard-iterator \
       --shard-id shardId-000000000000 \
       --shard-iterator-type TRIM_HORIZON \
       --stream-name my-first-kinesis-stream \
       --region us-east-1 \
       --profile admin
   ```

   If successful, you should get the following message back:

   ```
   {
       "ShardIterator": "AAAAAAAAAAFJUR6Bb1xkgWE+tvcfurlM+go8babQIZO2OZK67ENhFqur7mxkzzQ!RIwsyzCDWRJsP6/xzC+d3MKQ2gEGHvuMI8xfPnqeNu8cXo9ydoPriPOGxxN7/+jnPmz6AUytVStA=="
   }
   ```

2. Get the records using the shard iterator, as shown in the following code:

   ```
   aws kinesis get-records \
       --shard-iterator <shard iterator> \
       --region us-east-1 \
       --profile admin
   ```

Replace `<shard iterator>` with the shard iterator received in the previous step. This should return the following records:

```
{
    "Records": [
        {
            "SequenceNumber": "49591085571825738360783315497134932516437632568807915522",
            "ApproximateArrivalTimestamp": 1545473216.297,
            "Data": "dGVzdHBheWxvYWRmcm9tY2xpMQ==",
            "PartitionKey": "12345"
        },
```

I have not shown all the records here, only the first one. At the end, you will also get the next shard iterator, as shown in the following screenshot:

```
    ],
    "NextShardIterator": "AAAAAAAAAAHZdDSQw8SoeBsN32iLufI4EBTWbv3AqAR5YMRI2Xo00om/E7CmElTmn3Bs1B+rvHkheUbmivF9eiggujzFbOG5nfc+YboLOtKFWiYKFPvow2BNP+tZiSqPEg7Qa1Xko2IF4n4uiQ==",
    "MillisBehindLatest": 0
}
```

You may have to call `get-records` again with the shard iterator received in this step to retrieve further records.

8. Finally, you need to decode the Base64-encoded data using the following code:

```
$ echo dGVzdHBheWxvYWRmcm9tY2xpMQ== | base64 --decode
testpayloadfromcli1$
```

How it works...

In summary, we did the following in this recipe:

1. Created a Lambda function with basic Lambda permissions and Kinesis-specific permissions
2. Invoked Lambda with a payload as required by the input handler object (`Request.java`)
3. Verified that data was posted to the stream

From the Kinesis client, we retrieved `DescribeStreamResult` and from the `DescribeStreamResult`, we retrieved `StreamDescription`. The `StreamDescription` contains current status of the stream, the stream ARN, an array of shard objects of the stream, and information on whether there are more shards available. This was an optional step just to see the stream status.

The Kinesis client's `putRecords` method accepts a `PutRecordsRequest` object and the `PutRecordsRequest` object accepts a list of `PutRecordsRequestEntry` objects. We generated `PutRecordsRequestEntry` objects in a `for` loop and added them into a list. Once the list size crossed our defined batch size, we invoked the `putRecords` method of the Kinesis client and passed a `PutRecordsRequest` object with our list of `PutRecordsRequestEntry` objects.

There's more...

In this recipe, we used AWS Java SDK for Kinesis. We can also create producers using the **Kinesis Producer Library** (**KPL**). The KPL simplifies Kinesis producer application development and helps us to achieve high write throughput to a Kinesis data stream by aggregating smaller records into larger records, up to 1 MB in size. While the **Kinesis Client Library** (**KCL**) for Java can deaggregate records aggregated by KPL for regular applications, we need to use a special module to deaggregate records when using AWS Lambda as the consumer.

See also

- https://docs.aws.amazon.com/streams/latest/dev/developing-producers-with-kpl.html

Invoking Lambda with Kinesis events (Java)

There are different ways to manually read data from a KDS, such as using the SDK and KCL. We can also configure AWS to invoke a Lambda when records are put into a Kinesis stream. In this recipe, we will learn how to configure a lambda to be invoked when records are added to a Kinesis stream.

Getting ready

You will need the following prerequisites to complete this recipe:

- You need an active AWS account. You need to follow the section *Getting started* in the recipes *Your first AWS Lambda* and *Your first Lambda with AWS CLI* from Chapter 1, *Getting Started with Serverless Computing on AWS* to set up Java, Maven, the parent project, `serverless-cookbook-parent-aws-java` and AWS CLI, and may also read other notes there including code usage guidelines, S3 bucket creation and notes for the Windows users.
- Follow the recipe *Your first Kinesis data stream* and create a Kinesis stream named `kinesis-stream-for-event`.

How to do it...

We will now learn how we can implement a Java lambda function that will be invoked when records are added to a Kinesis stream. I will not show all the details of provisioning the lambda. You can refer to earlier recipes (mentioned in the *Getting ready* section).

Step 1 - Creating a Lambda project (Java)

In the previous recipes, we used a service interface and its implementation. In this recipe, we will create a `Lambda` function without a `service` class. As discussed in the previous chapter, you can follow any of the approaches that you prefer (or that your project prefers), but the underlying code will be the same.

> In this section, I will be discussing only the core application logic, and will not be discussing supporting code, such as imports, error handling, and Java doc comments; however, the complete working code will be provided along with the code files.

Let's start by defining the dependency for the AWS Kinesis SDK for Java in the POM file, as shown in the following code:

```
<dependency>
    <groupId>com.amazonaws</groupId>
    <artifactId>aws-java-sdk-kinesis</artifactId>
    <version>${aws.sdk.version}</version>
</dependency>
```

Chapter 7

The `POM` file also has dependencies for `aws-lambda-java-core`. The `aws.sdk.version` property is defined, along with other properties in the parent project `POM`, `serverless-cookbook-parent-aws-java`.

We can create the Java Lambda project with the following structure:

```
▼ ■ src
    ▼ ■ main
        ▼ ■ java
            ▼ ■ tech.heartin.books.serverlesscookbook
                  LambdaKinesisEventHandler
                  package-info.java
```

`LambdaKinesisEventHandler.java` can be implemented as follows:

```
public final class LambdaKinesisEventHandler implements
RequestHandler<KinesisEvent, Boolean> {
    public Boolean handleRequest(final KinesisEvent kinesisEvent, final
Context context) {
        LambdaLogger logger = context.getLogger();
        logger.log("Received Kinesis event: " + kinesisEvent);
        logger.log("Number of records: " +
kinesisEvent.getRecords().size());

        try {
            kinesisEvent.getRecords().forEach(r -> {
                final KinesisEvent.Record kr = r.getKinesis();
                logger.log("Record: " + kr.toString());
                logger.log("Data: " +
StandardCharsets.UTF_8.decode(kr.getData()).toString());
            });
        } catch (final Exception e) {
            logger.log("There was an exception: " + e.getMessage());
            return false;
        }
        return true;
    }
}
```

Step 2 - Provisioning and testing Lambda (AWS CLI)

Go through the following steps to deploy and invoke the lambda. You may also follow *Your first Lambda with AWS CLI* recipe of Chapter 1, *Getting Started with Serverless Computing on AWS* and use CloudFormation for Lambda provisioning:

1. Run `mvn clean package` from inside the Lambda project root folder to create the Uber JAR.
2. Upload the Uber JAR to S3.
3. Create a role named `lambda-invoke-kinesis-event-role` for the lambda with an appropriate trust relationship definition.
4. Create and attach a policy for basic logging permissions and attach it to the role.
5. Create a policy for the required Kinesis permissions using the following policy document and attach it to the role:

```
{
    "Version":"2012-10-17",
    "Statement":[
        {
            "Effect":"Allow",
            "Action":[
                "kinesis:GetRecords",
                "kinesis:GetShardIterator",
                "kinesis:DescribeStream",
                "kinesis:ListStreams"
            ],
            "Resource":[
                "arn:aws:kinesis:*:*:*"
            ]
        }
    ]
}
```

Save the file as `lambda-kinesis-producer-permissions.txt`, create a policy using this file, and attach it to the role.

6. Create the lambda function as follows:

```
aws lambda create-function \
    --function-name lambda-invoke-kinesis-event \
    --runtime java8 \
    --role arn:aws:iam::<account id>:role/lambda-invoke-kinesis-event-role \
    --handler tech.heartin.books.serverlesscookbook.LambdaKinesisEventHandler::handleRequest \
    --code S3Bucket=serverless-cookbook,S3Key=lambda-invoke-kinesis-event-0.0.1-SNAPSHOT.jar \
    --timeout 15 \
    --memory-size 512 \
    --region us-east-1 \
    --profile admin
```

7. Create an event source mapping for invoking the lambda function, as follows:

```
aws lambda create-event-source-mapping \
    --event-source-arn arn:aws:kinesis:us-east-1:<account id>:stream/kinesis-stream-for-event \
    --function-name lambda-invoke-kinesis-event \
    --starting-position LATEST \
    --batch-size 3 \
    --region us-east-1 \
    --profile admin
```

8. Verify the invocation by sending messages to the stream. You can do this by going through the following steps:

   1. Send messages with different payload text, following this:

      ```
      aws kinesis put-record \
          --stream-name kinesis-stream-for-event \
          --partition-key 12345 \
          --data sampledata01 \
          --region us-east-1 \
          --profile admin
      ```

   2. Check the CloudWatch logs.

We can check CloudWatch logs from Management console as follows:

1. Log in to the **Management** console and go to the Lambda service.
2. Click on your **Lambda** to see its configuration.
3. Click on the **Monitoring** tab.
4. Click on **View logs in CloudWatch**. Click on a **Log Stream** and check the logs.
5. You should see logs similar to those shown in the following screenshot:

CloudWatch > Log Groups > /aws/lambda/lambda-invoke-kinesis-event > 2018/12/24/[$LATEST]5479094867e

Filter events

Time (UTC +00:00)	Message
2018-12-24	
04:35:10	START RequestId: 3413b40a-063e-42c4-aa06-0205f104bd67 Version: $LATEST
04:35:10	Received Kinesis event: {[{eventSource: aws:kinesis,kinesis: {SequenceNumber: 49
04:35:10	Number of records: 1
04:35:10	Record: {SequenceNumber: 49591309472734779300945616534014129624248721
04:35:10	Data: sampledata01
04:35:10	END RequestId: 3413b40a-063e-42c4-aa06-0205f104bd67

How it works...

In summary, we did the following in this recipe:

1. Created a lambda that can be invoked when records are added to a Kinesis stream.
2. Added an event source mapping for invoking the lambda when records are added to a Kinesis stream.
3. Checked the `CloudWatch` logs. We will learn more about CloudWatch in the next chapter.

Event source mapping creates a mapping between an event source and an AWS lambda function. The lambda's `handler` function is then triggered by events on the event source. In our case, we created an event source mapping for our Lambda with a Kinesis event type.

The following are the three event source types that are currently supported:

- Amazon Kinesis
- Amazon SQS
- Amazon DynamoDB

We create all lambda triggers in a similar way to how we did it from UI. However, from CLI, we do this differently for different services. For example, Kinesis, SQS, and DynamoDB triggers are added using event source mapping, but for services such as API Gateway and Alexa Skills, triggers are defined when we use the `add-permission` subcommand of the lambda CLI command to add a permission policy, and for SNS, the lambda function is subscribed to the SNS topic using the `aws sns subscribe` command.

There's more...

We invoked the lambda function using triggers in this recipe. You can also use the AWS Kinesis SDK or the KCL to read from a Kinesis stream. However, a lambda trigger is the most common way to read from a stream in serverless applications. Refer to the *See also* section to read more about SDK and KCL approaches.

See also

You may read more about developing consumers using SDK at `https://docs.aws.amazon.com/streams/latest/dev/developing-consumers-with-sdk.html`.

You may read more about developing consumers with KCL at `https://docs.aws.amazon.com/streams/latest/dev/developing-consumers-with-kcl.html`.

Using Amazon ML for binary classification (AWS CLI)

This recipe will outline the steps to perform a simple machine learning service task following the AWS ML tutorial for the **Management** console, but also using AWS CLI APIs. The objective of this recipe is to get you started with using Amazon ML from an AWS CLI API perspective.

Getting ready

For the purpose of this demonstration, we will use the sample data CSV provided by AWS at `s3://aml-sample-data/banking.csv`. This CSV is provided by AWS for their **Management** console's step-by-step tutorial, as shown in the following screenshot:

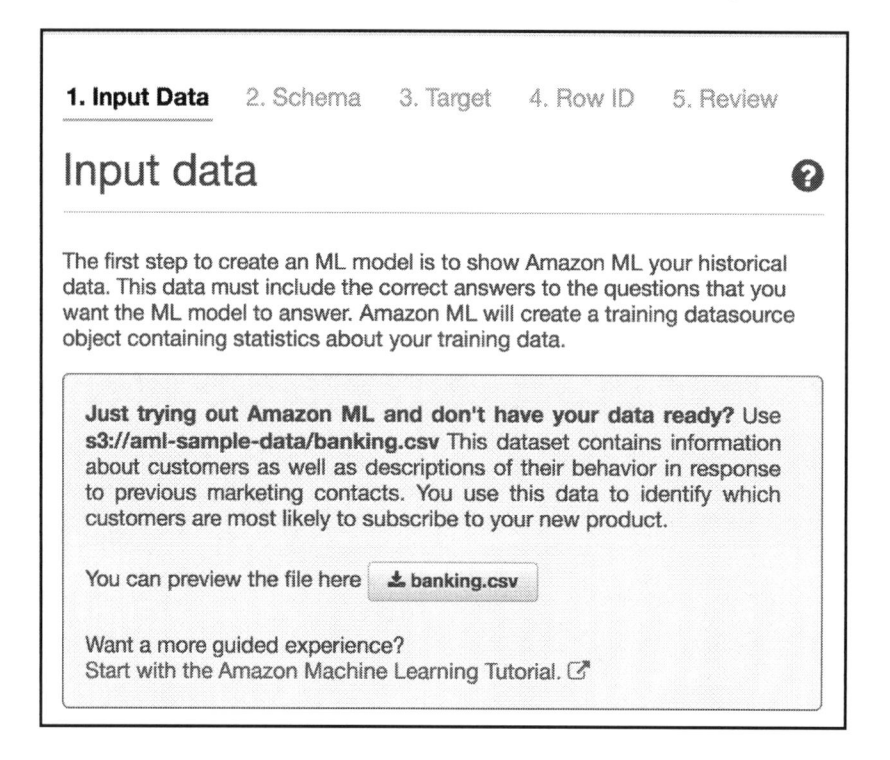

> You may download and familiarize yourself with the data, or simply directly use it in this recipe by going through the steps in the *How to do it* section.

How to do it...

In this recipe, we will learn how to make predictions with an AWS ML service for binary classification using AWS CLI by going through the following steps:

1. Prepare the data as a CSV and upload it to S3. Amazon ML requires a CSV with each row corresponding to an observation that may be used for training or testing. Each column also needs a name, which you can specify as the first row or specify separately using a schema file. You may also split data into multiple CSV files within the same bucket. If you have multiple files, you should provide a path ending with a forward slash (/).

   As mentioned in the *Getting ready* section, we will reuse the sample data available in AWS, which is already uploaded to S3 at `s3://aml-sample-data/banking.csv`.

2. Create the data source.

   > You should always split your data into two sets and create two data sources, one for training and one for evaluation. For example, you may use 70 percent of the data for training the system and creating the ML model, and the remaining 30 percent can be used for evaluating the ML model that was created. For this recipe, I will be using the same data source for both training and testing to keep things simple, but you should create two data sources in real world—one for training and one for evaluation—and use them accordingly.

   We can create an S3 data source object using the `aws machinelearning create-data-source-from-s3` command by going through the following steps:

   1. Create a sample JSON input using the `generate-cli-skeleton` subcommand, as follows:

      ```
      aws machinelearning create-data-source-from-s3 \
          --generate-cli-skeleton input
      ```

> **TIP:** Since the command input has nested JSON, it is a good practice to generate the sample input using the `generate-cli-skeleton` subcommand.

2. Prepare the input JSON with actual values, as follows:

```
{
    "DataSourceId": "my-first-s3-ds-id",
    "DataSourceName": "My First S3 DataSource",
    "DataSpec": {
        "DataLocationS3": "s3://aml-sample-data/banking.csv",
        "DataRearrangement": "{\"splitting\":{\"percentBegin\":10,\"percentEnd\":60}}",
        "DataSchemaLocationS3": "s3://aml-sample-data/banking.csv.schema"
    },
    "ComputeStatistics": true
}
```

Save this file as `create-data-source-from-s3-cli-input.json`.

3. Execute the `aws machinelearning create-data-source-from-s3` command, providing the input JSON file, as follows:

```
aws machinelearning create-data-source-from-s3 \
  --cli-input-json file://create-data-source-from-s3-cli-input.json \
  --region us-east-1 \
  --profile admin
```

This command works asynchronously, and immediately returns the data source ID, as shown in the following screenshot:

```
{
    "DataSourceId": "my-first-s3-ds-id"
}
```

You can check the status of your data sources with the `describe-data-sources` subcommand, as follows:

```
aws machinelearning describe-data-sources \
    --region us-east-1 \
    --profile admin
```

> **TIP**
> You can also filter the data sources returned in the response with additional options provided by the `describe-data-sources` subcommand. We did not use additional filtering here, as we only had one data source. You can check the *See more* section for a link to the AWS documentation for this sub command.

Once completed successfully, you should see the following response:

```
{
    "Results": [
        {
            "DataSourceId": "my-first-s3-ds-id",
            "DataLocationS3": "s3://aml-sample-data/banking.csv",
            "DataRearrangement": "{\"splitting\":{\"percentBegin\":10,\"percentEnd\":60}}",
            "CreatedByIamUser": "arn:aws:iam::            :user/heartin_admin",
            "CreatedAt": 1546059702.39,
            "LastUpdatedAt": 1546059946.154,
            "DataSizeInBytes": 2441459,
            "NumberOfFiles": 1,
            "Name": "My First S3 DataSource",
            "Status": "COMPLETED",
            "ComputeStatistics": true,
            "ComputeTime": 890000,
            "FinishedAt": 1546059946.154,
            "StartedAt": 1546059703.477
        }
    ]
}
```

Initially, when you run the commands, you will see the status as `INPROGRESS` until it is completed.

Alternatively, you can use the `get-data-source` subcommand to get the details for a particular data source.

3. Create a ML binary model based on the data source by using the following command:

```
aws machinelearning create-ml-model \
  --ml-model-id 'my-first-ml-model-id' \
  --ml-model-name 'My First ML Model' \
  --ml-model-type 'BINARY' \
  --training-data-source-id 'my-first-s3-ds-id' \
  --region us-east-1 \
  --profile admin
```

This command works asynchronously and immediately returns the ML model source ID, as shown in the following screenshot:

```
{
    "MLModelId": "my-first-ml-model-id"
}
```

You can check the status of your data sources with the `describe-ml-models` subcommand, as shown in the following code:

```
aws machinelearning describe-ml-models \
    --region us-east-1 \
    --profile admin
```

> **TIP**
> You can also filter the ML models returned in the response with additional options provided by the `describe-ml-models` subcommand. We did not use additional filtering here, as we only had one ML model. You can check the *See more* section for a link to the AWS documentation for this subcommand.

Once completed successfully, you should see the following response. The first part of the response contains the status and basic timestamp information:

```
{
    "Results": [
        {
            "MLModelId": "my-first-ml-model-id",
            "TrainingDataSourceId": "my-first-s3-ds-id",
            "CreatedByIamUser": "arn:aws:iam::          :user/heartin_admin",
            "CreatedAt": 1546062817.415,
            "LastUpdatedAt": 1546063005.486,
            "Name": "My First ML Model",
            "Status": "COMPLETED",
```

Initially, when you run the commands, you will see the status as INPROGRESS until it is completed.

The response also contains additional information of the model, including the defaults, as shown in the following screenshot:

```
            "SizeInBytes": 454760,
            "EndpointInfo": {
                "PeakRequestsPerSecond": 0,
                "EndpointStatus": "NONE"
            },
            "TrainingParameters": {
                "algorithm": "sgd",
                "sgd.l1RegularizationAmount": "0.0",
                "sgd.l2RegularizationAmount": "1E-6",
                "sgd.maxMLModelSizeInBytes": "100000000",
                "sgd.maxPasses": "10",
                "sgd.shuffleType": "none"
            },
            "InputDataLocationS3": "s3://aml-sample-data/banking.csv",
            "Algorithm": "sgd",
            "MLModelType": "BINARY",
            "ComputeTime": 76000,
            "FinishedAt": 1546063005.486,
            "StartedAt": 1546062818.784
        }
    ]
}
```

Alternatively, you can use the `get-ml-model` subcommand to get the details for a particular ML model.

4. Create an evaluation to verify your dataset. As mentioned before, I will be using the same dataset to keep things simple, as the aim of this recipe is to understand the process and syntax. However, you should always split your data into two sets and create two data sources, one for training and one for evaluation.

We can create an evaluation set using the `aws machinelearning create-evaluation` command, as follows:

```
aws machinelearning create-evaluation \
    --evaluation-id 'my-first-ml-evaluation-id' \
    --evaluation-name 'My First ML Evaluation' \
    --ml-model-id 'my-first-ml-model-id' \
    --evaluation-data-source-id 'my-first-s3-ds-id' \
    --region us-east-1 \
    --profile admin
```

> **TIP**
> You can also filter the ML evaluations returned in the response with additional options provided by the `describe-evaluations` subcommand. We did not use additional filtering here as we only had one ML model. You can check the *See more* section for a link to the AWS documentation for this subcommand.

Once completed successfully, you should see the following response:

```
{
    "Results": [
        {
            "EvaluationId": "my-first-ml-evaluation-id",
            "MLModelId": "my-first-ml-model-id",
            "EvaluationDataSourceId": "my-first-s3-ds-id",
            "InputDataLocationS3": "s3://aml-sample-data/banking.csv",
            "CreatedByIamUser": "arn:aws:iam::        :user/heartin_admin",
            "CreatedAt": 1546065380.356,
            "LastUpdatedAt": 1546065563.439,
            "Name": "My First ML Evaluation",
            "Status": "COMPLETED",
            "PerformanceMetrics": {
                "Properties": {
                    "BinaryAUC": "0.939753228565232"
                }
            },
            "ComputeTime": 122000,
            "FinishedAt": 1546065563.439,
            "StartedAt": 1546065381.673
        }
    ]
}
```

The closer the value of BinaryAUC is to 1, the better the model is. We got a very good result since we used the same dataset for training and evaluation.

Alternatively, you can use the `get-evaluation` subcommand to get the details of a particular evaluation.

5. Predictions can be real-time or batch. In this recipe, we will make a real-time prediction. First, we need to generate an endpoint.

   Execute the `get-ml-model` subcommand as follows:

   ```
   aws machinelearning get-ml-model \
       --ml-model-id 'my-first-ml-model-id' \
       --region us-east-1 \
       --profile admin
   ```

   The response will contain an endpoint section, shown in the following screenshot, denoting that no endpoint is generated:

   ```
   "EndpointInfo": {
       "PeakRequestsPerSecond": 0,
       "EndpointStatus": "NONE"
   },
   ```

   1. Create the real-time endpoint using the following code:

      ```
      aws machinelearning create-realtime-endpoint \
          --ml-model-id 'my-first-ml-model-id' \
          --region us-east-1 \
          --profile admin
      ```

      This will immediately return an endpoint with a status of UPDATING, as shown in the following screenshot:

```
{
    "MLModelId": "my-first-ml-model-id",
    "RealtimeEndpointInfo": {
        "PeakRequestsPerSecond": 0,
        "CreatedAt": 1546139685.587,
        "EndpointUrl": "https://realtime.machinelearning.us-east-1.amazonaws.com",
        "EndpointStatus": "UPDATING"
    }
}
```

You can use the `get-ml-model` subcommand as we did earlier in this section to get the details of the ML model, including the endpoint status. Once completed, the status and endpoint details should look as follows:

```
{
    "MLModelId": "my-first-ml-model-id",
    "TrainingDataSourceId": "my-first-s3-ds-id",
    "CreatedByIamUser": "arn:aws:iam:::user/heartin_admin",
    "CreatedAt": 1546062817.415,
    "LastUpdatedAt": 1546063005.486,
    "Name": "My First ML Model",
    "Status": "COMPLETED",
    "SizeInBytes": 454760,
    "EndpointInfo": {
        "PeakRequestsPerSecond": 200,
        "CreatedAt": 1546139745.192,
        "EndpointUrl": "https://realtime.machinelearning.us-east-1.amazonaws.com",
        "EndpointStatus": "READY"
    },
```

The response will also contain additional information, such as `TrainingParameters`, `InputDataLocationS3`, `MLModelType` (which in our case is `Binary`), `LogUri`, `ComputeTime`, `FinishedAt`, and `StartedAt`.

2. You can predict the target field (`0` or `1` for `Binary`) using the endpoint of the `predict` subcommand to provide the other record fields, as shown in the following code:

```
aws machinelearning predict \
    --ml-model-id 'my-first-ml-model-id' \
    --record 'age=44,job=blue-collar,marital=married,education=basic.4y,default=unknown,housing=yes,loan=no,contact=cellular,month=aug,day_of_week=thu,duration=210,campaign=1,pdays=999,previous=0,poutcome=nonexistent,emp_var_rate=1.4,cons_price_idx=93.444,cons_conf_idx=-36.1,euribor3m=4.963,nr_employed=5228.1' \
    --predict-endpoint 'https://realtime.machinelearning.us-east-1.amazonaws.com' \
    --region us-east-1 \
    --profile admin
```

This will return the following response:

```
{
    "Prediction": {
        "predictedLabel": "0",
        "predictedScores": {
            "0": 0.015805380418896675
        },
        "details": {
            "Algorithm": "SGD",
            "PredictiveModelType": "BINARY"
        }
    }
}
```

I just picked up a record from the data that we have. However, you can create a random record or pick one based on your use case and apply the preceding syntax.

> Binary classification ML models use a `ScoreThreshold` to mark the boundary between a positive prediction and a negative prediction. Output values greater than or equal to the ScoreThreshold will receive a positive result from the ML model (such as 1 or true). Output values less than the ScoreThreshold receive a negative response from the ML model (e.g. 0 or false). We have not altered the default threshold score for this recipe, which was 0.5. However, you may change it using the `update-ml-model` subcommand.

How it works...

In summary, we did the following in this recipe:

1. Learned how to prepare the data as a CSV and upload it to S3
2. Created an S3 data source
3. Created an ML model
4. Created an evaluation and verified the model
5. Created an endpoint for real-time prediction
6. Predicted the target value for a sample record

Let's discuss some of the concepts we learned in the recipe in a bit more detail.

Types of models

Amazon ML is used primarily for the following prediction use cases:

- **Binary classification:** Classifies values as one of two categories, such as true or false (or 1 or 0)
- **Multivalue classification:** Classifies values into multiple groups
- **Regression:** Predicts a numeric value

DataSource object

A `DataSource` object can reference data from different sources, such as S3, Redshift, and RDS. We used an S3 data source in this recipe. A `DataSource` object needs to be specified for operations such as `CreateMLModel`, `CreateEvaluation`, or `CreateBatchPrediction`.

Receiver Operating Characteristic and Area Under the ROC

A **Receiver Operating Characteristic (ROC)** curve is a graph that shows the performance of a classification model at different classification thresholds. The **Area Under the ROC** Curve measures the entire two-dimensional area underneath the entire ROC curve, aggregating the measure of the performance across all classification thresholds.

The AUC value denotes the ability of the model to predict a higher score for positive examples compared to negative examples. The AUC value is a decimal value from 0 to 1. The higher the value of the AUC, the better the ML model is. We use the AUC to measure the quality of the binary classification model. For our recipe, since I used the same dataset for training and testing, the AUC value was very close to 1.

There's more...

We used the AUC value to measure the accuracy of our binary classification model. For multivalue classification models, AWS uses the macroaverage F1 score to evaluate the predictive accuracy of a multiclass metric. A larger F1 score indicates better predictive accuracy for a regression model; AWS uses the **root mean square error** (**RMSE**) metric. The smaller the value of the RMSE, the better the accuracy of the model.

A detailed discussion of ML concepts is beyond the scope of this book. The aim of this recipe was to get you started with Amazon ML using AWS CLI APIs, and to familiarize you with a few ML terms that you can explore further. You can follow the reference links or other books on ML to learn more and experiment with the concepts further. I have also added links to some datasets in the *See also* section that you can use for your experiments.

See also

- http://archive.ics.uci.edu/ml/index.php
- https://www.kaggle.com/datasets
- https://docs.aws.amazon.com/machine-learning/latest/dg/understanding-the-data-format-for-amazon-ml.html
- https://docs.aws.amazon.com/cli/latest/reference/machinelearning/describe-data-sources.html
- https://docs.aws.amazon.com/cli/latest/reference/machinelearning/describe-ml-models.html
- https://docs.aws.amazon.com/cli/latest/reference/machinelearning/describe-evaluations.html
- https://docs.aws.amazon.com/machine-learning/latest/dg/evaluating_models.html

Building and testing an Alexa skill (Java for Lambda, CLI for Alexa skill)

Conversational user interfaces (**CUI**) are platforms that support conversations similar to real human conversations. They help humans to talk to a system using their natural language rather than using a new programming language or a **domain-specific language** (**DSL**). Smart appliances, such as TVs, smart speakers, and smart chatbots, that can understand and interpret natural language are examples of conversational interfaces.

Amazon Alexa is a virtual assistant that lives on the cloud. Alexa can listen to our requests and provide voice responses or take actions, such as switching on a smart bulb. Amazon ships Alexa along with its Echo devices, but Alexa can be used with other devices as well, making use of its APIs. You can extend the default Alexa functionality by creating your own Alexa skills.

In this recipe, we will create a simple Alexa skill that will introduce a person. This is a very basic skill, but it can still be useful for any events you might be hosting at work or even outside. We can use an Echo device to interact with Alexa through our Alexa skill. To demonstrate the Alexa skill, you can use any Alexa-enabled device, and for learning and testing purposes you can also use a simulator, such as `echosim.io`.

Getting ready

You should have the following prerequisites to go through this recipe:

- You need an active AWS account. You need to follow *Getting started* in the recipes *Your first AWS Lambda* and *Your first Lambda with AWS CLI* sections from Chapter 1, *Getting Started with Serverless Computing on AWS* to set up Java, Maven, the parent project, `serverless-cookbook-parent-aws-java`, and AWS CLI, and may also read other notes there, including code usage guidelines, S3 bucket creation, and notes for Windows users.
- Knowledge of how to install and configure the Alexa skills Kit CLI.
- An Echo device to talk to Alexa using the skill that we create. However, if you do not have an Echo device, you can use a simulator, such as `echosim.io`.
- A basic understanding of Java and Maven, and the steps for creating and invoking Lambda, as given in `Chapter 1, Getting Started with Serverless Computing on AWS`.

Installing and configuring the ASK CLI

> If you are working on a Windows platform, you need to first install the `Node.js` Windows build tools before installing `ask-cli`.

You can install `ask-cli` using the following code:

```
npm install -g ask-cli
```

Configuring ask-cli for the first time

Once `ask-cli` is installed, you can initialize it as follows:

```
ask init
```

`ask-cli` will ask you to choose the AWS profile that you want. You can choose the profile that you created as part of *Your first Lambda with AWS CLI* recipe in `Chapter 1`, *Getting Started with Serverless Computing on AWS*.

Once you select the profile, it will open a browser window where you have to sign in with your AWS credentials, and you will be shown a confirmation screen, as shown in the following screenshot:

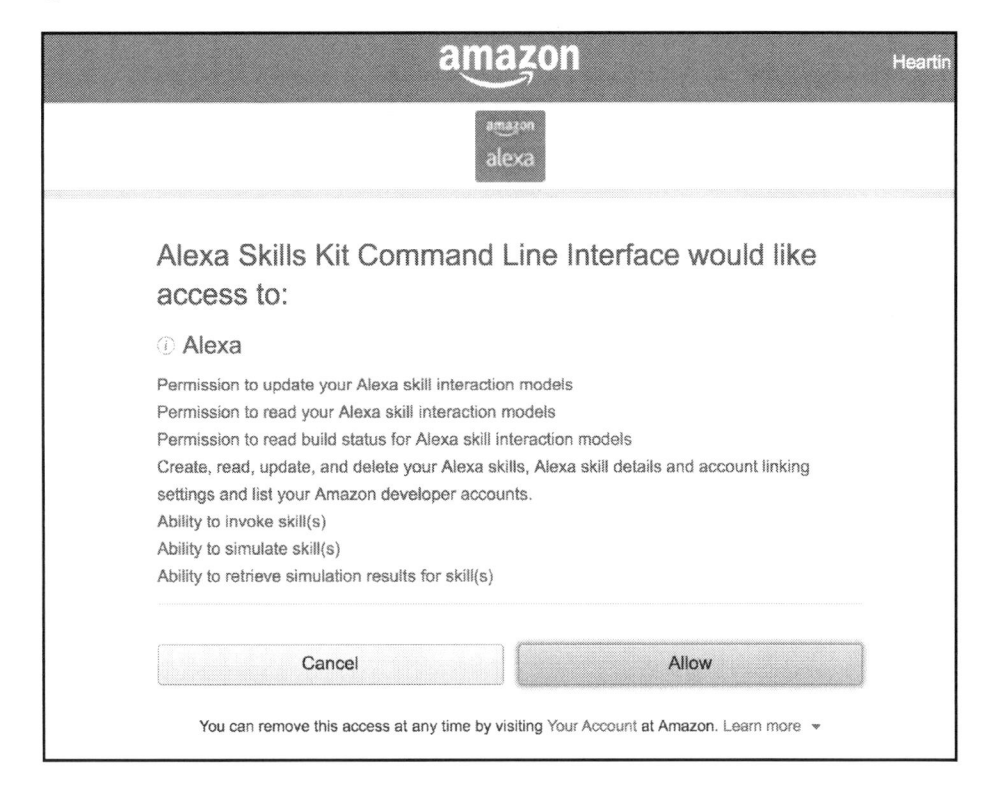

Once you click **Allow**, you will be redirected to a success page, as shown in the following screeenshot:

```
← → C   ⓘ 127.0.0.1:9090/cb?code=ANFIlWItEPKtqQkfFndl&scope=alexa%3A%3Aask%3Askills

Sign in was successful. Close this browser and return to the command line interface.
```

You can close the window and return to the Terminal, as shown in the following screenshot:

```
$ ask init
---------------------- Initialize CLI ----------------------
Setting up ask profile: [default]
? Please choose one from the following AWS profiles for skill's Lambda function
deployment.
  admin
Switch to 'Login with Amazon' page...
Tokens fetched and recorded in ask-cli config.
Vendor ID set as M334P5DTKSV0GP

Profile [default] initialized successfully.
```

> If you want to complete the initialization without opening a browser, you can use the `ask init --no-browser` command.

How to do it...

In this recipe, we will create a simple Alexa skill. When you ask Alexa to say introduction for a person, it will read out an introduction. You can use this simple skill in your company to introduce a guest or to introduce yourself in a talk or presentation. You can make changes to the recipe's code files and deploy it into your AWS account.

Alexa skill building has two parts: a Lambda backend that does the actual processing (returning the introduction text in our case) and the Alexa skill in the developer portal that interpret user requests, talks to the backend and returns the response.

Step 1 - Creating the Lambda project (Java)

The ASK SDK requires intent handlers for each of the expected intents. We will create intent handlers for our application-specific intent (for example, a self-intro intent), the launch intent—as well as help, stop, and cancel intents for the inbuilt intents—a fallback intent, and a session end request intent. We will then create a parent lambda handler class that registers all these intent handlers.

> I will be discussing only the core application logic and will not be discussing supporting code, such as imports, error handling, and Java doc comments in the book. However, the complete working code is provided along with the code files.

Let's start by defining the dependency of ASK SDK for Java in the POM file, as follows:

```xml
<dependency>
    <groupId>com.amazon.alexa</groupId>
    <artifactId>ask-sdk</artifactId>
    <version>${ask.sdk.version}</version>
</dependency>
```

The POM file also has dependencies for `aws-lambda-java-core`. The `ask.sdk.version` property is defined along with other properties in the parent project, POM `serverless-cookbook-parent-aws-java`:

```xml
<ask.sdk.version>2.11.2</ask.sdk.version>
```

We can create the Java Lambda project with the following package structure:

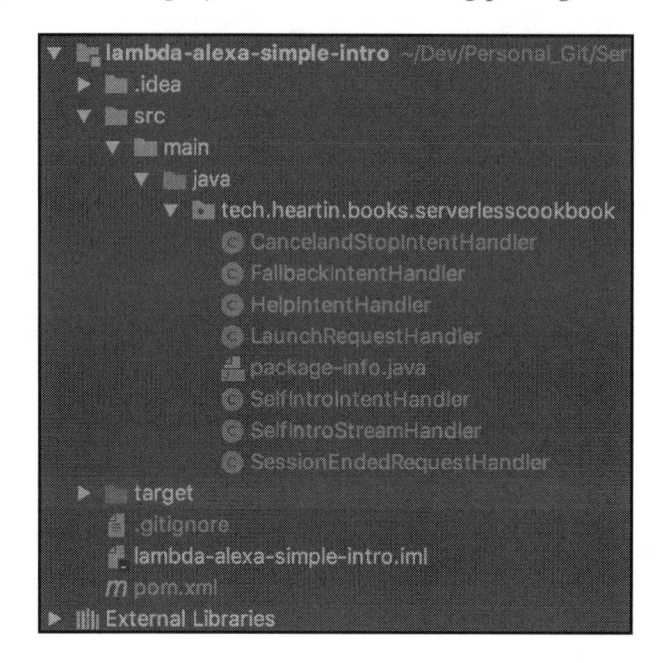

```
lambda-alexa-simple-intro  ~/Dev/Personal_Git/Ser
  .idea
  src
    main
      java
        tech.heartin.books.serverlesscookbook
          CancelandStopIntentHandler
          FallbackIntentHandler
          HelpIntentHandler
          LaunchRequestHandler
          package-info.java
          SelfIntroIntentHandler
          SelfIntroStreamHandler
          SessionEndedRequestHandler
  target
  .gitignore
  lambda-alexa-simple-intro.iml
  pom.xml
External Libraries
```

The `SelfIntroIntentHandler` class defines the speech text that does the introduction, as follows:

```
public class SelfIntroIntentHandler implements RequestHandler {

    @Override
    public final boolean canHandle(final HandlerInput input) {
        return input.matches(Predicates.intentName("SelfIntroIntent"));
    }

    @Override
    public final Optional<Response> handle(final HandlerInput input) {
        String speechText = "Hello, this is Alexa saying intro for Heartin Kanikathottu. "
            + "Heartin is a senior software engineer and blogger with around 11 years of IT experience. "
            + "He likes to share his technical knowledge through his blogs such as CloudMaterials.com "
            + "and Java J EE dot com. "
            + "He also likes to mentor juniors and take sessions at meetups and conferences.";

        return input.getResponseBuilder()
```

```
                .withSpeech(speechText)
                .withSimpleCard("SelfIntro", speechText)
                .build();
    }

}
```

The `LaunchRequestHandler` class defines the speech text for the app launch, as follows:

```
public class LaunchRequestHandler implements RequestHandler {

    @Override
    public final boolean canHandle(final HandlerInput input) {
        return input.matches(Predicates.requestType(LaunchRequest.class));
    }

    @Override
    public final Optional<Response> handle(final HandlerInput input) {
        String speechText = "Welcome to the Self Intro Alexa Skill for Heartin, you may say 'please say intro'";
        return input.getResponseBuilder()
                .withSpeech(speechText)
                .withSimpleCard("SelfIntro", speechText)
                .withReprompt(speechText)
                .build();
    }
}
```

The `HelpIntentHandler` class defines the speech text for the inbuilt intent `AMAZON.HelpIntent`, as follows:

```
public class HelpIntentHandler implements RequestHandler {

    @Override
    public final boolean canHandle(final HandlerInput input) {
        return input.matches(intentName("AMAZON.HelpIntent"));
    }

    @Override
    public final Optional<Response> handle(final HandlerInput input) {
        String speechText = "You you may say 'please say intro'!";
        return input.getResponseBuilder()
                .withSpeech(speechText)
                .withSimpleCard("SelfIntro", speechText)
                .withReprompt(speechText)
                .build();
    }
}
```

The `CancelandStopIntentHandler` class defines the speech text for the for the inbuilt intents `AMAZON.StopIntent` and `AMAZON.CancelIntent`:

```
public class CancelandStopIntentHandler implements RequestHandler {

    @Override
    public final boolean canHandle(final HandlerInput input) {
        return
input.matches(intentName("AMAZON.StopIntent").or(intentName("AMAZON.CancelI
ntent")));
    }

    @Override
    public final Optional<Response> handle(final HandlerInput input) {
        return input.getResponseBuilder()
                .withSpeech("Goodbye buddy")
                .withSimpleCard("SelfIntro", "Goodbye")
                .build();
    }

}
```

The `FallbackIntentHandler` class defines the speech text for the fallbacks when no intents match, as follows:

```
public class FallbackIntentHandler implements RequestHandler {

    @Override
    public final boolean canHandle(final HandlerInput input) {
        return input.matches(intentName("AMAZON.FallbackIntent"));
    }

    @Override
    public final Optional<Response> handle(final HandlerInput input) {
        String speechText = "Sorry buddy, I don't know that. You can say
try saying help!";
        return input.getResponseBuilder()
                .withSpeech(speechText)
                .withSimpleCard("SelfIntro", speechText)
                .withReprompt(speechText)
                .build();
    }

}
```

We will also define a `SessionEndedRequestHandler` class for handling session termination requests, as shown in the following code:

```
public class SessionEndedRequestHandler implements RequestHandler {

    @Override
    public final boolean canHandle(final HandlerInput input) {
        return input.matches(requestType(SessionEndedRequest.class));
    }

    @Override
    public final Optional<Response> handle(final HandlerInput input) {
        //any cleanup logic goes here
        return input.getResponseBuilder().build();
    }

}
```

Finally, we will create the Lambda handler class that extends `SkillStreamHandler`, as follows:

```
public class SelfIntroStreamHandler extends SkillStreamHandler {

    private static Skill skill = Skills.standard()
            .addRequestHandlers(
                    new CancelandStopIntentHandler(),
                    new SelfIntroIntentHandler(),
                    new HelpIntentHandler(),
                    new LaunchRequestHandler(),
                    new SessionEndedRequestHandler())
            .build();

    public SelfIntroStreamHandler() {
        super(skill);
    }

}
```

Step 2 - Provisioning Lambda (AWS CLI)

Go through the following steps to deploy and invoke the lambda. Refer to previous recipes or code files if you need more details on any of the steps. You can also follow *Your first Lambda with AWS CLI* recipe in Chapter 1, *Getting Started with Serverless Computing on AWS* and use CloudFormation for Lambda provisioning:

1. Run `mvn clean package` from inside the Lambda project root folder to create the Uber JAR.
2. Upload the Uber JAR to S3.
3. Create a role called `lambda-alexa-simple-intro-role` for the lambda, with an appropriate trust relationship definition.
4. Create a policy for basic logging permissions and attach it to the role.
5. Create the lambda function as follows:

```
aws lambda create-function \
    --function-name lambda-alexa-simple-intro \
    --runtime java8 \
    --role arn:aws:iam::<account id>:role/lambda-alexa-simple-intro-role \
    --handler tech.heartin.books.serverlesscookbook.SelfIntroStreamHandler::handleRequest \
    --code S3Bucket=serverless-cookbook,S3Key=lambda-alexa-simple-intro-0.0.1-SNAPSHOT.jar \
    --timeout 15 \
    --memory-size 512 \
    --region us-east-1 \
    --profile admin
```

6. Give permission for the Alexa skill to invoke this Lambda as follows:

```
aws lambda add-permission \
  --function-name lambda-alexa-simple-intro \
  --statement-id "12345" \
  --action "lambda:InvokeFunction" \
  --principal "alexa-appkit.amazon.com" \
  --region us-east-1 \
  --profile admin
```

We have given permission to any Alexa skill to invoke this lambda. Once you create a skill, you can remove this lambda and add a permission that allows only a particular skill to invoke this lambda, as shown in the following code:

```
aws lambda remove-permission \
    --function-name lambda-alexa-simple-intro \
    --statement-id "12345" \
    --region us-east-1 \
    --profile admin

aws lambda add-permission \
    --function-name lambda-alexa-simple-intro \
    --statement-id "12345" \
    --action "lambda:InvokeFunction" \
    --principal "alexa-appkit.amazon.com" \
    --event-source-token <skill id from lambda> \
    --region us-east-1 \
    --profile admin
```

Step 3 - Building an Alexa skill with ASK CLI

We can build an Alexa skill by going through the following steps:

1. Prepare the skill manifest JSON file, as shown in the following code:

```
{
    "manifest": {
        "publishingInformation": {
            "locales": {
                "en-US": {
                    "summary": "A simple skill to say introduction for someone",
                    "examplePhrases": [
                        "Alexa please say intro",
                        "say intro",
                        "help"
                    ],
                    "name": "self-intro",
                    "description": "Simple Intro Skill"
                }
            },
            "isAvailableWorldwide": true,
            "testingInstructions": "1) Say 'Alexa, say intro'.",
            "category": "ORGANIZERS_AND_ASSISTANTS",
            "distributionCountries": []
        },
        "apis": {
```

```
                    "custom": {
                        "endpoint": {
                            "uri": "arn:aws:lambda:us-east-1:<account
    id>:function:lambda-alexa-simple-intro"
                        }
                    }
                },
                "manifestVersion": "1.0"
            }
        }
```

Save this file as `skill.json`.

I have shown only one locale section for US: `en-US`. You can add additional locales. For example, you can add `en-IN` if you are planning to test this with an echo with **English (IN)** set. I have added two locales in the code files to demonstrate this.

2. Create a skill using this JSON file, as shown in the following code:

    ```
    ask api create-skill --file skill.json
    ```

If the skill manifest JSON file was created successfully, you should get the following response:

```
Create skill request submitted.
Skill ID: amzn1.ask.skill.ab1fdfac-42eb-42ae-aeae-b761f3c903c1
Please use the following command to track the skill status:
    ask api get-skill-status -s amzn1.ask.skill.ab1fdfac-42eb-42ae-aeae-b761f3c903c1
```

You can execute the command that is provided to track the skill as follows:

```
$ ask api get-skill-status -s amzn1.ask.skill.ab1fdfac-42eb-42ae-aeae-b761f3c903c1
```

If the skill creation was successful, you should get the following message:

```json
{
  "manifest": {
    "eTag": "4d7be69ac8b33ececf1c5df9b9c6f9a4",
    "lastUpdateRequest": {
      "status": "SUCCEEDED"
    }
  }
}
```

3. Prepare the model file as follows:

```json
{
    "interactionModel": {
        "languageModel": {
            "invocationName": "self-intro",
            "intents": [
                {
                    "name": "AMAZON.CancelIntent",
                    "samples": []
                },
                {
                    "name": "AMAZON.HelpIntent",
                    "samples": []
                },
                {
                    "name": "AMAZON.StopIntent",
                    "samples": []
                },
                {
                    "name": "SelfIntroIntent",
                    "samples": [
                        "please say intro",
                        "say intro",
                        "please say intro for",
                        "say intro for",
                        "intro",
                        "intro for"
                    ]
                }
            ]
        }
    }
}
```

Save this file as `en-US.json`. If you need to support more locales, you can create model files for them as well.

For more details on invocation names, intents, and utterances, refer to the *How it works* section.

4. Update the skill with the preceding model file, as follows:

```
ask api update-model \
    --skill-id amzn1.ask.skill.ab1fdfac-42eb-42ae-aeae-b761f3c903c1 \
    --file en-US.json \
    --locale en-US
```

Replace the skill ID with the skill ID you receive in *Step 2: Provisioning Lambda (AWS CLI)*.

If the model JSON file was created successfully, you should get the following response:

```
Model for en-US submitted.
Please use the following command to track the model build status:
    ask api get-skill-status -s amzn1.ask.skill.ab1fdfac-42eb-42ae-aeae-b761f3c903c1
```

You can execute the command that is provided to track the skill as follows:

```
$ ask api get-skill-status -s amzn1.ask.skill.ab1fdfac-42eb-42ae-aeae-b761f3c903c1
```

If the model creation was successful, you should get the following message:

```
{
  "interactionModel": {
    "en-US": {
      "eTag": "16c613e1f1aadd74398120b8f1886ca3",
      "lastUpdateRequest": {
        "status": "SUCCEEDED"
      }
    }
  },
  "manifest": {
    "eTag": "4d7be69ac8b33ececf1c5df9b9c6f9a4",
    "lastUpdateRequest": {
      "status": "SUCCEEDED"
    }
  }
}
```

If you created more locale files in the previous step, you can use the `update-model` subcommand to update the skills with those models as well.

5. Enable the skill using the following code:

```
ask api enable-skill \
    --skill-id amzn1.ask.skill.a585bf93-15bb-4361-ab56-ffbdc66027fd
```

If successful, you should see the following message:

```
The skill has been enabled.
```

You can now ask Alexa to open our app ('self intro') and then say one of the sample utterances we defined ('please say intro').

Redshift, Amazon ML, and Alexa Skills

You can use the Alexa simulator available at `https://echosim.io` if you do not have an Echo device. The homepage for this simulator is shown in the following screenshot:

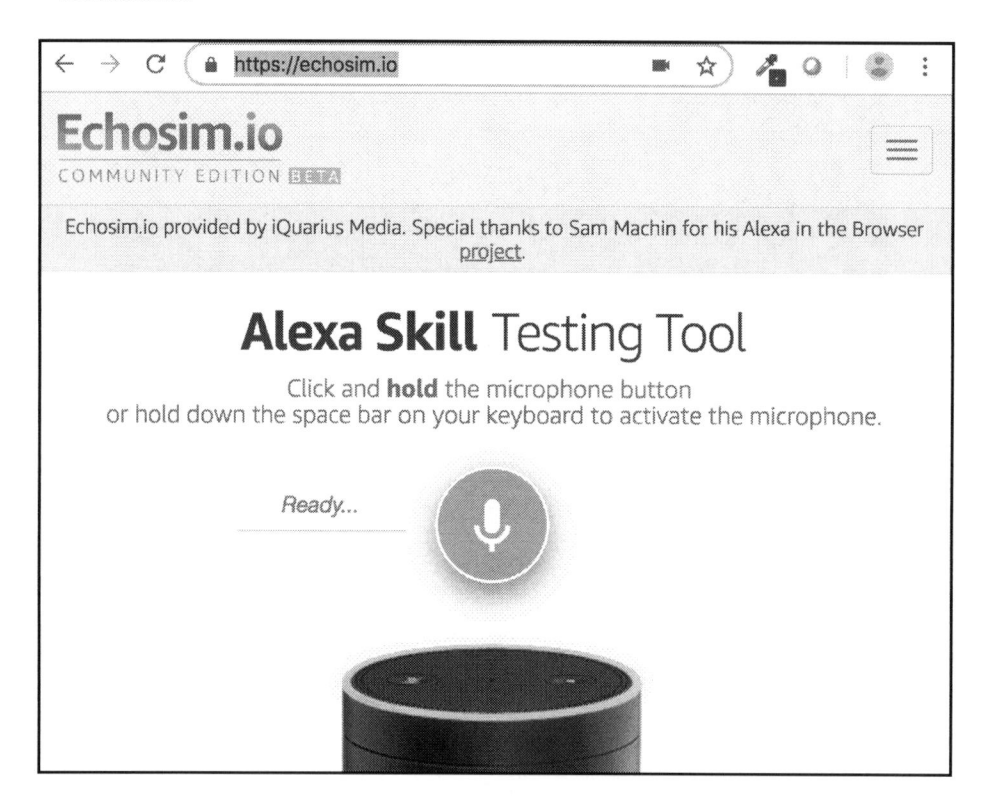

You can also log in to the AWS developer console and test your skill from the **Test** tab of your skill, as shown in the following screenshot:

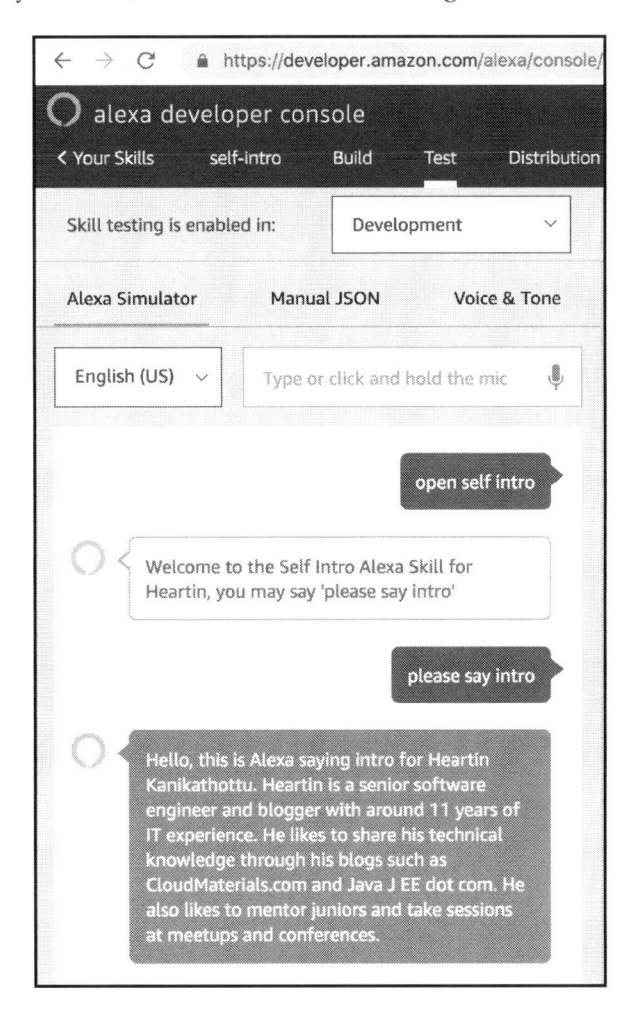

How it works...

Alexa uses **automated speech recognition** (**ASR**) followed by **natural language understanding** (**NLU**) to process user requests. Internally, Alexa makes use of Amazon Lex. Amazon Lex is the primary AWS service for building conversational interfaces with voice and text, using ASR and NLU.

In summary, we did the following in this recipe:

1. Created a Java lambda as the backend for the Alexa skill
2. Created an Alexa skill using the Alexa Skills Kit Command-Line Interface
3. Linked the Alexa skill and Lambda
4. Tested the skill

Now, let's learn some theory to understand these steps better.

Alexa skill invocation basics

You start a conversation with Alexa using an invocation name, or wake word. The default wake word is **Alexa**. These days, you can also use the wake words **Echo**, **Computer**, and **Amazon**. You can set the wake word from the Amazon Alexa app, which you can download from the Apple App Store or Google Play Store.

Once you activate Alexa, you can invoke a skill published by Amazon, or launch a custom skill published by other developers, using an invocation name. You can launch your own skills from your Echo devices without needing to publish them, as long as the device is linked to the same Amazon account as your developer portal.

Your Alexa skill can define different intents. Intents can be considered as different functionalities provided by your skill, such as welcoming someone to the app, responding to a question, taking an action, and so on. After you launch a skill, you need to say a phrase, and each phrase will be mapped to an intent.

For example, consider the sentence *Alexa, open Cloudericks and please say the intro*. *Alexa* is the wake work here, *Cloudericks* is our invocation name, and *please say the intro* is the utterance. The utterance will invoke an intent that performs the actual introduction. The intent can be defined within an AWS lambda or an external API.

You usually define more utterances for an intent, such as *please say intro*, *please say the intro*, *say intro*, and so on. You can define more utterances to make your application more flexible and then improve it further from the analytics data for failed utterances.

Instead of saying *open Cloudericks* to launch the skill, you can also use the invocation name in your sentence. For example, instead of saying *Alexa, open Cloudericks and please say the intro*, you can say *Alexa, please say intro for Cloudericks*, as we did in this recipe.

Explaining the Lambda project (Java)

We used ASK SDK v2 (Java) in this recipe. With this SDK version, you need to define handlers for each of your intents. Each handler has a `canHandle` function and a `handle` function. The `canHandle` function checks and confirms what intents the handler responds to and the `handle` function contains the actual logic for the intent.

Apart from the intent handler classes, you also need to define a parent handler class that extends the `SkillStreamHandler` class. From this handler class, you need to pass an `AlexaSkill` object that contains all the other intent handlers into the `SkillStreamHandler` parent constructor through a super call.

> If you are using the older version of the SDK, you can go to `https://alexa-skills-kit-sdk-for-java.readthedocs.io/en/latest/Migrating-To-ASK-SDK-v2-For-Java.html` to migrate to the version (v2) that we use in this recipe.

In the introduction, I wrote `CloudMaterials.com` and `javajee.com` differently so that Alexa says them in the way that I want. You can use **speech synthesis markup language** (SSML) for better control over how Alexa generates speech.

We first gave permission for any Alexa skill to invoke our lambda. This is because you can create a skill with a lambda endpoint only if the lambda has an Alexa trigger. Once you create a skill, you can remove this permission and add a permission that only allows this skill to invoke this lambda. The alternative is to create the skill without an endpoint, as shown in the following code, located in the `skill.json` file:

```
"apis": {
    "custom": {
    }
},
```

You can then create the lambda and add a trigger with this skill's ID. After that, you can update the `skill.json` with the endpoint and use the `update-skill` subcommand to update the skill, as shown in the following code:

```
ask api update-skill \
    --skill-id amzn1.ask.skill.6fed53f3-661e-4f26-8de8-4ee4844f899b \
    --file skill-update.json
```

Explaining the ASK CLI steps

We used ASK CLI to create our Alexa skill. We can also use the developer portal UI or a voice app platform (more information on this can be found in the *There's more* section).

ASK CLI provides a set of high-level commands, as well as a set of low-level commands. High-level commands include commands such as `ask new`, `ask deploy`, and so on that make the creation and deployment of skills very easy. The `ask new` command creates a sample skill, sample Lambda, and all the required files from a template that you can modify. The `ask deploy` command allows you to deploy the skill to the developer portal easily.

Low-level commands, on the other hand, provide more flexibility as to what you want to do with your skill. They allow you to work on only the skill or lambda. The low-level command steps also correspond to the steps we perform from the developer portal UI. In this recipe, we use the low-level set of commands to create and deploy the Alexa skill. We create and deploy the lambda in the same way that we have been doing in the previous recipes in this book.

To create a skill with ASK CLI, we created and used the following two files:

- `skill.json`: This is the skill manifest JSON file. It is the JSON representation of the skill and contains the required metadata for your skill.
- `en-US.json`: This is the locale-specific model file for the US locale. This file defines the invocation name, intents, and the sample utterances. We created the model file only for the US locale. You could, however, create model files for other supported locales as well. I have included more than one locale with code files to refer to.

There's more...

We created a simple Alexa skill, created a Lambda backend, linked both together, and tested it using the Echo device (or a simulator). You can now publish Alexa skills and get rewarded by Amazon through its Alexa promotional programs.

Amazon Lex is not just restricted to conversational interfaces that use voice inputs; it can also be used to build custom non-voice conversational interfaces, such as chatbots. Since the backends for both an Alexa skill and Lex-based chatbots can both be lambdas, you can reuse the same backend logic for both Alexa and a chatbot.

We created Alexa skills using ASK CLI. However, you can also use the developer portal to create and test Alexa skills easily. You can also explore the voice app platforms that make Alexa skill development even more easy.

Voice app platforms

There are various voice app platforms that let you create Alexa skills with much less code, or even no code at all. Most of these support drag-and-drop functionalities. These tools also let you build your skills once and then deploy them in multiple places. Examples of such tools include VoiceFlow, Bluetag, Conversation.one, Jovo, Witlingo, although there are many other.

See also

Detailed steps for installing and configuring ASK CLI are available at the following links:

- https://developer.amazon.com/docs/smapi/quick-start-alexa-skills-kit-command-line-interface.html
- https://developer.amazon.com/docs/smapi/skill-manifest.html

8
Monitoring and Alerting with Amazon CloudWatch

This chapter will cover the following topics:

- Checking logs, insights, and metrics (Console)
- Your first custom metric (AWS CLI)
- Setting up CloudWatch alarms (AWS CLI)
- CloudWatch alarms with dimensions (AWS CLI)
- Using CloudWatch metric log filters (AWS CLI and Console)

Introduction

DevOps is a mindset where the development team and the operations team responsible for a product or service collaborate together as a single, larger team to achieve their common goal of making a project successful. The actual implementation of DevOps practices differs from DevOps team to DevOps team. In practice, while core development activities may still be done by programmers and core operations activities may be still done by operations experts, many activities such as monitoring, debugging, and so on may be shared between both sides based on the work capacity available.

AWS provides many services that can help in monitoring and debugging projects deployed on the AWS cloud. Amazon CloudWatch is the most popular of these services, and without it we cannot be successful with AWS projects. CloudWatch can perform many functions, such as monitoring and alerting, gathering data and preparing metrics, visualizing the data sent to it using graphs, and so on. We have used CloudWatch for checking logs, and in `Chapter 1`, *Getting Started with Serverless Computing on AWS*, we used it for setting a billing alarm.

In previous chapters, we looked at services that can help us build serverless web applications, as well as services that extend the basic functionality with capabilities such as messaging, analytics, machine learning, and natural language processing. In this chapter, we will briefly discuss recipes for the CloudWatch service to start monitoring and debugging the services we looked at in the previous chapters. By doing this, we will better understand the role of CloudWatch in following DevOps practices with AWS.

Even programmers still spend a large amount of time monitoring and debugging the logs from the Management Console, and so most of the recipes in this chapter will use the Management Console with or without the corresponding AWS CLI commands.

Checking logs, insights, and metrics (Console)

In this recipe, we will learn how to log in and check the CloudWatch logs and metrics from the AWS Management Console. This is a simple recipe that is included in this chapter mainly to aid us in our other recipes where we can use CloudWatch to check logs or a metric. If you are familiar with checking logs and metrics from the console, you can skip this recipe.

In this recipe, we will only be discussing metrics that were automatically created by CloudWatch based on the resources we create—for example, Lambdas. In later recipes, we will learn how to create custom metrics from AWS CLI and how to use custom metrics in alarms.

Getting ready

The following are the prerequisites for this recipe:

- A working AWS account
- Access to AWS Management Console
- You should have created and tested at least one Lambda function to see the Lambda-related logs and metrics

How to do it...

We will first log in to the CloudWatch dashboard in AWS Management Console, check the logs, and then check the metrics.

Step 1: Logging in to the CloudWatch dashboard

We can log in to the CloudWatch dashboard by going through the following steps:

1. Log in to AWS Management Console.
2. From the **Service** dropdown select the **CloudWatch** service. We can also go directly to the CloudWatch dashboard by using `https://console.aws.amazon.com/cloudwatch`. The CloudWatch dashboard should look similar to the following screenshot; however, the actual alarms and their states may differ:

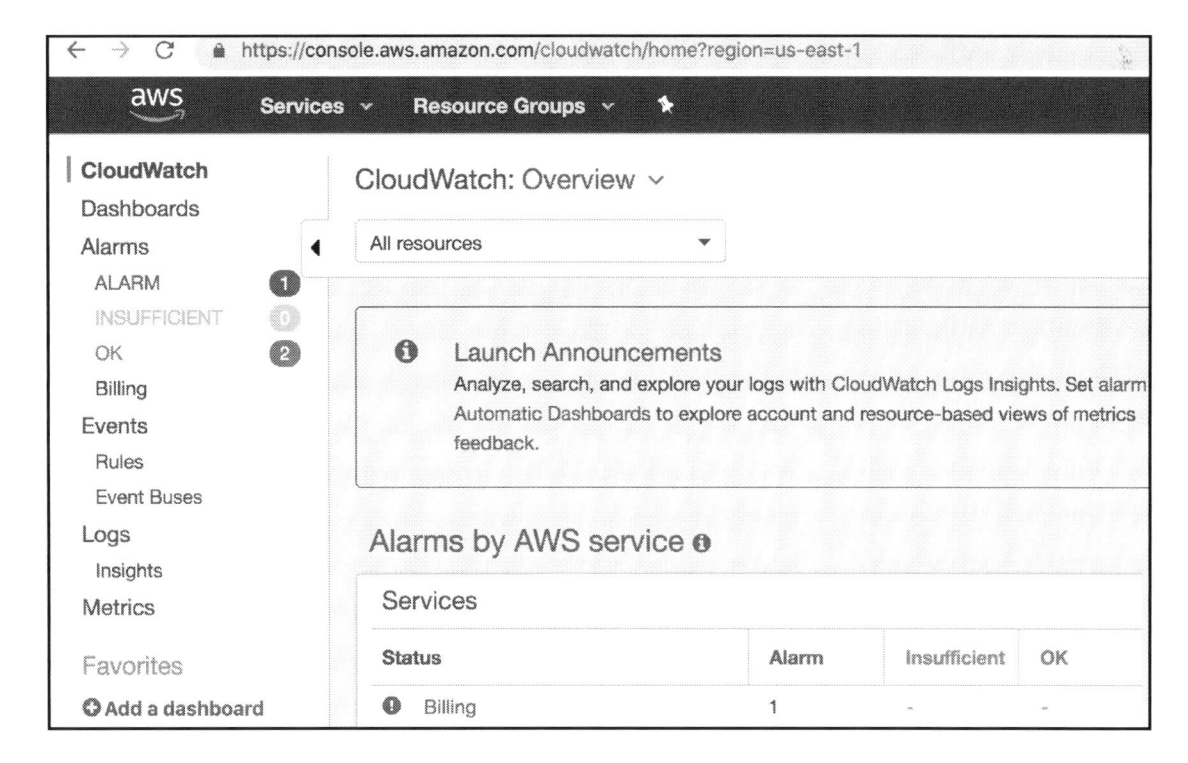

The dashboard will also contain information on recent alarms and their statuses.

Logs

From the Management Console we can check Lambda logs as follows:

1. From the CloudWatch dashboard, we can go the the logs page using the **Logs** link on the sidebar. It will show us all the log groups. We can also filter them by providing a prefix, as shown in the following screenshot:

Log Groups	Insights	Expire Events After	Metric Filters	Subscriptions
/aws/lambda/demo-lambda-with-cli	Explore	Never Expire	0 filters	None
/aws/lambda/demo-lambda-with-cli-new	Explore	Never Expire	0 filters	None
/aws/lambda/demoIAMOperationsWithSDK	Explore	Never Expire	0 filters	None
/aws/lambda/demoIAMOperationsWithSDKAndPOJO	Explore	Never Expire	0 filters	None
/aws/lambda/demoIAMOpsCLI	Explore	Never Expire	0 filters	None

2. Click on any of the log groups to get a list of all the log streams belonging to that log group, as shown in the following screenshot:

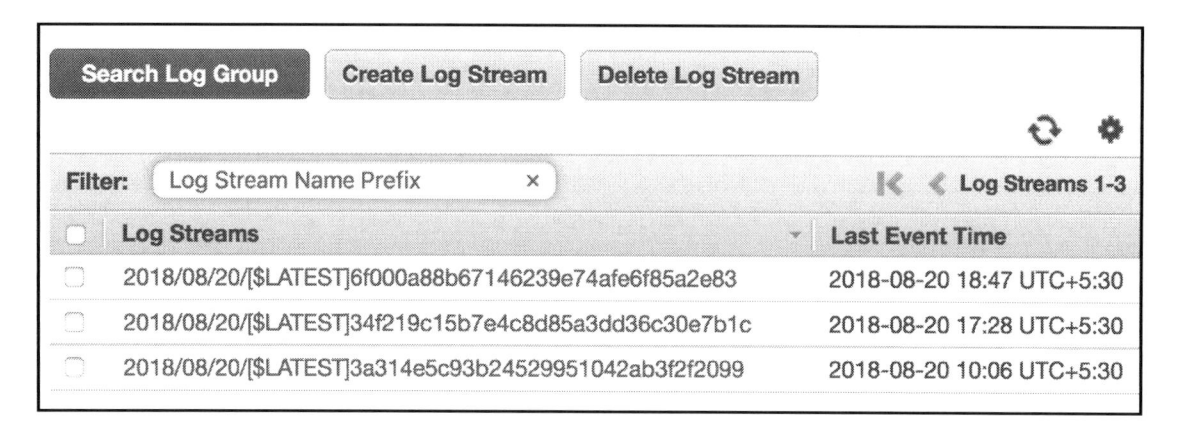

Log Streams	Last Event Time
2018/08/20/[$LATEST]6f000a88b67146239e74afe6f85a2e83	2018-08-20 18:47 UTC+5:30
2018/08/20/[$LATEST]34f219c15b7e4c8d85a3dd36c30e7b1c	2018-08-20 17:28 UTC+5:30
2018/08/20/[$LATEST]3a314e5c93b24529951042ab3f2f2099	2018-08-20 10:06 UTC+5:30

3. Click on any log stream to see the log events, as shown in the following screenshot:

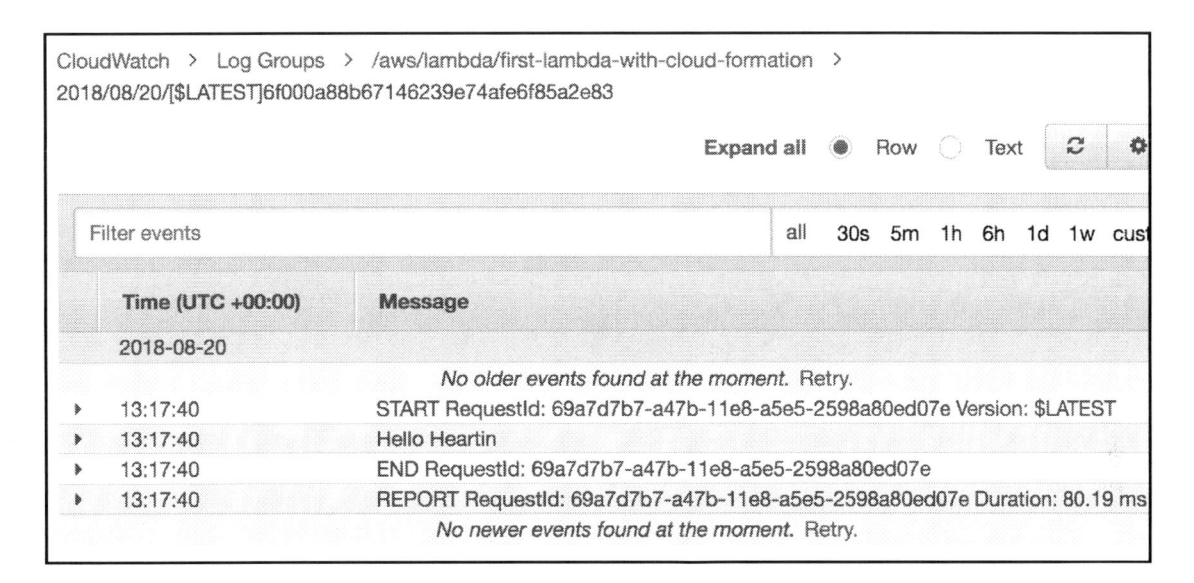

```
CloudWatch > Log Groups > /aws/lambda/first-lambda-with-cloud-formation >
2018/08/20/[$LATEST]6f000a88b67146239e74afe6f85a2e83
```

Time (UTC +00:00)	Message
2018-08-20	
	No older events found at the moment. Retry.
▶ 13:17:40	START RequestId: 69a7d7b7-a47b-11e8-a5e5-2598a80ed07e Version: $LATEST
▶ 13:17:40	Hello Heartin
▶ 13:17:40	END RequestId: 69a7d7b7-a47b-11e8-a5e5-2598a80ed07e
▶ 13:17:40	REPORT RequestId: 69a7d7b7-a47b-11e8-a5e5-2598a80ed07e Duration: 80.19 ms
	No newer events found at the moment. Retry.

Log insights

1. From the CloudWatch dashboard, we can go to the log insights page using the **Insights** sublink under the **Logs** link on the sidebar, as shown in the following screenshot:

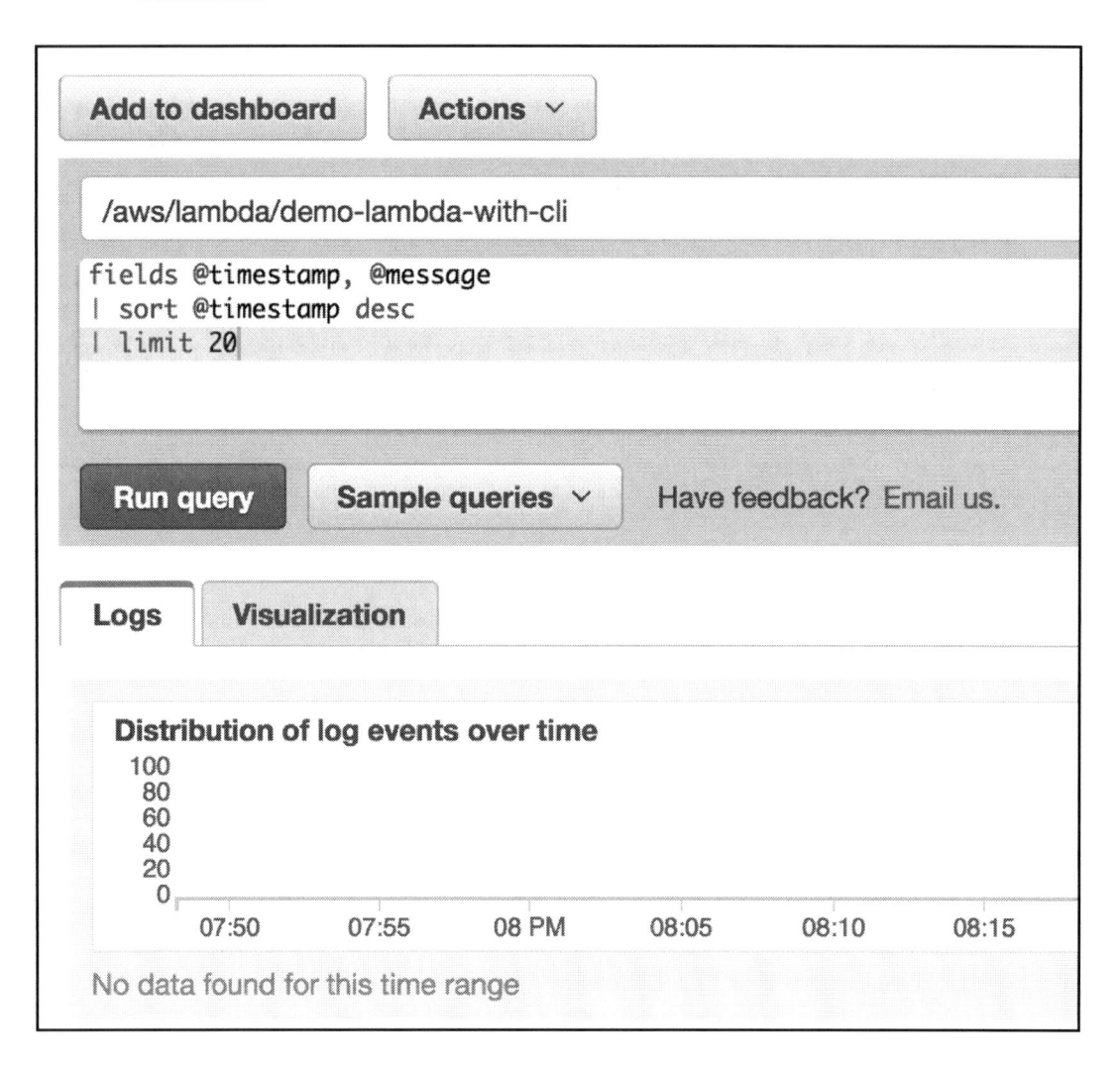

```
/aws/lambda/demo-lambda-with-cli

fields @timestamp, @message
| sort @timestamp desc
| limit 20
```

Run query **Sample queries** ˅   Have feedback? Email us.

Logs Visualization

Distribution of log events over time

```
100
 80
 60
 40
 20
  0
     07:50      07:55     08 PM     08:05     08:10     08:15
```

No data found for this time range

> Creating log insight queries is beyond the scope of this book, but I still wanted to bring this relatively new and powerful feature to your attention. You can refer to `https://docs.aws.amazon.com/AmazonCloudWatch/latest/logs/AnalyzingLogData.html` for more details.

Metrics

1. From the CloudWatch dashboard, we can go to the **Metrics** page by clicking on the **Metrics** link on the sidebar. This will list all the services with their metric counts, as shown in the following screenshot:

All metrics	Graphed metrics	Graph options	Source

Search for any metric, dimension or resource id

83 Metrics

Billing	DynamoDB
12 Metrics	16 Metrics

Firehose	Kinesis
2 Metrics	7 Metrics

Lambda	Logs
22 Metrics	6 Metrics

ML	S3
1 Metric	4 Metrics

SNS	SQS
5 Metrics	8 Metrics

Monitoring and Alerting with Amazon CloudWatch

2. Click on **Lambda**. This will give us the options to search for metrics **By Resource** or **By Function Name** and provides an option to view metrics **Across All Functions**, as shown in the following screenshot:

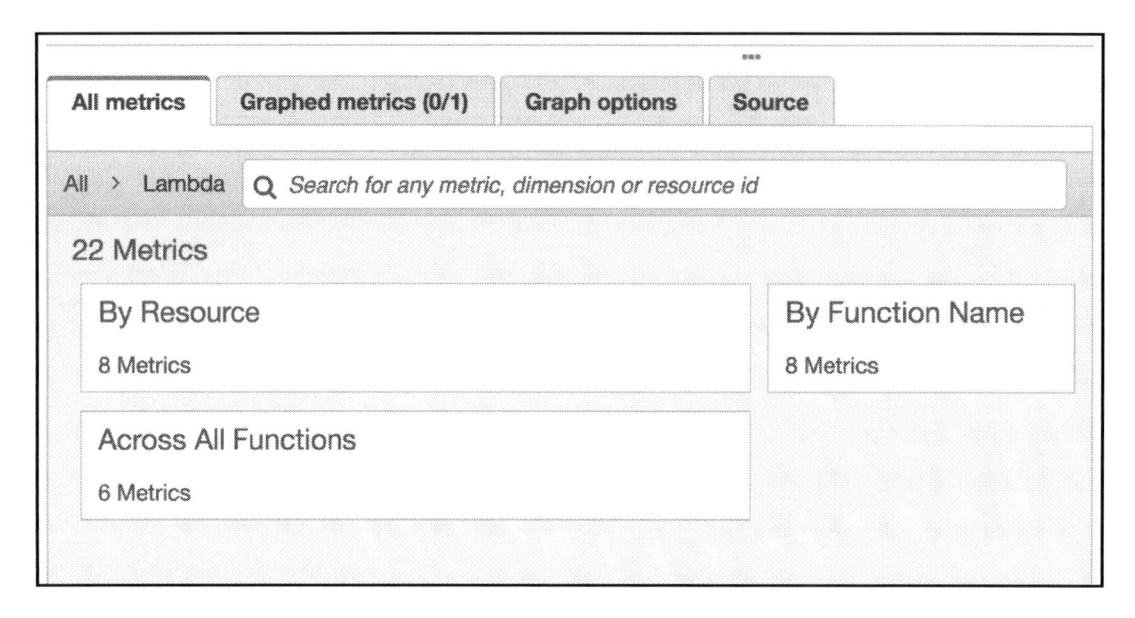

| All metrics | Graphed metrics (0/1) | Graph options | Source |

All > Lambda   Search for any metric, dimension or resource id

22 Metrics

| By Resource | By Function Name |
| 8 Metrics | 8 Metrics |

| Across All Functions |
| 6 Metrics |

3. Click on **By Function Name**. This will list all of the function names available, as shown in the following screenshot. We can also filter the results:

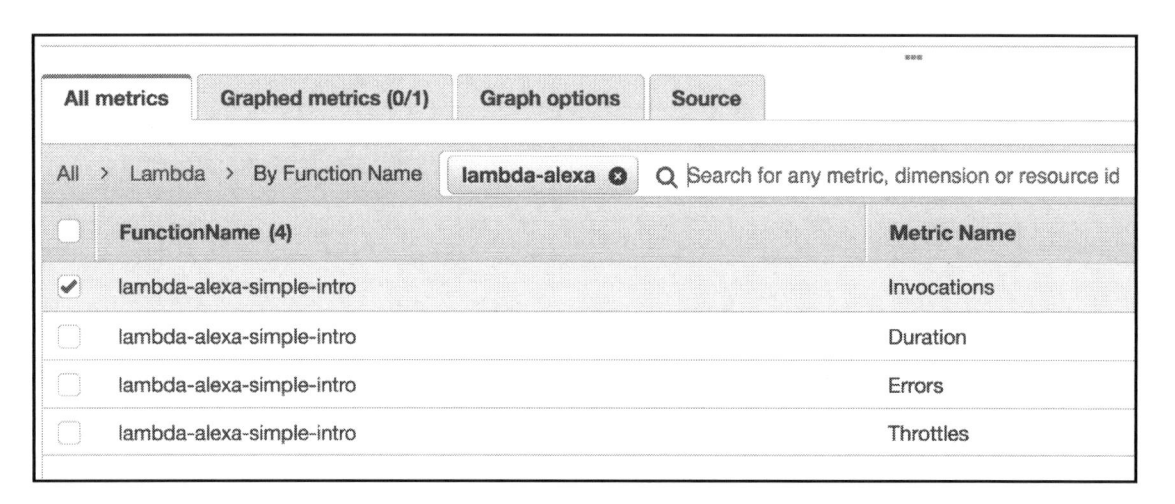

| All metrics | Graphed metrics (0/1) | Graph options | Source |

All > Lambda > By Function Name   **lambda-alexa**   Search for any metric, dimension or resource id

FunctionName (4)	Metric Name
lambda-alexa-simple-intro	Invocations
lambda-alexa-simple-intro	Duration
lambda-alexa-simple-intro	Errors
lambda-alexa-simple-intro	Throttles

4. Click on the metric name **Invocations** and from the options, click on **Add to graph** for our metric to appear in the graph shown. By default, it gives us time durations starting with 1 hour. But we can set it with time intervals starting with 1 minute using the dropdown next to **Custom**, as shown in the following screenshot:

I made a few invocations of the skill we created in the previous chapter and also set a 15-minute interval here.

You can go back to the **All metrics** page and go inside each of the other services and explore the various metrics available, along with the recipes for the corresponding service.

How it works...

Let's briefly look at some of the theory behind the more important terms we learned about in the previous section.

Log groups

A log group is a group of log streams that share the same settings, such as retention, monitoring, and access control. We can define log groups and specify which streams to put into each group. For Lambda functions, the log group is generated based on the Lambda names that we saw in the *How to do it...* section.

Log streams

Each log stream is a sequence of log events that shares the same source (for example, a Lambda). A new log stream is created every time we terminate our Lambda and deploy it again. AWS may delete empty log streams that are 2 months old.

Log insights

Log insights allow us to search and analyze CloudWatch logs. Log insights include a built-in query language with a simple set of commands. We can use log insights to identify the root cause of issues and even validate deployed fixes.

Log insights can automatically discover fields in logs from AWS services such as Route 53, Lambda, CloudTrail, VPC, and so on, even for a custom log that emits log events in JSON. Log insights can only be used to search log data that was sent to CloudWatch Logs on or after November 5, 2018.

Metrics

A metric is a time-ordered set of data points that is published to CloudWatch. A metric can be considered as a variable to monitor and the data points represent the values of that variable over a given time. The default metrics available for AWS Lambda functions include `Invocations`, `Errors`, `DeadLetterErrors`, `Duration`, `Throttles`, `IteratorAge`, `ConcurrentExecutions`, and `UnreservedConcurrentExecutions`.

Metrics are defined by a `name`, a `namespace`, and `zero` or more dimensions. For example, for the metric `Invocations` that we saw in this recipe, the namespace is `AWS/Lambda`. The dimensions are name–value pairs that can be associated with a CloudWatch metric. We can specify up to 10 dimensions for a given metric. The dimensions available for AWS Lambda CloudWatch include `FunctionName`, `Resource`, and `ExecutedVersion`.

There's more...

We have not explored metric and log insights much in this recipe. We will explore CloudWatch metrics more in later recipes. Log insights is a newer and powerful feature. For more information, you can refer to the link provided in the *See also* section and experiment with the log insights feature. We also didn't have a long-running Lambda with many invocations. Once we have such a Lambda, we can get more interesting metric graphs and insights.

See also

- https://docs.aws.amazon.com/AmazonCloudWatch/latest/logs/AnalyzingLogData.html

Your first custom metric (AWS CLI)

In the previous recipe, we learned how to check the automatically created CloudWatch metrics. We also learned some theory behind CloudWatch metrics. In this recipe, we will see how we can create a custom metric. We will create a simple functional scenario where we post a number of failed logins to the system. The sender may aggregate more requests within a set time, but we will not look at this in this recipe.

Getting ready

The following are the prerequisites for this recipe:

- A working AWS account.
- Access to AWS Management Console.
- You should have configured AWS CLI as discussed in the recipe *Your First Lambda with AWS CLI* in `Chapter 1`, *Getting Started with Serverless Computing on AWS*.

How to do it...

We can use the `aws cloudwatch put-metric-data` command to send metric data to CloudWatch. If the metric does not already exist, then this command will also create that metric.

Step 1–Create a simple metric without dimensions

Using the following code, we will first create a metric without specifying dimensions and then we will post data with dimensions. We can combine both *Step 1* and *Step 2* for real-world use cases:

```
aws cloudwatch put-metric-data \
    --namespace 'ServerlessProgrammingCookbook' \
    --metric-name 'FailedLogins' \
```

Monitoring and Alerting with Amazon CloudWatch

```
--value 1 \
--region us-east-1 \
--profile admin
```

We can verify our metric from AWS Management Console as follows:

1. Log in to Management Console and go to the CloudWatch dashboard.
2. Click on the **Metrics** link from the sidebar. We should now see a new custom namespace called `ServerlessProgrammingCookbook`, along with the AWS namespaces, as shown in the following screenshot:

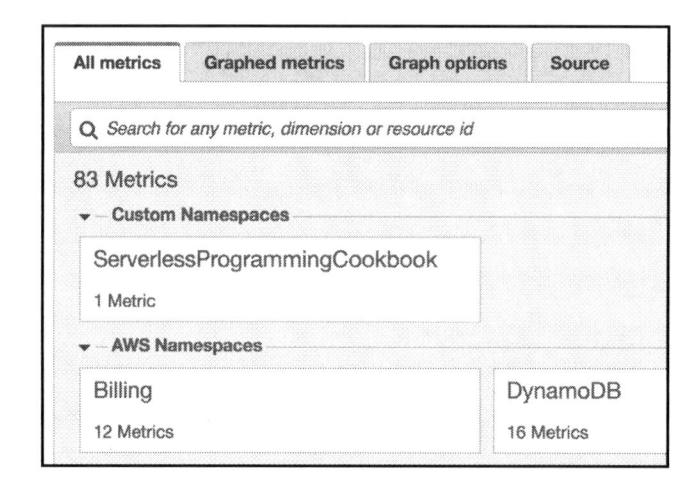

3. Click on the custom namespace `ServerlessProgrammingCookbook`. This will display a link called **Metric with no dimensions**, as shown in the following screenshot:

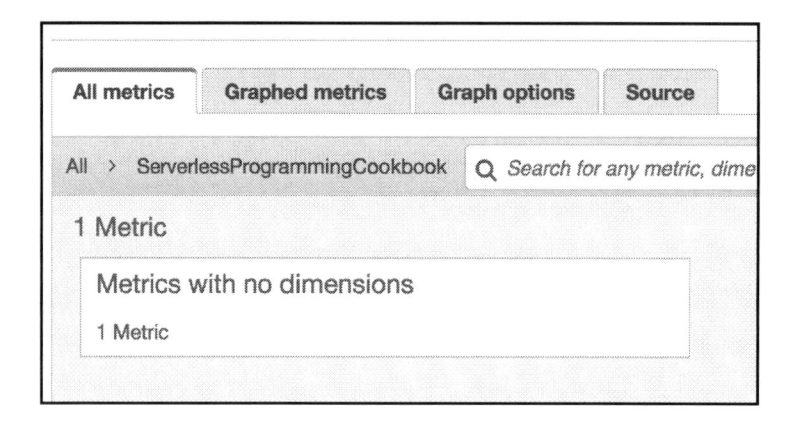

This is because we have not defined any dimensions for our metric.

4. Click on the **Metric with no dimensions** link. This will show us our new metric. We can now click on the dropdown next to the metric, as shown in the following screenshot, to perform all of the operations that we can perform on an automatically generated metric:

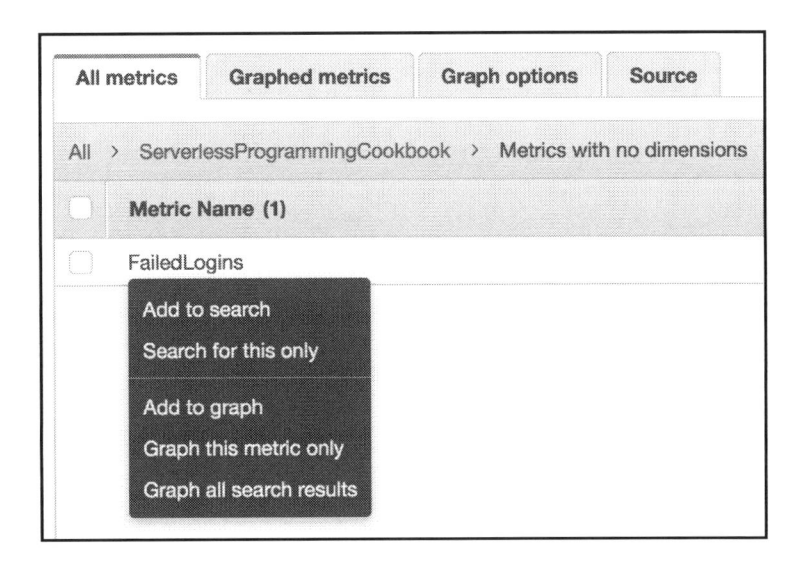

Step 2—Add dimensions to metric data

We can specify dimensions with the **put-metric-data** sub-command using its `dimensions` property. Add a dimension with two different values using the following code:

```
aws cloudwatch put-metric-data \
    --namespace 'ServerlessProgrammingCookbook' \
    --metric-name 'FailedLogins' \
    --value 1 \
    --dimensions 'Device=Mobile' \
    --region us-east-1 \
    --profile admin

aws cloudwatch put-metric-data \
    --namespace 'ServerlessProgrammingCookbook' \
    --metric-name 'FailedLogins' \
    --value 1 \
    --dimensions 'Device=Laptop' \
    --region us-east-1 \
```

Monitoring and Alerting with Amazon CloudWatch

```
    --profile admin

aws cloudwatch put-metric-data \
    --namespace 'ServerlessProgrammingCookbook' \
    --metric-name 'FailedLogins' \
    --value 1 \
    --dimensions 'Device=Laptop' \
    --region us-east-1 \
    --profile admin
```

We can verify our metric from AWS Management Console as follows:

1. When we click on our custom namespace, `ServerlessProgrammingCookbook`, we should see a link for our new dimension along with a link for the ones without a dimension, as shown in the following screenshot:

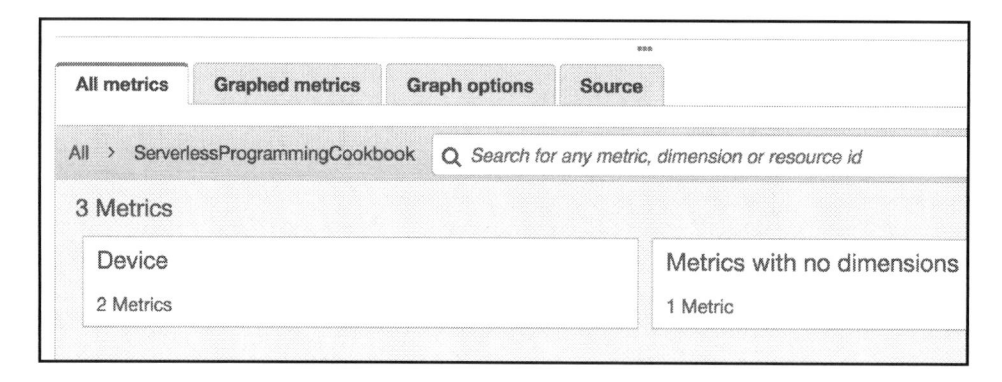

All metrics	Graphed metrics	Graph options	Source
All > ServerlessProgrammingCookbook	Search for any metric, dimension or resource id		
3 Metrics			
Device		Metrics with no dimensions	
2 Metrics		1 Metric	

2. Click on the **Device** link. This will show our metrics for each value of the **Device** dimension, as shown in the following screenshot:

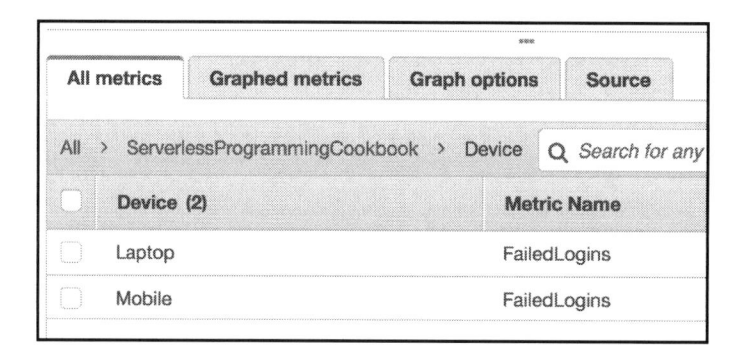

All metrics	Graphed metrics	Graph options	Source
All > ServerlessProgrammingCookbook > Device	Search for any		
Device (2)		Metric Name	
Laptop		FailedLogins	
Mobile		FailedLogins	

3. We can now click on the dropdown next to any of these dimension values (as shown in the following screenshot) to perform all operations that we can perform on an automatically generated metric:

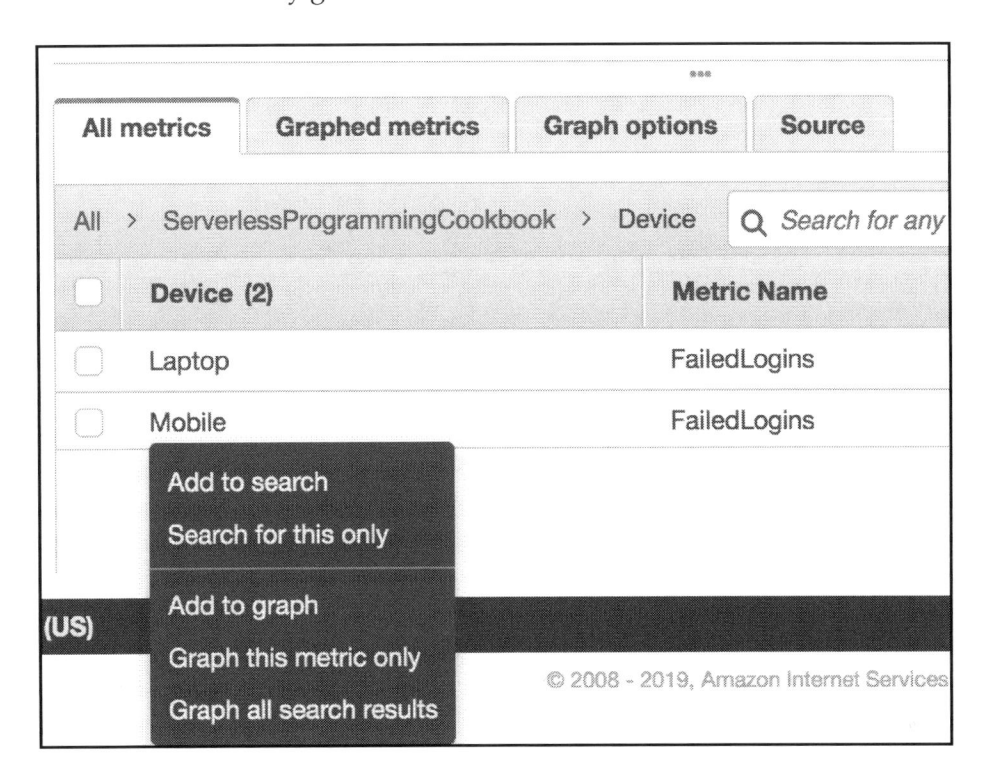

How it works...

In this recipe, we posted data to a custom metric that we wanted to create using the `aws cloudwatch put-metric-data` command and the metric was created for us. We first created the metric without specifying any dimension and then posted data to the metric specifying the dimensions. We also verified both cases. You can also refer to the previous recipe for the basic theory behind CloudWatch metrics, if you have not already done this.

The minimum granularity to which CloudWatch can aggregate metric data is 1 minute. So even if we post data to a CloudWatch metric in shorter intervals than 1 minute, CloudWatch will only aggregate with a minimum granularity of 1 minute.

There's more...

In this recipe, we created a custom metric using the `aws cloudwatch put-metric-data` command and specified the value and dimension using their respective properties. We can also use the `metric-data` property, which accepts a list of up to 20 metrics per call. Refer to the link on `put-metric-data` in the *See also* section for more details.

See also

- https://docs.aws.amazon.com/cli/latest/reference/cloudwatch/put-metric-data.html

Setting up CloudWatch alarms (AWS CLI)

CloudWatch alarms enable us to initiate actions based on the state of data within our metrics. These actions may be sent to the **Simple Notification Service** (**SNS**). For server-based applications that use autoscaling, CloudWatch alarms can also initiate actions to autoscaling groups.

Getting ready

The following are the prerequisites for this recipe:

- A working AWS account
- Access to AWS Management Console
- You should have configured AWS CLI as discussed in the recipe *Your First Lambda with AWS CLI* in `Chapter 1`, *Getting Started with Serverless Computing on AWS*
- You should have created a metric with the name `FailedLogins` and namespace `ServerlessProgrammingCookbook` following the previous recipe *Your first custom metric created from AWS CLI*
- You should have created an SNS topic with an email subscription following the recipe *Your first SNS topic for email and SMS* in `Chapter 6`, *Messaging and Notifications with SQS and SNS*

How to do it...

Let's create an alarm and simulate the conditions that will trigger it by going through the following steps:

1. We can create an alarm for a metric with the name `FailedLogins` and namespace `ServerlessProgrammingCookbook` as follows:

    ```
    aws cloudwatch put-metric-alarm \
        --alarm-name FailedRequestsAlarm \
        --alarm-description 'Alarm for failed login requests' \
        --metric-name 'FailedLogins' \
        --namespace 'ServerlessProgrammingCookbook' \
        --statistic 'Average' \
        --period 60 \
        --threshold 5 \
        --comparison-operator GreaterThanOrEqualToThreshold \
        --evaluation-periods 1 \
        --alarm-actions arn:aws:sns:us-east-1:<account id>:my-first-sns-topic \
        --region us-east-1 \
        --profile admin
    ```

2. Check the current status of the alarm using the `describe-alarms` command, as follows:

    ```
    aws cloudwatch describe-alarms \
        --alarm-names FailedRequestsAlarm \
        --region us-east-1 \
        --profile admin
    ```

Monitoring and Alerting with Amazon CloudWatch

If we try the `describe-alarms` command immediately after creation or if we have not sent any data for the metric within the specified period (60 seconds, in this case), we get the state `INSUFFICIENT_DATA`, as shown in the following screenshot:

```
{
    "MetricAlarms": [
        {
            "AlarmName": "FailedRequestsAlarm",
            "AlarmArn": "arn:aws:cloudwatch:us-east-1:            :alarm:FailedRequestsAlarm",
            "AlarmDescription": "Alarm for failed login requests",
            "AlarmConfigurationUpdatedTimestamp": "2019-01-15T08:57:50.072Z",
            "ActionsEnabled": true,
            "OKActions": [],
            "AlarmActions": [
                "arn:aws:sns:us-east-1:            :my-first-sns-topic"
            ],
            "InsufficientDataActions": [],
            "StateValue": "INSUFFICIENT_DATA",
            "StateReason": "Unchecked: Initial alarm creation",
            "StateUpdatedTimestamp": "2019-01-15T08:57:50.072Z",
            "MetricName": "FailedLogins",
            "Namespace": "ServerlessProgrammingCookbook",
            "Statistic": "Average",
            "Dimensions": [],
            "Period": 60,
            "EvaluationPeriods": 1,
            "Threshold": 5.0,
            "ComparisonOperator": "GreaterThanOrEqualToThreshold"
        }
    ]
}
```

3. Send some data to the metric with matching dimensions (none in this case), using the following code:

```
aws cloudwatch put-metric-data \
    --namespace 'ServerlessProgrammingCookbook' \
    --metric-name 'FailedLogins' \
    --value 1 \
    --region us-east-1 \
    --profile admin
```

We need to wait for at least the period you mentioned (or some more time). The `describe-alarms` command output should contain the status OK, as shown in the following screenshot:

```
"StateValue": "OK",
        "StateReason": "Threshold Crossed: 1 datapoint [1.0 (15/01/19 09:59:00)] was not greater than or equal to the threshold (5.0).",
        "StateReasonData": "{\"version\":\"1.0\",\"queryDate\":\"2019-01-15T10:00:31.461+0000\",\"startDate\":\"2019-01-15T09:59:00.000+0000\",\"statistic\":\"Average\",\"period\":60,\"recentDatapoints\":[1.0],\"threshold\":5.0}",
```

4. Send data so that the average crosses the threshold (5, in our case) using the `put-metric-data` command. We will send a value of 10, as shown in the following code:

```
aws cloudwatch put-metric-data \
    --namespace 'ServerlessProgrammingCookbook' \
    --metric-name 'FailedLogins' \
    --value 10 \
    --region us-east-1 \
    --profile admin
```

Based on the time taken to send after the previous command, you might get an average of 5.5 (an average of 10 and 1) or just 10 (if sent after 1 minute). In either case, the alarm should be triggered and the `describe-alarms` command output should contain the status ALARM.

```
"StateValue": "ALARM",
        "StateReason": "Threshold Crossed: 1 datapoint [10.0 (15/01/19 10:17:00)] was greater than or equal to the threshold (5.0).",
        "StateReasonData": "{\"version\":\"1.0\",\"queryDate\":\"2019-01-15T10:18:31.415+0000\",\"startDate\":\"2019-01-15T10:17:00.000+0000\",\"statistic\":\"Average\",\"period\":60,\"recentDatapoints\":[10.0],\"threshold\":5.0}",
```

If the SNS topic was configured correctly and we have subscribed to an email address successfully, we should get a message similar to the following:

> **ALARM: "FailedRequestsAlarm" in US East (N. Virginia)**
>
> **AWS Notifications** <no-reply@sns.amazonaws...   3:48 PM (7 minutes ago)
> to me
>
> You are receiving this email because your Amazon CloudWatch Alarm "FailedRequestsAlarm" in the US East (N. Virginia) region has entered the ALARM state, because "Threshold Crossed: 1 datapoint [10.0 (15/01/19 10:17:00)] was greater than or equal to the threshold (5.0)." at "Tuesday 15 January, 2019 10:18:31 UTC".
>
> View this alarm in the AWS Management Console:
> https://console.aws.amazon.com/cloudwatch/home?region=us-east-1#s=Alarms&alarm=FailedRequestsAlarm

The email will also contain the alarm details and state change action details, as shown in the following screenshot:

```
Alarm Details:
- Name:                    FailedRequestsAlarm
- Description:             Alarm for failed login requests
- State Change:            OK -> ALARM
- Reason for State Change: Threshold Crossed: 1 datapoint [10.0 (15/01/19 10:17:00)] was greater than or equal to the threshold (5.0).
- Timestamp:               Tuesday 15 January, 2019 10:18:31 UTC
- AWS Account:

Threshold:
- The alarm is in the ALARM state when the metric is GreaterThanOrEqualToThreshold 5.0 for 60 seconds.

Monitored Metric:
- MetricNamespace:         ServerlessProgrammingCookbook
- MetricName:              FailedLogins
- Dimensions:
- Period:                  60 seconds
- Statistic:               Average
- Unit:                    not specified
```

The change actions details are as follows:

```
State Change Actions:
- OK:
- ALARM: [arn:aws:sns:us-east-1:                    :my-first-sns-topic]
- INSUFFICIENT_DATA:
```

When the average goes below the threshold, the alarm automatically goes back to the `OK` state.

How it works...

In this recipe, we created an alarm for a metric using the `aws cloudwatch put-metric-alarm` command. The metric may not be available at the time of the alarm's creation, in which case the alarm will remain in the state `INSUFFICIENT_DATA`.

We used the following properties of the `put-metric-alarm` sub-command:

- `metric-name` is the name of the metric with which we want to associate this alarm.
- `namespace` is the namespace of the metric.
- `statistic` is the statistic operation for the metric and can have one of the following values: `SampleCount`, `Average`, `Sum`, `Minimum`, or `Maximum`. To find the percentile, we need to use the `extended-statistic` property instead.
- `period` is the length, in seconds, of each time that the specified metric is evaluated. Valid values are `10`, `30`, and any multiple of `60`. We specified `60`.
- `threshold` is the value that the comparison operator option value uses for calculating whether an `ALARM` state has been reached. We specified a value of `5`.
- `comparison-operator` specifies the comparison operator to use. We used `GreaterThanOrEqualToThreshold`.
- `evaluation-periods` is the number of periods over which the data is compared to the threshold. For example, we can set an alarm that triggers when five consecutive data points are breached. We specified a value of `1` for the alarm to be triggered when only one data point is breached.
- `alarm-actions` is the ARN of actions to execute when this alarm transitions to the `ALARM` state from any other state.

The alarm may belong to one of the following states:

- `OK` - Denotes that the alarm has not been triggered.
- `ALARM` - Denotes that the alarm was triggered.
- `NOT_SUFFICIENT` - Denotes that there is not enough data to determine the alarm state—for example, there is no data within the time period specified by the alarm. An alarm just created will also be in this state for a little bit of time.

When an alarm goes to the `INSUFFICIENT_DATA` state immediately after the alarm creation, it will give a `StateReason` of `Unchecked: Initial alarm creation`. Once the alarm is in an `OK` or `ALARM` state and then goes to the `INSUFFICIENT_DATA` state because there is not enough data within the evaluation period, it gives a `StateReason` as `Insufficient Data: 1 datapoint was unknown`, as follows:

```
"StateValue": "INSUFFICIENT_DATA",
"StateReason": "Insufficient Data: 1 datapoint was unknown.",
"StateReasonData": "{\"version\":\"1.0\",\"queryDate\":\"2019-01-15T10:24:31.408+0000\",\"statistic\":\"Average\",\"period\":60,\"recentDatapoints\":[],\"threshold\":5.0}",
```

There's more...

We created a simple alarm and learned how to trigger it. Some of the important things to remember regarding CloudWatch alarms include the following:

- The alarm period should be equal to or greater than the metric frequency.
- The state of the alarm should change (for example, `OK` to `ALARM`) for the alarm to trigger an action.
- The alarm and its actions must be in the same region.
- We can create an alarm before we create the metric. The alarm stays in the `INSUFFICIENT_DATA` state until the metric is available with data.

In this recipe, we created an alarm from only AWS CLI. However, if you have fully understood this recipe, then you can do the same easily with Management Console.

See also

- https://docs.aws.amazon.com/cli/latest/reference/cloudwatch/index.html

CloudWatch alarms with dimensions (AWS CLI)

In the previous recipe, we created a CloudWatch alarm for a metric without any dimensions. In this small recipe, we will learn how to create a CloudWatch alarm for a metric with dimensions, and we will then verify the alarm by sending some data with dimensions.

Getting ready

The following are the prerequisites for this recipe:

- A working AWS account.
- Access to AWS Management Console.
- You should have configured AWS CLI as discussed in the recipe *Your First Lambda with AWS CLI* in Chapter 1, *Getting Started with Serverless Computing on AWS*.
- You should have created a metric with the name FailedLogins and namespace ServerlessProgrammingCookbook following the previous recipe *Your first custom metric created from AWS CLI*.
- You should have created an SNS topic with an email subscription following the recipe *Your first SNS topic for email and SMS* in Chapter 6, *Messaging and Notifications with SQS and SNS*.

How to do it...

Let's create an alarm and simulate conditions that will trigger it:

1. We can create an alarm for a metric with the name FailedLogins and namespace ServerlessProgrammingCookbook as follows:

```
aws cloudwatch put-metric-alarm \
    --alarm-name FailedRequestsAlarmWithDimensions \
    --alarm-description 'Alarm for failed login requests' \
    --metric-name 'FailedLogins' \
    --namespace 'ServerlessProgrammingCookbook' \
    --statistic 'Average' \
    --period 60 \
    --threshold 5 \
```

```
        --comparison-operator GreaterThanOrEqualToThreshold \
        --evaluation-periods 1 \
        --dimensions Name=Device,Value=Laptop \
        --alarm-actions arn:aws:sns:us-east-1:<account id>:my-
first-sns-topic \
        --region us-east-1 \
        --profile admin
```

2. Check the current status of the alarm using the `describe-alarms` command as follows:

```
aws cloudwatch describe-alarms \
    --alarm-names FailedRequestsAlarm \
    --region us-east-1 \
    --profile admin
```

If we try the `describe-alarms` command immediately after the alarm's creation or if we have not sent any data for the metric within the specified period (60 seconds, in this case), we get the state `INSUFFICIENT_DATA` within the response.

Send the data with the dimension using the following code:

```
aws cloudwatch put-metric-data \
    --namespace 'ServerlessProgrammingCookbook' \
    --metric-name 'FailedLogins' \
    --value 1 \
    --dimensions Device=Laptop \
    --region us-east-1 \
    --profile admin
```

If we check with `describe-alarms` after some time, we can see that the state has changed to `OK`. We can now post data with a higher value (for example, `10`) so that the average is more than the threshold, as shown in the following screenshot. Based on the interval we take to send data, and based on when the average is calculated, we may get a `10` or `0.5` average:

```
            "StateValue": "ALARM",
            "StateReason": "Threshold Crossed: 1 datapoint [5.5 (15/01/19 19:10:00)] was greater than or equal to t
he threshold (5.0).",
            "StateReasonData": "{\"version\":\"1.0\",\"queryDate\":\"2019-01-15T19:10:36.535+0000\",\"startDate\":\
"2019-01-15T19:10:00.000+0000\",\"statistic\":\"Average\",\"period\":10,\"recentDatapoints\":[5.5],\"threshold\":5.
0}",
```

We will also receive a mail notification similar to the one we received in the previous recipe, *Setting up CloudWatch alarms (AWS CLI)*.

How it works...

In this recipe, we created an alarm for a metric with dimensions using the `dimensions` property of the `put-metric-alarm` command. We then used the `dimensions` property of the `put-metric-data` command to send the data. We also used a period of 10 seconds, smaller than we used in the previous recipe. The period has to be 10, 30, or a multiple of 60.

There's more...

If we mistype the dimension details either while creating the alarm or while sending data, it will not throw any error. Instead, the data will go to a separate dimension and the alarm will stay in the state `INSUFFICIENT_DATA`. The metric name and the dimension names and values are case sensitive.

See also

For more theory and explanation, please refer to the previous recipe, *Setting up CloudWatch alarms (AWS CLI)*.

Using CloudWatch metric log filters

We can use log filters to define search patterns within the logs. We can use log filters to turn logs into metrics and then use those metrics to trigger alarms.

Getting ready

The following are the prerequisites for this recipe:

- A working AWS account
- Access to AWS Management Console
- You should have configured AWS CLI and created the lambda `demo-lambda-with-cli` as discussed in the recipe *Your First Lambda with AWS CLI* in Chapter 1, *Getting Started with Serverless Computing on AWS*

How to do it...

Let's see how we can create metric log filters.

Creating metric filters from AWS CLI

Let's go through the following steps to create metric filters using AWS CLI:

1. We first need to prepare our metric transformations, as follows:

```
[
  {
    "metricName": "HelloCountMetric",
    "metricNamespace": "ServerlessProgrammingCookbook",
    "metricValue": "1"
  }
]
```

Save this into the `metric-transformations.json` file.

2. Use the `put-metric-filter` command to create a metric filter using the `metric-transformations.json` file, as follows:

```
aws logs put-metric-filter \
    --log-group-name /aws/lambda/demo-lambda-with-cli \
    --filter-name 'HelloCountFilter' \
    --filter-pattern 'Hello' \
    --metric-transformations file://metric-transformations.json \
    --region us-east-1 \
    --profile admin
```

3. Execute the Lambda a few times, either from the console or from AWS CLI, as follows:

```
aws lambda invoke \
    --invocation-type RequestResponse \
    --function-name demo-lambda-with-cli \
    --log-type Tail \
    --payload '{"name": "Heartin"}' \
    --region us-east-1 \
    --profile admin \
    outputfile.txt
```

The actual output of the invocation does not matter, as long as it is a success message.

4. Verify the metric from the console by going through the following steps:
    1. Log in to AWS Console and go to CloudWatch.
    2. Click on **Metrics** in the sidebar.
    3. Click on **Metrics with no dimensions**. We should now see a new metric with the name `HelloCountMetric`. We can also add `HelloCountMetric` to the graph or create an alarm for it, as shown in the following screenshot:

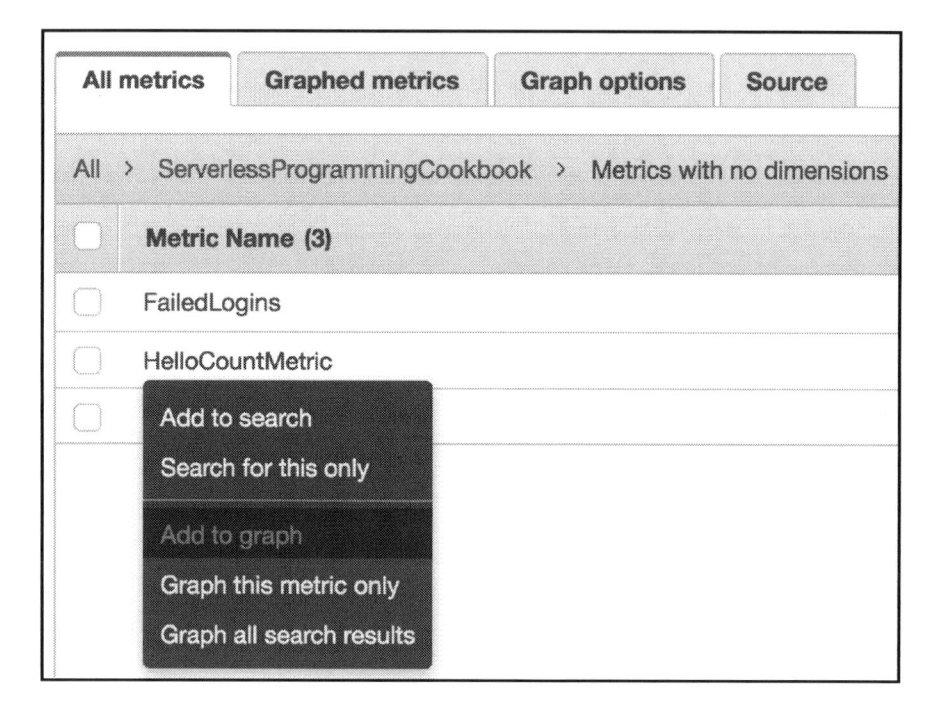

All metrics	Graphed metrics	Graph options	Source

All > ServerlessProgrammingCookbook > Metrics with no dimensions

	Metric Name (3)
☐	FailedLogins
☐	HelloCountMetric
☐	Add to search
	Search for this only
	Add to graph
	Graph this metric only
	Graph all search results

Creating metric filters from the console

When we create metric filters from the Management Console, we can first test filter patterns against existing log data and then create the filter by going through the following steps:

1. Log in to AWS Console and go to CloudWatch.
2. Click on **Logs** from the sidebar. This will display the log groups, as shown in the following screenshot:

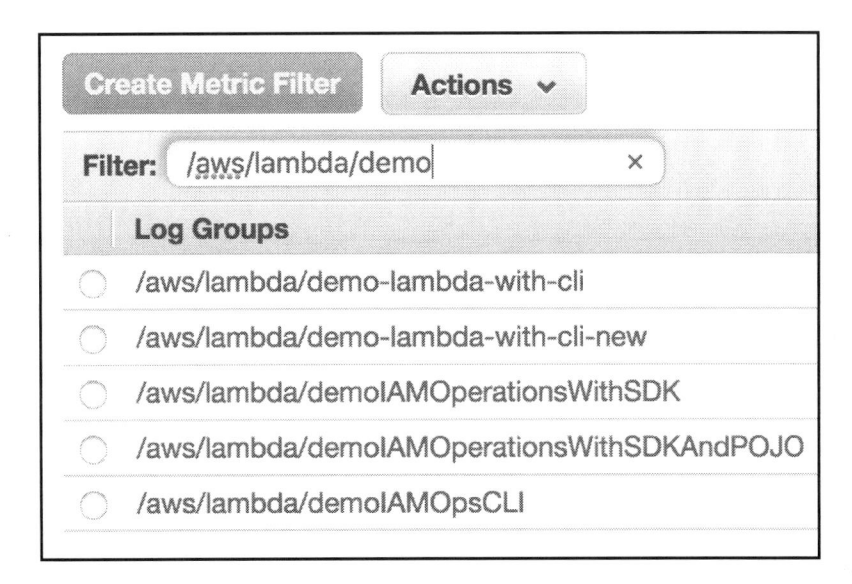

Log Groups
/aws/lambda/demo-lambda-with-cli
/aws/lambda/demo-lambda-with-cli-new
/aws/lambda/demoIAMOperationsWithSDK
/aws/lambda/demoIAMOperationsWithSDKAndPOJO
/aws/lambda/demoIAMOpsCLI

Filter: /aws/lambda/demo

Monitoring and Alerting with Amazon CloudWatch

3. Select a log group and click on **Create Metric Filter**. This will take us to the **Define Logs Metric Filter** page. Enter the filter pattern (for example, `Hello`), select a log stream, and click on **Test Pattern**, as shown in the following screenshot:

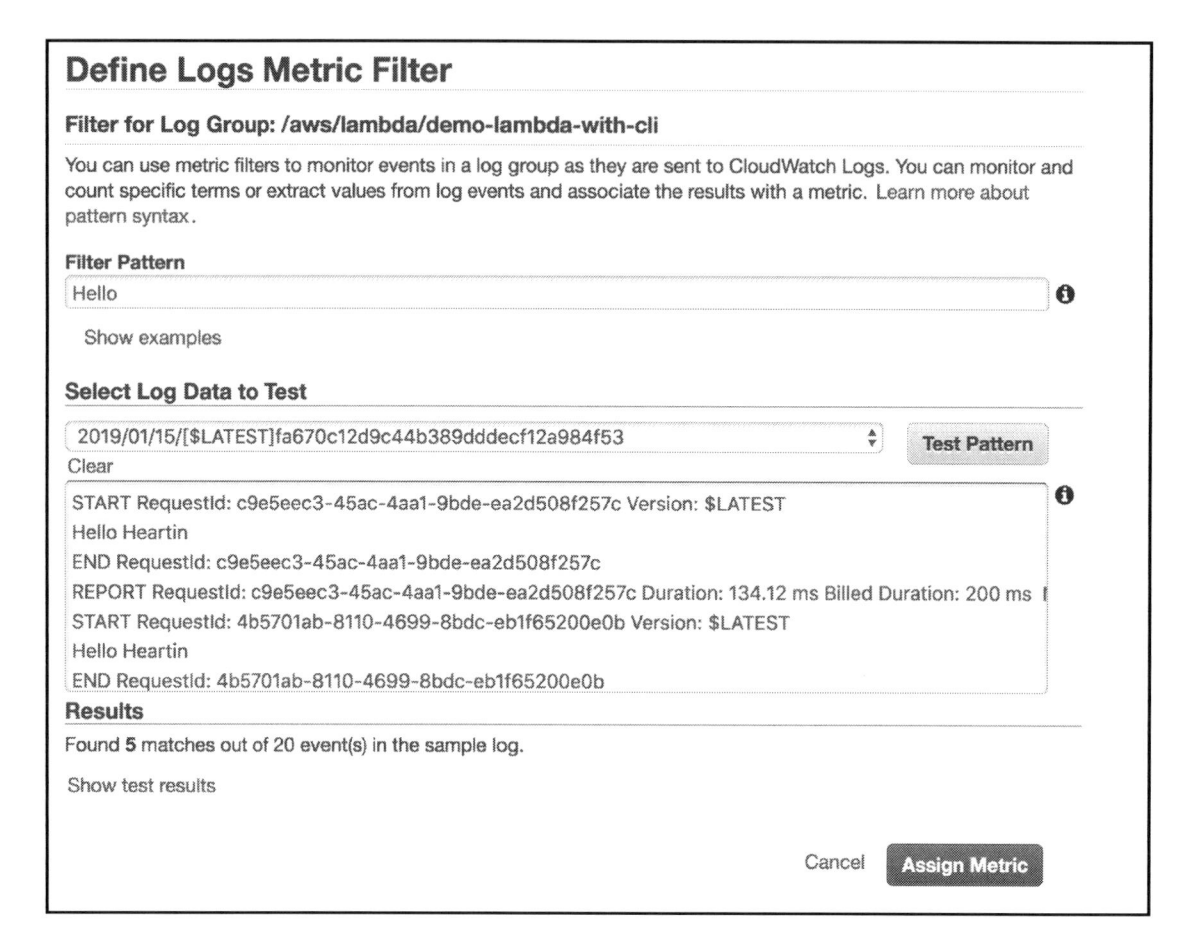

Define Logs Metric Filter

Filter for Log Group: /aws/lambda/demo-lambda-with-cli

You can use metric filters to monitor events in a log group as they are sent to CloudWatch Logs. You can monitor and count specific terms or extract values from log events and associate the results with a metric. Learn more about pattern syntax.

Filter Pattern

Hello

Show examples

Select Log Data to Test

2019/01/15/[$LATEST]fa670c12d9c44b389dddecf12a984f53

Clear   **Test Pattern**

START RequestId: c9e5eec3-45ac-4aa1-9bde-ea2d508f257c Version: $LATEST
Hello Heartin
END RequestId: c9e5eec3-45ac-4aa1-9bde-ea2d508f257c
REPORT RequestId: c9e5eec3-45ac-4aa1-9bde-ea2d508f257c Duration: 134.12 ms Billed Duration: 200 ms
START RequestId: 4b5701ab-8110-4699-8bdc-eb1f65200e0b Version: $LATEST
Hello Heartin
END RequestId: 4b5701ab-8110-4699-8bdc-eb1f65200e0b

Results

Found **5** matches out of 20 event(s) in the sample log.

Show test results

Cancel   **Assign Metric**

4. Click on **Assign Metric**. This will take us to the **Create Metric Filter and Assign a Metric** page. Enter `filter name`, `metric namespace`, and provide a `metric name`, as shown in the following screenshot:

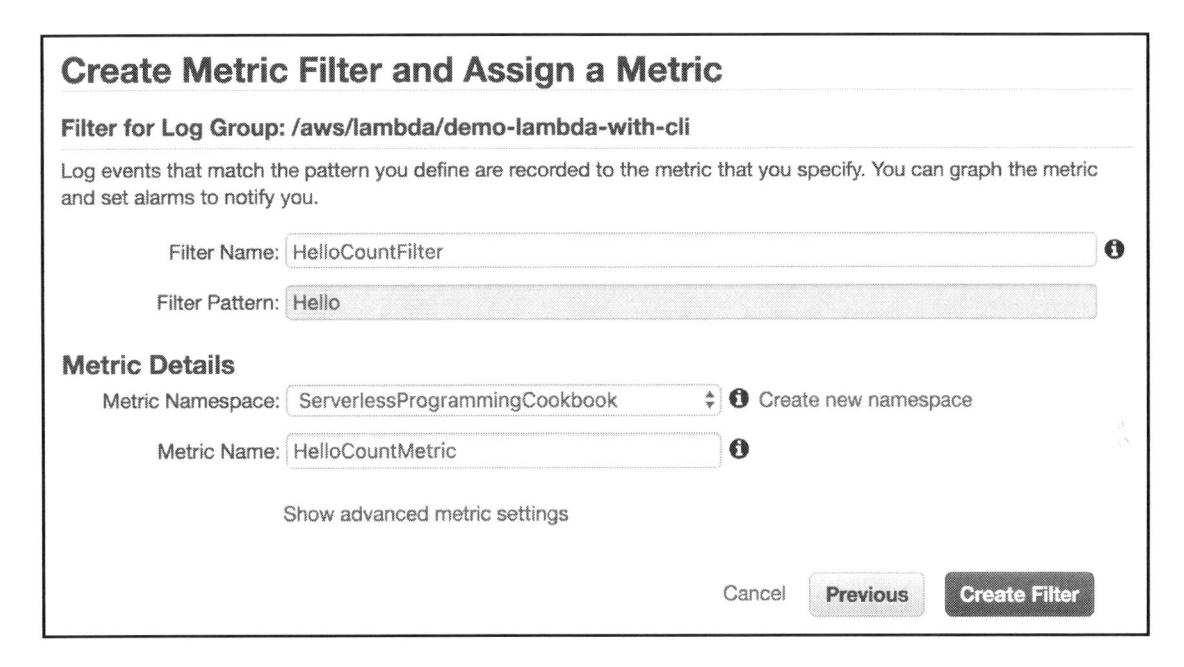

Create Metric Filter and Assign a Metric

Filter for Log Group: /aws/lambda/demo-lambda-with-cli

Log events that match the pattern you define are recorded to the metric that you specify. You can graph the metric and set alarms to notify you.

Filter Name: HelloCountFilter

Filter Pattern: Hello

Metric Details

Metric Namespace: ServerlessProgrammingCookbook ⟳ Create new namespace

Metric Name: HelloCountMetric

Show advanced metric settings

Cancel | Previous | **Create Filter**

5. Click on **Create Filter**. If successful, we should see the following message:

Add Metric Filter

✓ Your filter **HelloCountFilter** has been created.

Filter Name: HelloCountFilter
Filter Pattern: Hello
Metric: ServerlessProgrammingCookbook / HelloCountMetric
Metric Value: 1
Default Value: none

Create Alarm ✏️ ✖

How it works...

We used metric log filters in this recipe. We can use metric log filters to match terms, phrases, and values in the log events. When a match is made, we can increment the value of a CloudWatch metric. For example, we can create a metric log filter to count the occurrence of the word *ERROR*.

Metric filters can also extract numerical values from space-delimited log events, and in such cases, we can increment our metric value by the actual numerical value from the log. We can also use conditional operators and wildcards for matches.

We also looked at metric log creation from the CloudWatch console, and learned how it gives us the additional capability to test our search patterns against existing data.

Log filters do not work on data that was already sent to CloudWatch, but only on data sent after the filter was created. At the time of writing, log filters will only return the first 50 results.

There's more...

This was a very basic recipe to demonstrate the use of metric filters. You can now create alarms for the metric created in this recipe by following the recipe *Setting up CloudWatch alarms (AWS CLI)*.

See also

- https://docs.aws.amazon.com/cli/latest/reference/logs/put-metric-filter.html

9
Serverless Programming Practices and Patterns

This chapter will cover the following:

- Enabling **Cross-Origin Resource Sharing** (**CORS**) for the API and testing with CodePen
- Implementing and testing Cognito operations with the JavaScript SDK
- Federated identity with Amazon Cognito
- Creating a **Secure Sockets Layer** (**SSL**) certificate with **AWS Certificate Manager** (**ACM**)
- Fan-in and fan-out architectural patterns with AWS

Introduction

In the previous chapters, we saw many AWS services that can be used for building serverless applications. In this chapter, we will explore some general practices and patterns that involve one or more of those AWS services. We have been using AWS CLI APIs and Java Lambdas until now. Services such as API Gateway and Cognito generally interact mostly with UI components and hence we will discuss their use with the JavaScript SDKs. We will also enable and use CORS, and then test our JavaScript SDK code from a browser using CodePen.

Furthermore, we will see how to create a federated identity with Cognito. We did not try this recipe in `Chapter 4`, *Application Security with Amazon Cognito*, as federated identity requires a valid domain name. We registered a domain name in `Chapter 5`, *Web Hosting with S3, Route53, and CloudFront*. We will then discuss a pattern called the fan-out pattern, which involves the **Simple Notification Service** (**SNS**) and the **Simple Queue Service** (**SQS**). We covered SQS and SNS recipes in `Chapter 6`, *Messaging and Notifications with SQS and SNS*. Finally, we will conclude with a recipe on certificate generation using ACM.

Serverless Programming Practices and Patterns

This chapter tries to bridge the gap between the AWS serverless services we learned and how they are actually used in real-world projects. This chapter assumes that you are comfortable with all the services discussed in the previous chapters. We may not discuss in detail all the code and theory behind the practices and patterns we discuss, especially those that were already discussed.

Enabling CORS for the API and testing with CodePen

CORS is a mechanism that allows a web application running at one domain (origin) to access selected resources from a different server. Without CORS, the server will respond with a status code of `403` in such cases. We will create an API gateway service similar to what we did in Chapter 2, *Building Serverless REST APIs with API Gateway*, but will also enable CORS on the API.

We will first get familiar with the CodePen website and will test our API by invoking it using JavaScript SDK code from within the CodePen website. This will also be a revision of the API Gateway concepts that we learned in Chapter 2, *Building Serverless REST APIs with API Gateway*, but with the additional support for CORS. We will only discuss new concepts here; for theory on already discussed topics, you may refer to the recipes of Chapter 2, *Building Serverless REST APIs with API Gateway*.

Getting ready

The following are the prerequisites for this recipe:

- A working AWS account
- A configured AWS CLI, as discussed in the *Your first Lambda with the AWS CLI* recipe of Chapter 1, *Getting Started with Serverless Computing on AWS*
- You have followed the steps in the recipe *Your first API using the AWS CLI* from Chapter 2, *Building Serverless REST APIs with API Gateway*, and created and deployed an API with a GET URL of the form `https://<rest-api-id>.execute-api.us-east-1.amazonaws.com/dev/greeting/Heartin`
- You are familiar with CodePen or any browser-based tool from which we can send JavaScript requests to our API

[392]

Getting familiar with CodePen

Follow these steps to use CodePen to connect to our API through GET:

1. Go to `https://codepen.io`. This will take us to the CodePen website.
2. Click tab **Create** and then select the **Pen** option.
3. Click the **Settings** menu, select the **Behavior** tab, and uncheck the **Enabled** option under **Auto-Updating Preview**. This will enable us to **Run** our code.

Enter the following code in the JS section of the CodePen UI and click **Run**:

```
var xhr = new XMLHttpRequest();
xhr.open('GET',
'https://8vqyyjelad.execute-api.us-east-1.amazonaws.com/dev/greeting/Hearti
n');
xhr.onreadystatechange = function (event) {
console.log(event.target.response);
}
xhr.setRequestHeader('Content-Type', 'application/json');
xhr.send();
```

We should receive a blank response in the CodePen UI. But if we open the developer tools for our browser (for example, Chrome Developer tools), we should see the actual error message as follows:

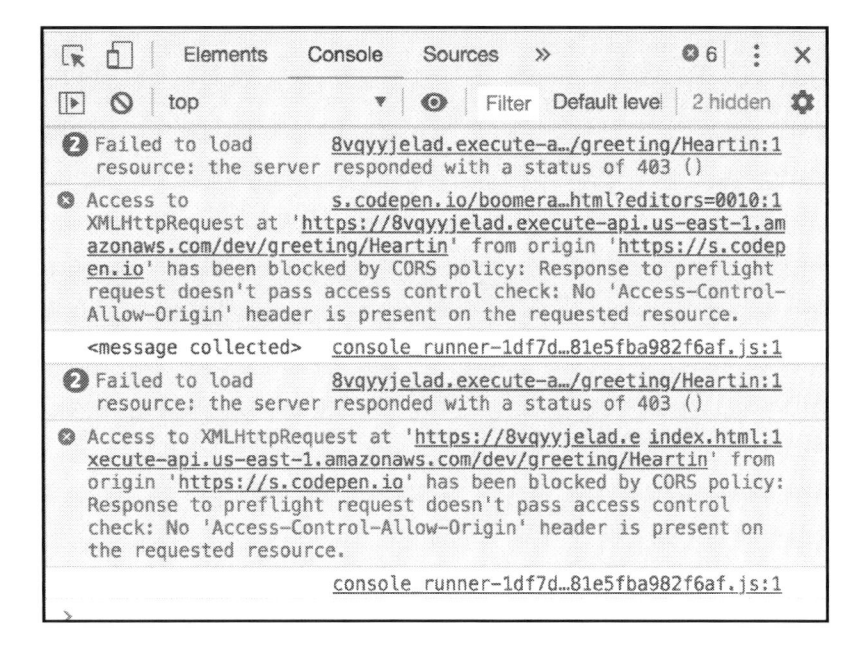

Serverless Programming Practices and Patterns

This is because CORS is not enabled. We will create an API with CORS enabled and test it again in the *How to do it...* section. We will also see how we can enable CORS on the current API.

How to do it...

Let's create an API with CORS enabled from scratch. Steps 1 to 4 are the same as we have seen in `Chapter 2`, *Building Serverless REST APIs with API Gateway*:

1. Create an API:

    ```
    aws apigateway create-rest-api \
        --name 'API WITH CORS' \
        --region us-east-1 \
        --profile admin
    ```

    > I will not display the region and profile parameters for further commands. You may either add them manually to every command or configure them as the defaults with the AWS CLI configuration.

2. Get the ID of the root resource path \:

    ```
    aws apigateway get-resources \
        --rest-api-id xenqybowjg
    ```

3. Create a resource `greeting` under the root path:

    ```
    aws apigateway create-resource \
        --rest-api-id xenqybowjg \
        --parent-id p8yd8xde55 \
        --path-part greeting
    ```

4. Create a subresource with a path parameter that can accept a string:

    ```
    aws apigateway create-resource \
        --rest-api-id xenqybowjg \
        --parent-id xkjhh7 \
        --path-part "{name}"
    ```

[394]

5. Next, we will create the GET method:

   1. Execute put-method for the GET method:

      ```
      aws apigateway put-method  \
          --rest-api-id xenqybowjg \
          --resource-id sfgfk6 \
          --http-method GET \
          --authorization-type "NONE"
      ```

   2. Execute put-method-response for the GET method:

      ```
      aws apigateway put-method-response \
          --rest-api-id xenqybowjg \
          --resource-id sfgfk6 \
          --http-method GET \
          --status-code 200 \
          --response-parameters file://put-method-response-get.json
      ```

      put-method-response-get.json should look as follows:

      ```
      {
        "method.response.header.Access-Control-Allow-Origin": false
      }
      ```

   3. Execute put-integration for the GET method:

      ```
      aws apigateway put-integration \
          --rest-api-id xenqybowjg \
          --resource-id sfgfk6 \
          --http-method GET  \
          --type MOCK  \
          --integration-http-method GET \
          --request-templates "{\"application/json\": \"{"statusCode": "200"}\"}"
      ```

   4. Execute put-integration-response for the GET method:

      ```
      aws apigateway put-integration-response \
          --rest-api-id xenqybowjg \
          --resource-id sfgfk6 \
          --http-method GET \
          --status-code 200 \
          --response-templates file://response-template-get.json \
      ```

[395]

```
        --response-parameters file://put-method-integration-
    get.json \
        --selection-pattern "" \
        --region us-east-1 --profile admin
```

The `response-template-get.json` file should have the following contents:

```
{"application/json": "Hello $input.params('name')"}
```

The `put-method-integration-get.json` file should have the following contents:

```
{
    "method.response.header.Access-Control-Allow-Origin":
"'*'"
}
```

6. Now, we will create the OPTIONS method:

   1. Execute `put-method` for the OPTIONS method:

      ```
      aws apigateway put-method \
          --rest-api-id xenqybowjg \
          --resource-id sfgfk6 \
          --http-method OPTIONS \
          --authorization-type "NONE"
      ```

   2. Execute `put-method-response` or the OPTIONS method:

      ```
      aws apigateway put-method-response \
          --rest-api-id xenqybowjg \
          --resource-id sfgfk6 \
          --http-method OPTIONS \
          --status-code 200 \
          --response-parameters file://put-method-options.json
      ```

      `put-method-options.json` should look like this:

      ```
      {
          "method.response.header.Access-Control-Allow-Origin":
      false,
          "method.response.header.Access-Control-Allow-Headers":
      false,
      "method.response.header.Access-Control-Allow-Methods":
      false
       }
      ```

Chapter 9

3. Execute `put-integration` for the OPTIONS method:

```
aws apigateway put-integration \
    --rest-api-id xenqybowjg \
    --resource-id sfgfk6 \
    --http-method OPTIONS \
    --type MOCK  \
    --integration-http-method OPTIONS \
    --request-templates "{\"application/json\":
\"{\"statusCode\": \"200\"}\"}"
```

4. Execute `put-integration-response` for the OPTIONS method:

```
aws apigateway put-integration-response \
    --rest-api-id xenqybowjg \
    --resource-id sfgfk6 \
    --http-method OPTIONS \
    --status-code 200 \
    --response-parameters file://put-method-integration-response-options.json \
    --selection-pattern ""
```

The `put-method-integration-response-options.json` file should contain the following content:

```
{
   "method.response.header.Access-Control-Allow-Origin":
"'*'",
   "method.response.header.Access-Control-Allow-Headers":
"'Content-Type,Authorization,X-Amz-Date,X-Api-Key,X-Amz-Security-Token'"
}
```

7. Deploy the API:

```
aws apigateway create-deployment \
    --rest-api-id xenqybowjg \
    --stage-name dev \
    --stage-description "Dev stage" \
    --description "Dev deployment"
```

Execute the following URL from the browser: `https://xenqybowjg.execute-api.us-east-1.amazonaws.com/dev/greeting/Heartin`.

[397]

Serverless Programming Practices and Patterns

8. Execute the URL from CodePen as follows:

```
var xhr = new XMLHttpRequest();
xhr.open('GET', 'https://qngs4lsxob.execute-api.us-
east-1.amazonaws.com/dev/greeting/Heartin');
xhr.onreadystatechange = function (event) {
console.log(event.target.response);
}
xhr.setRequestHeader('Content-Type', 'application/json');
xhr.send();
```

In the Chrome developer console, we should now see a success message as follows, instead of the errors we saw in the *Getting ready* section.

```
                    console_runner-1df7d...81e5fba982f6af.js:1
② Hello Heartin    console_runner-1df7d...81e5fba982f6af.js:1
```

> Components within the CloudFormation template correspond to what we have seen with AWS CLI commands and are mostly self-explanatory. The corresponding CloudFormation template is provided with the code files for reference.

How it works...

We created an API from scratch with CORS enabled. We did it using both AWS CLI commands and the CloudFormation template. Let's first understand the CLI steps in detail.

The first four steps with the CLI are similar to what we have seen in recipes in `Chapter 2, Building Serverless REST APIs with API Gateway`:

1. Create an API
2. Get the ID of the root resource
3. Create a resource `greeting`
4. Create a subresource with a path parameter

The next four steps create the GET method:

5. `put-method` for the `GET` method
6. `put-method-response` for the `GET` method
7. `put-integration` for the `GET` method
8. `put-integration-response` for the `GET` method

[398]

Chapter 9

The `put-method` subcommand and `put-integration` subcommand are similar to what we have seen in the recipes of Chapter 2, *Building Serverless REST APIs with API Gateway*. The `put-method-response` and `put-integration-response` subcommands now also should specify the `response-parameters` property.

The `response-parameters` property of the `put-method-response` subcommand contains a key-value map specifying required or optional response parameters that the API can send back in the response. The key of this map is a method response header name and the value is a Boolean flag indicating whether the method response parameter is required or not (true for required and false for optional).

The `response-parameters` property of the `put-method-integration` subcommand contains a key-value map that specifies the response parameters that are passed to the method response from the backend (mock integration in our case). The key is a method response header parameter name and the value is an integration response header value, a static string value enclosed within single quotes, or a JSON expression from the integration response body.

As we can see from the previous section, we need to use four subcommands to configure an HTTP method with API Gateway when using the AWS CLI. However, with a CloudFormation template, we needed only one resource of type `AWS::ApiGateway::Method`:

The next four steps create an OPTIONS HTTP method for the resource:

9. `put-method` for the OPTIONS method
10. `put-method-response` for the OPTIONS method
11. `put-integration` for the OPTIONS method
12. `put-integration-response` for the OPTIONS method

OPTIONS is required for the preflight requests.

For Ajax and HTTP request methods, especially for ones that can modify data, such as non-GET methods, or for POST method with certain MIME types, the specification mandates browsers to preflight a request to server, asking for supported methods with an HTTP OPTIONS request. The server responds back with a header `Access-Control-Allow-Methods` that lists all support methods other than GET (for example, DELETE). The browser will then send the actual request only for the supported HTTP request methods.

The `OPTIONS` response should also contain the headers `Access-Control-Allow-Origin` and `Access-Control-Allow-Headers`. The `Access-Control-Allow-Origin` header specifies the servers (origins) that can access a particular resource. A value of `*` in our case indicates that any other domain name can access it with CORS. In practice, you may make it more specific to particular domains. The `Access-Control-Allow-Headers` header specifies the headers that are allowed in the actual request. We just specified the basis headers `Content-Type, Authorization, X-Amz-Date, X-Api-Key,` and `X-Amz-Security-Token`.

Even if we only use a `GET URI`, we still need the OPTIONS method configured as we are making an AJAX call with the `XMLHttpRequest` object. With the `XMLHttpRequest` object, we can exchange data with a web server without reloading the whole page. All modern web browsers have a built-in support for the `XMLHttpRequest` object. In our case, the `Access-Control-Allow-Methods` header may be empty or not specified with the `put-method-integration` subcommand, since we are not supporting any other methods than `GET` (it still has to be defined with the `put-method-response` subcommand, but we can specify it as optional).

Finally, we deploy the API and then test it using CodePen:

13. Deploy the API
14. Execute the URL from CodePen

There's more...

In this recipe, we did a `GET` request from another domain through CORS. We can also try out other HTTP methods. One of the important changes we need to make is to specify the HTTP methods that are allowed using the `Access-Control-Allow-Methods` header in the CORS response.

See also

- https://developer.mozilla.org/en-US/docs/Glossary/Preflight_request

Implementing and testing Cognito operations with the JavaScript SDK

We saw Cognito operations with AWS CLI commands in Chapter 4, *Application Security with Amazon Cognito*. With web applications, Cognito is generally used with the JavaScript SDK from the frontend. Hence, we will see various uses of Cognito using the JavaScript SDK and then test it using CodePen. We may use CodePen or any other tool, or use it within our application (for example, an Angular app) and then test it.

Getting ready

The prerequisites for this recipe are as follows:

1. A working AWS account
2. The Node.js and npm installed on your machine
3. Download the amazon-cognito-identity.min.js file
4. Create an S3 bucket and upload the amazon-cognito-identity.min.js file
5. Create a Cognito user pool and a client

We also need to complete the following setup before we follow the steps outlined in the *How to do it...* section:

Download the amazon-cognito-identity.min.js file

Create a temp folder and go inside the folder.

Run this:

```
npm i amazon-cognito-identity-js
```

We should see a response similar to this:

```
+ amazon-cognito-identity-js@3.0.7
added 7 packages from 20 contributors and audited 7 packages in 4.791s
found 0 vulnerabilities
```

If we do an `ls`, we should see the following two folders created:

```
$ ls
node_modules            package-lock.json
```

If we go inside `node_modules/amazon-cognito-identity-js/dist`, we should see these files:

```
$ cd node_modules/amazon-cognito-identity-js/dist/
$ ls
amazon-cognito-identity.js              amazon-cognito-identity.min.js.gz
amazon-cognito-identity.min.js
```

Create an S3 bucket and upload the amazon-cognito-identity.min.js file

Create an `S3` bucket as follows:

```
aws s3api create-bucket \
    --bucket serverlesscookbook-cognito-files \
    --profile admin
```

Upload the `amazon-cognito-identity.min.js` file:

```
aws s3 cp amazon-cognito-identity.min.js s3://serverlesscookbook-cognito-files \
    --profile admin
```

Execute the bucket policy that allows public read access to the bucket:

```
aws s3api put-bucket-policy \
    --bucket serverlesscookbook-cognito-files \
    --policy file://s3-website-policy.json \
    --profile admin
```

The `s3-website-policy.json` file should have these contents:

```
{   "Version":"2012-10-17",
    "Statement":[
        {   "Sid":"PublicReadGetObjectAccess",
            "Effect":"Allow",
            "Principal": "*",
            "Action":["s3:GetObject"],
            "Resource":["arn:aws:s3:::serverlesscookbook-cognito-files/*"]
```

Creating a Cognito user pool and client

We can create a Cognito user pool as follows:

```
aws cognito-idp create-user-pool \
    --cli-input-json file://create-user-pool-cli-input.json \
    --region us-east-1 \
    --profile admin
```

The `create-user-pool-cli-input.json` file has the following contents:

```
{
    "PoolName": "javscript_pool",
    "Policies": {
        "PasswordPolicy": {
            "MinimumLength": 8,
            "RequireUppercase": true,
            "RequireLowercase": true,
            "RequireNumbers": true,
            "RequireSymbols": true
        }
    },
    "AutoVerifiedAttributes": [
        "email"
    ],
    "AliasAttributes": [
        "email"
    ],
    "EmailVerificationMessage": "Your verification code from MyApp is {####}",
    "EmailVerificationSubject": "Your verification code from MyAp",
    "UserPoolTags": {
        "Team": "Dev"
    }
}
```

This is the same as what we have seen in *Chapter 4, Application Security with Amazon Cognito*, which we can refer to for more details and explanations.

Create a user pool client:

```
aws cognito-idp create-user-pool-client \
    --user-pool-id us-east-1_P8srRzYqn \
    --client-name javscript-pool-client \
```

```
--explicit-auth-flows USER_PASSWORD_AUTH \
--region us-east-1 \
--profile admin
```

Replace the user pool ID value with the ID of the user pool you created in the previous step.

How to do it...

We will use CodePen to execute the JavaScript SDK code for Cognito operations, following these steps:

1. Open CodePen and add locations to the required files.
2. Go to `https://codepen.io/`.
3. Click the **Create** tab and then select the **Pen** option.
4. In the new window, click the **Settings** menu, select the **Behaviour** tab, and uncheck the **Enabled** option under **Auto-Updating Preview.**
5. In the **Settings** menu, select the **JavaScript** tab and do the following:
    1. Search for `aws sdk` and select the appropriate SDK:

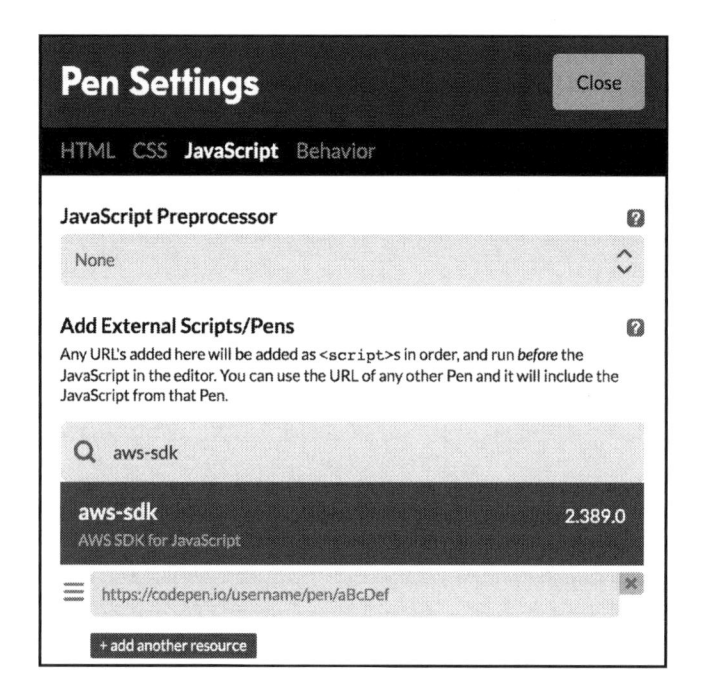

CodePen will populate the SDK URL (as we will see in the next screenshot).

6. Add the URL of our `amazon-cognito-identity.min.js` file (for example, `https://s3.amazonaws.com/cognito-min-bucket/amazon-cognito-identity.min.js`):

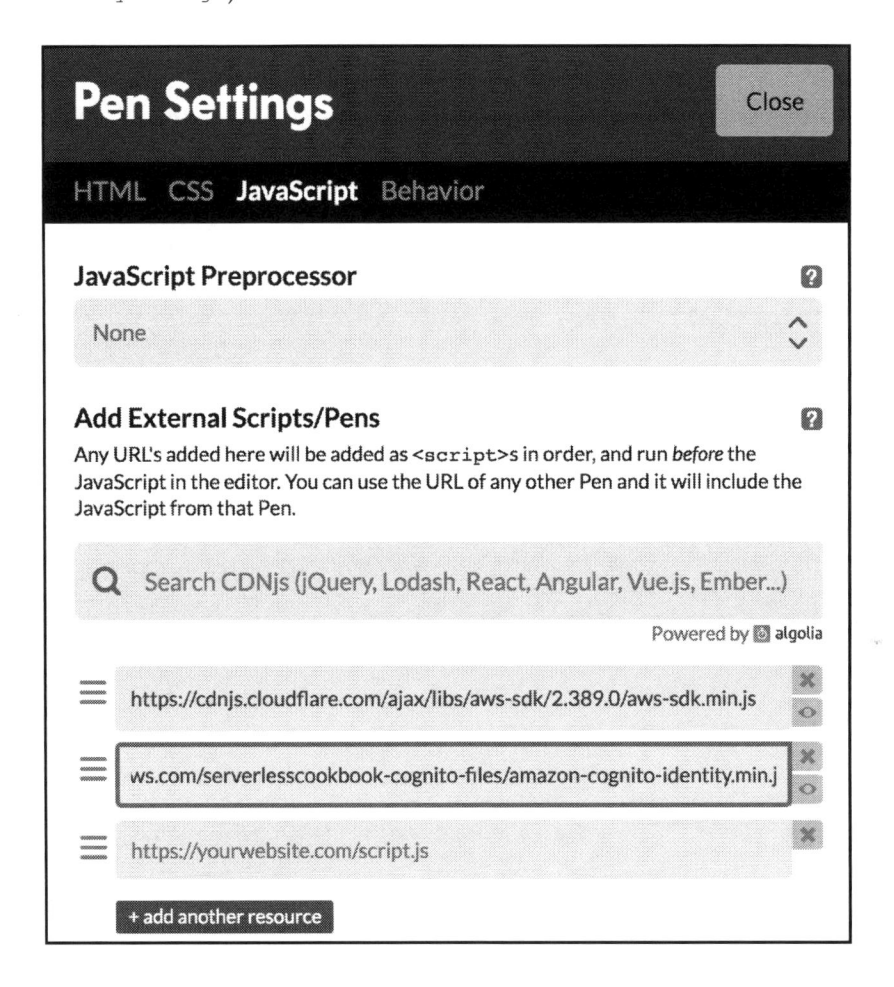

Pen Settings

HTML CSS **JavaScript** Behavior

JavaScript Preprocessor

None

Add External Scripts/Pens

Any URL's added here will be added as `<script>`s in order, and run *before* the JavaScript in the editor. You can use the URL of any other Pen and it will include the JavaScript from that Pen.

Search CDNjs (jQuery, Lodash, React, Angular, Vue.js, Ember...)

Powered by algolia

https://cdnjs.cloudflare.com/ajax/libs/aws-sdk/2.389.0/aws-sdk.min.js

ws.com/serverlesscookbook-cognito-files/amazon-cognito-identity.min.j

https://yourwebsite.com/script.js

+ add another resource

[405]

7. Click **Close**. We can now run JavaScript code from within the **Cognito JS** tab, as we did in the previous recipe:

```
var poolData = {
    UserPoolId: 'us-east-1_P8srRzYqn',
    ClientId: '3sk2emj3thcp6mdg43he50k4qn'
};
var userPool = new AmazonCognitoIdentity.CognitoUserPool(poolData);
var attributeList: CognitoUserAttribute[] = [];
var emailAttribute = {
```

8. We can sign up/register the user with the following code:

```
var poolData = {
    UserPoolId: '<user pool id>',
    ClientId: '<client id>'
};
var userPool = new AmazonCognitoIdentity.CognitoUserPool(poolData);
var attributeList: CognitoUserAttribute[] = [];
var emailAttribute = {

Name : 'email',
Value : '<user email>'
};

attributeList.push(new
AmazonCognitoIdentity.CognitoUserAttribute(emailAttribute));

userPool.signUp('heartin', 'Passw0rd$1', attributeList, null,
function(err, result){
    if (err) {
        console.log(JSON.stringify(err));
        alert(err.message || JSON.stringify(err));
        return;
    }
    var cognitoUser = result.user;
    console.log('user name is ' + cognitoUser.getUsername());
});
```

9. Update the code with correct userpool ID, client ID, username, and password, and click **Run**.
We can view the log messages in the developer console as follows:

```
<message collected>   console_runner-1df7d...81e5fba982f6af.js:1
user name is heartin  console_runner-1df7d...81e5fba982f6af.js:1
```

10. Confirm the registered user by using the code received in the email provided during registration:

```
var poolData = {
   UserPoolId: '<user pool id>',
   ClientId: '<client id>'
};
var userPool = new AmazonCognitoIdentity.CognitoUserPool(poolData);
var userData = {
       Username : 'heartin',
       Pool : userPool
   };

var cognitoUser = new AmazonCognitoIdentity.CognitoUser(userData);
   cognitoUser.confirmRegistration('698099', true, function(err, result) {
       if (err) {
           alert(err.message || JSON.stringify(err));
           return;
       }
       console.log('call result: ' + result);
   });
```

Replace `698099` with the code you received. Run the script from CodePen and we should receive a response similar to this in the developer logs:

```
call result: SUCCESS  console_runner-1df7d...81e5fba982f6af.js:1
```

11. Sign in to the application using the registered email ID and password:

```
var authenticationData = {
       Username : 'heartin',
       Password : 'Passw0rd$1',
   };
   var authenticationDetails = new
AmazonCognitoIdentity.AuthenticationDetails(authenticationData);
   var poolData = {
       UserPoolId: '<user pool id>',
```

[407]

```
        ClientId: '<client id>'
    };
    var userPool = new
AmazonCognitoIdentity.CognitoUserPool(poolData);
    var userData = {
        Username : 'heartin',
        Pool : userPool
    };
    var cognitoUser = new
AmazonCognitoIdentity.CognitoUser(userData);
    cognitoUser.authenticateUser(authenticationDetails, {
        onSuccess: function (result) {
            var accessToken =
result.getAccessToken().getJwtToken();
            console.log('access token is:' + accessToken);
        },
        onFailure: function(err) {
          console.log(JSON.stringify(err));
            alert(err.message || JSON.stringify(err));
        },

    });
```

If successful, we should receive the access token in the response and we can verify it from the browser developer console:

```
access token           console_runner-1df7d…81e5fba982f6af.js:1
is:eyJraWQiOiI3V0FrUVQ4Z082eXg3RjN4SHBTbnZkNnRjZjBBcHJEZXo1WXN
jS1VDNzZFPSIsImFsZyI6IlJTMjU2In0.eyJzdWIiOiJmM2M3ZmMxOS03MTI2L
TRlNWYtOTlmZS1mMTIxMzYxNjBmYmIiLCJldmVudF9pZCI6IjI3MGQ0MjdjLTF
hMTAtMTFlOS1hMTViLTNkMzVlY2FkYWQ1ZiIsInRva2VuX3VzZSI6ImFjY2Vzc
yIsInNjb3BlIjoiYXdzLmNvZ25pdG8uc2lnbmluLnVzZXIuYWRtaW4iLCJhdXR
oX3RpbWUiOjE1NDc2MTkyMjgsImlzcyI6Imh0dHBzOlwvXC9jb2duaXRvLWlkc
C51cy1lYXN0LTEuYW1hem9uYXdzLmNvbVwvdXMtZWFzdC0xX1A4c3JSellxbiI
sImV4cCI6MTU0NzcwMjgyOCwiaWF0IjoxNTQ3Njk5MjI4LCJqdGkiOiJhMTQ3N
Dg2NS04NjI0LTQwNjktYWE4YS1jNjljOGI1NTUxOGUiLCJjbGllbnRfaWQiOiI
zc2syZW1qM3RoY3A2bWRnNDNoZTUwazRxbiIsInVzZXJuYW1lIjoiaGVhcnRpb
iJ9.ChGkYGm9KIisgMOuOaU2EhEic241IFcgoYZNhfSknSG1qhGcOiC7nX9s3S
4XJleSpJOgZkXR_9ZqfEp-
eT3LpXwGGMvCfekV7RACPcUPcux407KtD2ABHVKMGqSNz1ygNip3zmN9u2aJcP
hyiQFIPj9QGesUII7bSwa8B_Z-I6fLR8GaK2ixwwkk-
VOp7OLBP7nZVGpPO4oyTELvwQM9KMx-8dhGvujvPXY-CYB-
V0SIrbju6Wj7lZS0TJ62sSO-
JT9VCtxdxGuVm207lUOOZMUTHjWUJyyz_C7RqtkN84sWx0dxtAIPhNoMHn-
ETTD6FdQEmzPwEAm_ifF_z_z6Ug
```

We can now use this access token for further operations.

How it works...

We used CodePen to execute a basic user signup and login flow using the JavaScript SDK for Cognito. The APIs used correspond to the AWS CLI APIs used in `Chapter 4`, *Application Security with Amazon Cognito*, which we can refer to for more details and explanations.

There's more...

We have implemented the JavaScript SDK-based code for Cognito and executed it from CodePen. We can use the code with any JavaScript application, or a framework such as Angular. We implemented only one login flow. You may follow this recipe and the recipes in `Chapter 4`, *Application Security with Amazon Cognito*, and do the same for all the other flows discussed.

See also

- https://docs.aws.amazon.com/cognito/latest/developerguide/using-amazon-cognito-user-identity-pools-javascript-examples.html

Federated identity with Amazon Cognito

`Federated identity` is a process where a user's identity and attributes are stored across different identity management systems. For example, we can use federated identity to allow users to log in to our system with another identity provider's credentials. In this recipe, we will see how to use federated identity with Cognito user pools. For the purpose of demonstration, we will be using Google Plus as the identity provider and Cognito will act as the identity broker. The general process will be the same for any other providers, such as Facebook or Amazon.

Getting ready

The following are the prerequisites for this recipe:

- A working AWS account.
- An S3 static website with a real domain name pointing to it. You may follow the recipes in `Chapter 5`, *Web Hosting with S3, Route53, and CloudFront* to create a static website, register a domain, and link the domain name to the static website.
- A basic understanding of HTML and JavaScript is good to have.

How to do it...

We first need to configure the identity provider (Google Plus in our case) to be used for federated identity login.

Step 1 - Configuring Google Plus

Before we can use Google Plus for federated identity logins with Cognito, we need to follows these steps:

1. Navigate to `https://console.developers.google.com`.
2. Click **Library** on the left sidebar and accept the **terms and conditions** (of course after reading them) if displayed.
3. Scroll down, Select **Google+ API**, and click **Enable** on the new page:

2. Click on **Credentials** on the left sidebar menu, then click **Create** to create a new credential. If we have not created a project yet, this should show us a new project window:

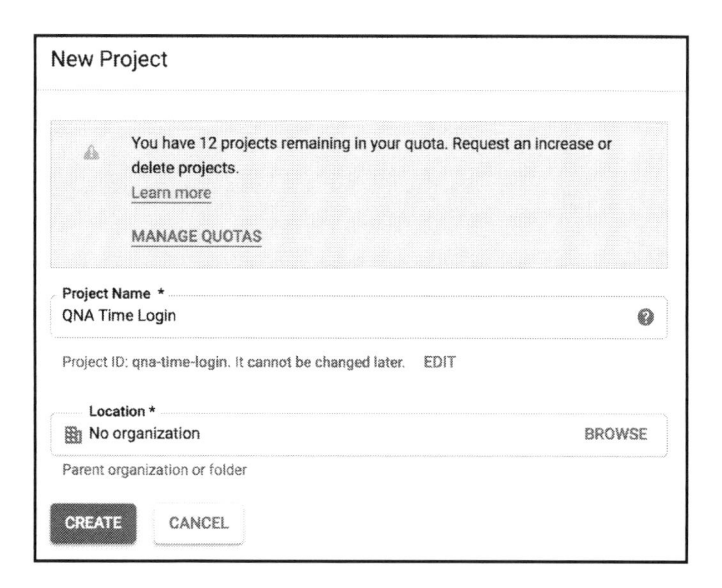

3. In the **New Project** window, do the following:
   1. Provide a **Project Name**
   2. Leave the default value for **Location** as it is
   3. Click the **CREATE** button

Now, click **Create credentials** in the **Credentials** popup:

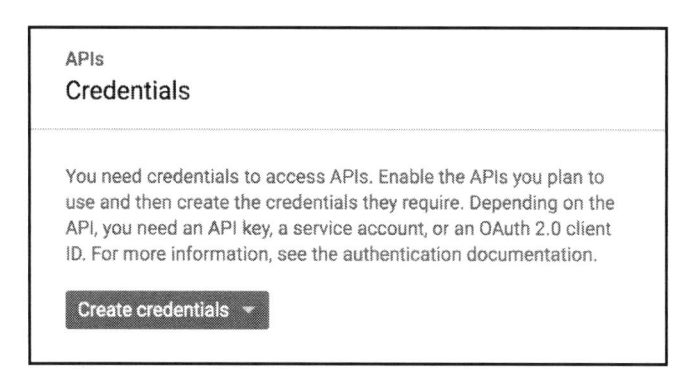

6. From the **drop-down** menu, select **OAuth Client ID**:

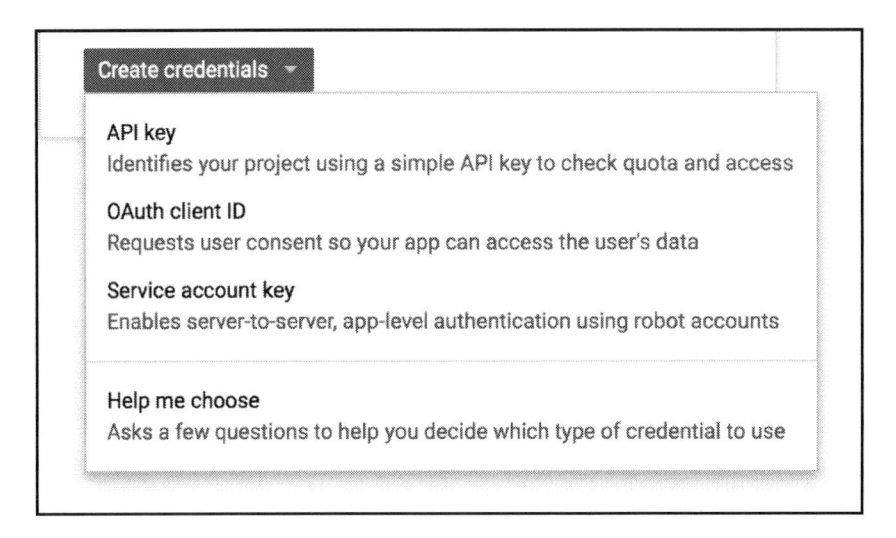

Create credentials

API key
Identifies your project using a simple API key to check quota and access

OAuth client ID
Requests user consent so your app can access the user's data

Service account key
Enables server-to-server, app-level authentication using robot accounts

Help me choose
Asks a few questions to help you decide which type of credential to use

7. There may be a warning message: **To create an OAuth client ID, you must first set a product name on the consent screen**:
    1. Click **Configure consent screen** to the right of it
    2. In the **OAuth consent screen** tab, do the following:
        1. Give an application name
        2. In the **Authorized domains** section, add a valid domain name:

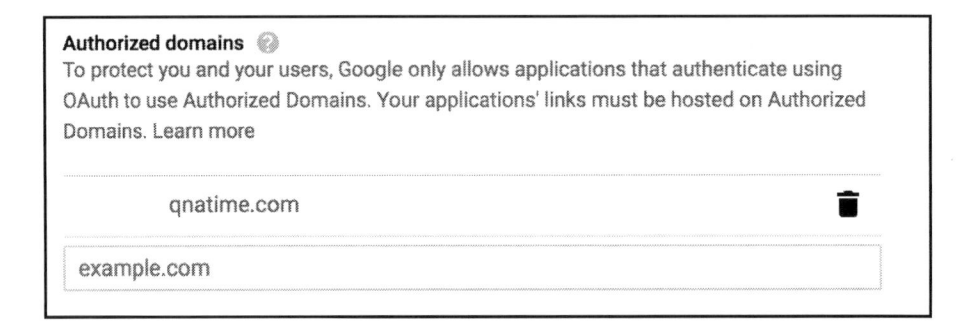

Authorized domains
To protect you and your users, Google only allows applications that authenticate using OAuth to use Authorized Domains. Your applications' links must be hosted on Authorized Domains. Learn more

qnatime.com

example.com

3. Click **Save** at the bottom of the form to save

[412]

Chapter 9

8. We will be redirected to the page for creating an **OAuth client ID**. Set Application Type as **Web application** and enter our domain under Authorized JavaScript origins:

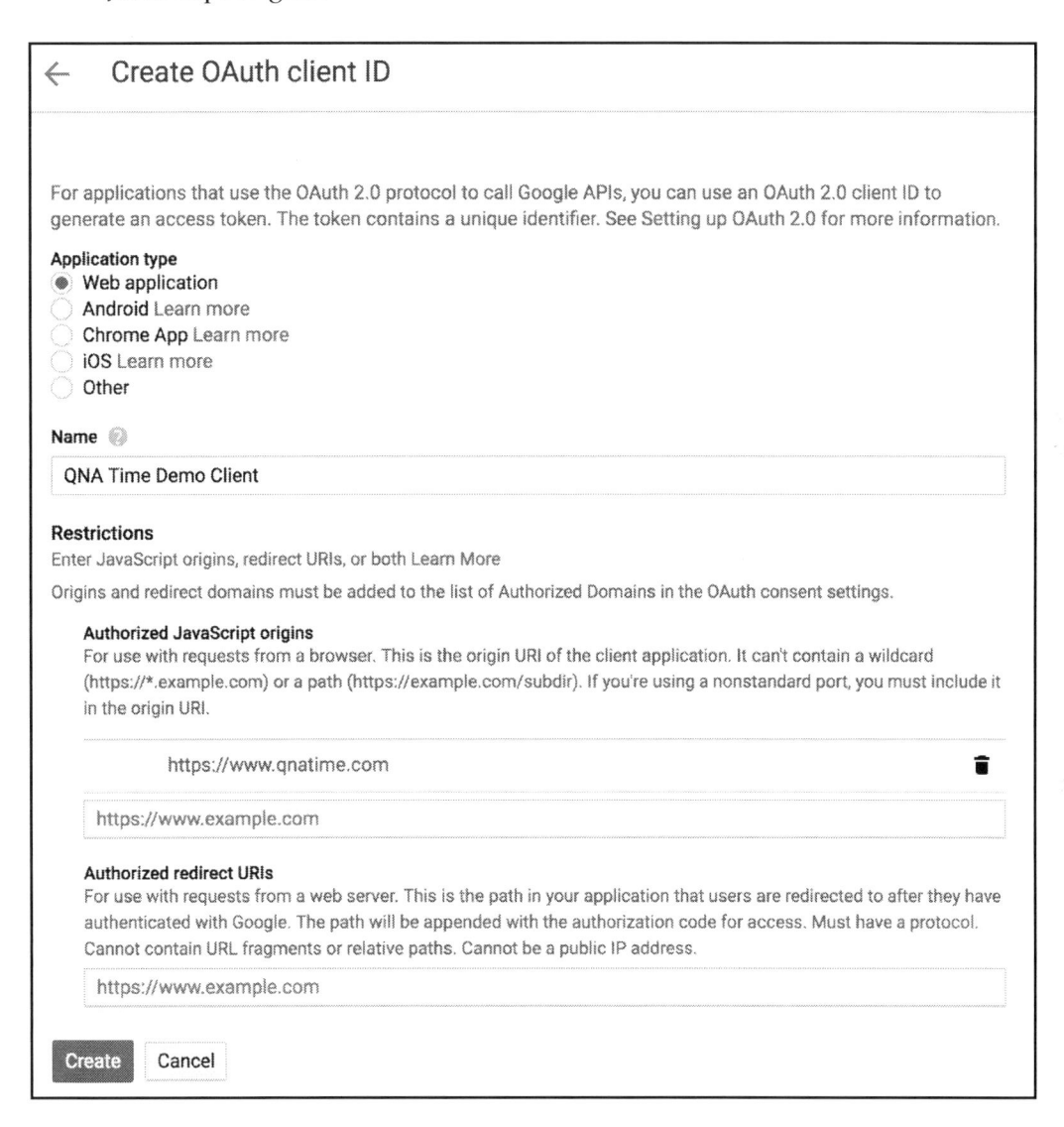

← Create OAuth client ID

For applications that use the OAuth 2.0 protocol to call Google APIs, you can use an OAuth 2.0 client ID to generate an access token. The token contains a unique identifier. See Setting up OAuth 2.0 for more information.

Application type
- ● Web application
- ○ Android Learn more
- ○ Chrome App Learn more
- ○ iOS Learn more
- ○ Other

Name

QNA Time Demo Client

Restrictions

Enter JavaScript origins, redirect URIs, or both Learn More

Origins and redirect domains must be added to the list of Authorized Domains in the OAuth consent settings.

Authorized JavaScript origins
For use with requests from a browser. This is the origin URI of the client application. It can't contain a wildcard (https://*.example.com) or a path (https://example.com/subdir). If you're using a nonstandard port, you must include it in the origin URI.

https://www.qnatime.com

https://www.example.com

Authorized redirect URIs
For use with requests from a web server. This is the path in your application that users are redirected to after they have authenticated with Google. The path will be appended with the authorization code for access. Must have a protocol. Cannot contain URL fragments or relative paths. Cannot be a public IP address.

https://www.example.com

Create   Cancel

[413]

9. Click **Create** and we will be provided with a client ID:

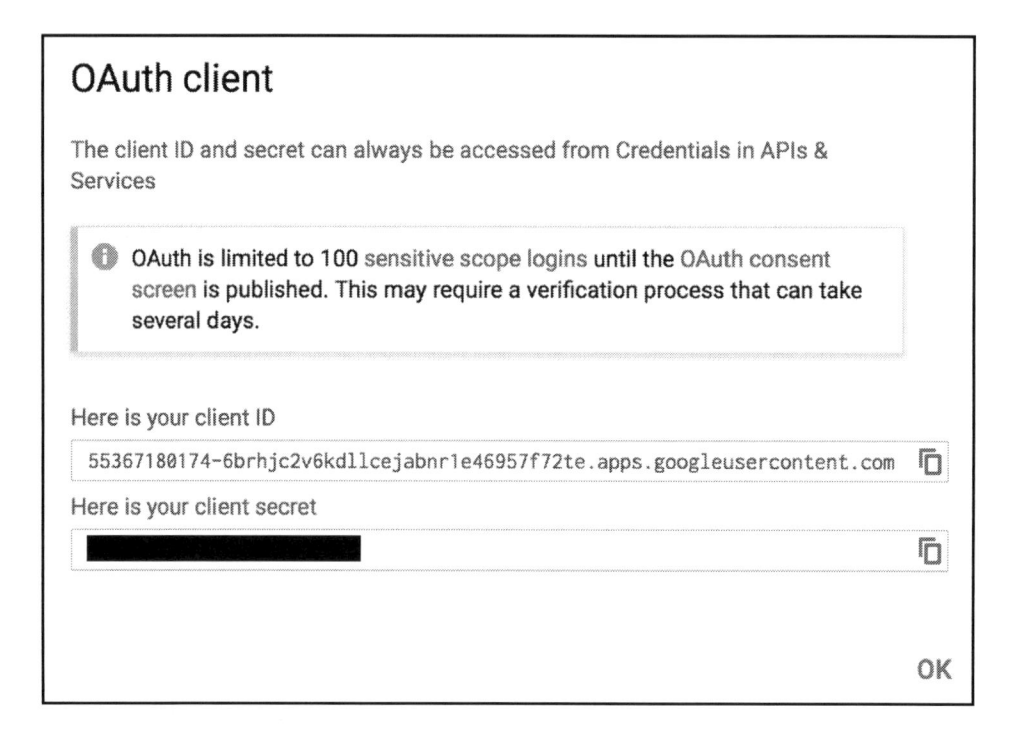

OAuth client

The client ID and secret can always be accessed from Credentials in APIs & Services

> OAuth is limited to 100 sensitive scope logins until the OAuth consent screen is published. This may require a verification process that can take several days.

Here is your client ID

`55367180174-6brhjc2v6kdllcejabnr1e46957f72te.apps.googleusercontent.com`

Here is your client secret

OK

Step 2 - Creating and Configuring an Identity Pool

Let's now create and configure an identity pool from the AWS CLI:

1. Create a `provider.json` file, with Google as the provider name and the client ID received from the previous step:

    ```
    { "accounts.google.com" :
    "55367180174-6brhjc2v6kdllcejabnr1e46957f72te.apps.googleuserconten
    t.com" }
    ```

2. Create an identity pool:

    ```
    aws cognito-identity create-identity-pool \
        --identity-pool-name qnatimepool \
        --no-allow-unauthenticated-identities \
        --supported-login-providers file://provider.json
        --profile admin
    ```

Chapter 9

You should get a response similar to this:

```
{
    "IdentityPoolId": "us-east-1:0f692fe2-c799-4334-b29b-54fd6544f2fb",
    "IdentityPoolName": "qnatimepool",
    "AllowUnauthenticatedIdentities": false,
    "SupportedLoginProviders": {
        "accounts.google.com": "55367180174-6brhjc2v6kdllcejabnr1e46957f72te.apps.googleusercontent.com"
    }
}
```

3. Create a policy that allows the necessary permissions to the user:

   ```
   aws  iam  create-policy \
       --policy-name  identity-pool-policy \
       --policy-document file://role_policy.txt \
       --profile  admin
   ```

4. The `role_policy.txt` file has the following contents:

   ```
   {
       "Version": "2012-10-17",
       "Statement": [
           {
               "Effect": "Allow",
               "Action": [
                   "mobileanalytics:PutEvents",
                   "cognito-sync:*",
                   "cognito-identity:*"
               ],
               "Resource": [
                   "*"
               ]
           }
       ]
   }
   ```

   There should be a role associated with a user who uses public APIs to log in, so that AWS can issue a token to access AWS services.

5. Create a role named `identity-pool-role` and attach a policy to the role.
6. Create a `roles.json` file with the ARN role as follows:

   ```
   {"authenticated":"arn:aws:iam::<account id>:role/identity-pool-role"}
   ```

[415]

7. Attach the role to the pool:

```
aws cognito-identity set-identity-pool-roles \
  --identity-pool-id <your identity pool id> \
  --roles file://roles.json \
  --region us-east-1 \
  --profile admin
```

Step 3 - Preparing and uploading code files

We need two HTML files, `index.html` for primary landing page and `error.html` for errors. We will see the important components within the `index.html` here. We will use JavaScript SDK code from within the `index.html` file. A completed `index.html` file with required JavaScript code and `error.html` file are available with code files.

Preparing the index.html file

The `index.html` file should have the following contents:

Start defining the HTML file with a `DOCTYPE` declaration and the `<html>` tag:

```
<!DOCTYPE html>
<html>
```

The `<head>` section of the HTML file should have contents as follows:

```
<head>
  <meta http-equiv="Content-Type" content="text/html; charset=utf-8" />
  <title>QNA Time</title>
  <script src="https://apis.google.com/js/platform.js" async defer></script>
  <script src="https://cdnjs.cloudflare.com/ajax/libs/aws-sdk/2.390.0/aws-sdk.min.js"></script>
  <meta
    name="google-signin-client_id"
    content="1056864857699-i6ami0u5oevpn9bro2k3r095jtqohdi7.apps.googleusercontent.com"
  />
</head>
```

Start defining a `<script>` section with the following variables:

```
<script type="text/javascript">
  var id_token;
  var identity;
  var cognitoidentity = new AWS.CognitoIdentity({ region: "us-east-1" });
```

Define the `getCredentials` method to get the access token from Cognito:

```
function getCredentials() {
    var params1 = {
        IdentityId: identity,
        Logins: {
            "accounts.google.com": id_token
        }
    };
    cognitoidentity.getCredentialsForIdentity(params1, function(err, data)
{
        if (err) console.log(err, err.stack);
        else {
            console.log(data);
            console.log(data.Credentials.AccessKeyId);
        }
    });
}
```

Add an `onSignIn` method that will be invoked on the success of Google authentication. This method is specified within the HTML body:

```
    function onSignIn(googleUser) {
      id_token = googleUser.getAuthResponse().id_token;
      console.log("google_id_token:" + id_token);

      var params = {
        IdentityPoolId:
          "us-east-1:f36a0555-fd35-43d6-bafa-187ecdef0f04" /* required */,
        Logins: {
          "accounts.google.com": id_token
        }
      };

      cognitoidentity.getId(params, function(err, data) {
        if (err) console.log(err, err.stack);
        // an error occurred
        else {
          console.log(data);
          identity = data.IdentityId;
          getCredentials();
```

```
        }
    });
}
</script>
```

Add the HTML body:

```
<body>
<span style="text-align:center;"><h1>Welcome to QNA TIME</h1></span>
<form>
  <div
        style="width:200px;"
        class="g-signin2"
        data-onsuccess="onSignIn"
  ></div>
</form>
</body>
```

Deploying and testing the index.html file

Follow these steps to deploy the HTML file:

1. Copy `index.html` and `error.html` to the S3 bucket. Create an `error.html` with dummy contents or follow earlier chapter recipes. It is also available with the code files.
2. Hit the website URL:

3. Click on the Google **Sign in** button. If not already signed in to our Google account, we will be provided with an option to log in to your Google account. Once logged in, we should see the **Signed in** message.

How it works...

A Cognito Federated Identity authentication flow to access AWS services has two forms: classic flow and enhanced flow.

Classic flow can be summarized as follows:

1. The user logs in with an external IDP such as Amazon, Google, or Facebook
2. The IDP returns an OAuth token
3. The client will then make a request to Cognito with the OAuth token
4. Cognito will validate the OAuth token with the IDP and if successful, return a token back
5. The client will then make an `AssumeRoleWithWebIdentity` call to STS, passing this token
6. STS will validate the token and return with temporary credentials (access key ID and secret access key)
7. The client can now use the temporary credentials to access AWS services

Enhanced flow can be summarized as follows:

1. User logs in with an external IDP such as Amazon, Google, or Facebook
2. The IDP returns an OAuth token
3. The client will then make a request to Cognito with the OAuth token
4. Cognito will validate the OAuth token with the IDP and if successful, return a token back
5. The client will then make a `GetCredentialsForIdentity` call with Cognito itself
6. Cognito will validate the token, negotiate with STS, and return temporary credentials (access key ID and secret access key)
7. The client can now use the temporary credentials to access AWS services

We followed the enhanced flow in this recipe.

There's more...

We created a simple application to demonstrate the Cognito authentication flow. You may follow this recipe and implement the same thing, as per your application needs.

See also

- https://docs.aws.amazon.com/cognito/latest/developerguide/cognito-identity.html
- https://docs.aws.amazon.com/cognito/latest/developerguide/authentication-flow.html

Creating SSL/TLS certificate with ACM

In the Using HTTPS with CloudFront domain recipe of Chapter 5, *Web Hosting with S3, Route53, and CloudFront,* we used an SSL certificate. In this recipe, we will see how we can create such an SSL certificate using ACM. ACM is a free service for domains with a HostedZone in Route 53. ACM can also be used to import certificates created outside of AWS.

Getting ready

We should have a domain registered with AWS or with an outside registrar, and the domain should have a HostedZone available in Route 53. You may register a domain by following the Registering a domain with Route 53 recipe of Chapter 5, *Web Hosting with S3, Route53, and CloudFront.*

How to do it...

We will create certificates using both AWS CLI API commands and a CloudFormation template in this section. I have also included the steps for the AWS Management Console in the There's more section.

For certificates to work with CloudFront, AWS requires the certificates to be available in `us-east-1 region` and will get replicated to other required regions.

AWS CLI Commands

1. We can request a certificate from AWS Certificate Manager, passing the domain name and a validation method:

   ```
   aws acm request-certificate \
     --domain-name www.qnatime.net \
     --validation-method DNS \
     --profile admin
   ```

   Validation methods available at DNS and email. With DNS, we need to create a `CNAME` record in our domain's DNS records to verify the ownership of the domain. With email, we can verify using an email address. DNS is the preferred way, as per the AWS documentation.

   This command will return the ARN certificate:

   ```
   {
     "CertificateArn": "arn:aws:acm:us-east-1:[REDACTED]:certificate/42b3ba99-66e9-4e71-8c1c-4239c1e81c84"
   }
   ```

2. We can now use the `describe-certificate` subcommand to see the status, along with validation information:

   ```
   aws acm describe-certificate \
       --certificate-arn arn:aws:acm:us-east-1:218317422462:certificate/42b3ba99-66e9-4e71-8c1c-4239c1e81c84 \
       --profile admin
   ```

This command will return the validation status along with validation information:

```
{
    "Certificate": {
        "CertificateArn": "arn:aws:acm:us-east-1:███████████:certificate/42b3ba99-66e9-4e71-8c1c-4239c1e81c84",
        "DomainName": "www.qnatime.net",
        "SubjectAlternativeNames": [
            "www.qnatime.net"
        ],
        "DomainValidationOptions": [
            {
                "DomainName": "www.qnatime.net",
                "ValidationStatus": "PENDING_VALIDATION",
                "ResourceRecord": {
                    "Name": "_f086ad8e4c10e38385c3c36394a06182.www.qnatime.net.",
                    "Type": "CNAME",
                    "Value": "_ee9788f2dcf3eaefaa85bb096163ffd4.tljzshvwok.acm-validations.aws."
                },
                "ValidationMethod": "DNS"
            }
        ],
```

The response also contains some additional information about the certificate, but will be incomplete at this point:

```
        "Subject": "CN=www.qnatime.net",
        "CreatedAt": 1543673401.0,
        "Status": "PENDING_VALIDATION",
        "KeyAlgorithm": "RSA-2048",
        "SignatureAlgorithm": "SHA256WITHRSA",
        "InUseBy": [],
        "Type": "AMAZON_ISSUED",
        "KeyUsages": [],
        "ExtendedKeyUsages": [],
        "RenewalEligibility": "INELIGIBLE",
        "Options": {
            "CertificateTransparencyLoggingPreference": "ENABLED"
        }
    }
}
```

3. Create a change resource record set JSON for updating the CNAME record as required for DNS validation:

```
{
  "Comment": "change batch request for dns validation www.qnatime.net",
  "Changes": [
    {
      "Action": "CREATE",
      "ResourceRecordSet": {
        "Name": "_f086ad8e4c10e38385c3c36394a06182.www.qnatime.net.",
        "Type": "CNAME",
        "TTL": 300,
        "ResourceRecords": [
          {
            "Value": "_ee9788f2dcf3eaefaa85bb096163ffd4.tljzshvwok.acm-validations.aws."
          }
        ]
      }
    }
  ]
}
```

4. Execute the `change-resource-record-sets` subcommand of `route53` CLI command:

```
aws route53 change-resource-record-sets \
    --hosted-zone-id Z3G50MON7IDA18 \
    --change-batch file://resources/change-resource-record-sets-dns-validation.json \
    --profile admin
```

This command will return a change ID with the status as **PENDING**.

We can then use the `get-change` subcommand of `route53` CLI command to check the status. The status should change to **INSYNC** when successful.

5. Check the status of certificate creation using the `describe-certificate` subcommand. It might take some time before the validation is completed and the certificate is ready to use. If successful, we should get a response as follows:

```
{
    "Certificate": {
        "CertificateArn": "arn:aws:acm:us-east-1:            :certificate/42b3ba99-66e9-4e71-8c1c-4239c1e81c84",
        "DomainName": "www.qnatime.net",
        "SubjectAlternativeNames": [
            "www.qnatime.net"
        ],
        "DomainValidationOptions": [
            {
                "DomainName": "www.qnatime.net",
                "ValidationStatus": "SUCCESS",
                "ResourceRecord": {
                    "Name": "_f086ad8e4c10e38385c3c36394a06182.www.qnatime.net.",
                    "Type": "CNAME",
                    "Value": "_ee9788f2dcf3eaefaa85bb096163ffd4.tljzshvwok.acm-validations.aws."
                },
                "ValidationMethod": "DNS"
            }
        ],
```

The initial part of the response contains a message about DNS validation success.

Next, the response contains additional info about the certificate and issuer:

```
        "Serial": "0d:                                          :c9",
        "Subject": "CN=www.qnatime.net",
        "Issuer": "Amazon",
        "CreatedAt": 1543673401.0,
        "IssuedAt": 1543675489.0,
        "Status": "ISSUED",
        "NotBefore": 1543622400.0,
        "NotAfter": 1577880000.0,
        "KeyAlgorithm": "RSA-2048",
        "SignatureAlgorithm": "SHA256WITHRSA",
        "InUseBy": [],
        "Type": "AMAZON_ISSUED",
```

Chapter 9

The final part of the response contains `KeyUsages`, `ExtendedKeyUsages`, `RenewalEligibility`, and `Options`:

```
"KeyUsages": [
    {
        "Name": "DIGITAL_SIGNATURE"
    },
    {
        "Name": "KEY_ENCIPHERMENT"
    }
],
"ExtendedKeyUsages": [
    {
        "Name": "TLS_WEB_SERVER_AUTHENTICATION",
        "OID": "1.        .1"
    },
    {
        "Name": "TLS_WEB_CLIENT_AUTHENTICATION",
        "OID": "1.        .2"
    }
],
"RenewalEligibility": "INELIGIBLE",
"Options": {
    "CertificateTransparencyLoggingPreference": "ENABLED"
}
}
```

CloudFormation Template

The certificate request process requires user interaction to verify the domain and hence it cannot be fully automated with CloudFormation scripts. However, I will still provide two templates to request for a certificate and verify the DNS. In the real world, you may just verify from the AWS Management Console or AWS CLI:

1. Use the following CloudFormation template for requesting a certificate from CloudFormation:

    ```
    ---
    AWSTemplateFormatVersion: '2010-09-09'
    Description: 'Certificate Manager'
    Parameters:
      RootDomainName:
        Description: Domain name for generating certificate
        Type: String
    Resources:
      RootDomainCert:
        Type: AWS::CertificateManager::Certificate
    ```

```
      Properties:
        DomainName: !Ref RootDomainName
        ValidationMethod: DNS
Outputs:
  CertificateArn:
    Value: !Ref RootDomainCert
```

2. Execute the template using the `create-stack` subcommand in `us-east-1 region` (the default).

   The stack will be created in the CREATE_IN_PROGRESS state, as we can verify with the `describe-stacks` subcommand.

3. Use the `describe-stack-events` subcommand to get the CNAME values for DNS validation:

   ```
   aws cloudformation describe-stack-events \
       --stack-name cnamerecordsetstack \
       --profile admin
   ```

   The CloudFormation stack with a resource of type `AWS::CertificateManager::Certificate` stays in the response state of CREATE_IN_PROGRESS until we verify the DNS with CNAME. CNAME is provided as an event during stack creation. If successful, the preceding command will return the list of events along with the details for the CNAME record in one of the event as shown here:

   ```
   {
       "StackEvents": [
           {
               "StackId": "arn:aws:cloudformation:ap-south-1:218317422462:stack/mycertstack/a02e4ce0-f6e6-11e8-90f7-0a791b5fd632",
               "EventId": "RootDomainCert-0df88ead-da2f-4c0d-a1b6-823dba08bae7",
               "StackName": "mycertstack",
               "LogicalResourceId": "RootDomainCert",
               "PhysicalResourceId": "",
               "ResourceType": "AWS::CertificateManager::Certificate",
               "Timestamp": "2018-12-03T10:32:18.100Z",
               "ResourceStatus": "CREATE_IN_PROGRESS",
               "ResourceStatusReason": "Content of DNS Record is: {Name: _7d2add77f3493141152bc8765e40401c.quizzercloud.com.,Type: CNAME,Value: _9376279cf263f4ec3ced17d9b08122ce.tljzshvwok.acm-validations.aws.}"
           },
   ```

4. Add a CNAME record for DNS validation in the domain's HostedZone.

You can use the `RecordSetGroup` resource to add a `CNAME` record in a new template file:

```
CNAMERecordSetGroup:
  Type: AWS::Route53::RecordSetGroup
  Properties:
    HostedZoneName: !Ref HostedZone
    Comment: Zone apex alias.
    RecordSets:
      -
        Name: !Ref CNAMEname
        Type: CNAME
        TTL: 900
        ResourceRecords:
          - !Ref CNAMEValue
```

Note that this is not a complete template. We also need to define three parameters, `HostedZone`, `CNAMEname`, and `CNAMEValue`, of type string. We can also define the template version and a description. The completed template is available in the code files.

5. After adding the `CNAME` record with the second stack, we can execute the `describe-stacks` subcommand against the first stack (certificate stack) and check the status until it is completed.

How it works...

In summary, we did the following in this recipe:

1. Created a request for an SSL certificate
2. Verified that we own the domain through DNS updates and got the certificate issued

Most of the steps in the recipe are self-explanatory. To see the generated certificate in action, you may refer to the Using HTTPS with CloudFront domain within recipe of `Chapter 5`, Web Hosting with S3, Route53, and CloudFront.

There's more...

We saw how to create SSL/TLS certificates using ACM. We can also import certificates created outside of AWS. We can use these certificates with services such as AWS Load Balancer, API Gateway API, and a CloudFront distribution.

Apart from using SSL certificates and HTTPS, we can also add additional security to our web applications using services such as AWS WAF, AWS Shield, AWS Shield Advanced, and AWS Firewall Manager.

You may also explore Let's Encrypt for creating free SSL/TLS certificates for your AWS deployments. Let's Encrypt is a certificate authority that provides free SSL certificates.

See also

- To understand more about the use of a dedicated IP and SNI for serving HTTPS requests, you may refer to the following link: `https://docs.aws.amazon.com/AmazonCloudFront/latest/DeveloperGuide/cnames-https-dedicated-ip-or-sni.html`
- Current ACM availability in different regions can be found at the following link: `https://docs.aws.amazon.com/general/latest/gr/rande.html#acm_region`

Fan-in and fan-out architectural patterns with AWS

Fan-in generally refers to the process where multiple producers produce data and pass it into a single service or message router. The term is most commonly used in digital electronics to denote the number of inputs that a logic gate can handle. For example, an AND gate with four inputs has a fan-in of 4.

Fan-out generally refers to the process where a service or message router delivers messages to multiple consumers, mostly in parallel. In digital electronics, the fan-out of a logic gate output is equal to the number of gate inputs it can drive. For example, one output may be connected to several inputs.

Fan-in and fan-out patterns can be used together with distributed messaging applications to decouple producers and consumers. A fan-in process decouples producers from the service, and a fan-out process decouples the service from the consumer. The fan-in and fan-out patterns may be used with producers and consumers of the same type (if their throughput requirements differ) or with producers and consumers of different types.

Getting ready

We need a working AWS account with the necessary permissions if we want to implement the following suggestions.

We also need to be familiar with the following services and the steps we followed to use them in this book:

- AWS Lambda from `Chapter 1`, *Getting Started with Serverless Computing on AWS*
- Amazon SQS and Amazon SNS from `Chapter 6`, *Messaging and Notifications with SQS and SNS*
- Amazon Kinesis from `Chapter 7`, *Redshift, Amazon ML, and Alexa Skills*

How to do it...

Let's see approaches to implement fan-in and fan-out architectural patterns in AWS.

Please note that there is no single correct solution to most of these architectural problems. Architectural problems and their solutions also evolve over time, based on experience and research. Therefore, do a search on popular search engines or have discussions with your peers before implementing a scenario outlined here in the real world.

Scenario 1 - Pub-Sub with multiple producers and consumers

We have producer services that produce data and more than one consumer will need that data.

Approach: We can use SNS as the service router between the producer services and consumer services as follows:

1. Producers publish messages to SNS (fan-in)
2. Consumers subscribe to SNS and consume messages from SNS (fan-out)

Scenario 2 - Parallel processing without duplicates

We have a producer service that produces service requests and more than one consumer can process those requests in parallel, but the same service request should not be delivered to more than one consumer.

Approach: We can use SQS as the service router between the producer service and consumer services as follows:

1. The producer publishes messages to SQS
2. SQS delivers each message only to one of the consumers (fan-out)
3. Multiple consumers publish their results to another service, such as S3 or DynamoDB, and results are aggregated (fan-in)

Scenario 3 - Streaming real-time data for processing

For processing streaming data in real time, we may have to use a service designed specifically for such use cases.

Approach: We can use Kinesis streams for the stream, with Kinesis Analytics for routing, as follows:

1. Producers produce data in Kinesis Stream, configured for high throughput (fan-in)
2. Kinesis Analytics routes it into an appropriate stream with a lower throughput (fan-out)

Scenario 4 - Streaming real-time data for storing

For processing streaming data in real time, we may have to use a service designed specifically for such use cases.

Approach: We can use Kinesis firehose as follows:

1. Producers produce data in Kinesis firehose (fan-in)
2. Kinesis firehose stores the data in a supported data store such as S3, Redshift, ES, or Splunk

How it works...

This recipe suggests various approaches to implement the fan-in/fan-out architectural patterns in AWS. The fan-in and fan-out patterns may be used together, or even separately. They may also be used in a different order, fan-in followed by fan-out or fan-out followed by fan-in. The first scenario occurs when multiple producers send data to a single scalable service (fan-in) and consumers consume data in parallel (fan-out) and process it. The latter scenario, of fan-out followed by a fan-in, can be used in situations where we want to process a task in parallel (fan-out) through different services, and then combine the individual outputs into a single output (fan-in) for generating the final result. We may even combine these scenarios into a fan-in, fan-out, fan-in combo.

Real-world example scenarios

Let's see some examples of the scenarios we discussed in the *How to do it...* section.

Scenario 1 - Pub-Sub scenario with multiple producers and consumers

Consider a social media website. Producers are users who post data and consumers are users who follow other users. Users' posted details can be published to the service router and the router service may then break down the task further and deliver it to all followers.

Scenario 2 - Parallel processing

Consider that we need to find people belonging to some category from within a country. We can do this calculation for each state or even districts in parallel, and then combine all the results together. The map-reduce algorithm used by Hadoop is an example.

Scenario 3 - Streaming real-time data for processing

Streaming real-time data has many use cases such as log analytics and IOT analytics. In most of these cases, however, the throughput requirement for the producer may be high and actual consumption rate might require only a lower throughput. We could use a single stream with a high throughput, but then we will also be wasting throughput. Therefore, we can have different streams with different throughputs, as required, and then, using Kinesis Analytics' capabilities (for example, analyzing data streams with SQL), we can route the request into an appropriate stream.

Scenario 4 - Streaming real-time data for storage

Consider a case where multiple producers produce streaming data that just needs to be stored in one of the Kinesis Firehose supported data stores, such as S3, Redshift, ES, or Splunk. We may not want to do any processing or analytics immediately, but this can be done in parallel or at a later point of time from these data stores.

There's more...

In this recipe, we discussed some scenarios and a possible approach to handle the fan-in and/or fan-out patterns in those scenarios. The idea of the recipe was to get you familiar with the fan-in and fan-out patterns and scenarios. The exact services shown in the approaches are not the only solutions available. You may explore more and for services already covered in previous recipes, you may implement these scenarios.

Serverless programming in AWS is a huge topic. But I believe we have touched upon most of the essential services in Chapters 1 to 8. We also saw some general practices and patterns in Chapter 9 that involve those services. If you have completed all the recipes up to now, you should have enough knowledge to contribute significantly to your work or personal projects in the area of serverless computing with AWS.

In the next chapter, we will quickly see some of the other cloud provider services that correspond to the AWS services that we have seen up to now.

Building a full stack web application on AWS

You can build a full stack serverless web application using the services that we learned in this book. UI may be built using Angular or any JavaScript-based frameworks you are comfortable with and then deployed into an S3 bucket configured as a static website. A domain can be bought and its DNS can be configured to point to the S3 bucket with Route 53.

Backend APIs can be built using API gateway. UI code can interact with the API and the API then invoke Lambda. Lambda can write and read data from DynamoDB. Lambda can be created using Java programming language following the recipes in this book or you may use any other Lambda-supported languages you are comfortable with.

User management and application-level authentication can be done with Cognito. Cognito can be integrated with your UI code following the Cognito JavaScript SDK code that we saw. You can support federated identity logins through identity providers such as Google, Facebook, or Amazon. You can improve the performance of your website using CloudFront CDN.

You may also follow or participate in developing a real-world, full stack, serverless web application called **QNA Time** using most of the services we saw within this book at `https://github.com/heartin/qnatime`.

See also

You can read about Cognito and Cognito authentication flows in `Chapter 4`, *Application Security with Amazon Cognito*. You may read more about them from the following links.

- `https://docs.aws.amazon.com/cognito/latest/developerguide/cognito-identity.html`
- `https://docs.aws.amazon.com/cognito/latest/developerguide/authentication-flow.html`

10
Other Cloud Providers

This chapter will cover the following topics:

- Your first Serverless application on Azure
- Your first Serverless application on Google Cloud Platform
- Your first Serverless application on IBM Cloud

Introduction

I believe that most people who are following a technological career path would like to be good architects one day. A good architect should not only have deep knowledge on their expert areas, but should also have good breadth of knowledge about a lot of other things, including competing technologies.

From Chapters 1 to 9, we learned about many services that can help us build Serverless applications on the AWS cloud. In this chapter, we will briefly discuss Serverless services from some of the other popular cloud providers corresponding to the various AWS services that we saw.

Knowing the Serverless services from various cloud providers can help us make better architectural decisions. Having this knowledge can also gives us an edge over others in discussions related to Serverless computing, both meetings at work as well as less formal meetings, such as conferences and meetups.

Your first Serverless application in Azure

Microsoft Azure is a cloud computing service from Microsoft and provides services similar to AWS in the areas of **software as a service (SaaS)**, **platform as a service (PaaS)**, **infrastructure as a service (IaaS)**, and Serverless computing. It supports many different programming languages, tools and frameworks. In this recipe, we will create a simple Serverless application on Azure. We will also learn about the most appropriate managed Serverless services in Azure for the various use cases discussed in this book.

Getting ready

Following are the prerequisites for this recipe:

- JDK 8 or above.
- Apache Maven 3 or above.
- A working account on Azure.
- Azure CLI.
  You can install Azure CLI by using the installer available at: `https://docs.microsoft.com/en-us/cli/azure/install-azure-cli?view=azure-cli-latest`. Verify installation and login by running: `az login`. This command will open a browser window where you can login to your Microsoft account.
- Azure Functions CORE Tools.
  You can install Azure Functions CORE Tools using npm as:
  `npm install -g azure-functions-core-tools`

How to do it...

We will create a simple Azure Java project as follows:.

1. Create a new directory for the project and run the `mvn archetype:generate` command, given as follows:

   ```
   mvn archetype:generate \
     -DarchetypeGroupId=com.microsoft.azure \
       -DarchetypeArtifactId=azure-functions-archetype
   ```

> **TIP**: Note: If you are using Windows, you may replace \ with ^.

Provide values for the variables, as follows:

- Define the value for the `'groupId'`: `tech.heartin.books.serverless-cookbook` property
- Define the value for the `'artifactId' : helloworld-azure-fn` property
- Define the value for the `'version' 1.0-SNAPSHOT :` : property
- Define the value for the `'package'`: `tech.heartin.books.serverlesscookbook` property
- Define the value for the `'appName' : HelloWorldAzureFn` property
- Define the value for the `'appRegion' 'westus'`: property
- Define the value for the `'resourceGroup' java-functions-group: :` property
- Confirm the properties configuration using: `Y: :`

This will create a project in the `helloworld-azure-fn` directory that is the same as our artifact ID.

2. Go inside the project directory and run `mvn clean package`
3. Next, run `mvn azure-functions:run`

We should see the following within the output:

```
Now listening on: http://0.0.0.0:7071
Application started. Press Ctrl+C to shut down.

Http Functions:

        HttpTrigger-Java: [GET,POST] http://localhost:7071/api/HttpTrigger-Java
```

Other Cloud Providers

4. Invoke the following URL: `http://localhost:7071/api/HttpTrigger-Java?name=Heartin`

   We should see the response in the browser as follows:

   ```
   localhost:7071/api/HttpTrigger-Java?name=Heartin
   Hello, Heartin
   ```

Deploying the function to Azure

To deploy the Azure function follow these steps:

1. Open Azure CLI and run

   ```
   az login
   ```

2. Go to the project folder and run the following command:

   ```
   mvn azure-functions:deploy
   ```

   You will get an output similar to the following:

   ```
   [INFO] Scanning for projects...
   [INFO]
   [INFO] ------< tech.heartin.books.serverless-cookbook:helloworld-azure-fn >------
   [INFO] Building Azure Java Functions 1.0-SNAPSHOT
   [INFO] --------------------------------[ jar ]--------------------------------
   [INFO]
   [INFO] --- azure-functions-maven-plugin:1.2.1:deploy (default-cli) @ helloworld-azure-fn ---
   [INFO] Authenticate with Azure CLI 2.0
   [INFO] The specified function app does not exist. Creating a new function app...
   [INFO] Successfully created the function app: helloworld-azure-fn
   [INFO] Trying to deploy the function app...
   [INFO] Trying to deploy artifact to helloworld-azure-fn...
   [INFO] Successfully deployed the artifact to https://helloworld-azure-fn.azurewebsites.net
   [INFO] Successfully deployed the function app at https://helloworld-azure-fn.azurewebsites.net
   [INFO]
   [INFO] BUILD SUCCESS
   [INFO]
   [INFO] Total time: 03:11 min
   [INFO] Finished at: 2019-01-24T07:44:07+05:30
   [INFO]
   ```

Getting function info from UI and verifying the deployment

We can get the url to invoke from UI as follows:

1. Login to `https://portal.azure.com/`
2. Click on App Services from left sidebar or the main page
3. Click on our app name
4. In the App's page click on the function name `HttpTrigger-Java`

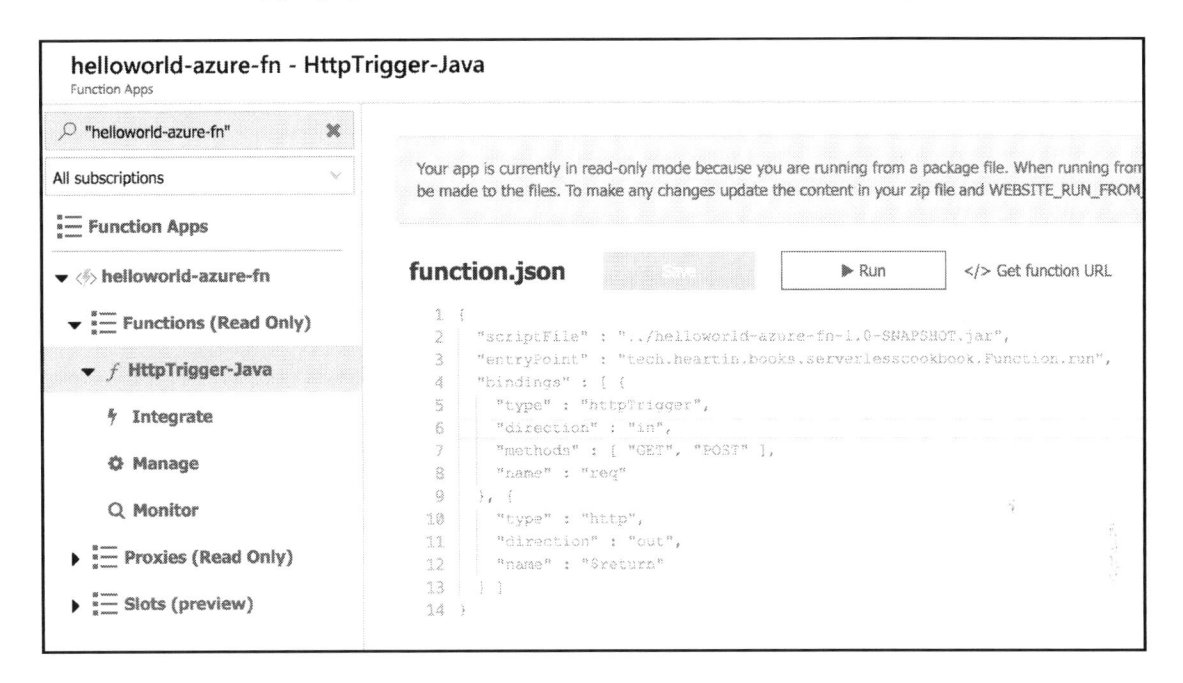

![helloworld-azure-fn - HttpTrigger-Java screenshot showing Function Apps sidebar with helloworld-azure-fn expanded to show Functions (Read Only) > HttpTrigger-Java, Integrate, Manage, Monitor, Proxies (Read Only), Slots (preview). Main panel shows function.json with Save, Run, and Get function URL buttons, and JSON content defining scriptFile, entryPoint, and bindings.]

Other Cloud Providers

5. Click on `Get function URL`. This will return the public URL for your function.

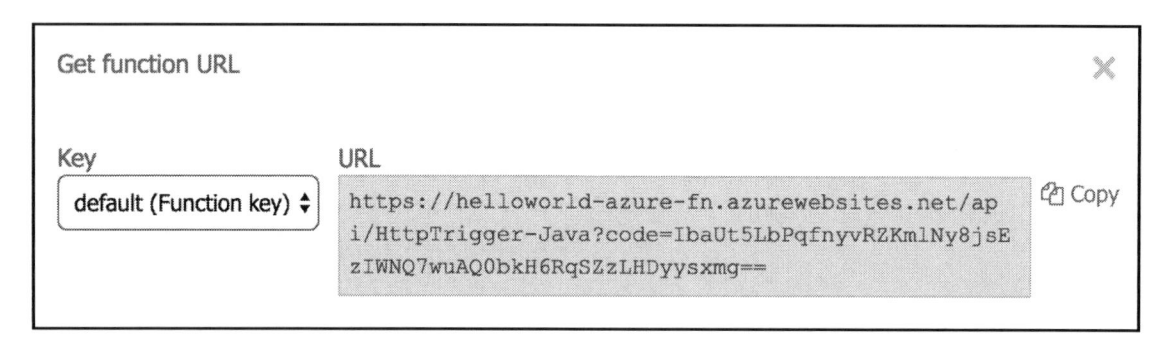

Get function URL

Key: default (Function key)

URL: https://helloworld-azure-fn.azurewebsites.net/api/HttpTrigger-Java?code=IbaUt5LbPqfnyvRZKmlNy8jsEzIWNQ7wuAQ0bkH6RqSZzLHDyysxmg==

Copy

We can run the public URL from a browser specifying the required path parameter (similar to what we did with localhost).

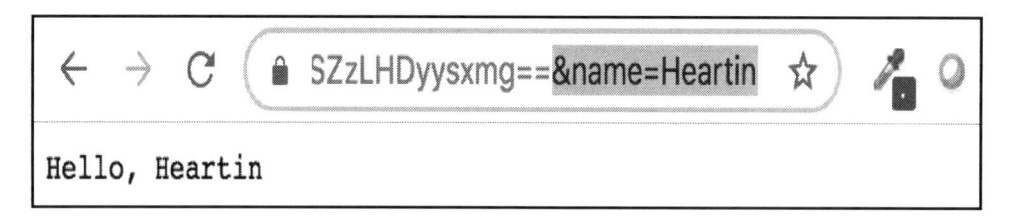

`SZzLHDyysxmg==&name=Heartin`

`Hello, Heartin`

How It works...

The goal of this recipe was become familiar with Azure cloud and write our first Serverless application on Azure. In the next two sections, we will list the Azure Serverless services corresponding to the AWS Serverless services we saw in this book. You can refer to the links provided for each service to learn more and get started with them.

There's more...

Let's look at some of the Azure services that we can use to implement Serverless applications:

- **Serverless computing on AWS**:
  Azure functions are event-driven, Serverless compute functions that can scale on demand. We need to pay only for the resources we consume. The corresponding AWS service is AWS Lambda.

- **Access management**:
  Azure Active Directory is Microsoft's identity and access management service. The corresponding AWS service is IAM.

- **Resource provisioning and management**:
  The Azure Resource Manager service enables us to define the infrastructure and dependencies for our app in a single declarative template and then repeatedly deploy the app using the template. The corresponding AWS service is CloudFormation.

- **Simple object store**:
  Blob Storage is a scalable object storage for unstructured data. The corresponding service in AWS is Amazon S3.

- **API management**:
  The API Management service in Azure helps in publishing, managing, securi
- ng, and analyzing APIs. The corresponding service in AWS is API Gateway.

- **Storage tier**:
  Azure Cosmos DB is a distributed multi-model database service. The corresponding service that we used in this book is Amazon DynamoDB.

- **User management**:
  Azure Active Directory B2C in Azure is a customer identity and access management service. It enables us to use social accounts, emails, and custom IdPs. The corresponding service in AWS that helps with user management is Amazon Cognito.

- **Domain hosting and DNS management**:
  Azure DNS can be used to host domains in Azure. The Traffic Manager service in Azure can route incoming traffic for high performance and availability. Amazon Route 53 can be used for both domain hosting and DNS management.

- **Content Delivery Network**:
  The Content Delivery Network service in Azure is used for global content delivery and acceleration. The corresponding service in AWS is Amazon CloudFront.
- **Queue service**:
  The Queue Storage service in Azure can be used to create simple message queues for large workloads. The corresponding service in AWS is Amazon SQS.
- **Notification service**:
  The Notification Hubs service in Azure can be used to send push notifications to different platforms in response to API calls. The corresponding service in AWS is Amazon SNS.
- **Managing events and streams**:
  The Event Hubs service in Azure can be used for real-time data ingestion. The corresponding service from Amazon that we have discussed in this book is Amazon Kinesis Data Streams.
- **Machine learning service**:
  Azure Machine Learning Studio is a fully managed service that we can use to build, deploy, and share predictive analytics solutions. The corresponding service in AWS that we have discussed in this book is the Amazon Machine Learning service.
- **Monitoring**:
  With the Azure Monitor service, we can monitor applications in Azure with analytics and machine learning support. The corresponding service in AWS that we have discussed in this book is Amazon CloudWatch.
- **Data warehouse management**:
  SQL Data Warehouse is Azure's data warehouse solution. The corresponding service in AWS is Amazon Redshift.
- **Data integration/data pipeline**:
  The Data Factory service in Azure can be used to create, schedule, and monitor data pipelines. In AWS, we can use the Data Pipeline service for building data pipelines.
- **Mobile**:
  The Mobile Apps service helps in building engaging iOS, Android, and Windows apps. It also enables single sign-on functionality with Azure Active Directory. AWS AppSync is a Serverless backend for mobile, web, and enterprise applications.

See also

You can read more about the services discussed in the previous section by using the following links:

- **Azure Functions**: https://azure.microsoft.com/en-in/services/functions/
- **Azure Active Directory:** https://azure.microsoft.com/en-in/services/active-directory/
- **Azure Resource Manager:** https://azure.microsoft.com/en-in/features/resource-manager/, https://docs.microsoft.com/en-us/azure/azure-resource-manager/resource-group-overview
- **Blob Storage:** https://azure.microsoft.com/en-in/services/storage/blobs/, https://docs.microsoft.com/en-us/azure/storage/blobs/storage-blobs-introduction
- **API Management:** https://azure.microsoft.com/en-us/services/api-management/
- **Azure Cosmos DB:** https://azure.microsoft.com/en-us/services/cosmos-db/
- **Azure Active Directory B2C:** https://azure.microsoft.com/en-us/services/active-directory-b2c/
- **Azure DNS:** https://azure.microsoft.com/en-us/services/dns/
- **Traffic Manager:** https://azure.microsoft.com/en-us/services/traffic-manager/
- **Content Delivery Network:** https://azure.microsoft.com/en-us/services/cdn/
- **Queue Storage:** https://azure.microsoft.com/en-us/services/storage/queues/
- **Notification Hubs:** https://azure.microsoft.com/en-in/services/notification-hubs/
- **Event Hubs:** https://azure.microsoft.com/en-us/services/event-hubs/
- **Azure Machine Learning Studio:** https://azure.microsoft.com/en-us/services/machine-learning-studio/
- **Azure Monitor**: https://azure.microsoft.com/en-us/services/monitor/
- **SQL Data Warehouse:** https://azure.microsoft.com/en-us/services/sql-data-warehouse/
- **Redshift:** https://aws.amazon.com/redshift/
- **Data Factory:** https://azure.microsoft.com/en-us/services/data-factory/
- **Data Pipeline:** https://aws.amazon.com/datapipeline/

- **Mobile Apps:** https://azure.microsoft.com/en-us/services/app-service/mobile/
- **AWS AppSync:** https://aws.amazon.com/appsync/

Your first serverless application on Google Cloud Platform

Google Cloud is a set of software solutions from Google and its primary components are **Google Cloud Platform (GCP)** and G Suite. GCP is a suite of cloud computing services that deal with SaaS, PaaS, IaaS and Serverless computing. GSuite is a set of business applications including Gmail, Google Docs and Google Drive. In this recipe, we will build a simple serverless application on GCP. We will also look at the appropriate managed services in GCP for various serverless use cases.

Getting ready

Following are the prerequisites for this recipe:

1. Node.js and `npm` installation can be verified with following commands:

    ```
    node -v
    npm -v
    ```

2. You need to have a working account in the Google Cloud Platform. You need a credit card to create an account. However, Google will give you a credit of 300$ for a 1-year duration at the time of writing this book and won't charge you until the credit is over.
3. Install Google Cloud SDK. To install Google Cloud SDK, you may follow this link: https://cloud.google.com/sdk/docs.

How to do it...

We can create a simple Google Cloud function from command line following these steps:

1. Create a project with project ID as `my-first-gcp-project-id`

    ```
    gcloud projects create 'heartin-gcp-project-id' --name='My First GCP Project'
    ```

You should see a response similar to as follows:

```
$ gcloud projects create 'heartin-gcp-project-id' --name='My First GCP Project'
Create in progress for [https://cloudresourcemanager.googleapis.com/v1/projects/
heartin-gcp-project-id].
Waiting for [operations/cp.6887929382572106326] to finish...done.
```

2. Set the property project. You may set it for the current workspace by running:

    gcloud config set project 'heartin-gcp-project-id'

You should see a response similar to the following:

```
$ gcloud config set project 'heartin-gcp-project-id'
Updated property [core/project].
```

3. Enable Cloud Functions.

    gcloud services enable cloudfunctions.googleapis.com

You should see a response similar to the following:

```
$ gcloud services enable cloudfunctions.googleapis.com
Operation "operations/acf.3da249de-430e-45ac-bcac-81585011e18b" finished
successfully.
```

4. Clone or download the Sample Code from the Git URL:

    git clone
    https://github.com/GoogleCloudPlatform/nodejs-docs-samples.git

5. Go to `functions` directory.

    cd nodejs-docs-samples/functions/helloworld/

6. Deploy the function.

    gcloud functions deploy helloGET --runtime nodejs6 --trigger-http

Other Cloud Providers

You should see a response, as follows:

```
$ gcloud functions deploy helloGET --runtime nodejs6 --trigger-http
Deploying function (may take a while - up to 2 minutes)...done.
availableMemoryMb: 256
entryPoint: helloGET
httpsTrigger:
  url: https://us-central1-heartin-gcp-project-id.cloudfunctions.net/helloGET
labels:
  deployment-tool: cli-gcloud
name: projects/heartin-gcp-project-id/locations/us-central1/functions/helloGET
runtime: nodejs6
serviceAccountEmail: heartin-gcp-project-id@appspot.gserviceaccount.com
sourceUploadUrl: https://storage.googleapis.com/gcf-upload-us-central1-b3ee4388
-40db-4843-a2eb-f39f19f65043/fa1eac61-38f1-4f82-b4a4-4ac41d76a1fe.zip?GoogleAcc
essId=service-948172233016@gcf-admin-robot.iam.gserviceaccount.com&Expires=1548
886369&Signature=M2Jv0tcVJfF23yKgBnA7JyooC1XOS2K8lb83E%2B1eh8BFaOzUyCbXs7%2FR7c
eAGugSamSaBWXZoWM1Wr2RK%2BGvvhhO9%2BNZuF0vDuB30acwrOuiBU7faF%2BFbbwhwcsgXgOhrj0
TsEgIIhxzg9WE3e%2B5SmwGNvW9cKlt3U0H4Xg7pp9gBlDV8j0nL1WZW%2FEGtM46j2qUhF30CIqRec
M5F2%2Fd7OmmETREJyn7sZFfdUvqwnk9x6p1qjlMjAjZgcpVBDylDiplAg%2FuUOEejcM%2FxVLfwpW
%2BVChVGBuUPi2j4cN1NunFletKcImHPPyhcjFXPeHjfCVstH9Y%2BnV19RxXObELYA%3D%3D
status: ACTIVE
timeout: 60s
updateTime: '2019-01-30T21:43:18Z'
versionId: '2'
```

7. Run the `httpsTrigger` URL from the previous section in a browser. You should see `Hello World` printed on the browser screen as follows:.

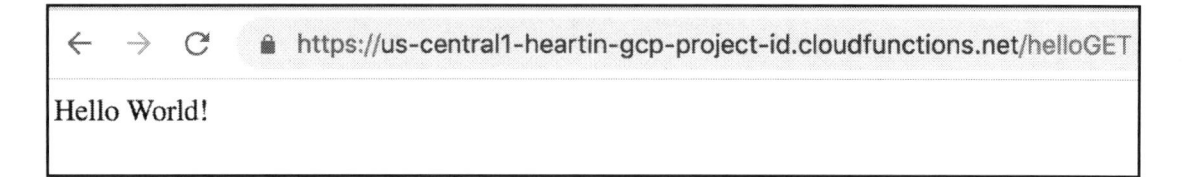

← → C 🔒 https://us-central1-heartin-gcp-project-id.cloudfunctions.net/helloGET

Hello World!

How it works...

The goal of this recipe was to become familiar with GCP. The code repository from Google that we used in this recipe has more code examples to get you going further with GCP. In the next two sections, we will list the GCP serverless services for various use cases. You can refer to the links provided for each service to learn more and get started with them.

Unlike AWS free tier where you get some services free upto some limits, GCP gives you a credit amount and you are free to use it until it expires and is not limited to any specific set of services.

There's more...

Let's look at some of the GCP services that we can use to implement Serverless applications:

- **Serverless computing on AWS**:
  Google Cloud Functions is an event-driven, Serverless compute platform and corresponds to Lambdas in AWS.
- **Access management**:
  Cloud Identity & Access Management provides fine-grained access control for cloud resources.
- **Resource provisioning and management**:
  Cloud Deployment Manager allows us to create and manage cloud resources with templates.
- **Simple object store**:
  Google Cloud Storage is a unified object storage.
- **API management**:
  Apigee API Platform helps in developing, securing, deploying, and monitoring your APIs. Cloud Endpoints is another service that help in developing and maintaining APIs. While Cloud Endpoints is service-specific to GCP and has better native support for integrations with GCP backend services, Apigee API Platform is generic and can be used across GCP, on-premises, and with other clouds.
- **Storage tier**:
  Cloud Datastore is a highly scalable NoSQL database and can be used for standard data storage use cases. Cloud Bigtable is a petabyte-scalable NoSQL database used mostly for analytical workloads.
- **User management**:
  Cloud Identity helps you manage users, devices, and apps from a single console.
- **Domain hosting and DNS management**:
  Cloud DNS is Google's DNS service.

- **Content Delivery Network:**
  Cloud CDN accelerates the content delivery for websites and applications hosted with Google Compute Engine and Google Cloud Storage using Google's edge points across the globe. Google Compute Engine is Google's virtual machine service and corresponds to the EC2 service in AWS. We did not look at the EC2 service much as the focus of this book is Serverless services.
- **Queue service:**
  Cloud PUB/SUB allows you to ingest event streams at any scale, and can be used for simple, reliable, real-time stream analytics. Cloud PUB/SUB is the closest service there is that corresponds to SQS in AWS.
- **Notification service:**
  Cloud PUB/SUB is also the closest service there is that corresponds to SNS in AWS.
- **Managing events and streams:**
  Cloud PUB/SUB from Google is again the closest service there is that corresponds to Kinesis Data Streams in AWS. Cloud Dataflow is another service from Google that allows stream and batch data processing.
- **Machine learning service:**
  Cloud Machine Learning Engine helps in building superior models and deploying them.
- **Monitoring:**
  Stackdriver Monitoring helps in monitoring the performance, uptime, and overall health of cloud applications hosted in GCP and AWS.
- **Data warehouse management:**
  Google BigQuery is a highly scalable data warehouse solution, and is used for analytics similar to Redsihft in AWS.
- **Mobile:**
  Firebase helps in building mobile apps more quickly and is also the primary mobile development platform in GCP.

See also

You can read more about the services discussed in the previous section by using the following links:

- **Google Cloud Functions:** https://cloud.google.com/functions/
- **Cloud Identity & Access Management:** https://cloud.google.com/iam/
- **Cloud Deployment Manager:** https://cloud.google.com/deployment-manager/

- **Google Cloud Storage:** https://cloud.google.com/storage/
- **Apigee API Platform:** https://cloud.google.com/apigee-api-management/
- **Cloud Endpoints:** https://cloud.google.com/endpoints/
- **Cloud Datastore:** https://cloud.google.com/datastore/
- **Cloud Bigtable:** https://cloud.google.com/bigtable/
- **Cloud Identity:** https://cloud.google.com/identity/
- **Cloud DNS:** https://cloud.google.com/dns/
- **Cloud CDN:** https://cloud.google.com/cdn/
- **Cloud PUB/SUB:** https://cloud.google.com/pubsub/
- **Cloud Dataflow:** https://cloud.google.com/dataflow/
- **Cloud Machine Learning Engine:** https://cloud.google.com/ml-engine/
- **Stackdriver Monitoring:** https://cloud.google.com/monitoring/
- **Google Bigquery:** https://cloud.google.com/bigquery/
- **Firebase:** https://firebase.google.com/, https://firebase.google.com/firebase-and-gcp/

Your first Serverless application on IBM cloud

IBM Cloud provides a set of cloud computing services that deal with SaaS, PaaS, IaaS and Serverless computing. For virtualization, IBM uses the IBM Websphere application infrastructure. The management layer of the IBM cloud uses IBM Tivoli middleware. In this recipe, we will build a simple serverless application on IBM Cloud. We will also look at the IBM cloud services for the various serverless use cases.

Getting ready

Following are the prerequisites for this recipe:

- Create an account at IBM cloud: https://www.ibm.com/cloud/.
- Using the IBM id, create account at https://console.bluemix.net/registration/. This will create a Lite account.
- We need to upgrade our account by adding credit card details, which will help us in creating orgs and spaces in IBM cloud.

Other Cloud Providers

- If you are not able to add a credit card, then you may send an e-mail to `verify@us.ibm.com` with your credit card's last 4 digits so that they can verify the account and enable the upgrade functionality.
- Download and install IBM Cloud CLI. Installer is currently downloadable from `https://console.bluemix.net/docs/cli/reference/ibmcloud/download_cli.html#install_use`.
- Log in to the IBM Cloud CLI and create a space for the default org (if not already created).
    1. Login to `https://console.bluemix.net`.
    2. Click **Manage** > **Account** > **Cloud Foundry Organizations**.
    3. Click on `default` as `org name` and click **Add a space** button.
    4. Select a region where you want to create a space and provide a name, and click **Save**.

> **TIP**
> My first experience with IBM Cloud was not very smooth. Most cloud providers usually try to improve themselves based on feedback and hence your experience might be smoother. If you have entered credit card details and upgraded your account, you can raise a ticket with IBM cloud team for any issues you may face.

How to do it...

We will login through IBM Cloud CLI and deploy a function following the as follows: steps. Exact outputs for these steps may differ slightly when you run these commands for the first time and further executions.

1. Execute `ibmcloud login` and enter the username and password as follows:

```
ibmcloud login
```

Chapter 10

You should see an output as follows with further prompts:

```
$ ibmcloud login
API endpoint: cloud.ibm.com

Email> ████████gmail.com

Password>
Authenticating...
OK


Targeted account


Targeted resource group Default


Select a region (or press enter to skip):
1. au-syd
2. jp-tok
3. eu-de
4. eu-gb
5. us-south
6. us-east
Enter a number>
```

Other Cloud Providers

2. Enter the option number for `us-south`

   You should see further response as:

```
Enter a number> 5
Targeted region us-south


API endpoint:      https://cloud.ibm.com
Region:            us-south
User:              ████████gmail.com
Account:

Resource group:    Default
CF API endpoint:
Org:
Space:

Tip: If you are managing Cloud Foundry applications and services
- Use 'ibmcloud target --cf' to target Cloud Foundry org/space interactively, or
 use 'ibmcloud target --cf-api ENDPOINT -o ORG -s SPACE' to target the org/space
.
- Use 'ibmcloud cf' if you want to run the Cloud Foundry CLI with current IBM Cl
oud CLI context.
```

> ℹ️ If you have not updated credit card and using a lite account, you may see a different screen with lesser options.

3. Run:

   ```
   ibmcloud target -cf
   ```

[452]

Chapter 10

There should be an organization with your email address. Select it.

```
$ ibmcloud target --cf
Targeted Cloud Foundry (https://api.ng.bluemix.net)


Select an organization (or press enter to skip):
1.
2.
Enter a number> 2
Targeted org

Targeted space dev1



API endpoint:      https://cloud.ibm.com
Region:            us-south
User:
Account:

Resource group:    Default
CF API endpoint:   https://api.ng.bluemix.net (API version: 2.106.0)
Org:
Space:             dev1
```

4. Install the cloud functions plug-in:

    ibmcloud plugin install cloud-functions

5. Create a file name `hello.js` with following contents:

    ```
    function main(params) {
        var name = params.name || 'World';
        return {payload: 'Hello, ' + name + '!'};
    }
    ```

> I have used Node.js code as provided in IBM samples.

[453]

Other Cloud Providers

6. Create `hello` action:

   ibmcloud fn action create hello hello.js

7. Invoke the function without passing parameters:

   ibmcloud fn action invoke helloworld --blocking --result

   You should see an output, as follows:

   ```
   {
       "payload": "Hello, World!"
   }
   ```

8. Invoke action with parameters:

   ibmcloud fn action invoke hello --blocking --result --param name Heartin

   ```
   {
       "payload": "Hello, Heartin!"
   }
   ```

How It works...

The goal of this recipe was become familiar with IBM Cloud and write our first serverless application on IBM cloud. In the next two sections, we will list the IBM Cloud serverless services for various use cases. You can refer to the links provided for each service to learn more and get started with them.

There's more...

Let's look at some of the IBM Cloud services that we can make use of when implementing Serverless applications:

- **Serverless computing on AWS**:
  IBM Cloud Functions allow you to execute code on demand similar to AWS Lambda.

- **Access management**:
  IBM Cloud Identity and Access Management (IAM) supports authenticating users for both platform services and controlling access to resources across IBM Cloud.
- **Resource provisioning and management**:
  The IBM Continuous Delivery service helps you provision an integrated toolchain using customizable, shareable templates with tools from IBM and third parties.
- **Simple object store**:
  IBM Cloud Object Storage is IBM's object storage solution in the cloud for unstructured data.
- **API management**:
  IBM API Connect helps in creating and managing APIs.
- **Storage tier**:
  IBM Cloudant is a distributed NoSQL database that is optimized for handling heavy workloads. IBM Db2 on Cloud is a relational database in IBM Cloud.
- **User management**:
  The closest corresponding service to Amazon Cognito that we can currently obtain from IBM is IBM Cloud Identity from the IBM Cloud marketplace.
- **Domain hosting and DNS management**:
  IBM Domain Name Services provides simple domain registration and DNS management.
- **Content Delivery Network**:
  IBM Content Delivery Network caches content in various locations for faster retrieval using the Akamai network.
- **Queue service**:
  IBM MQ on Cloud is one of the queue service that IBM Cloud supports. IBM cloud also supports RabbitMQ as a managed service.
- **Notification service**:
  The IBM Push Notifications service allows you to send real-time notifications to mobile and web applications.
- **Managing events and streams**:
  The IBM Streaming Analytics service can be used to analyze streaming data from different sources and types.
- **Machine learning/AI service**:
  There is no service that directly corresponds with Amazon ML within IBM. However, we can use IBM Watson within IBM Cloud for artificial intelligence (AI). IBM Watson is IBM's popular deep learning AI platform.

- **Monitoring**:
  IBM Cloud Event Management helps in identifying, notifying, and resolving critical incidents more quickly. IBM Cloud Availability Monitoring is integrated to the DevOps toolchain, and runs tests from locations around the world to proactively detect and fix performance issues. IBM Cloud also supports monitoring with Sysdig as a managed service. Sysdig allow you to monitor containers across their entire life cycle.
- **Data warehouse management**:
  IBM Db2 Warehouse on Cloud is an elastic data warehouse in the cloud that is built for analytics use cases.
- **Data integration/data pipeline**:
  The IBM Message Hub Object Storage bridge can be used to build end-to-end IoT data pipelines in IBM Cloud.

See also

You can read more about the services that are discussed in the previous section by using the following links:

- **IBM Cloud Functions:** https://www.ibm.com/cloud/functions
- **IBM Cloud Identity and Access Management:** https://console.bluemix.net/docs/iam/index.html#iamoverview, https://www.ibm.com/security/identity-access-management
- **Continuous Delivery:** https://www.ibm.com/cloud/continuous-delivery
- **IBM Cloud Object Storage:** https://www.ibm.com/cloud/object-storage
- **IBM API Connect:** https://www.ibm.com/cloud/api-connect
- **IBM Cloudant:** https://www.ibm.com/cloud/cloudant
- **IBM Db2 on Cloud:** https://www.ibm.com/cloud/db2-on-cloud
- **IBM Cloud Identity:** https://www.ibm.com/in-en/marketplace/cloud-identity
- **Domain Name Services:** https://www.ibm.com/cloud/dns
- **IBM Content Delivery Network:** https://www.ibm.com/cloud/cdn
- **IBM MQ:** https://www.ibm.com/cloud/mq
- **Messages for RabbitMQ:** https://www.ibm.com/cloud/messages-for-rabbitmq
- **Push Notifications:** https://www.ibm.com/cloud/push-notifications
- **Streaming Analytics:** https://www.ibm.com/cloud/streaming-analytics

- **IBM Watson with IBM Cloud:** `https://www.ibm.com/cloud/ai`
- **Event Management:** `https://www.ibm.com/cloud/event-management`
- **Availability Monitoring:** `https://console.bluemix.net/catalog/services/availability-monitoring`
- **Monitoring with Sysdig:** `https://cloud.ibm.com/docs/services/Monitoring-with-Sysdig/index.html`
- **IBM Db2 Warehouse on Cloud:** `https://www.ibm.com/cloud/db2-warehouse-on-cloud`
- **Message Hub Object Storage:** `https://www.ibm.com/blogs/bluemix/2017/03/end-to-end-iot-data-pipelines-introducing-the-message-hub-object-storage-bridge/`

In this chapter, we went through some simple recipes on other cloud platforms, namely Azure, Google Cloud, and IBM Cloud. We also briefly looked at the names and descriptions of some of the serverless services available with these cloud platforms. In the rest of this book, we had covered most of the essential serverless services from AWS in detail.

Serverless cloud computing is a huge and fast-growing field. Some of the services or commands we saw in this book might be upgraded in the near future. You can check for the details of these updates from their respective documentation. We will try to update the code files in the repository for any important updates that come to our notice.

To continue learning about serverless cloud computing and to keep an eye on the latest trends, you can pick up an advanced book on serverless cloud computing from Packt or follow my notes on cloud computing (particularly serverless computing) at `http://cloudmaterials.com/en/books`.

Other Books You May Enjoy

If you enjoyed this book, you may be interested in these other books by Packt:

Hands-On Serverless Applications with Go
Mohamed Labouardy

ISBN: 9781789134612

- Understand how AWS Lambda works and use it to create an application
- Understand how to scaleup serverless applications
- Design a cost-effective serverless application in AWS
- Build a highly scalable and fault-tolerant CI/CD pipeline
- Understand how to troubleshoot and monitor serverless apps in AWS
- Discover the working of APIs and single page applications
- Build a production-ready serverless application in Go

Other Books You May Enjoy

Hands-On Serverless Applications with Kotlin
Hardik Trivedi

ISBN: 9781788993708

- Design a serverless architecture
- Use AWS Lambda to contain your serverless API
- Explore the various ways to keep serverless apps safe and secure
- Understand how a serverless API allows you to use huge infrastructure and cut costs
- Discover how to handle distributed systems in Kotlin
- Design the data flow between cloud services and custom business logic
- Secure your Kotlin AWS serverless application
- Master Kotlin design patterns for serverless applications

Leave a review - let other readers know what you think

Please share your thoughts on this book with others by leaving a review on the site that you bought it from. If you purchased the book from Amazon, please leave us an honest review on this book's Amazon page. This is vital so that other potential readers can see and use your unbiased opinion to make purchasing decisions, we can understand what our customers think about our products, and our authors can see your feedback on the title that they have worked with Packt to create. It will only take a few minutes of your time, but is valuable to other potential customers, our authors, and Packt. Thank you!

Index

#
#set
  using 95

A
access token 173
admin authentication flow 172
ADMIN_NO_SRP_AUTH
  versus USER_PASSWORD_AUTH 173
Alexa simulator
  reference 352
Alexa skill
  ask-cli, configuring 339
  ASK CLI steps 356
  ASK CLI, configuring 338
  ASK CLI, installing 338
  building 338, 340
  building, with ASK CLI 347, 350
  invocation basics 354
  Lambda (AWS CLI), provisioning 346
  Lambda project (Java) 355
  Lambda project (Java), creating 341, 345
  testing 338, 353
  voice app platforms 357
  working 353
Amazon API Gateway 12
Amazon Certificate Manager (ACM) 238
Amazon CloudFormation
  alternatives 40
  benefits 39
  Cloud Formation Designer 39
  CloudFormation Template Components,
    reference 38
  intrinsic functions 38
  JSON 32
  Lambda 36
  policy 36
  project, setting up 32
  pseudo-parameters 48
  resource component 38
  roles, cleaning up 36
  S3 bucket 32
  Template Components 37
  used, for building API 67, 70, 72
  used, for creating Lambda 31
  used, for provisioning Lambda infrastructure 31, 32
  using, with Lambda 40
  YAML 32
Amazon CloudFront 12
Amazon CloudWatch 11
Amazon Cognito
  federated identity, using with 409
Amazon DynamoDB 12
Amazon ML
  Area Under the ROC (AUC) 336
  DataSource object 336
  prediction use cases 336
  Receiver Operating Characteristic (ROC) 336
  using, for binary classification 326, 327, 330, 333, 335
Amazon Route 53 207
Amazon Simple Storage Service (S3) 12
Apache Velocity Language
  about 96
  reference 96
API gateway
  Cognito, integrating with 187
  reference 112
API
  configuring, for acting as proxy for Lambda 103
  creating, with CLI commands 83, 91
  creating, with CloudFormation template 85, 92

testing 93
application programming interface (API) 59
automated speech recognition (ASR) 353
AWS CLI commands
  used, for creating REST API 75
AWS CLI
  about 21
  API gateway sub-commands 64
  configuring 22, 24
  data, reading from DynamoDB 132
  data, working with 126
  documentation, reference 67
  in Windows machine 24
  items, adding 127
  items, deleting 131
  items, reading 127, 130
  items, updating 131
  memory-size 30
  operations, adding 132
  operations, deleting 132
  operations, updating 132
  policy, attaching 30
  return-consumed-capacity 133
  role, creating 30
  S3 bucket, creating 24
  timeout 30
  used, for building API 60, 64
  used, for deploying AWS Lambda 21, 25
  using, with Lambda 40
AWS Command Line Interface (CLI)
  cleaning up 30
  key 30
  S3 Bucket 30
AWS Identity and Access Management (IAM) 11, 12
AWS Lambda
  about 12
  code repository usage guidelines 14
  code, deploying ways 20
  creating 13, 16
  creating, from management console 20
  dependencies 19
  JSON, parsing from Lambda handler 20
  parent POM 18
  roles 18

  runtimes 18
AWS platform
  services 12
  services, reference 12
  starting with 8, 9, 11
AWS SDK
  using, with Lambda 40
AWS Serverless Application Model (AWS SAM) 38
Azure services
  for implementing Serverless applications 441
  references 443
Azure
  serverless application, creating 436

B

Bearer Token 173

C

certificate, with domain
  associating, AWS CLI commands used 251
  associating, CloudFormation template used 253, 255
client-side authentication flow
  about 174
  Cognito user pool client, creating 175
  using 176, 178
CloudFront domain
  using, with HTTPS 250
CloudFront, setting up for S3 website
  about 214
  AWS CLI commands, using 215
  CloudFormation template, using 218, 220
  DistributionConfig defaults 216
CloudFront, using with custom domain name
  about 239
  AWS CLI commands, using 239, 242
  CloudFormation template, using 243
  CloudFront distribution stack 244
  distribution, deleting 249
  distribution, disabling 249
  HTTPS, used for securing domain URL 248
  template, creating for RecordSet stack 246
CloudFront
  setting up, for S3 website 214
  using, with custom domain names 239

[464]

CloudWatch alarms (AWS CLI)
  setting up 374, 377, 380, 381
CloudWatch alarms
  creating, for metric with dimension 382, 384
CloudWatch dashboard
  logging in 361
CloudWatch metric log filters
  creating, from AWS CLI 385
  creating, from console 387, 390
  using 384
CodePen
  reference 404
  used, for testing API 392, 394, 399, 400
  using 393
Cognito operations
  amazon-cognito-identity.min.js file, downloading 401
  amazon-cognito-identity.min.js file, up, loading 402
  implementing, with JavaScript SDK 401, 409
  S3 bucket, creating 402
  testing, with JavaScript SDK 401
  user pool and client, creating 403
Cognito user pool client
  creating 167, 175
  creating, with AWS CLI 168, 175
  creating, with CloudFormation template 168, 175
Cognito user pool
  AliasAttributes, versus UsernameAttributes 166
  creating 158
  creating, with AWS CLI 158, 196
  creating, with CloudFormation template 161, 163, 165, 200
  JSON templates, generating with CLI commands 165
  JSON templates, using with CLI commands 165
Cognito, integration with API gateway
  AWS CLI, using 187, 191
  claim-based identity approach 194
  CloudFormation template, using 192
Cognito
  integrating, with API gateway 187
  used, for setting up user sign-up flow 178
Content Delivery Network (CDN) 207, 238
conversational user interfaces (CUI) 337

Cross-Origin Resource Sharing (CORS)
  about 391
  enabling, for API 392, 396, 399, 400
custom domains, using with S3 static websites
  about 232
  AWS CLI commands, using 232
  CloudFormation template, using 235, 237
custom metric
  creating 369
  dimensions, adding to data 371
  simple metric, creating without dimensions 369

D

Dagger 53
dependency injection
  about 48
  code refactoring 49
dev practices, Lambdas
  dependency injection 48, 50, 53
  unit testing 48, 50, 53
DevOps 359
DNS propagation time 230
domain-specific language (DSL) 337
domain
  name, registering with Route 53 220
  registering, from AWS Management Console 225
  registering, with AWS CLI commands 221, 224
DynamoDB SDK
  AmazonDynamoDB client, versus DynamoDB wrapper client 139
  IAM actions 139
  IAM policy 139
  Single Lambda, versus Multiple Lambdas 140
  using, from Lambda 134, 136, 138
DynamoDB table
  asynchronous operations, waiting for 120
  creating 114
  creating, ways 121
  creating, with CLI commands 115
  creating, with CloudFormation template 117
  data model 119
  datamodel limits 119
  features 121
  keys and partitions 120

[465]

limitations 122
local and global secondary indexes 122
read and write capacity units 120
reference 120
DynamoDB
  reference 155

E

edge locations 214

F

federated identity
  Google Plus, configuring 410, 413
  using, with Amazon Cognito 409
Function as a Service (FaaS) 7

G

GCP services
  for implementing Serverless applications 447
  references 448
global secondary index (GSI)
  about 121
  reference 122
Google Cloud Platform
  serverless application, creating 444
groups
  working with 183, 186

H

hash key 120
hosted zone 225
HTTPS
  using, with CloudFront domain 250
hypermedia as the engine of application state (HATEOAS) 66
Hypertext Transfer Protocol (HTTP) 65

I

IBM Cloud services
  for implementing Serverless applications 454
  references 456
IBM Cloud
  serverless application, creating 449
Identity and Access Management (IAM) 9

identity token (ID token) 173
identity tokens 194
Infrastructure as a Service (IaaS) 7
insights
  checking 360
intrinsic function
  reference 39

J

Java Development Kit (JDK) 13
JavaScript SDK
  used, for implementing Cognito operations 401, 409
  used, for testing Cognito operations 401, 409
JSON schema
  reference 102
JSONPath expressions
  about 96
  reference 96

K

Key Management Service (KMS) 310
Kinesis Client Library (KCL) 319
Kinesis data stream
  about 302
  creating 302, 307
  creating, with AWS CLI 302
  creating, with CloudFormation template 304
  data, adding 305
  data, retrieving 305
  shard iterator types 308, 310
Kinesis Producer Library (KPL) 310
  Lambda project, creating 319
Kinesis Stream, with SDK
  data, writing into 310
  Lambda project, creating 311, 318
  Lambda, provisioning 315
  Lambda, testing 315

L

Lambda function
  creating, fro proxy integration 104
Lambda integration
  CLI commands 80
  CloudFormation template components 81

used, for building API 73, 79
Lambda logs
　checking 362
Lambda proxy integration
　ANY HTTP method 110
　API, creating with CloudFormation templates 108
　greedy path 110
　input and output format 111
　Lambda function, creating 104
　Lambda, deploying 105
　Proxy API, creating with 105
　RequestStreamHandler, versus RequestHandler 110
Lambda, invoking with Kinesis events
　about 319, 324
　lambda function, creating without service class 320
　lambda, provisioning 322
　lambda, testing 322
Lambda
　creating 74
　data items, adding 145, 148
　data, reading 149, 154, 155
　invoking, with SNS events (Java) 294
　invoking, with SQS event (Java) 277
　tables, creating 141, 145
local secondary index (LSI)
　about 121
　reference 122
log groups 367
log insights 364, 368
log streams 368
logs
　checking 360

M

Machine Learning (ML) 301
mapping templates
　reference 96
metrics
　about 368
　checking 360, 365, 367
models
　used, for validating request payloads 96

Multi-Factor Authentication (MFA) 11

N

nameserver (NS) 225
Natural Language Processing (NLP) 256
natural language understanding (NLU) 353
Not Secure message 250

O

one time passwords (OTP) 284

P

plain old Java objects (POJOs) 74
　creating, for requests and response 42, 46
Platform as a service (PaaS) 7
POST API method
　building 82
　testing 82
Postman
　used, for testing 86
put-integration response
　options 88

R

range key 120
read capacity unit (RCU) 120
refresh token 173
Representational State Transfer (REST) 66
request payloads
　API, creating with CLI commands 98
　API, testing 101
　CloudFormation template 100
　request data format 97
　validating, with models 96, 102
requests
　mapping, with mapping templates 89, 90
responses
　mapping, with mapping templates 89, 90
REST API
　creating, with AWS CLI commands 75
　creating, with CloudFormation template 78
Route 53, using with domains registered with other registrars
　about 227

DNS propagation 230
DNS, configuring from AWS Management Console 230
hosted zone, creating from AWS CLI commands 228
hosted zones, creating from CloudFormation template 229
Route 53
  reference 250
  used, for registering domain name 220
  using, with domains registered with other registrars 227, 230

S

S3 static website
  AWS CLI commands, using 208, 211
  CloudFormation template, using 211, 213
  custom domains, using with 232
  setting up 208
S3 website
  CloudFront, setting up 214
SDK (Java)
  used, for receiving SQS messages in batch 269
  used, for sending messages 262
  used, for sending SQS messages in batch 269
Secure Remote Password (SRP) 172
Server Name Identification (SNI) 256
server-side authentication flow
  about 172
  Cognito user pool client, creating 167
  using 167, 169, 170
serverles framework
  used, for deploying Lambda 54, 57, 58
serverless application
  creating, in GCP 444
  creating, on IBM Cloud 449
Simple Notification Service (SNS) 284, 374, 391
Simple Queue Service (SQS) 391
Simple Storage Service (S3) 24, 208
single sign-on 194
SNS events (Java)
  Lambda (AWS CLI), provisioning 297
  Lambda (AWS CLI), testing 298
  Lambda project code (Java) 295
  used, for invoking Lambda 294

SNS topic
  creating, for email and SMS 284
  creating, with AWS CLI 285
  creating, with CloudFormation template 285
  email subscription, creating 287
  Lambda (AWS CLI), provisioning 292
  Lambda (AWS CLI), testing 292
  Lambda project code (Java) 290
  message, publishing 288
  publishing to, with SDK (Java) 289
  SMS subscriptions, creating 286
Software as a Service (SaaS) 7
speech synthesis markup language (SSML) 355
SQS event (Java)
  data, setting up 280
  Lambda (AWS CLI), provisioning 280
  Lambda (AWS CLI), testing 283
  Lambda project code (Java) 278
  Lambda, invoking 277
  queues, setting up 280
SQS messages
  data, setting up 273
  Lambda (AWS CLI), provisioning 273
  Lambda (AWS CLI), testing 273
  Lambda project code (Java) 270
  queues and data, setting up 273
  sending, in batch with SDK (Java) 269
  working 276
SQS queue (AWS CLI + CloudFormation)
  (AWS CLI) data, receiving 260
  (AWS CLI) data, sending 260
  AWS CLI commands 258
  CloudFormation template 259
  creating 258, 261
SQS queue
  creating 262
  Lambda (AWS CLI), provisioning 265, 269
  Lambda (AWS CLI), testing 265, 269
  Lambda project code (Java), creating 263, 265
Start Of Authority (SOA) 225
Structured Query Language (SQL) 113

T

templates
  mapping 94

Test Driven Development (TDD) 53
TestNG 53
throughput provisioning example
 about 123
 limits, reference 125
 scenarios 123, 124
 strongly consistent, versus eventually consistent
  reads 125

U

unit testing 48
URL
 parts 66
user pool, with SMS verification
 creating 196

user sign-up flow
 setting up, with admin confirmation 182
 setting up, with MFA 195
 setting up, with MFA verification 202, 205
 setting up, with self confirmation 179, 181, 183
 setting up, with SMS verification 195, 202, 205

V

variables
 mapping 94
Velocity Template Language (VTL) 89

W

write capacity unit (WCU) 120

Made in the USA
Monee, IL
10 October 2020